Echoes of Jesus

Does the New Testament Reflect What He Said?

Jonathan P Clerke

PUBLISHING

Foreword by Rev Dr Peter Christofides

Copyright © 2013, 2017 by Jonathan Clerke. All rights reserved. No part of this book may be used or reproduced or transmitted in any form or by any means, electronic or mechanical, including photocopying, or by any information storage and retrieval system, without the written permission of the publisher. The only exception is brief quotations in reviews.

Publisher: IceFire Publishing PO Box 618 Albany Creek Qld 4035 Australia
Original publication date: 2014. Revised 2017.
ISBN: 9780992338305
eISBN: 9781925177022

Cover design: Stay Media Productions & Jonathan Clerke
Cover Photograph: Resurrection of Jesus by Keith Reicher
Editing: Rebecca Gollan
For further information, visit *echoesofjesus.com*

Clerke, Jonathan
Echoes of Jesus

Unless otherwise indicated, Scripture quotations are from the HOLY BIBLE, NEW INTERNATIONAL VERSION®, NIV® Copyright © 1973, 1978, 1984, 2011 by Biblica, Inc.® Used by permission. All rights reserved worldwide. Scripture quotations marked New American Standard Bible or NASB are taken from the NEW AMERICAN STANDARD BIBLE®, Copyright © 1960, 1962, 1963, 1968, 1971, 1972, 1973, 1975, 1977, 1995 by The Lockman Foundation. Used by permission. Scripture quotations marked ESV are taken from the ESV® Bible (The Holy Bible, English Standard Version®) copyright © 2001 by Crossway, a publishing ministry of Good News Publishers. ESV® Text Edition: 2011. The ESV® text has been reproduced in cooperation with and by permission of Good News Publishers. Unauthorized reproduction of this publication is prohibited. All rights reserved.

National Library of Australia Cataloguing-in-Publication entry:
Author: Clerke, Jonathan P., author.
Title: Echoes of Jesus : does the New Testament reflect what he said? / Jonathan Clerke.
ISBN: 9780992338305 (paperback)
Subjects: Jesus Christ–Historicity.
Jesus Christ–Biography–Sources
Bible. New Testament–Evidences, authority, etc.
Authority–Religious aspects–Christianity.
Dewey Number: 232.908

Typeset in 11/13 Times by Australian eBook Publisher

Table of contents

Praise for *Echoes of Jesus*	xiii
Abbreviations, symbols, glossary and distance calculations	xix
Foreword	xxiii
Preface	xxvii
Dedication	xxix
Acknowledgements	xxxi
Introduction	1

Part I: Literacy and gullibility in the world of Jesus — 9

Chapter 1: Writing history and creating libraries — 11

Evaluating the skills of ancient writers	12
Herodotus	12
Thucydides	14
Lucian	16
Others	17
Ancient history-writing techniques	17
The abundance and availability of historical writings	18
The ability to source ancient books	19
Vast numbers of historians	21
Ancient libraries	23
Conclusion	27

Chapter 2: Literacy in the ancient world — 29

Literacy and gullibility	29
Assessing literacy in the Greco–Roman world	30

Functional indicators	33
Variety of genres	36
Geographic dispersion	37
Graffiti	40
Lost words in lost worlds	43
Literacy across the Roman Empire	44
Literacy in Roman-occupied Greece	44
Literacy in Roman-occupied Egypt	46
Literacy in Roman-occupied Britain	51
The affordability of reading and writing	54
The cost of books	54
The cost of writing	57
Conclusion	58

Chapter 3: Literacy in Jesus' world — 59

Reading and writing in Jewish society	60
Reading and writing as part of Jewish expectations and practices	60
Scribes	62
Dead Sea Scrolls	63
Documentation everywhere	64
The farmers' need for literacy	66
Graffiti in graveyards and houses	67
Christian literacy	69
Availability of writing materials	70
Surviving Christian manuscripts and letters	70
Christian libraries	72
Christianity among the well educated	72
Conclusion	75

Chapter 4: Illiteracy and gullibility, miracles and reasoning — 77

Learning without reading	79
Christian beliefs, miracles and gullibility	81
Jesus' miracles	81

Miracles performed by early disciples	83
Conclusion	84

Part II: From Jesus' mouth to the disciples' hands — 85

Chapter 5: Jesus the teacher — 87

If Jesus wasn't an author, how do we know what he said?	87
Making an accurate translation	88
Interpretation	89
Did Jesus motivate his disciples to preserve what he taught?	90
Jesus the teacher	90
Jesus the movement founder	92
Jesus claimed to be God the Son	93
Jesus' teaching methods	93
Were Jesus' disciples capable of taking notes?	95
Note-taking and shorthand in the Greco–Roman world	95
Note-taking and shorthand in Jewish society	96
The Gospel of Luke based on earlier writings	98
A chief note-taker?	99
Where did Luke and Mark source their information?	101
But weren't the disciples uneducated?	102
Conclusion	103
Appendix 1: But why didn't Jesus write his own message?	103
Appendix 2: Examples of various Greek words for 'love'	105

Chapter 6: Jesus' teaching methods — 107

Could the disciples have memorised Jesus' teachings?	107

Deductions about the disciples' capacity to memorise	108
Memorisation in the ancient world	109
Did Jesus cast his message in ways designed to aid memorisation?	111
Parables	112
Actions speak louder than words	113
Poetry	113
Miscellaneous techniques	115
Why do the Gospels differ from each other?	116
Flexibility in describing background material	117
Flexibility in Jesus' non-essential words	118
Variation inherent in Jesus' teachings	119
Variations in Aramaic to Greek translations	120
Freedom to select, but not freedom to fabricate	122
Why four Gospels instead of one?	123
Conclusion	125
Appendix: Did Jesus discourage memorisation amongst his disciples?	126

Part III: Accuracy in the copying of the New Testament accounts   129

Chapter 7: Ancient copies of the New Testament: from Egypt to the Vatican   131

Ancient extensive copies: Codices Sinaiticus, Vaticanus, Alexandrinus and Bezae	132
Codex Sinaiticus	133
Codex Vaticanus	137
Codex Alexandrinus	138
Codex Bezae Cantabrigiensis	139
Ancient partial copies	140
Chester Beatty Papyri	141

Bodmer Papyri　　　　　　　　　　　　　144
　　　Conclusion: Reconstructing the autographs　145

Chapter 8: Making copies without photocopiers　　　　　　　　　　　　　　　　147

　How accurately could Christian communities
　make copies of the New Testament?　　　　148
　　　A deeper comparison of P75 and Codex
　　　Vaticanus　　　　　　　　　　　　　148
　What do the ancient, less-accurate copies of the
　New Testament teach?　　　　　　　　　153
　　　Minor errors and deliberate changes
　　　found in P45　　　　　　　　　　　153
　　　Minor errors caused by copyists: a look at P46　159
　Conclusion　　　　　　　　　　　　　　164

Chapter 9: Deliberate changes and their cumulative impact on Jesus' words　　　165

　What were the causes of variations among the
　many manuscripts?　　　　　　　　　　166
　Changes made deliberately by copyists　　167
　　　Deliberate and simple changes　　　　169
　　　Deliberate and complex changes　　　170
　Variations in the content of all of the Gospels　171
　　　Regarding the book of Matthew　　　174
　　　Regarding the book of Mark　　　　　174
　　　Regarding the book of Luke　　　　　175
　　　Regarding the book of John　　　　　177
　Conclusion　　　　　　　　　　　　　　179

Chapter 10: Prominent variations and their impacts on Christian living　　　　181

　A variation impacting Christians considering
　marriage after divorce　　　　　　　　　181
　Variations to the ending for Mark's Gospel　185

The tenacity of the scribes	186
Are new teachings found in the short ending?	189
Are new teachings found in the long ending?	189
Another variation involving a large number of words: Jesus and the woman caught in adultery	192
Conclusion	194

Chapter 11: Boundaries of divergence between ancient manuscripts and an English New Testament — 195

Comparing the Codex Vaticanus and the Codex Bezae	195
Comparing verses on Jesus, the crucifixion and forgiveness	198
Comparing verses on the resurrected Jesus	201
Comparing verses on doctrines relating to who Jesus is and his uniqueness	204
Conclusion	206
Appendix 1: Foundational teachings of mainstream Christianity	206
Appendix 2: Jesus considered as God, as taught in Acts chapters 2 to 4	207

Part IV: Evidence from early Christian and non-Christian witnesses — 209

Chapter 12: Christian beliefs as revealed by Christian and non-Christian writers prior to 200 AD — 211

Was the pre–200 AD New Testament the same as today's?	211
Did the New Testament authors record the truth about Jesus?	217
Bias due to partiality causing excessive disdain	218

Bias due to partiality causing excessive glorification	220
Canvassing Christian beliefs during the first 150 years	221
Tacitus the historian	223
Thallus the historian	229
Conclusion	235
Appendix: Sextus Julius Africanus	236

Chapter 13: Lucian and his view on Christianity — 241

Lucian's religious and philosophical beliefs	242
The Passing of Peregrinus	243
Two portraits of Christianity	247
Alexander the Oracle-Monger	264
Conclusion	265
Appendix: Examples of sebō being chosen to indicate worship of divinities	266

Chapter 14: Lucian's book about Peregrinus: history or fantasy? — 269

Four ways to examine *The Passing of Peregrinus*	270
Was Lucian capable of writing a historically accurate account?	270
Did Lucian intend his readers to regard the work as true?	271
Was the content of *The Passing of Peregrinus* in fact true?	274
Is Lucian's account consistent within itself?	277
Other areas of interest in Lucian's work	278
Does Lucian's account contain elements that disagree with the New Testament?	279
What were Lucian's sources of Christian information?	281

Could Lucian have been referring to someone other than Jesus as the instigator of Christianity?	284
Conclusion	285

Chapter 15: Pliny the Younger — 287

Extracts from Pliny's letters describing the investigation of Christians	288
Insights into Pliny's character	291
Pliny's interest in the Christians	294
Does Pliny's letter reflect content found in the New Testament?	297
Authenticity of the letters	300
Conclusion	304

Chapter 16: Was Josephus a capable historian? — 305

Who was Josephus?	305
Why and for whom did Josephus write?	307
Josephus' accuracy in using other written sources	310
Josephus' accuracy as an eyewitness	313
Accuracy in portraying architectural details	313
Ability as a military historian	315
Did Josephus use other eyewitnesses?	318
Conclusion	319

Chapter 17: Josephus and the New Testament — 321

The first reference to Jesus: crucified by Pilate	321
Authenticity of the first reference	322
Conclusion to the first reference about Jesus	329
The second reference to Jesus: James the brother of Jesus	330

Authenticity of the second reference	333
Conclusion to the second reference about Jesus	336
Josephus' comments about other New Testament people	337
Josephus and John the Baptist	337
Josephus and the beliefs of the Sadducees	338
Josephus and the New Testament's descriptions of legal proceedings	339
Did Luke copy information from Josephus' books?	340
Conclusion	344
Appendix 1: Digressions in book 18 of The Antiquities of the Jews	345
Appendix 2: Deliberate changes by Christian copyists?	346

Chapter 18: Implications   349

What about me?	349
A hypothetical map for those who are interested in investigating Jesus	350
Implications for Muslims	353
Conclusion	360

End-of-book appendices   361

Appendix 1: A brief background of first-century Judea	363
Appendix 2: Points of agreement between biblical and non-biblical sources	373
Appendix 3: Did Jesus really grow up in the town of Nazareth?	379

Praise for *Echoes of Jesus*

Endorsements

This is a book for those who like to question and think and who are not satisfied with pat answers. It explores the consistency of the biblical records about Jesus with profound insight and honest evaluation. It describes the author's personal quest for truth with no stone left unturned. Everything is carefully explained. Everything is well documented. This is an excellent resource for theological faculty and students as well as for anyone genuinely searching for truth. If you have questions or doubts about the identity of the real Jesus or the reliability of the Bible, this is the book for you.

> Rev Dr John Sweetman, BSc, DipEd, BD, GradTheol, DMin (Denver Seminary, USA); Principal of Malyon College, Brisbane, Australia

Echoes of Jesus examines the vital question of the reliability of the New Testament, in particular the Gospels' record of the words of Christ. It is a wide-ranging and comprehensive study, yet at the same time accessible and readable for those without a scholarly knowledge of the Bible. It answers many of the questions that both Christians and non-Christians raise, particularly Muslim objections to the Christian faith. It is my prayer that the Lord will use Jonathan Clerke's book to encourage and strengthen the faith of many.

> Dr Patrick Sookhdeo, PhD (London University's School of Oriental and African Studies), International Director of the Barnabas Fund, Adjunct Professor at the George C. Marshall European Center for Security Studies, Visiting Professor at the Defence Academy of the United Kingdom and at Cranfield University, United Kingdom

Echoes of Jesus is a very insightful and much-needed book in the area of apologetics, particularly as the reliability of the Bible is increasingly challenged. I use it as a text in Australia's only theologically-accredited Apologetics to Islam course run at the Melbourne School of Theology.

> Dr Bernie Power, D.Th, lecturer in Islamic Studies, Melbourne School of Theology, Australia.

This well written work on the biblical account of the historical Jesus exposes the reader to key issues that are often overlooked in popular Christian apologetics. *Echoes of Jesus* raises the believer's confidence levels in the reliability of the Gospels and the apostolic writings, and should be taken seriously by scholars.

> Dr James M. Leonard, PhD (Cambridge), former Adjunct Professor (LSU, Notre Dame Seminary, Loyola University, John Brown University, Arkansas, US).

For anyone interested in the truth claims of Christianity, *Echoes of Jesus* by Jonathan Clerke is a helpful and interesting read and an excellent resource. Based on extensive, robust and systematic research of primary and secondary sources, the author persuasively argues that the New Testament accurately and faithfully records what Jesus said and taught in his lifetime. Clerke's research establishes the following: (a) there was a high-level of literacy in the ancient world including Jesus's; (b) people in the ancient world were not as gullible as critics of Christianity have claimed; (c) ancient historians were both professional and credible in their task of recording history; (d) as a master-teacher, Jesus employed methods which facilitated the remembrance and easy recall of his teachings; (e) the autographs of the New Testament were faithfully transmitted despite variant readings and textual traditions; and, (f) extra-biblical sources like Lucian, Pliny the Younger and Josephus contain reliable evidences which attest to the veracity of the New Testament. Clerke has done a great service to the church in writing this book to defend the truth claims of Christianity. His research has also significant implications for Christian-Muslim dialogue. This book is not for the faint of heart as it requires much patience and critical thinking to grapple with all the research. But, for the cause of truth, the effort is worth it!

> Rev. Dr. Bernard Low, former Associate Professor in Systematic Theology at Singapore Bible College; PhD (University of Nottingham). Former Director of SBC's Centre for Continuing Theological Education.

The biblical worldview is rooted in Scripture, which speaks with authority and logical consistency on matters of epistemology, cosmology and ethics. The earthly words of Christ are an integral component of Scripture, and Jonathan Clerke has provided us a meticulously researched evidentialist account of how the logos of God has been accurately documented and preserved.

Dr Ting Wang, PhD (Hebrew Union College, Jewish Institute of Religion, Cincinnati, US); former Lecturer in Biblical Hebrew, Stanford University; Translator, Oxford English Version (Luke, forthcoming).

Jesus was a historical person. He gained an immense following in the Greco–Roman world of the first four centuries. Countless people embraced him not only as a valued religious teacher, but as the Son of God. It wasn't gullibility, illiteracy or a denial of the realities of life that paved the way for these convictions. Jon Clerke's book shows that you don't have to take a degree in theology or history to discover the obvious. The history of early Christianity and its sacred writings is one of the best documented on this planet. Time to find out for yourself!

Professor Benno A. Zuiddam, DTh (University of the Orange Free State), PhD (North-West University, South Africa), School of Ancient Languages and Text Studies, North-West University, South Africa, Greenwich School of Theology (UK); Centre for Patristic Research (the Netherlands); Member of the South African Academy of Science and Arts

Testimonials

The Bible is under attack, as it always has been, but with the advent of 'New Atheism', combined with modern means of communication, this attack is reaching more people, including those who would not normally take an interest. Christians need to have the tools to defend the Bible and this is what has impressed me about *Echoes of Jesus*. The detail in the table of contents enables the reader to be able to go directly to the page of interest and thereby be readily provided with information for a robust defence. Early Greek New Testament documents is an area normally heavy with jargon. Jonathan Clerke's coverage of these documents (chapters 7, 8 and 9), their grouping and his explanation of their variances is the clearest I have come across. The book is written in a scholarly manner with each piece of new information adequately referenced, thereby giving confidence to the reliability of the statement. *Echoes of Jesus* will hold a valuable place in my library.

> Dr Gary J Baxter, PhD (Monash University); author of A Defence of the Bible

As a scientist and a Christian, I often find myself in interesting discussions about issues such as evolution versus creation and the historical accuracy of the Bible. Objectivity is critical in these discussions, so wherever possible, I try to focus on accurate scientific and historical data and facts; for example, in relation to evolution, one of my interests is quantitative genetics, particularly the probability associated with mutation and selection rates, and the likelihood of known information coding sequences having developed by chance. Jonathan's book enables me to use the same objective approach in relation to evaluating the New Testament and determining whether it accurately records the life and teachings of Jesus.

In his book, *Echoes of Jesus: Does the New Testament Reflect What He Said?*, there is a wealth of factual information from a range of sources, including archaeological records, ancient manuscripts and the writings of both early Christians and non-Christians. *Echoes of Jesus* also provides valuable contextual information on the times and circumstances during which the New Testament was written, and the likelihood that events and teachings could, and probably were, accurately recorded and retained for 2000 years. As a scientist, I found Jonathan's approach very objective, which undoubtedly also reflects his scientific background! I am really looking forward to using this information in discussions with people genuinely interested in the life, times and teachings of Jesus — and, of course, what it all means if indeed it has been accurately recorded!

> Dr Owen Nichols, PhD (University of Western Australia); mining environmental consultant, Brisbane, Australia

This book will appeal to all those who have a desire to know more about the cultural setting in which Jesus both lived and taught. The value of this book is that it draws upon information from both Christian and non-Christian records, and the author is not afraid of delving into perspectives and formal records from 'both sides of the fence'. The book underpins its arguments with easily understood concepts using a multitude of reference documents, all recorded in a substantial running bibliography.

With my training as a civil engineer, and now with significant experience in major multi-million-dollar project delivery, I have a keen appreciation for the need for everything to 'add up' before I commit to or place my faith in any aspect of project delivery. This is also my approach to my faith in the God of the Bible, and the author provides me with a solid foundation on which to further develop my faith in the authenticity and accuracy of the Bible.

This book will appeal to anyone who is looking for a defence to the common belief that Jesus was born into a world of illiteracy. It will specifically appeal to Bible students of all kinds who are looking for a concise and well-referenced book that gives sound reasons for believing that the early chapters of the New Testament are entirely believable, if only because they were generated at a time when people were very capable of recording information both reliably and accurately.

This book is yet another beacon of light in a post-God world that has convinced itself there is no God. May it open many people's eyes to He who is 'the Way, the Truth and the Life'.

> Peter Ham, BEng(Civil) (University of Queensland), PGradDipBus(Mgt) (Deakin University); registered professional engineer, Wyong, Australia

Jon's wonderful book elegantly addresses many of the searching questions I have regarding the veracity of Scripture with meticulous scholarship and personable wit. I share many of the concerns of folks who challenge the integrity and therefore the relevance of the Gospels. Jon's systematic, evidence-based defence of the capture and preservation of Jesus' life and teachings in the New Testament is compelling. Thanks Jon for providing a text that balances approachability with solid, detailed evidence. I'm renewed in fervour to defend the Bible's record and relevance in this post-Christian age.

> Bill Robertson, BCom, CISA, CRISC, GradDipDiv; IT audit, risk and controls specialist, Brisbane, Australia

This book is a valuable addition to the library of anyone interested in Christian apologetics, or indeed anyone who wants to know how Jesus' teaching has been passed down to us. The book has been meticulously researched and is a work of considerable scholarship, yet written in accessible language. It reads like a quest, as Jonathan takes us from the ancient world to today, seeking answers to the questions surrounding the veracity of the Gospels. This book provides the context in which the words of Jesus were recorded and preserved and concludes with the certainty that the Gospels, as we know them today, are trustworthy. A great read, it will also be a useful book of reference.

   J Nott

Echoes of Jesus is a 'must-have' book for all those interested in the person of Jesus, the credibility of the Bible, and in particular the New Testament. Written in an easy-to-understand and logical format Jonathan answers the pertinent questions a person may have about literacy in the ancient world, the teaching methods of Jesus, and the amazing accuracy and credibility of the New Testament accounts as well as including a selection of ratifying evidence for Jesus from early Christian and non-Christian witnesses. Whether you're a layperson wanting for proof for Jesus or a theological student researching the accuracy of the Bible *Echoes of Jesus* will more than satisfy your needs.

   P Jayawardhana

Abbreviations and Glossary

Abbreviations

AD	Anno Domini. Derived from the Latin for 'in the year of the Lord', 1 AD being the year calculated as when Jesus was born. However, when it was developed in about 1582 it contained some errors. Hence, Jesus Christ was actually born c. 4 BC.
b.	The date a person was born, for example: Cassius Dio (b. 163 AD)
BC	'Before Christ' was born. (*See also* AD.)
BCE	Before the Christian Era, or Before the Common Era. (*See also* CE.)
CE	Christian Era or Common Era. BCE and CE are used in this book only when they exist within a quote or a title of a referenced work. It has become fashionable in some quarters to abandon AD and BC in order to appear more secular. Critics of this approach argue that not using AD or BC is to deny the historical nature of the dating system.
c.	Approximately. Derived from the Latin word *circa*, meaning 'around' or 'about'. Unless stated otherwise, it may apply to both dates with which it is associated. For example, 'c. 114–165 AD' means that at least one of the stated years is approximate.
ESV	English Standard Version of the Bible
NASB	New American Standard Bible
NIV	New International Version of the Bible, 2011
P45, P^{45}	A Greek papyrus manuscript containing parts of the four Gospels and the New Testament book of Acts, written between 200 AD and 250 AD. The superscript convention has been dropped to avoid confusion with footnotes, except when used in quotations and titles of publications.

P46, P⁴⁶	A Greek manuscript containing parts of the New Testament, but not the Gospels or Acts, written c. 200 AD. The superscript convention has been dropped to avoid confusion with footnotes, except when used in quotations and titles of publications.
P47, P⁴⁷	A Greek manuscript containing parts of the New Testament book of Revelation, written between 200 AD and 250 AD. The superscript convention has been dropped to avoid confusion with footnotes, except when used in quotations and titles of publications.
P66, P⁶⁶	A Greek manuscript containing parts of the Gospel of John, written between 175 AD and 200 AD. The superscript convention has been dropped to avoid confusion with footnotes except when used in quotations and titles of publications.
P72, P⁷²	A Greek manuscript containing the New Testament books of 1 Peter, 2 Peter and Jude, written c. 300 AD. The superscript convention has been dropped to avoid confusion with footnotes, except when used in quotations and titles of publications.
P75, P⁷⁵	A Greek manuscript containing parts of the Gospels of Luke and John, written c. 200 AD. The superscript convention has been dropped to avoid confusion with footnotes, except when used in quotations and titles of publications.
r.	The dates during which a person reigned or held office, for example: Emperor Hadrian (r. 117–138 AD)
RSV	Revised Standard Version of the Bible

Symbols

§	Section sign, indicating the numbering found in the Greek text of the works of Josephus. This numbering has been sourced from the translation by W Whiston, who also used paragraph numbering.
[ ]	The use of square brackets, such as [OT], indicates that the contents enclosed by the brackets have been added by myself to a quote made by someone else.
( )	Curved brackets found within a quote belong to the originator of the quote.
Mark 12:2–4	This format typically refers to a passage from the Bible, although any book can be referenced this way. In the example given, Mark 12:2–4 indicates verses 2 to 4 inclusive of the twelfth chapter of the book of Mark. If a book has only one chapter, then its reference will appear as, for example, Philemon 7, 18, 21, indicating verses 7, 18 and 21 of the book of Philemon. When there are two books by the same name, then they are differentiated using a number before the name of the book, such as 2 Peter 3:15.
[sic]	Indicates that the words quoted really are found in the original quote. It is typically used to point out that a mistake of some kind, such as a spelling or grammatical error, exists in the original source of the quote.

Glossary

Alexandrinus	See *Codex Alexandrinus*.
Bezae	See *Codex Bezae Cantabrigiensis*.
Bodmer Papyri	A collection of codices found in Egypt, including three important New Testament manuscripts dating from about 175 AD to the early 300s AD

Chester Beatty Papyri	A collection of 12 codices that were probably found in northern Egypt. Three of the codices are important New Testament manuscripts dating from 200 AD to 300 AD.
Codex	A document made in the form of a book
Codices	Plural of codex
Codex Alexandrinus	A nearly complete Greek manuscript, written in the 400s AD
Codex Bezae Cantabrigiensis	Often abbreviated to Codex Bezae. This Greek and Latin manuscript, written c. 400 AD, contains much of the New Testament.
Codex Sinaiticus	A complete Greek manuscript of the New Testament, dating from c. 350 AD. It also contains large portions of the Old Testament.
Codex Vaticanus	A complete Greek manuscript of the New Testament, dating from the 300s AD. It also contains large portions of the Old Testament.
Septuagint	An ancient Greek version of the Old Testament
Sinaiticus	See *Codex Sinaiticus*.
Synoptic	An adjective used to describe the first three New Testament gospels: Matthew, Mark and Luke
Vaticanus	See *Codex Vaticanus*.

Distance calculations

Distances between cities or other points of interest were calculated using MapCrow (www.mapcrow.info) and represent the distance measured in a straight line, that is, 'as the crow flies'.

Foreword

By Rev Dr Peter Christofides, Vose Seminary, Perth, Australia

As a lecturer in New Testament studies at a seminary and the teaching pastor at a local church, I have appreciated *Echoes of Jesus* and the way Jonathan Clerke displays a unique combination of scholarship in archaeology, history and theology, along with a remarkable simplicity of expression. This excellent work demonstrates his enormous capacity for research and his unusual ability to write things down so that the ordinary person, as well as the student of biblical studies, can understand them.

There are a number of different ways of reading and searching the Scriptures. When it comes to the devotional reading of the Bible, hearing from God is the focus. The academic study of Scripture, however, focuses on understanding the text in relation to its historical context. These two approaches and their results are often posed antagonistically against one another. There are critical scholars who devalue the devotional reading of Scripture and the quest to hear the voice of the living God in it. There are others who dismiss the academic study of these texts as inconsequential, since the Spirit is 'all they need' to interpret the Scriptures. The former reduce the witness of Scripture to a basic, workable, rational morality that does not interfere with the modern agenda. The latter privilege their potentially idiosyncratic and erroneous readings and applications with divine authority. In my opinion, neither of these positions, in their extreme, results in effective learning.

Both kinds of inquiry can and should work together in the community of faith. The academic study of the Scriptures can be used by people of faith as a means to allow the text to speak its own word on its own terms. But this avenue of inquiry is also best pursued prayerfully and in connection with the God who continues to speak through these texts. With these spiritual disciplines, the fruits of academic study are brought back into the conversation with God and with other Christians about what God would say to God's people today through these texts. The critical study of the New Testament acknowledges the distance between the modern reader — in his or her cultural, political, theological and economic setting — and the author and immediate readers of a New Testament text. The devotional use of the New Testament presumes the immediacy and accessibility of the Word for the worshipper. Pursuing both avenues of inquiry, allowing neither to overwhelm the other and bringing the results of each into vigorous interaction with the other, puts the Christian leader on the surest ground, enjoying the riches of both while being less liable to the limitations of either.

Echoes of Jesus seeks to nurture this kind of integrated approach to Scripture, attending to both the methods and results of academic and critical study of the New Testament as well as to the ways that these texts continue to speak a word from the Lord about discipleship, community and ministry. After reading this book, I can assure readers that they will be prepared to, firstly, more fully engage the critical and prayerful study of the New Testament and, secondly, more reliably discern the direction the Spirit would give through these texts for nurturing disciples and building communities of faith that reflect the heart and character of their Lord. These objectives have been especially highlighted in this book.

Jonathan has written an introduction to the New Testament that gives very close attention to the historical, social, cultural and rhetorical dimensions of those ancient writings as well as the ancient settings. *Echoes of Jesus* gives its readers comprehensive background and instruction on the interpretive approaches for present-day readers of the Bible. This book is a 'must get' for anyone interested in digging deeper during their journey through the New Testament.

I will be recommending *Echoes of Jesus* to my students and church friends as it invites its readers to carefully study in order to carefully apply. It stimulates thought and discussion, which is valuable and purposeful for shaping disciples and supporting communities of faith and ministry to the world.

Rev Dr Peter Christofides, DipTheol, BTh(Hons), MA (Bib. Studies), D. Litt et Phil (Doctor of Literature and Philosophy, University of Johannesburg), PhD (University of Pretoria), Cert IV TAE

Peter has two doctorates and was previously Principal of Rosebank Bible College and head of biblical languages at the Baptist Theological College of Southern Africa. Most recently, he has served as Senior Pastor at Casuarina Baptist Church (Australia) during a time of significant growth. An effective communicator, Peter is the teaching pastor at Riverton Baptist Community Church. Peter is of Greek ancestry (and speaks Greek fluently).

Preface

Many of the people I come across are unaware of the vast amount of historical evidence there is for the trustworthiness of the New Testament — that section of the Bible that discusses Jesus and the first Christians. They reasonably assume that the accounts of Jesus are mere fables, stories that are not historically true. Often they consider that the original wording of the New Testament has been distorted as copies were made of copies over and over again for hundreds of years. Other comments include the belief that the bias of the original authors would have distorted their written records of Jesus' teachings and actions.

Many of these same individuals, when shown evidence for the reliability of the New Testament, are eager to learn more. However, they often do not have any background knowledge of the subjects of history or Christianity. So this book has been written with as little jargon as possible, and with explanatory comments when technical language is unavoidable. I have supplied background information whenever experience — from the many conversations I have had over the decades — has taught me that it can't be assumed.

Although there are a number of other excellent books that focus on the reliability of the New Testament, like all books, they can't be 'all things to all people'. For example, many of the books that present evidence for the reliability of the copying of the New Testament do so using many technical terms and assume that the reader has a good understanding of the topic already. Some are written for an audience that is competent in ancient Greek. Those books that do cover this topic in a more accessible way often don't present much of the actual evidence, leaving the reader to rely heavily on the reassuring words of a scholar.

Credentials

My qualifications have nurtured a strong research-based approach to examining information. These qualifications are mainly in physiotherapy and parasitology, resulting in a BSc(Hons) and a BPhty, both from the University of Queensland. Because I am not qualified as a historian, a critic of the New Testament or a philosopher, I have provided the evidence that has formed the basis of my conclusions. In this way, readers can independently evaluate whether such conclusions are reasonable. Similarly, when I have had to rely on the conclusions of others, I have sought out those scholars who have the relevant qualifications. Readers should have the opportunity to be discerning. Judges do not have to be experts in forensics, ballistics and criminal psychology in order to weigh up well-presented evidence from experts on a murder by shooting.

Dedication

To Anita, Roshan and Sharmini Clerke. Three amazing people who show their passion for Jesus in many diverse and tangible ways.

To Jack and Gloria Clerke for instilling in me a love for books from a very young age, and for encouraging me to follow Jesus.

Acknowledgements

Special thanks go to my best friend and wonderful wife Anita, for helping create time and space for me to write this book over a period of more than eight years. My chief editor, Rebecca Gollan, was always quick to respond to my drafts and had an incredible eye for detail and consistency. Rebecca's vast experience as a professional non-fiction editor meant that her frequent encouragement was very inspiring. Roshan was an excellent assistant editor, covering a lot of material in a short period of time. I also wish to thank Dr Owen Nichols, Grant, Angela and others who often had the dubious honour of looking over the early drafts. If it were not for the assistance given by Trish and Roshan in obtaining numerous books and articles from university libraries this book would still be unfinished. Many people who have attended my talks over the years have spurred me on to make this book a reality. Mark Stay from Stay Media Productions generously applied his professional skills to producing the cover. Amanda and Julia at Australian eBook Publisher skillfully performed the task of turning a very large and plain word processing document into its present stylish and attractive form. I am indebted to Rev Dr Peter Christofides for enthusiastically writing the foreword with great insight. I gladly accept the blame for any errors that have slipped through into the final pages despite all of the help I have received.

Introduction

Can we hear echoes of Jesus' words when we read the New Testament?

Many questions arise when looking at the life and teachings of Jesus Christ as found in the New Testament. The importance of these questions is evident by the fact that there are few issues more emotive than whether this part of the Bible contains a real and accurate description of Jesus. This is partly because of two reasons. Firstly, individual people and governments around the world use, or have used, the Bible as their foundation for deciding what is right and what is wrong. Secondly, hundreds of millions of men, women and children understand the Bible as being God's ultimate revelation of himself to us, describing how God became human flesh and dwelt among people in the person of Jesus Christ. It is this same Jesus that they believe offers them forgiveness and a relationship whereby he indwells them and becomes their friend and master.

How scholars view the reliability of the New Testament

Despite the importance of these Biblical passages about Jesus to so many people, I have met many who believe that no intelligent person would spend time considering the life and teachings of Jesus. Often this is because they are convinced that the biblical records about Jesus merely represent a collection of folk tales. To them the New Testament accounts about Jesus represent fanciful stories that have been so entwined with reality that it is impossible to discern anything but a small remnant of historical truth about what Jesus actually said and did.

On the other hand, I have found that there have been extraordinarily brilliant individuals who have discovered that Jesus' life was at least very fascinating, even though they appear to have never given their allegiance to him. One of the most famous scientists of the 20th century was greatly impressed by the figure of Jesus Christ. Although he did not profess to be a Christian, the Nobel Prize-winning physicist Albert Einstein made the following comments in an interview in 1929:

> *As a child I received instruction in the Bible and the Talmud. I am a Jew, but I am enthralled by the luminous figure of the Nazarene [Jesus] ... Jesus is too colossal for the pen of phrasemongers, however artful ...*[1]

When asked if he accepted the historical existence of Jesus, he replied:

> *Unquestionably. No one can read the Gospels without feeling the actual presence of Jesus. His personality pulsates in every word. No myth is filled with such life ... legendary heroes of antiquity ... lack the authentic vitality of Jesus.*[2]

When such a great genius of physics as Einstein speaks so favourably about the accounts of Jesus found in the Gospels of the New Testament, it should at least encourage us to read them and decide for ourselves just how colossal is Jesus. Einstein did, like all of us, have a bias about the existence of God, and so his belief in a 'spirit vastly superior to man'[3] may have predisposed him to arrive at his conclusions about Jesus. However, it should be kept in mind that Einstein began life

---

1 GS Viereck, 'What life means to Einstein: an interview by George Sylvester Viereck', *Saturday Evening Post,* 26 October 1929, pp. 17, 110, 113, 114 & 117.
2 GS Viereck, , pp. 17, 110, 113, 114 & 117.
3 H Dukas & B Hoffman (eds), *Albert Einstein the Human Side,* Princeton University Press, Princeton, 1981. At least at one point in his life, Einstein did not believe in a personal God. Based on *New York Times* magazine article from 1930, according to the same book. At the present time, a variety of scientists are publishing popular books on theological issues, often denouncing the existence of God.

as a practising Jew (a religion that does not regard Jesus as God the Son) nor did he believe in a personal God. The thought did also occur to me that Einstein's judgment about Jesus may be regarded as inconsequential insofar as inspiring us to read the New Testament given he was a specialist in physics and not in history or theology. The flipside of this concern is that if an intelligent person who is not a specialist in history, nor a Christian, could conclude that the Gospels present a reliable account about Jesus, then maybe one does not need to be a rocket scientist to reach a similar conclusion.

Of course it is not only brilliant scientists who consider that the Gospels contain valuable information about Jesus. There are scholars of history and ancient literature who have also concluded that the Bible provides a reliable account about Jesus. I have selected quotations from two such scholars; the first is from another secular scholar and the second from a Christian.

Will Durant, a philosopher and Pulitzer Prize–winning writer of history, wrote:

> *Despite the prejudices and theological preconceptions of the evangelists [who wrote the Gospels], they record many incidents that many inventors would have concealed. No one reading these scenes can doubt the reality of the figure [Jesus] behind them. That a few simple men should in one generation have invented so powerful and appealing a personality, so lofty an ethic and so inspiring a vision of human brotherhood, would be a miracle far more incredible than any recorded in the Gospels. After two centuries of Higher Criticism [attacking the authenticity and veracity of the Bible] the outlines of the life, character, and teaching of Christ, remain reasonably clear, and constitute the most fascinating feature in the history of Western man.[4]*

---

4 W Durant, 'Caesar and Christ: a history of the Roman civilization and of Christianity from beginnings to A.D. 325', in *The Story of Civilization*, vol. 3 " Simon and Schuster, New York, 1944, p. 557. It should be kept in mind that Durant referred to himself as an agnostic and was critical of belief in a supernatural God. He also believed that the gospels were not a perfect record of Jesus' life. For example he stated that 'there are many contradictions between one gospel and another... [However the] contradictions are of minutiae, not substance; in essentials the synoptic gospels agree remarkably well.' p. 557

Professor Edwin Yamauchi, who has received masters and doctoral degrees in Mediterranean studies, stated in an interview that:

> ...my studies have greatly strengthened and enriched my spiritual life ... This doesn't mean that I don't recognize that there are some issues that still remain; within this lifetime we will not have full knowledge. But these issues don't even begin to undermine my faith in the essential trustworthiness of the New Testament ... For me, the historical evidence has reinforced my commitment to Jesus Christ as the Son of God who loves us and died for us and was raised from the dead.[5]

But what does the evidence say?

However, the decision of whether or not to investigate the life of Jesus should not be based solely on the testimonies of several scholars. One reason for this is that it is easy to find scholars who have quite different opinions about the historical trustworthiness of the New Testament accounts. For example, one scholar wrote that even Jesus' birth town (Bethlehem) had been deliberately reassigned from the real place of birth, so as to make Jesus appear very significant in the eyes of the Jews.[6]

Because of this divergence of scholarly opinion, I wanted to embark on a study of the actual evidence for the reliability of the New Testament. This is based on the concept that it is not so much opinions that matter, but the foundations for these opinions. The evidence that I was particularly interested in related to three broad questions that are commonly asked:

1. The New Testament was written hundreds of years ago, so it had to be copied by hand, over and over again, until the printing press was invented in the 1400s. Has all this repeated copying caused many changes in the message of the New Testament and, if so, how much has it changed? If there were changes, were they all accidentally made by copyists or were some intentional?

---

5 L Strobel, *The Case for Christ: A Journalist's Personal Investigation of the Evidence for Jesus,* Zondervan, Michigan, US, 1988, p.119. Prof. Yamauchi has published 80 articles in 37 scholarly journals.

6 BD Ehrman, *Jesus, Interrupted: Revealing the Hidden Contradictions in the Bible (and Why We Don't Know About Them),* HarperCollins e-books, 2009, pp. 235–6. http://www.scribd.com/doc/22916607/Jesus-interrupted-Bart-D-ehrman, accessed 11/08/2013.

2. Were the people who wrote the New Testament reliable and honest? Because these authors were biased towards Jesus, has their bias twisted the original story?

3. Given that Jesus did not write down his teachings into a book, how is it possible that Jesus' spoken words were recorded accurately by his disciples? Was not reading and writing 2000 years ago the preserve of only an elite few?

Parts of this book

My investigative journey took a path involving several successive stages, which are discussed in parts I to IV. The book then finishes with a look at the implications of the discoveries made along the way, followed by three appendices. The following is a brief outline of the book.

Part I: Literacy and gullibility in the world of Jesus

This part consists of four chapters that explore several related beliefs that I have encountered frequently. The first is that people who lived around the time of Jesus were unable to write accurate history and that as a consequence the small amount of literature that was produced is probably very inaccurate. The second belief is that literacy was rare among the people. This illiteracy created an environment conducive to people being easily duped, which in turn aided the spread of Christianity.

In chapter 1, I will demonstrate that there existed people, during and before the time of Jesus, who were able to write reliable historical records. Chapter 2 will look at how widespread literacy was in the Greco–Roman Empire. This geographical consideration is important as it was from the province of Judea that Christianity grew. Chapter 3 will seek to uncover evidence for literacy amongst the Judean inhabitants specifically, as these are the people with which Jesus shared his life the most. It will also examine the literacy of the early Christian community. Finally, chapter 4 will examine the relationship between illiteracy and gullibility.

Part II: From Jesus' mouth to the disciples' hands

This explores in two chapters whether it was possible for Jesus' actions and teachings to be recorded accurately by the early disciples. It analyses the idea that the disciples casually followed Jesus around the countryside and tried to recall what he said and what he did only after he had died. With these half-hearted remembrances, they then began to travel the highways and byways spreading their stories.

In chapter 5 I will examine the likelihood that Jesus was a teacher who was diligent in teaching his disciples, and that they in turn were equally dedicated to preserving what he said and did.

Chapter 6 will illustrate how Jesus taught using various techniques that would have greatly aided the accurate retention of all that he said. It will also look at why it is that sometimes the same account, when described in more than one Gospel, has variations.

Part III: Accuracy in the copying of the New Testament accounts

Unfortunately, the original handwritten books and letters of the New Testament no longer exist. However, copies of these documents were made before they disintegrated, and as the centuries passed, copies of these copies were also made. This process of making copies of copies has resulted in changes to the original wording. The extent and impact of these changes are explored in this part. Chapter 7 examines the oldest complete, and incomplete, copies of the New Testament. Chapter 8 looks closely at the accuracy of copying by comparing several ancient important copies made in the 200s and 300s AD, while chapter 9 explores ways of comparing many ancient copies. The impact of three portions of the New Testament that have been copied differently in the early centuries AD is studied in chapter 10. Chapter 11 responds to the question of how different the Christian message would be if our New Testament was solely based on one particular ancient copy that is considered by many scholars to be very different and inferior in terms of accuracy to other highly regarded copies.

Part IV: Evidence from early Christian and non-Christian witnesses

Because the oldest significant portions of the New Testament are dated later than 200 AD, it is important to establish whether the New Testament was copied accurately before this time. One way to explore this matter is to compare the teachings of Christian leaders who wrote before 200 AD with the teachings of the New Testament. Another way is to delve into the writings of non-Christians who also wrote before 200 AD and commented on Christian beliefs. The comments of these non-Christians can also be used to determine if the bias of the authors of the New Testament had a negative impact on their truthfulness. Who these non-Christian authors were, why they commented on Jesus and the Christians, and what they had to say is one of the main focuses of this part.

Chapter 12 compares Christian teachings found in a letter composed by the Christian leader Polycarp with statements found in the New Testament. It also considers the work of two non-Christian historians — Tacitus and Thallus. The credibility and writings of three more authors from the ancient world — Lucian, Pliny and Josephus — are examined over chapters 13 to 17.

Implications and the appendices

The final chapter outlines the implications of the New Testament being reliable for those who have non-Christian beliefs, including agnostics and Muslims.

I have also composed three appendices, the first of which provides a brief background of political and religious life in first-century Judea. The second appendix consists of a table showing points of agreement between the New Testament and the non-Christian writers mentioned in part IV. Appendix 3 considers claims that the town named in the New Testament as being Jesus' home town did not exist during his lifetime.

I hope that those who finish reading this book will see that it is reasonable to conclude, based on an understanding of historical evidence, that the New Testament accounts of Jesus and the first Christians are trustworthy and vitally important.

Part I

Literacy and gullibility in the world of Jesus

This part consists of four chapters that explore several related beliefs that I have encountered frequently. The first is that people who lived around the time of Jesus were unable to write accurate history and that as a consequence the small amount of literature that was produced is probably very inaccurate. The second belief is that literacy was rare among the people. This illiteracy created an environment conducive to people being easily duped, which in turn aided the spread of Christianity.

Chapter 1 will demonstrate that there existed people, during and before the time of Jesus, who were able to write reliable historical records. Chapter 2 will look at how widespread literacy was in the Greco–Roman Empire. This geographical consideration is important as it was from the province of Judea that Christianity grew. Chapter 3 will seek to uncover evidence for literacy amongst the Judean inhabitants specifically, as these are the people with which Jesus shared his life the most. It will also examine the literacy of the early Christian community. Finally, chapter 4 will examine the relationships between illiteracy and gullibility, miracles and reasoning.

1
Writing history and creating libraries

Archaeology has shown that the New Testament has the hallmarks of being an account of real people in real places, as opposed to a work of pure fantasy. But I still wished to know whether the New Testament reliably passes on more than the bare facts that there was once a man called Jesus who taught in Judea. I wanted to know whether its pages could contain accurate details about what Jesus said and did. Such a possibility goes against a common assumption that people who lived around the time of Jesus were unable to write accurate history. As a consequence, it is believed by many that the small amount of literature that was produced at that time is probably very inaccurate.

In this chapter I will delve into how much ancient authors knew about the actual process of investigative reporting. What did they know about how to put together a historical account? Is it possible that writers of 2000 years ago, be they pagan or Christian, were aware of the pitfalls inherent in producing a reliable historical account? (The study of the methodology used to write history is called historiography.[1]) These and other relevant subjects are addressed in this and subsequent chapters. In this way, the implications of the evidence from the non-Christian sources, discussed later in the book, can be better appreciated.

---

1 Many ancient historians wrote in an annalistic style, whereby the story was put into a chronological order, year by year. This caused difficulties when it came to overlapping issues that spanned many years.

Evaluating the skills of ancient writers

My research revealed that writers of thousands of years ago were very skilled when it came to writing about current and past events. They were aware of the influence of bias and the importance of good source material. In many ways it could be said that they knew the essence of modern-day historiography. The following three ancient writers serve as examples.

Herodotus

Herodotus is often regarded as the father of history.[2] His famous work is called *The Histories*, which was written from Athens between the years c. 448 and 422 BC.[3] This was mostly concerned with the Greco–Persian wars that occurred only a few decades earlier. Herodotus wrote in narrative form with digressions describing a diverse range of people and places. These digressions included details about 'topography, climate, flora, fauna, natural resources, customs, past history and the like'.[4] He gathered much of his information through first-hand inquiry in many different countries. His ability to arrange this information:

> *in one grand historical scheme is one of the great achievements of his or any other age ... The word for 'inquiry' that Herodotus uses is* historia *... The noun and its verb ... denote on-the-spot-inquiry of what one sees and hears.*[5]

Herodotus sometimes applied logic to determine which of two historical accounts of a particular event was true. This is seen when reading how he evaluated the two conflicting accounts of how an army led by Croesus had crossed the river Halys. He judged that the version involving the use of bridges was correct, in contrast to the conflicting account based on the digging of trenches to divert the river.[6]

---

2 LL Grabbe, 'Who were the first real historians? On the origins of critical historiography', in LL Grabbe (ed.), *Did Moses Speak Attic*, Sheffield Academic Press, Sheffield, UK, 2001, p. 163. Lester Grabbe was Professor of Hebrew Bible and Early Judaism at the University of Hull in 2001.
3 JE Powell, *The History of Herodotus*, Adolf M Hakkert, Amsterdam, 1967, p. 38.
4 TJ Luce, 'Herodotus and Historia', in *The Greek Historians*, Routledge, London, 1997, p. 16.
5 TJ Luce, 'Herodotus and Historia', p. 21.
6 Herodotus, *The History of Herodotus*, trans. GC Macaulay, vol. 1, book 1, para. 75, www.gutenberg.org/files/2707/2707-h/2707-h.htm, accessed 16/01/2014.

He was cautious when considering the supernatural, saying that:

> *all men are equally ignorant of these matters [i.e. tales of the gods]: and whatever things of them I may record, I shall record only because I am compelled by the course of the story.*[7]

This caution was partly due to his awareness of how personal bias impacts discernment. Herodotus went so far as to say that only a deranged person would lampoon the religion of another. This statement was made after noting how Cambyses the Persian had, among other incidents, visited a temple in Memphis (in Egypt) and made fun of the image of an Egyptian god. Herodotus explained:

> *It is clear to me therefore by every kind of proof that Cambyses was mad exceedingly; for otherwise he would not have attempted to deride religious rites and customary observances. For if one should propose to all men a choice, bidding them select the best customs from all the customs that there are, each race of men, after examining them all, would select those of his own people; thus all think that their own customs are by far the best: and so it is not likely that any but a madman would make a jest of such things.*[8]

Herodotus then supplied an example, or as he called it, a proof, demonstrating how bias affects the judgments of other cultures:

> *Dareios [King Darius I of Persia] in the course of his reign summoned those of the Hellenes [Greeks] who were present in his land, and asked them for what price they would consent to eat up their fathers when they died; and they answered that for no price would they do so. After this Dareios summoned those Indians who are called Callatians, who eat their parents, and asked them in presence of the Hellenes, who understood what they said by help of an interpreter, for what payment they would consent to consume with fire the bodies of their fathers when they died; and they cried out aloud and bade him keep silence from such words.*[9]

---

7   Herodotus, *The History of Herodotus*, trans. GC Macaulay, vol. 1, book 2, para. 3, www.gutenberg.org/files/2707/2707-h/2707-h.htm, accessed 16/01/2014.
8   Herodotus, *The History of Herodotus*, trans. GC Macaulay, vol. 1, book 3, para. 38, www.gutenberg.org/files/2707/2707-h/2707-h.htm, accessed 16/01/2014.
9   Herodotus, vol. 1, book 3, para. 38.

The above examples reveal how Herodotus used logic and evidence to support his conclusions. This desire to ascertain the truth motivated him to interview individuals even if it meant travelling extensively. He once deliberately went to consult the priests in three different cities in Egypt in order to see if their accounts were harmonious.[10] Similarly, Herodotus wrote how he had travelled from Memphis in Egypt to Tyre in present-day Lebanon (540 kilometres as the crow flies). He did this simply because he was 'desiring to know'[11] with as much certainty as possible the origins of the name of the god Heracles.[12] Herodotus also understood the need to look at motives when seeking understanding of what people said.[13]

This is not to say that Herodotus always got it right. However, his numerous accurate comments outweigh his mistaken ones.[14] Some of those errors may have arisen from his interest in what was bizarre, amazing and astonishing, and such matters often have dubious origins. Nevertheless, some of his weird accounts have turned out to be true.[15] For example, he described how goats in Arabia were allowed to graze among certain bushes that produced a sweet aromatic substance called ledanon. Later the owners harvested the ledanon from the goats' beards to use in perfumes. Even today it is possible to watch the harvesting of ledanon on the island of Crete by locals combing leather or plastic thongs through the Cistus creticus (rockrose) bushes. Goats can still be found grazing among the plants.[16]

Thucydides

Another Greek historian was Thucydides (460–400 BC), who became famous for his book on the war between the Greek city-states of Athens and Sparta, the latter based in the region that is still called Peloponnese. Thucydides was especially concerned with the destruction caused by the war.[17] Thucydides warned those who wanted to obtain a reliable

---

10 Herodotus, vol. 1, book 2, para. 3.
11 Herodotus, vol. 1, book 2, para. 44.
12 Herodotus, vol. 1, book 2, paras 43–44.
13 TJ Luce, 'Herodotus and Historia', p. 23. Citing Herodotus' *Historia* 3.2,16.
14 TJ Luce, 'Herodotus and Historia', p. 28.
15 TJ Luce, 'Herodotus and Historia', pp. 27–8.
16 In Latin these bushes are called labdanum or ladanum. Visit www.labdanum.gr for more information. Accessed 29/11/2008.
17 TJ Luce, 'Thucydides: Subject and methods', in *The Greek Historians*, Routledge, London, 1997, p. 70.

account of events to avoid those 'chroniclers who composed their works to please the ear rather than to speak the truth'.[18] Furthermore, he wrote:

And with reference to the narrative of events [in the Peloponnesian war], far from permitting myself to derive it from the first source that came to hand, I did not even trust my own impressions, but it rests partly on what I saw myself, partly on what others saw for me, the accuracy of the report being always tried by the most severe and detailed tests possible. My conclusions have cost me some labour from the want of coincidence between accounts of the same occurrences by different eye-witnesses, arising sometimes from imperfect memory, sometimes from undue partiality for one side or the other.[19]

Thucydides has proved to be quite a reliable historian. This is based on the fact that:

some bits of information from other sources [apart from Thucydides] do survive that enable us to check his accuracy, and it is to his credit that there are few points on which he can be shown to be in error and a great many on which he has been proven correct.[20]

Thucydides' style does vary, and in one particular section, titled 'Archaeology', he does in fact name sources and 'openly discusses what evidence he finds trustworthy and why he makes the deductions he does'.[21] In fact, he tests the truthfulness of what some of the much earlier writers of Greek history said:

with an impressive piece of analysis, strikingly modern in many of its methods. His evaluation of written evidence is remarkable, for he endeavours wherever possible to check it by material evidence, by analogy with contemporary Greece, as well as by appealing to probability and internal consistency.[22]

---

18 B Jowett (trans.), *Thucydides: The Peloponnesian Wars, Revised and Abridged with an Introduction by PA Bunt*, Book 1:21, Twayne Publishers, New York, 1963, 1.21, p. 12.
19 D Lateiner (rev.), The History of the Peloponnesian War / Thucydides, (trans. R. Crawley), Barnes & Noble Classics, New York, 2006, 1.22, pp. 18–19.
20 TJ Luce, 'Thucydides: Subject and methods', p. 71.
21 TJ Luce, 'Thucydides: Subject and methods', p. 74.
22 TJ Luce, 'Thucydides: Subject and methods', p. 75.

An example of Thucydides' method of analysis is how he discerned the truthfulness of one of his sources. He noted that the poet Homer, who wrote some 400 years earlier than Thucydides' own time, had described various Greek customs. Thucydides found these practices still existed in backward regions in his own time and concluded that they were once much more widespread.[23] To him, this in turn validated at least some of the writings of Homer.[24]

Thucydides also used archaeology to discover aspects of history. He discussed the exhuming of graves on the island of Delos, which was carried out by the more recent inhabitants as a means of purifying it. Thucydides understood that the cultural identity of the deceased could be determined based on the methods of burial and types of weapon. He concluded that the remains belonged to the Carian people, and that they were the early colonists of the island.[25]

Lucian

Although Lucian (c. 120–180 AD)[26] did not compose a lengthy and detailed account of history covering a particular period of time, he did write on the proper way to produce a historical account. (Lucian is one of the non-Christian writers examined in depth in part IV of this book.) The following is an excerpt from his book *How to Write History*, written in about 165 AD:

> *Here is a serious fault to begin with by some writers; it is their fashion to neglect the examination of facts, and give the space gained to eulogies of generals and commanders; those of their own side they exalt to the skies, the other side they disparage intemperately ... History, on the other hand, abhors the intrusion of any least falsehood ... The historian's task is to tell the thing as it happened ... A fair historian may nurse private dislikes, but he will ... set the truth high above his hate; he may have some favourites, but he will not spare their errors.*[27]

---

23 B Jowett, *Thucydides: The Peloponnesian Wars*, Book 1:5–7, pp. 3–4.
24 TJ Luce, 'Thucydides: Subject and methods', pp. 74–5.
25 B Jowett, *Thucydides: The Peloponnesian Wars*, Book 1:8, p. 4.
26 CP Jones, *Culture and Society in Lucian*, Harvard University Press, London, 1986, p.6
27 HW Fowler & FG Fowler, The Works of Lucian of Samosata, vol. 2:7, 39, Clarendon Press, Oxford, 1905, pp. 112, 128.

Others

Since these three authors represent Greco–Roman historians, the question arises as to how widespread were these practices of good historical writing. One author noted that in the Near East critical and accurate historical writing — including details of many battles that had been lost — has been found in Babylon as early as the eighth century BC.[28] Much later, and among the Jews, Josephus is regarded as a critical historian.[29] I have devoted chapters 16 and 17 to his history as he makes mention of many characters and events found in the New Testament.

Ancient history-writing techniques

These findings make it clear that ancient historians were aware that when it came to writing reliable history certain requirements needed to be met. These requirements included interviewing eyewitnesses who had participated in the events; limiting the narrative to the confines of good-quality evidence; where possible, travelling to the sites where the action had taken place; checking details with contemporary documents; and faithfully recording the truth as it actually happened.[30] As Professor Grabbe noted:

> *It was a commonplace expectation that the [Greco–Roman] historian's first concern was faithfulness to the data and accuracy in presenting them, even if it was generally anticipated that he would also write an interesting and elevating account.*[31]

Later, writing about various ancient historians, not just Greco–Roman ones, he stated:

> *there are many examples of critical historical writing in antiquity, with a few comparing quite favourably with the products of historians in the last couple of centuries.*[32]

---

28 LL Grabbe, pp. 171–3.
29 LL Grabbe, pp. 176–8. Grabbe notes that Josephus exempts the Jewish holy scriptures from critical questioning.
30 CJ Hemer, *The Book of Acts in the Setting of Hellenistic History,* ed. CH Gempf, Eisenbrauns, Winona Lake, Indiana, 1990, p. 100.
31 LL Grabbe, p. 168.
32 LL Grabbe, p. 180.

Although no one can prove that a particular writer of ancient times always used these techniques (successfully or not) to obtain and record the truth, it should be borne in mind that they could have and may well have. This reasonable supposition should be considered when reading the works of the ancient authors discussed in part IV of this book.

Similarly, it is reasonable to allow the possibility that the New Testament authors, who purported to write a truthful account that incorporated historical details, did actually follow such a set of precedents or guidelines to the best of their ability. Like other historians, they explicitly state that they were writing about real events that happened in places and with people that existed at that time. Such statements are found scattered through the various books of the New Testament, such as:

> *Therefore, since I myself have carefully investigated everything from the beginning, it seemed good also to me to write an orderly account for you, most excellent Theophilus, so that you may know the certainty of the things you have been taught. (Luke 1:3–4)*
>
> *We did not follow cleverly invented stories when we told you about the power and coming of our Lord Jesus Christ, but we were eyewitnesses of his majesty. (2 Peter 1:16)*

The abundance and availability of historical writings

Next I wanted to learn how much was written in the Greco–Roman societies that the early Christians inhabited 2000 years ago. Was the ability to write confined to only a few people and how substantial were their books? Were many people in those societies able to read, and how much access was there to books in general? Finding answers to these questions would help me to understand whether such societies[33] were capable of discerning the differences between fictitious stories and reliable factual accounts. If there was very little literature in circulation, it might have been possible for the authors of the New Testament to get away with fictitious or exaggerated accounts of Jesus. This is because their readers would not have been able to compare the

---

33 The societies I was interested in were the Greco–Roman ones that had influenced greatly the world of Jesus and the first generations of Christians.

content of the New Testament to other historical literature commenting on Christianity. This may have lead to a popular acceptance that wasn't warranted.

What I learnt through my investigations made me quite astonished at the enormous amount of literature that existed in ancient times. Sometimes it was even found washed up on the beach. This is recounted by the historian Xenophon (430–354 BC), who wrote about the wrecks of Greek ships in the southern region of the Black Sea. He said that among the flotsam and jetsam 'were found great numbers of beds and boxes, quantities of written books'.[34]

There were even books with coloured pictures. Pliny the Elder (23 BC – 79 AD) mentioned an illustrated book relating to the medicinal value of plants: 'The Greek writers have delineated it [the plant moly] as having a yellow flower ...'. A translator's footnote indicates that 'delineates' refers to illustrations.[35]

The ability to source ancient books

Being able to study books written years earlier is important when writing about historical events that predate any living witnesses. If ancient historians were diligent in this manner, it would further illustrate the value they gave to books.

I decided to search for examples of authors sourcing literature that was many years old by their own standards. One of the first I came across was the Greek author Athenaeus, who lived in the Egyptian town of Naucratis, about 150 kilometres north-west of Cairo. This second century AD author was found to have named about 260 plays from 44 poets from the fifth century BC alone.[36] So Athenaeus had the ability to access publications that were originally composed 500 years earlier than his era.

---

34 Xenophon, *Anabasis* VII 5–14, cited by EA Parsons, *The Alexandrian Library: Glory of the Hellenic World: Its Rise, Antiquities, and Destruction*, Cleaver-Hume Press, London, 1952, p. 25.
35 Pliny Secundus, *The Natural History*, book 25, chapter 8, n. 4.
36 K Sidwell, 'Athenaeus, Lucian and fifth-century comedy', in D Braund & J Wilkins (eds) *Athenaeus and His World: Reading Greek Culture in the Roman Empire,* University of Exeter Press, Exeter, UK, 2000, p. 137

I discovered a longer interval by reading the work of one modern-day historian who reported on a religious proclamation found in the town of Sardis, whose ruins lie in Turkey. The proclamation was from a governor and is 'a Greek translation of an Aramaic edict [i.e. a proclamation from a magistrate] promulgated c. 365 BC ... Our inscription is a copy made some 500 years afterwards'.[37]

Some books were used by quite a few famous ancient figures for hundreds of years. The book by Aeneas Tacticus called *Military Preparations* was originally penned in about 380 BC.[38] It was referred to by various famous Greek writers in subsequent centuries, such as the historian Polybius (203–120 BC), the philosopher Onasander in the first century AD and the writer Polyaenus in the second century AD. Aeneas Tacticus wrote another war manual called *How to Survive under Siege*. Although written in 357 BC, large portions of it were copied in the third century AD by the African Christian historian Sextus Julius Africanus.[39] It's unlikely that Africanus used a 500-year-old copy of the original book and more probable that he used one of the various copies of the war manual that had been made over the intervening years. It still surprised me that despite great turmoils in the history of the region, scholars living hundreds of years later could source ancient books.

As an aside, *How to Survive under Siege* makes interesting reading. The following quote is from a chapter titled 'How a large city can be guarded by a few men':

> *Moreover, you should disguise the most-able bodied of the women, old men, and boys that are in the town, and arm them as much like men as you can. And in place of arms [that is weapons] give them their jars and similar bronze utensils, and march them around the wall, but do not by any means allow them to throw missiles or yet to hurl a javelin, for even a long way off a female betrays her sex when she tries to throw.*[40]

---

37 GHR Horsely, *New Documents Illustrating Early Christianity: A Review of the Greek Inscriptions and Papyri Published in 1976*, Ancient History Documentary Research Centre, Macquarie University, 1981, p. 22.
38 TE Page et al. (eds), *Aeneas Tacticus, Asclepiodotus, Onasander: With an English Translation by Members of The Illinois Greek Club*, The Loeb Classical Library, William Heinemann, London, 1948, p. 13.
39 TE Page et al., pp. 5, 13.
40 TE Page et al., p. 223.

These examples reveal that those living in Greco–Roman cultures valued books and had the ability to preserve them for posterity's sake. This is relevant to investigating the reliability of the New Testament. It shows that it is reasonable to believe that the first Christians had the mindset of treasuring their books about Jesus for the sake of future generations. This in turn positively impacts on how readily later Christians could access very old copies of their scriptures when needing to make new copies.

Vast numbers of historians

The genre of historical writing was incredibly vast in these societies. At least 856 names of ancient Greek historians whose works have been mostly lost have been compiled based on 'fragments of their works, whether in quotation and paraphrase, or through *testimonia*: that is, comments about their lives and writings'.[41] For example, the Latin author Aulus Gellius (born c. 125 AD) wrote a series of books called *Attic Nights*, which supplies:

> valuable information in many fields of knowledge, and it contains extracts from a great number of Greek and Roman writers (275 are mentioned by name), the works of many of whom are otherwise wholly or in great part lost.[42]

Only the writings of six of the top-10 well-known ancient Greek historians have survived.[43] We know of the other four based on the mentions they receive in ancient writings. Between 323 BC and 146 BC (the Hellenistic age) many histories consisted of 30 volumes or more.[44] The writing of history continued after the birth of Christianity, and in geographically diverse regions.

The books of Appian of Alexandria (c. 95–165 AD) in Greece can still be read today, as can the books of Cassius Dio (c. 163–235 AD) from the Roman province of Bithynia in present-day Turkey.[45]

---

41 TJ Luce, 'Fourth-century and Hellenistic historiography', in *The Greek Historians*, Routledge, London, 1997, p. 106.
42 Gellius, *The Attic Nights of Aulus Gellius: with an English Translation by John C Rolfe*, vol. 1, William Heinemann, London, 1970, pp. xvi–xvii.
43 TJ Luce, 'Fourth-century and Hellenistic historiography', pp. 105–6.
44 TJ Luce, 'Fourth-century and Hellenistic historiography', pp. 107–8.
45 Bithynia would now be part of central and northern Turkey.

These are a few examples of the history books produced in ancient times:

- Polybius of Megalopolis (203–120 BC) wrote about the history of the Mediterranean. Although his publication only covered the period 264–145 BC, it consisted of 40 books.[46]
- The Syrian called Nicholas of Damascus (born c. 64 BC) wrote a world history comprising 144 books.[47]
- Livy (c. 59 BC to 17 AD) wrote a history of Rome called *From the Founding of the City*, which consisted of 142 books. It might be conjectured by some that these were small books. However, some simple calculations estimated that in book 10 alone there are over 24,600 words.[48] To help put this in perspective, the book you are reading now consists of about 105,000 words exclusive of the footnotes.
- The Jewish historian Josephus (37 AD to c. 100 AD) wrote several books, *The Antiquities of the Jews* being his largest and containing approximately 360,000 words.[49]
- The Roman historian Tacitus (c. 56 AD to c. 125 AD) wrote two major historical works, *The Annals* being his latest although in reality it was a prequel to his *Histories*. The two of them together comprised about 30 books. Although most of *The Annals* have been lost (four complete books and part of four others survive), this series originally consisted of at least 16 books and book 1 alone consists of approximately 13,000 words.[50]

---

46 TJ Luce, 'Polybius', in *The Greek Historians*, Routledge, London, 1997, p. 123.
47 S Bowman, 'Josephus in Byzantium', in LH Feldman & G Hata (eds), *Josephus, Judaism, and Christianity*, Wayne State University Press, Detroit, 1987, p. 367.
48 This is based on the English translation edited by Rev Canon Roberts as found on Tufts University's Perseus Digital Library (www.perseus.tufts.edu/hopper), where I calculated the number of words in the first 10 chapters, and then noted that there were 47 chapters.
49 This is based on *The Works of Josephus: Complete and Unabridged Translated by William Whiston*, Hendrickson Publishers, Massachusetts, 1989. I calculated the number of words in the preface (excluding footnotes of the translator), noted that there were 515 pages and then subtracted 5% to be conservative in allowing for variable lengths of footnotes made by the translators.
50 This word count based on *The Annals by Tacitus: Translated by Alfred John Church and William Jackson Brodribb*, accessed from http://classics.mit.edu/Tacitus/annals.1.i.html on 6/04/2008.

Ancient libraries

Writing in general also had a very prominent cultural value as reflected in some large and geographically diverse libraries. In Egypt's prestigious city of Alexandria, there was a vast library that had been accumulating scrolls since c. 220 BC. Aulus Gellius said that this library housed 'nearly seven hundred thousand volumes [or scrolls]' in 48 BC.[51] At around the same time, the library at Pergamum (the ruins of which lie in present-day Turkey) housed 200,000 scrolls.[52] This collection of books began in earnest with Eumenes II (r. 197–159 BC), though his predecessor Attalus I (r. 241–197 BC) started the collection. These two great libraries became serious competitors for purchasing books, and when books couldn't be purchased they copied them. Egypt was not only the home of the older library, but also the major manufacturer of the papyrus used for making paper. In order to diminish its rival's capacity, Egypt's government banned further exports of papyrus![53]

The Roman Emperor Augustus, who reigned from 31 BC to 14 AD, founded two libraries, one for Greek books and the other for Latin ones. Subsequent first-century Roman emperors, such as Tiberius, Vespasian and Trajan, also built libraries in Rome. The remains of Trajan's library are quite extensive and have allowed archaeologists to reconstruct on paper many of its details. Completed in about 112 AD, the library was extremely ornate, spacious and comfortable for visitors, and housed

---

51 Gellius, 1968, vol. 2, book 8, ch. 17.3, p. 139. See also pp. 138–9, n. 4. A scroll may have contained more than one book, and some books may have used more than one scroll. It has been suggested that the 700,000 scrolls may have represented 100,000 different titles as the library also housed duplicate copies (pp. 64–5). Mostly it was a collection of Greek literature, though some foreign books were translated into Greek (pp. 65, 67). History, philosophy, law and medical literature appear to have been present (pp. 68, 100). The library allowed people to read its books in nearby passages and colonnades (p. 67). There is no evidence that people could borrow books.
52 Plutarch, *Antonius*, pp. 58–9. This library was founded by Eumenes II, c. 160 BC (see JO Ward, 'Alexandria and its Medieval Legacy: The Book, the Monk and the Rose', in R MacLeod (ed.), *The Library of Alexandria: Centre of Learning in the Ancient World*, IB Tauris Publishers, New York, 2001, p. 165.
53 EA Parsons, *The Alexandrian Library: Glory of the Hellenic World: Its Rise, Antiquities, and Destruction*, Cleaver-Hume Press, London, 1952, p. 25.

about 20,000 scrolls.[54] By 350 AD there were 28 public libraries in Rome.[55] Sometimes libraries were built in honour of an emperor, such as the library built in Athens sometime between 98 and 102 AD by a wealthy man named Titus Pantainos and dedicated to Trajan.[56] The Emperor Hadrian (r. 117–138 AD) also built a great library in Athens.[57]

Libraries could also be found in other cities, such as Corinth, Ephesus and Smyrna, which had some of the earliest Christian communities.[58] The Ephesian library was completed around 135 AD [59] and was only 132 kilometres (82 miles) from the library in Pergamum. Yet the size of the Ephesian library was still considerable, having a capacity for about 9,500 scrolls. This would be equivalent to 730 books the size of the *Iliad*.[60] The *Iliad* has approximately 175,830 words when translated into English.[61] By comparison, *Harry Potter and the Prisoner of Azkaban* by JK Rowling has 107,253 words.[62]

The original construction of the Ephesian building was designed to create a grandiose library and a magnificent tomb for its benefactor, the famous Roman senator Celsus.[63] Unfortunately, the interior was destroyed by fire during an earthquake in 262 AD and the façade succumbed to another earthquake hundreds of years later. The library's

---

54 L Casson, *Libraries in the Ancient World*, Yale University Press, London, 2001, pp. 84–8.
55 HL Pinner, *The World of Books in Classical Antiquity*, AW Sijthoff, Leiden, The Netherlands, 1958, p. 56.
56 J Camp, *The Athenian Agora*, Thames and Hudson, London, 1986, pp. 187–91.
57 EA Parsons, p. 7, quoting Pausanius, *Attika*, Book 1 XVIII-9.
58 EA Parsons, p. 17.
59 J McRay, *Archaeology and the New Testament*, Baker Academic, Grand Rapids, Michigan, 1991, p. 261.
60 DR Johnson, *The Library of Celsus, an Ephesian Phoenix*, Wilson Library, Bulletin 54, 1980, pp. 651–3. Johnson based his calculations on vellum scrolls of about 6 metres length, written on both sides.
61 This word count is based on my calculations from the English translation by AT Murray, 1924, from Tufts University's Perseus Digital Library (www.perseus.tufts.edu/hopper) accessed 12/04/2012. I first calculated the average numbers of words per line (11.37) based on over 240 lines from two separate books, and then calculated the average number of lines per book (644.37) from eight of the 24 books.
62 Harry Potter Lexicon, www.hp-lexicon.org/about/books/pa/book_pa.html, accessed 12/04/2012.
63 L Casson, p. 115.

architecture is so magnificent that, even in its partially restored state, it is a major Turkish tourist attraction.

Although it seems that most public libraries allowed people to read the books only within the library walls, some lending libraries existed. Aulus Gellius mentions how in the library of Tibur (now modern-day Tivoli, 27 kilometres, or 17 miles, from Rome), which he says was 'well supplied with books', an acquaintance was able to take a book from the library. The book was by Aristotle (384–322 BC) and the friend quoted a portion of it that argued that water from melted snow was harmful to drink, as the good portion of the water evaporated away when it first became snow.[64] Athens also had a library that allowed borrowing.[65] Even if most libraries didn't lend books out to the people, some were built as if to ensure the people came to the libraries. Various emperors built lavishly decorated free bathing complexes, complete with steam rooms, massage chambers, gardens, cold-water plunge pools, and libraries.[66] These free public baths, along with other commercial baths, were:

> *patronised by all Romans, men and women, young and old, rich and poor. They came there not only for the bathing facilities but to pass time in leisurely activities, to walk in the gardens, play ball ... listen to lectures, chat with friends — or browse the library. The contents of the bath libraries must have reflected this state of affairs, namely that the readership would consist primarily of people who turned to the books as a pastime ... and only secondarily of professionals ...*[67]

Private libraries also existed, not just on land but also at sea! There was a library housed on board the gigantic pleasure ship owned by the tyrant of the Sicilian province of Syracuse, Heiron I (478–467 BC).[68] The remains of one large private library have been discovered in the south of Italy. This Villa Suburbana dei Papiri (Villa of the Papyri) housed 1787 scrolls when Mount Vesuvius erupted in 79

---

64 Gellius, vol. 3, book 19, ch. 5, p. 363.
65 L Casson, pp. 106–7.
66 L Casson, p. 89.
67 L Casson, pp. 91–2.
68 Athenaeus, *The Deipnosophists: With an English Translation by CB Gulick*, vol. 2, book 5, 207.e, pp. 438–9.

AD, swallowing Pompeii and the nearby town of Herculaneum in lava.[69] This was the same eruption that destroyed Pompeii. During the late second century AD, Larensis, once the procurator of the region Moesia, had an extremely large private library in Rome. Also, the Larensis library 'is typical of the private collections of books gathered by rich Romans from the second century BC ...'[70]

Private libraries became so numerous that the Roman philosopher Lucius Annaeus Seneca (4 BC – 65 AD) wrote disparagingly about some of these collections. The context of the following remarks were made whilst espousing the benefits of controlling one's own desires, avoiding excesses and fostering frugality:

> *What is the use of having countless books and libraries, whose titles their owners can scarcely read through in a whole lifetime? ... [Those kings responsible for the collection of books at the Alexandrian library] had collected the books, not for the sake of learning, but to make a show, just as many who lack even a child's knowledge of letters use books, not as the tools of learning, but as decorations for the dining room ... What excuse have you to offer for a man who seeks to have bookcases made of citrus-wood and ivory ... and sits yawning in the midst of so many thousand books, who gets most of his pleasure from the outsides of volumes and their titles? Consequently it is in the houses of the laziest men that you will see a full collection of orations and histories with the boxes piled right up to the ceiling; for by now among cold baths and hot baths a library also is equipped as a necessary ornament of a great house.*[71]

---

69 JJ Deiss, *Herculaneum: Italy's Buried Treasure*, J Paul Getty Museum, Malibu, California, 1989, p. 68.
70 C Jacob, 'Athenaeus the librarian', in D Braund & J Wilkins (eds), *Athenaeus and His World: Reading Greek Culture in the Roman Empire*, University of Exeter Press, Exeter, UK, 2000, p. 87.
71 Seneca, 'On Tranquility of Mind', in *Seneca in Ten Volumes*, vol. 2 *Moral essays with an English translation by JW Basore*, Harvard University Press, Cambridge, 1970, Book 9, pp. 202–285, quote from pp. 247–9.

Conclusion

These findings make it apparent that there were people in those Greco–Roman societies who could produce reliable historical writings and many who could also read the prodigious number of books available from a wide variety of genres. It seems that at least some people of these societies would have been well able to discern the difference between fanciful tales and factual accounts. Many of the New Testament writers could have been aware of the basic requirements of producing a reliable historical account, and were capable of doing so. However, if only a mediocre proportion of those societies could read and write, then valid concerns can be raised about whether it was *likely* that such aims could have been met. I now wanted to examine these and other related issues.

2

Literacy in the ancient world

Literacy and gullibility

The previous chapter established the existence of a plethora of written books housed in a multitude of libraries across the ancient Greco–Roman[1] world of the first Christians. However, some consider that the evidence of literacy based on books and libraries indicates only the presence of literacy in the elite members of those empires. These critics also claim that Christianity flourished in the first few centuries only because the vast majority were illiterate and, therefore, gullible. This supposed situation enabled the masses to be easily duped into believing anything, as they were largely ignorant of the world around them.

Others have taken the belief in mass illiteracy to arrive at a different conclusion: that it is unlikely that Jesus and his disciples were able to read or write competently. As a result, they claim that Jesus' life story and teachings were rapidly distorted as they were passed from one person to the next. I will examine the issue of distortion in later chapters,[2] but first the matter of illiteracy clearly needed further investigation.

Venturing outside the walls of the ancient libraries, I found that the assertions regarding illiteracy and gullibility proved to be false on several grounds. This chapter and the next two will explore three of the reasons that negate these arguments, namely that:

- literacy was widespread
- people can learn much about their world without being able to read

---

1 Greco-Roman and Graeco-Roman are simply spelling variants.
2 See parts III and IV.

- many of the people taught by Jesus, and many who became the first Christians, were discerning rather than gullible.

This chapter will look first at broad issues and then focus in on literacy in various geographic regions. The next chapter will concentrate on literacy in the countries where Jesus taught. Finally chapter 4 will delve into the relationship between literacy and gullibility.

Assessing literacy in the Greco-Roman world

From the overall abundance of historical writing described in the previous chapter, it is not too surprising to learn that many people living during and around the time of Jesus did have the ability to read. One scholar noted that there was a '... wide use of shorthand and the carrying of notebooks in the Greco–Roman world, [as well as] the school practice of circulating lecture notes and utilizing them in published works...'[3]

Although formal education was most accessible to the children of the wealthy in the Roman Empire, it is accepted that many learnt to read and write in their own homes. Even among the wealthy there was debate as to whether it was best to teach a budding young scholar in the home one-on-one with a teacher or to send them to a large school.[4] Despite the wealthy having a financial advantage over the poor in educating their children, they were not the only ones to engage in this activity. Just as in today's world, poorer parents 'were prepared to make sacrifices for their children's education'.[5] Pupils may have been required to pay as little as half a denarius per month in an Italian country town to a primary teacher.[6] Teaching may have occupied only eight months

---

3   RH Gundry, *The Use of the Old Testament in St. Matthew's Gospel: With Special Reference to the Messianic Hope*, EJ Brill, Leiden, The Netherlands, 1967.
4   Quintilian, *The Institutio of Oratoria of Quintilian with an English Translation*, trans. HE Butler, William Heinemann, London, 1963, vol. 1, book 1, ch. 2, p. 39. Quintilian lived between c. 35 AD to c. 100 AD.
5   SF Bonner, *Education in Ancient Rome: From the Elder Cato to the Younger Pliny*, Methuen & Co, London, 1977, p. 328.
6   SF Bonner, pp.149–50. Bonner cited the work of Horace (65–8 BC), referring to conditions in his hometown of Venusia in the south of Italy.

per year. Given that an ordinary workman could expect a denarius a day, parents didn't have to be very wealthy to pay for an education.[7] That the poor did manage to learn such skills is evidenced from the fact that many of the teachers had themselves arisen out of destitute circumstances. Many seemed to have achieved this through self-help.[8]

Girls are often thought of as being excluded from education in the ancient world. Yet this was not universally the case. Girls had been taught reading and writing before the Roman Empire conquered Greece. Vases dating from around 490 BC frequently depict women reading.[9] One writer of Greek comedy, Menander (342–291 BC), used the reality of women being able to read and write to belittle those who couldn't.[10] In the period between the first century BC and 200 AD, Latin inscriptions have been found that speak of women as 'scribes';[11] some of these women were slaves and others freed slaves.[12]

The teaching of reading and writing was performed in a very methodical and detailed fashion. In the beginning stages, reading was taught progressively starting with letters, then syllables, then monosyllabic words. Writing was taught 'equally conscientiously'.[13] One ancient Greek author advised that children be taught to write using letters carved in wood, which then acted as a three-dimensional template guiding the child's pen. Quick legible writing was encouraged as a 'sluggish pen delays our thoughts, while an unformed and illiterate hand cannot be deciphered ...'[14]

This is not to say that every ancient Greek and Roman was literate (even today illiteracy among adults in Greece is about 4%). When attempting

---

7 SF Bonner, pp. 149–50.
8 SF Bonner, p. 328.
9 L Casson, *Libraries in the Ancient World*, Yale University Press, London, 2001, pp. 19–21.
10 JW Thompson, *Ancient Libraries*, Archon Books, London, 1962, pp. 17–18, 104, n. 25, citing Greek dramatist Menander without any specific reference.
11 K Haines-Eitzen, 'Girls trained in beautiful writing': Females scribes in Roman antiquity and early Christianity, *Journal of Early Christian Studies*, 6(4), 1998, pp. 629–46, quote from p. 634.
12 K Haines-Eitzen, pp. 634–6.
13 SF Bonner, p. 329.
14 Quintilian, vol. 1, book 1, ch. 1, p. 35.

to understand the extent of literacy within a society, the different levels of literacy need to be kept in mind. One way of grading literacy is to consider what degree of literacy is required for an individual to function within their society. In England, it is estimated that 16% of adults are functionally illiterate. This equates to about 5.2 million who:

> *have literacy levels at or below those expected of an 11-year-old. They can understand short straightforward texts on familiar topics accurately and independently, and obtain information from everyday sources, but reading information from unfamiliar sources, or on unfamiliar topics, could cause problems.*[15]

Many factors conspire to make it difficult to establish the prevalence of literacy in an ancient culture. Much of the historic record has been lost. Discussion is further complicated by the multi-lingual societies of the Greco–Roman Empire. In the world inhabited by Jesus and the early Christians, it was possible that:

> *A Christian in first-century Palestine might have been thoroughly literate in Aramaic, largely literate in Hebrew, semi-literate in Greek, and illiterate in Latin, while a Christian in Rome in the late second century might have been literate in Latin ... but ignorant of Aramaic and Hebrew.*[16]

To establish the prevalence of literacy I looked at a number of indicators. When I speak of the ability to read and write, I was particularly interested in literacy that extended beyond a vocabulary of a few dozen words. A limited ability to read would enable a person to recognise their own name, words to do with their occupation, and numbers. I wanted to know if they could read a variety of genres that ranged from official documents to amusing poetry. This type of literacy would require a larger vocabulary and encompass concepts rather than just facts. Similarly with the ability to write, I wanted to know about those who could write more than just their signature and numbers. To determine these aspects of literacy, four different types of evidence will be investigated:

---

15 National Literacy Trust, 'How many illiterate adults are there in England?', www.literacytrust.org.uk/adult_literacy/illiterate_adults_in_england, accessed 12/05/2012.
16 HY Gamble, *Books and Readers in the Early Church: A History of Early Christian Texts*, Yale University Press, London, 1995, p. 3.

1. functional indicators
2. varieties of genres
3. the geographical dispersion of books
4. graffiti.

Functional indicators

Apart from libraries and the evidence of schooling, another way of determining literacy in societies is to consider functional indicators. This is because it is more worthwhile to examine the impact that written words had on individuals from within a society, than simply attempting to estimate the proportion of people that could read.[17]

Functional indicators of literacy would include such items as the use of written contracts, and whether or not the issuing of receipts was common practice. Similarly, if the social fabric of a society included the use of letters and other forms of written communication between individuals, then these are also functional indicators of literacy. As will be shown in later sections of this chapter, and throughout the next chapter, abundant examples of these typical forms of literary expression have been discovered. What I will delve into now are two atypical functional indicators that immediately caught my attention, namely curse tablets and epitaphs.

Curse tablets

Curse tablets were extremely popular in ancient societies. Such tablets, called *defixiones,* are found throughout the ancient world. Over a thousand of these have been found in regions as far apart as northern Africa and England, and from Syria in the east to Spain in the west. The defixiones were typically made of lead and were composed in the hope that the person(s) named on the tablet would be influenced in particular ways. Curses were made against rivals in areas of life as diverse as business, sport, theatre and love. These tablets were embedded in the tapestry of life of citizens from all classes. It has been said that 'almost everyone, from aristocrats and philosophers to slaves and jockeys,

---

17 AK Bowman, *Life and Letters on the Roman Frontier: Vindolanda and its People*, Routledge, New York, 1994, p. 82.

seems to have known the *defixio* as a social fact'.[18] Their mere existence points to the abundance of those who could read and write. At times, the person desiring to impose the curse on a human target may have inscribed the tablets themselves. More commonly, the curse tablets appear to have been written for clients by professional and amateur scribes associated with the business of cursing.[19] There seems to have been no shortage of scribes able to compose defixiones. A different person wrote each of the 130 curse tablets discovered in the city of Bath, England.[20]

To illustrate the nature of curse tablets, I have provided a sample of the text from one of a dozen tablets found in present-day northern France. These Latin defixiones were all written sometime in the 200s AD. The target of this jinx is an actor called Sosio, probably orchestrated by a rival actor named Eumolpus:

> *May Sosio become delirious, may Sosio suffer from fevers, may Sosio suffer pain every day. May Sosio not be able to speak ... May Sosio not be able to outshine the pantomime actor Eumolpus. May he not be able to play [the role of] a married woman in a fit of drunkenness on a young horse ...*[21]

Spells were often composed in very similar ways, following a recipe or a formula. These patterns were taken from written handbooks that were used in regions as far apart as Britain and Italy.[22] If most clients were unable to read the actual curses, then it would seem unlikely that the composers would be so diligent in rigidly sticking to the formula. This is particularly pertinent for at least some of the towns where curse tablets have been found because the majority 'of the clients [of the defixiones found in Bath] appear to have come from the lower social classes ...'[23]

---

18 JG Cager, *Curse Tablets and Binding Spells from the Ancient World*, Oxford University Press, Oxford, 1992, p. 21.
19 JG Cager, pp. 4–5.
20 JG Cager, pp. 5, 13.
21 JG Gager, p. 75.
22 JG Gager, pp. 177, 193.
23 JG Gager, p. 193. Gager here heavily cites the work of RSO Tomlin, *Tabellae Sulis: Roman Inscribed Tablets of Tin and Lead from the Sacred Spring at Bath*, Oxford University Committee for Archaeology, Oxford, 1988.

Epitaphs

Like curse tablets, epitaphs are another atypical indicator of literacy that readily catch the imagination. Epitaphs are inscribed messages, usually found on tombs, which are addressed to the living from the 'dead'. Such messages speak volumes about the widespread nature of literacy within their respective communities. Epitaphs from as early as the seventh century BC have been brought to light.[24] Some have an exquisite amount of detail, describing the occupation of the deceased, the length of their marriage, and for how many years, months and days they lived. Latin inscriptions frequently include the number of hours left in the unfinished dying day of the person entombed.[25] The existence of these mundane details assumes that there would be at least some in the community who could read.

Some epitaphs may argue only for the existence of literacy among the elite. If the content of the epitaph provides only those details mentioned above, it is possible that the intended readers would be the relatives and peers of the deceased. If in turn, the tomb was clearly built by someone with more than adequate wealth, then the intended readers may have been only those of similar status.

Other epitaphs are clearly aimed for readers who are not peers of the deceased. The following example has the message aimed directly at the passersby:

> *My name, wayfarer, is Aphrodisius; I am an Alexandrian, and my coffin is the middle one. I am dead by a most pitiful death, all through my wife, a vile, false mate, may Zeus destroy her utterly. Her secret lover, who was disgracing my name, dragged me to a cliff and threw me off like a discus, young as I was: for I was in my twentieth year when the spinning Fates made Hades a present of me. Farewell.*[26]

Tombs that lay alongside the roads were frequently inscribed to ward travellers off from tampering.[27] Sometimes the message was

---

24 R Lattimore, *Themes in Greek and Latin Epitaphs*, University of Illinois Press, Urbana, US, 1962, p. 15.
25 R Lattimore, p. 16 and n.19.
26 R Lattimore, p. 118. According to p. 117, this epitaph was discovered in Troad, in modern-day Turkey.
27 R Lattimore, p. 106.

quite simple: Do not open this resting place.[28] Oftentimes it was threatening:

> *Whoever in passing gives me in tribute a rose or some other flower, may he have grace from all the heavenly gods. But if another comes with wicked designs, may he have the hostility of all the underworld gods.*[29]

Written requests for tombs to be left untouched are found in very diverse places. The quote above is taken from central Turkey, whilst another has been found in west Jerusalem, dated to the first century BC.[30] The composers of these epitaphs clearly considered that large numbers of those likely to meddle with the tombs were able to read, otherwise there would have been little point in directly addressing the would-be offenders.

These curse tablets and epitaphs provide indications of the active role literacy played in the day-to-day functioning of various ancient societies. The implication from these functional indicators is that literacy was found in all levels of society.

Variety of genres

Another way to delve into a society's ability to read is to find out what they actually read. If they read only books on philosophy and history, it could be argued that book reading was mainly the province of the academic elite. I discovered that not only were there a great quantity of books in the ancient world, but also that there existed an amazing variety of genres, each of which had vast quantities of material. For example, as mentioned in the previous chapter, a second century AD author called Athenaeus was found to have named about 260 plays from

---

28 R Lattimore, p. 106.
29 R Lattimore, p. 107. According to n. 145 on the same page, this epitaph was discovered in Cappadocia and dates from the second century AD.
30 A Millard, *Reading and Writing in the Time of Jesus*, Sheffield Academic Press, Sheffield, UK, 2001, p. 98.

44 poets from the fifth century BC alone.[31] He also cited from other poetic works outside of this period, including 210 titles from only two poets.[32] He had read popular and obscure medical works, quoting from nine different doctors.[33] It is apparent from reading Athenaeus that 'the Greeks had the greatest variety of books on cookery, gastrology, angling and horse-breeding...'[34]

Biographies were a popular genre, typically aimed at delivering moral lessons,[35] and not written solely for the intelligentsia. One ancient Roman biographer wrote a series of 16 books, covering kings, military leaders, 'philosophers, poets, historians, lawgivers and orators'.[36] Sometimes biographies were illustrated. The prolific ancient scholar, Pliny the Elder, recommended that his friend's biographical work be illustrated with 700 pictures of outstanding personalities.[37] It has been said that this publication was 'emphatically an edition for the general public'.[38]

Geographic dispersion

Another way to examine literacy is to look at how far books were distributed geographically, especially those not involving complex philosophy. I found that at least some works of history travelled far and wide. Livy's enormous publication of history seems to have made

---

31 K Sidwell, 'Athenaeus, Lucian and fifth-century comedy', in D Braund & J Wilkins (eds), *Athenaeus and His World: Reading Greek Culture in the Roman Empire*, University of Exeter Press, Exeter, UK, 2000, p. 137.
32 K Sidwell, p. 137.
33 J-N Corvisier, 'Athanaeus, medicine and demography', in D Braund & J Wilkins (eds), *Athenaeus and His World: Reading Greek Culture in the Roman Empire*, University of Exeter Press, Exeter, UK, 2000, p. 499.
34 HL Pinner, *The World of Books in Classical Antiquity*, AW Sijthoff, Leiden, The Netherlands, 1958, p. 27.
35 R Mellor, *The Historians of Ancient Rome*, Routledge, New York, 2004, p. 8.
36 R Mellor, p. 9.
37 The friend was Marcus Varro (116 BC – 27 BC) and the book's title *Imagines*.
38 HL Pinner, p. 16.

it from Italy to Cadiz in the south-west of Spain.[39] Some may consider that a work of history would be mostly read by the academics of the day; however, there is no need to assume that the general populace was as disinterested in history as some pockets of society are today. But even if we assume that both philosophy and history were not of interest to the general public, were books of a more light-hearted nature being circulated outside of the major intellectual centres, such as Rome and Alexandria?

I found some answers from looking into the world of poetry. The Roman poet Horace (65–8 BC), famous in his own time, wrote on love, wine, nature, friends and the need for mutual tolerance.[40] He boasted that his poems were read widely: 'Spain shall hear my warbling, and the banks of Rhone'.[41] Rhone is a river that runs from Switzerland to France. Horace also penned:

The Colchian, and the Dacian ...
and the Geloni at the end of the world will know me, the learnéd Spaniard will study me, and the drinker of the Rhône.[42]

---

39 Pliny the Younger wrote to his friend Nepos: 'Did you never read of a man from Gades [modern day Cadiz] who was so roused by the name and fame of Titus Livy that he came from the end of the earth to set eyes on him, and as soon as he had seen him he departed? To fail to regard as worthwhile an acquaintance which is as pleasant, charming, and civilized as can be, is an attitude which is *malappris*, uneducated, sluggish, and virtually degrading. You will respond: "But I have authors no less eloquent to read". True enough, but reading is always on the cards, whereas listening is not.' Pliny the Younger, *Complete Letters: Translated with an Introduction and Notes*, trans. PG Walsh, book 2, epistle 3, sections 8–9, Oxford University Press, New York, 2009, p. 32. By permission of Oxford University Press.
40 Poet Seers, 'Horace', www.poetseers.org/the_great_poets/the_classics/horace/, accessed 2/5/10.
41 Horace, *The Odes and Carmen Saeculare of Horace*, book 2, poem 20,trans. J Conington, George Bell and Sons, London, 1882, http://www.perseus.tufts.edu/hopper/text?doc=Perseus%3Atext%3A1999.02.0025%3Abook%3D2%3Apoem%3D20, accessed 29/1/2013.
42 Horace, *Odes*, book 2, poem 20, lines 17–20, translation in HN Parker, 'Books and reading Latin poetry', in eds WA Johnson & HM Parker, *Ancient Literacies: the Culture of Reading in Greece and Rome*, Oxford University Press, UK, 2009, p. 186.

Colchis was on the eastern shore on the Black Sea,[43] Dacia was in the region north of the Danube as it pours into the Black Sea, and the Geloni lived in the region of present-day Ukraine. Elsewhere, Horace writes how his book makes money for the famous booksellers in Rome called the Sosii, and crosses the sea, presumably the Mediterranean.[44]

The prolific Roman poet, Martial, wrote a total of 1561 poems,[45] many of them obscene. He claimed that his poems were read in Britain and Vienne (a part of France) and throughout the Roman Empire.

Another poet from the same era and region was Propertius (c. 50–15 BC), whose first anthology consisted solely of love poems to his girlfriend Cynthia. Propertius was so popular that in his second anthology he was able to write:

> *It's only my love for you that has made my name and fame. They know who I am in the frozen Scythian tundra.*[46]

This frozen area was literally the Borysthenides,[47] which referred to the Dnieper River running from Russia to the Black Sea. In this poem and others, Propertius expressed feelings that mirror those still harboured by some men (I think sadly so) even today:

> *I'd sooner have them cut off my head than marry, [and] be ordered around by a wife ...*[48]

Horace, Martial and Propertius certainly illustrate that not all books composed in the first century AD dealt with academic matters. It is unlikely that the poets' description of their far-reaching fame is idle boasting. Horace's works were part of the Latin reading program in schools.[49] A Roman poet who lived about 100 years after Horace

---

43 'Colchis', *Encyclopaedia Britannica*, vol. 5, William Benton, London, 1962, p. 945.
44 Horace, *The Art of Poetry*, line 345.
45 S Johnson, 'The obituary epigrams of Martial', *The Classical Journal*, 1954, 49(6), pp. 265–72.
46 Sextus Propertius, *Propertius in Love: The Elegies*, trans. DR Slavitt, University of California Press, Berkeley, US, 2002, book 2, poem 7, pp. 61–2.
47 The Latin Library, www.thelatinlibrary.com/prop2.html#7, accessed 15/05/2010.
48 Sextus Propertius, book 2, poem 7, p. 61.
49 SF Bonner, p. 216, citing Quintilian I 5 72.

wrote of how grammar schooling started before adequate daylight had arrived, so that 'Horace was all discoloured ...'[50]

Some have wondered if the poetic works were composed with the expectation that they would become popular through being recited to others. If this was the case, then the books themselves would not have had such a large geographic dispersion. Others have maintained that the anthologies were produced with the expectation that they would be read, and read silently. In response it has been argued cogently that:

> *Not only did Romans read silently to themselves, they read silently to themselves even when other people were present ...*[51] *Did the Republican and Augustan poets write with readers or listeners in mind? The evidence is overwhelming ... all claims to poetic immortality or worldwide fame must rest on the existence of written, physically enduring texts. That books — not performances — were the medium through which all poets made themselves known to the world is the unmistakable testimony of [the various poets].*[52]

Graffiti

The last yardstick for literacy that I will look at is one that I have found very interesting and amusing: the study of ancient graffiti. There is a vast extent of this form of writing, especially in the town of Pompeii. Located about 270 kilometres south of Rome, it was destroyed by a massive volcanic eruption in August 79 AD. Incredibly, almost 5000 examples of graffiti scratched into walls have been found.[53] Another type of graffiti that was actually painted onto walls is also present in large numbers.[54]

---

50 SF Bonner, p. 126, citing Juvenal VII, 227 with commentators.
51 HN Parker, 'Books and reading Latin poetry', in WA Johnson & HN Parker (eds), *Ancient Literacies: The Culture of Reading in Greece and Rome*, Oxford University Press, Oxford, UK, 2009, p. 198. Emphasis in the original.
52 HN Parker, p. 219.
53 H Mourtisen, *Elections, Magistrates and Municipal Élite: Studies in Pompeian Epigraphy*, Analecta Romana Instituti Danici, supplement 15, Rome, p. 9. This count was based on two references, the last of which was dated 1979.
54 H Mourtisen, pp. 9–10.

The Pompeian graffiti writers themselves were aware of the prodigious volume of their workmanship, as shown by the following sample found on the wall of the amphitheatre:[55]

I'm amazed, wall, that you haven't fallen down in ruins,
Since you bear the tedious outpourings of so many writers.[56]

With so much writing on walls, it is probable that a variety of people from many walks of life were involved in the production, and the same could be said for the nature of the intended audience. One scholar noted that:

To my mind, the sheer volume of graffiti and its wide variation in style, orthography, and placement would seem to argue for a community of both writers and readers from a fairly wide range of social and educational backgrounds.[57]

Whilst some graffiti was of a simple erotic nature (so-and-so slept here with so-and-so), others were poetic:

Long life to whoever is in love
and death to whoever is ignorant of love.
Death twice over to whoever forbids being in love.[58]

What I found particularly interesting is that much of the graffiti consisted of quotes from books famous at that time, especially poetic works. These books covered a large time frame, from the works of Euripides (480–406 BC) and Ennius (239–169 BC), to Vergil (70–19 BC) and Propertius (c. 50–15 BC). Many of the quotes are from Vergil's epic called *Aeneid*, which consists of over 10,000 lines. Apart from such direct quotations:

there is other evidence of a connection between the wall texts and elite literature: uses of meter [rhythmic structure] ...; invocations

---

55 M Hartnett, *By Roman Hands: Inscriptions and Graffiti for Students of Latin*, Focus Publishing, Newburyport, US, 2008, p. 63. This carries an illustration of the graffiti.
56 K Milnor, 'Literary literacy in Roman Pompeii: the case of Virgil's Aeneid', in WA Johnson & HN Parker (eds), *Ancient Literacies: The Culture of Reading in Greece and Rome*, Oxford University Press, Oxford, 2009, p. 293, citing CIL 4.1904.
57 K Milnor, p. 292, n. 9.
58 L Casson, p. 110.

> *of mythological characters like Pasiphai, Danae, and Dionysus ...; [and] the use of 'literary' words, figures, and modes of expression ... The [graffiti represents] in a certain sense, the meeting point between ... pragmatic, urban, everyday texts and those that emerged from the sphere of elite cultural production.*[59]

Aside from the thousands of graffiti samples found scratched on the walls in Pompeii, there are also abundant remains of writing of a very different nature, being painted onto walls rather than scratched. Over 2600 of these *dipinti* have been found in Pompeii. About 75 of them announce gladiatorial competitions, and the remainder endorse numerous political candidates. The use of dipinti for electioneering was extremely popular, with 2466 examples being made in a space of only 17 years.[60] The politically motivated dipinti seem to have largely been painted by professionals called *scriptores*.[61] Counting the graffiti, dipinti and other written forms, altogether over 11,000 inscriptions have been found in Pompeii.[62]

Considering the town's population was somewhere between 6400 and 30,000 just before its demise, the prodigious amount of writing indicates a very literate society.[63] Pompeii's artists depicted:

> *scenes that included figures reading rolls ... and women holding notes ... writing instruments and materials — pen, ink, rolls, tablets.*

> *Clearly reading and writing were not limited to an elite upper crust of the town's population. And there is no reason to think that Pompeii was exceptional; other Italian communities must have been equally literate.*[64]

Graffiti certainly existed in other Italian regions. In a shrine in the town of Spoleto, about 100 kilometres north of Rome, Pliny the Younger

---

59 K Milnor, p. 294.
60 H Mourtisen, pp. 9–10.
61 H Mourtisen, p. 31.
62 H Mourtisen, p. 9.
63 M Beard, *Pompeii: The Life of a Roman Town*, Profile Books, London, 2008, p. 10. Estimates vary based on assumptions of how many people lived in the houses. Beard described it as: 'A small town community with ... a citizen body of just a few thousand men ...' (p. 25).
64 L Casson, p. 110.

was able to write in about 109 AD that there were 'many inscriptions written by many hands on all the pillars and on all the walls, which hym [give praise to] the waters and the god'.[65]

Graffiti was such a popular form of self-expression in various towns that one very popular Roman poet of the time wrote:

> *I tell you, if you want to be read about, you should look for a drunk poet of the dark brothel, who, with crude charcoal and crumbling chalk, writes poems which people read while they [defecate].*[66]

Graffiti is certainly a very ancient expression of literacy by common people in many diverse regions. It's quite possible that graffiti found in an underground passage to a temple in Cyrene, on the coast of Libya, dates back to the fifth century BC. This group consists of nearly 60 names of visitors scratched in the mud of the walls and roof.[67] Graffiti in the lands of Transjordan and Syria, where Jesus sojourned, are discussed in the next chapter in the section titled 'Graffiti in graveyards and houses' (pp. 67–9).

Lost words in lost worlds

When we look at the evidence for literacy in societies that flourished 2000 years ago, I am mindful of the fact that we are looking only at the tip of an iceberg. We know that large amounts of literature have disintegrated over the many centuries. Some of these losses have been recorded by ancient historians who refer to books that no longer exist, libraries that were destroyed, and the activities of authorities aimed at destroying Christian literature.

An estimate of the amount of administrative paperwork that has disappeared can be calculated because of the discovery of military-related documentation. These payment records included very specific

---

65 Pliny the Younger, p. 195. By permission of Oxford University Press.
66 Martial, book 1, 12.61.7–10, in *Martial Epigrams*, vols 1–3, ed. & trans. DRS Bailey, Harvard University Press, Cambridge, Massachusetts, 1993.
67 M Beard, 'Writing and religion: ancient literacy and the function of the written word in Roman religion', in M Beard et al. (eds), *Literacy in the Roman World*, Ann Arbor, Michigan, 1991, pp. 41–2, 46.

details. Record number 68 contained the three payments given during one year (81 AD) for the wages of two named soldiers. (As an aside, imagine the uproar that would arise today if military personnel were to receive their wages only three times a year.) Record number 68 also included how much they spent and how much they had on deposit. Based on an examination of the handwriting, three different individuals wrote the record.[68] It is staggering to look at the estimate of what has perished:

> *A minimum figure of 25 legions of 5000 men each, with an equal number of auxiliaries, with three pay-records annually for each man, would have produced, in the 300 years from Augustus to Diocletian [roughly 27 BC to 305 AD], at the very least 225,000,000 individual pay-records. Of these all that survive in intelligible form are [pay-records numbered] 68 and 70.*[69]

Literacy across the Roman Empire

To gain a better appreciation of literacy across the vast Roman Empire, I will now examine evidence for literacy in three geographically diverse regions: Greece, Egypt and Britain. Since this book is concerned with the ability of the first Christians to make accurate recordings of Jesus' life, I've devoted a subsequent chapter to literacy in their lands (Judea and nearby regions), and among the Jews. After all, many of the first Christians were Jews and Jesus was a Jew.

Literacy in Roman-occupied Greece

Rome conquered much of the Greek Empire in 146 BC, although some cities retained forms of self-government. Years later parts of the region revolted, and so in about 86 BC Rome responded by attacking the famous Greek city of Athens.[70] In Athens, as in many Greek cities, there was a large meeting and civic area called the Agora.[71] The Athenian Agora was probably the most grandiose of all, and consisted of a large open area roughly square in shape, containing many important

---

68 RO Fink, *Roman Military Records on Papyrus*, American Philological Association, 1971, pp. 243–9.
69 RO Fink, p. 242.
70 J Camp, *The Athenian Agora*, Thames and Hudson, London, 1986, p. 181.
71 J Camp, p. 14.

buildings. These included long open colonnades (one being 147 metres long),[72] law courts, markets, a mint, monuments and altars.[73] The law courts were large, with the smallest Athenian jury comprising 201 men and the largest 2500.[74]

Among the ruins of these buildings an incredible treasure trove of inscriptions (i.e. writings carved in stone) has been found. The 7500 or so inscriptions include: 'laws, treaties, honorary decrees, dedications, building accounts, temple inventories, boundary stones and statue bases'.[75] Some inscriptions are quite long, such as the dedication found on the Library of Pantainos, built around 100 AD. It consists of 69 words (when translated into English).[76]

Impressive as the vast number of inscriptions may be, it needs to be noted that the Agora existed for many hundreds of years until the fourth century AD when invading forces resulted in a 'large-scale abandonment'.[77] Nevertheless, it is fair to say that the profusion of inscriptions, situated so that they would be read by those passing by, indicates a significant percentage of the populace in Athens enjoyed literacy during these centuries.

Some may suggest that the Agora is not representative of Greece, as Athens was world famous for being an intellectual giant. Certainly Athens was famous for its academics. 'Dozens of philosophers, sophists, rhetoricians, grammarians, and the like crowded Athens during ... [the second century AD]'.[78] Aristotle (384–322 BC) was quoted by the Greek historian Dionysius of Halicarnassus (b. c. 60 BC) as saying that in Athens the speeches of famous orators were sold in the hundreds.[79]

However, Greece at this time had many prominent cities exhibiting the hallmarks of literate societies; Athens wasn't an oasis in an intellectual desert. A long inscription found in the Greek city of

---

72 J Camp, p. 175.
73 J Camp, pp. 7, 14.
74 J Camp, p. 108. About 100,000 coins have also been discovered (refer to p. 113).
75 J Camp, p. 17.
76 J Camp, p. 190.
77 J Camp, p. 198.
78 J Camp, p. 196.
79 HL Pinner, p. 24.

Amphipolis consists of 139 lines dating to 21 BC.[80] Ephesus was also a very populous Greek city, the ruins of which lie on the west coast of Turkey. About 300 bilingual Greek and Latin inscriptions have been found to date.[81]

Christians certainly lived within the Greek borders. Given that cities such as Athens (Acts 17:16–34), Thessalonica and Ephesus are mentioned in the New Testament as having Christian communities, it is reasonable to infer that many of these Greek Christians could well have been literate.

Literacy in Roman-occupied Egypt

Egypt, having already been occupied by the Greeks, surrendered to Roman control upon the death of Cleopatra in August of 30 BC. Roman rulers remained in control for over five centuries after this. Although the first word many people associate with Egypt is pyramids, it should perhaps be Oxyrhynchus. This Egyptian town has one of the most startling examples of the prevalence of literacy as it was 2000 years ago. The town still exists today, and is about 160 kilometres south of Cairo. The ancient rubbish dumps from around this town have furnished a massive number of papyrus fragments since their initial discovery in 1896. During one season of exploration, the chief explorers had to employ over 200 men and boys for nearly 14 weeks to carry out the excavation.[82] By 2008 it was reported that 5476 documents (such as letters) and 2918 literary manuscripts (such as excerpts of books) from Oxyrhynchus had been published.[83] Of course, many fragments remain to be published.

---

80 Archaeological Reports 31 (1984–85) 48, cited by J McRay, 'Archaeology and the book of Acts', *Criswell Theological Review*, 1990, 5(1), pp. 69–82, especially p. 72.
81 B Burrell, 'Reading, hearing, and looking at Ephesos', in WA Johnson & HN Parker (eds), *Ancient Literacies: The Culture of Reading in Greece and Rome*, Oxford University Press, Oxford, 2009, p. 70.
82 A Luijendijk, *Greetings in the Lord: Early Christian and the Oxyrhynchus Papyri*, Harvard Theological Studies, Cambridge, US, 2008, pp. 7–9.
83 A Luijendijk, p. 9.

By 1975 over 1060 published documents from Oxyrhynchus were available.[84] A list of document types sourced from only the period of the first two centuries AD furnishes a staggering diversity of topics. The following is a partial list of document descriptions: contract for marriage, complaint against a husband, complaint against a wife, deed of divorce, application for remarriage, agreements on the nurturing of a child, apprenticeship contracts including one to a shorthand writer and another to a weaver, examination of a slave before a sale, complaint of extortion from a weaver against a tax-collector, trials concerning inheritance, birth and death notices, promise to attend court, receipts for beer, accident reports, monthly meat bill from a cook, receipt of wages for nursing, order for household utensils and supplies, dinner invitations, reports on mummifying, wrestling rules and medical prescriptions. This long list certainly illustrates the breadth of literacy in that society!

In terms of overall cultural achievements, the town itself may have been similar to other towns in Egypt, pointing to a significant degree of literacy among several towns in Egypt at that time. This can be seen from the following quote about Oxyrhynchus:

We have evidence, actually, of twenty temples, of gymnasia, of courts for playing ball and a racecourse, of a theatre — seating 8,000 to 12,000 people — as well as a script on papyrus of Euripides ... This is in addition to the correspondence and literary activity alluded to earlier, all of which adds up to a city full of cultural and intellectual pursuits ... Similar data could be compiled for other cities ... farther up the Nile, where papyri have been found, but what we have outlined will be sufficient to make the point that these were places not only of literacy but literary activity ...[85]

---

84   RLB Morris, 'A study in the social and economic history of Oxyrhynchus for the first two centuries of Roman rule', PhD dissertation, Department of Classical Studies, Duke University, 1975, pp. 6–7

85   EJ Epp, 'The significance of the papyri for determining the nature of the New Testament text in the second century: A dynamic view of textual transmission', in *Gospel Traditions in the Second Century: Origins, Recensions, Text, and Transmission*, ed. William B Petersen, University of Notre Dame Press, London, 1989, p. 83, citing CH Roberts & TC Skeat, *The Birth of the Codex*, Oxford University Press, Oxford, 1983 p. 35.

Certainly those in the Egyptian government had to be literate, even well before Roman occupation. Anyone working in a government department today knows how quickly vast quantities of documents are produced. Ancient Egyptian government was no different. The finance minister in the period of 258–257 BC had three offices, and in one month they had 'used 434 rolls of papyrus, some of them ... up to 12 metres long (40 feet)'.[86]

Writing was even carried out by those who probably knew they could not write well! This was shown by the discovery in Egypt of the following letter written sometime between 100 and 200 AD:

> *Ammonous to her sweetest father, greeting.*
>
> *When I received your letter, and recognised that by the will of the gods you were preserved, I rejoiced greatly. And as at the same time an opportunity has presented itself, I am writing you this letter, being very anxious to pay my respects to you ... If the bearer of this letter hands over a small basket to you, it is I who send it. All your friends greet you by name. Celer greets you and all who are with him. I pray for your health.*[87]

The letter is described as being 'very illiterate, the original Greek abounding in false concords'.[88] A false concord is a discrepancy in grammar where words disagree in aspects such as number and gender. (The sentence 'My brother ordered six banana for herself' includes two false concords.) Such eagerness to write by someone who is only semi-literate indicates that writing wasn't restricted to those highly skilled in grammar.

The discoveries outlined above make it readily apparent that Pliny the Elder wasn't exaggerating when he wrote the following in about 77 AD:

---

86   A Millard, p. 36.
87   G Milligan, *The New Testament Documents: Their Origin and Early History*, MacMillan and Co., London, 1913, p. 91. George Milligan was at the time Professor of Divinity and Biblical Criticism, University of Glasgow.
88   G Milligan, p. 90.

> *But before we leave Egypt we shall also describe the nature of papyrus, since our civilisation or at all events our records depend very largely on the employment of paper.*[89]

An Egyptian's desire to write wasn't entirely limited to accessing papyrus, as many other materials were also used. One material that was popular for short texts were *ostraca*, which were typically broken pieces of pottery. In the ancient city of Apollinopolis Magna (Edfu in more recent times, about 100 kilometres south of Oxyrhynchus), 254 ostraca were found recording taxes paid by Jews. The bulk of these are from the period 70–116 AD.[90] Another ostracon from this city, dating from the first century AD, is a love letter, most likely from a wife to her soldier husband. The 50 or so words that remain finish with: 'but if you love me come ... let us rejoice'.[91]

As discussed in the previous chapter, Alexandria in Egypt had a library of immense proportions, which would have encouraged Egyptians from near and far to be proud of their academic prowess. Surely this pride acted as a catalyst to encourage literacy. That reading wasn't restricted to those who visited libraries is evidenced by the fact that 'a Roman prefect [governor] received 1804 petitions in three days in AD 210, which were to be publicly displayed in Alexandria'.[92]

One form of literature that circulated widely outside of the libraries was the oracle. These were messages composed by those who could supposedly perceive the future or dispense wisdom. The authors of oracles claimed to receive their messages directly from the gods. Such practices created abundant opportunities for manipulators and deceivers. Oracles were so prominent in Egyptian society that the

---

89 Pliny, *Natural History: In Ten Volumes with an English Translation*, trans. H Rackham, William Heinemann, London, 1945, Book XIII:69 (also referred to as Book XIII, para. XXI), p. 139.
90 C Haas, *Alexandria in Late Antiquity: Topography and Social Conflict*, John Hopkins University Press, Baltimore, 2006, p. 412, n. 46.
91 GHR Horsely, *New Documents Illustrating Early Christianity: A Review of the Greek Inscriptions and Papyri Published in 1976*, Ancient History Documentary Research Centre, Macquarie University, 1981, pp. 58–9.
92 A Millard, p. 37.

Roman Emperor Septimius Severus (r. 193–211 AD) was compelled to act. He commanded:

> *let no man through oracles, that is by means of written documents supposedly granted under divine influence, nor by means of the parade of images or suchlike charlatanry, pretend to know things beyond human ken and profess [to know] the obscurity of things to come ...*[93]

One reason for the prevalence of literacy during Roman times may be the legacy of education that was left behind by the earlier Greek conquerors. From surviving lists of censuses taken in about 250 BC, some villages had as many as one teacher for every 110 adults.[94] A Greek school teacher's manual from the 200s BC has been discovered, which contains information about the literature that was being taught. Students learnt Greek from famous authors such as Homer (who wrote the *Iliad* and *Odyssey* in the 800s BC) and Alexandrian poets.[95]

In its very early years, an organised and literate Christianity thrived in Egypt. For example, Oxyrhynchus had at least three churches in the late 200s to early 300s AD.[96] Numerous ancient copies of the New Testament have been discovered in Egypt, and some of these are discussed in chapter 7, titled 'Ancient copies of the New Testament: from Egypt to the Vatican'. For now it is enough to note a few examples of Christian literature just from Oxyrhynchus alone: a portion of Matthew's Gospel and another of John's Gospel, both

---

[93] JR Rea, 'A new version of P. Yale inv. 199', Zeitschrift für Papyrologie und Epigraphik (Journal for Papyrology and Epigraphy), vol. 27, pp. 151–6. Cited by AK Bowman & G Woolf, 'Literacy and power in the ancient world', in AK Bowman & G Woolf (eds), *Literacy and Power in the Ancient World*, Cambridge University Press, Cambridge, UK, 1996, p. 7.

[94] DJ Thompson, 'Literacy and power in Ptolemaic Egypt', in AK Bowman & G Woolf (eds), *Literacy and Power in the Ancient World*, Cambridge University Press, Cambridge, UK, 1996, pp.75–6.

[95] DJ Thompson, p. 76.

[96] A Luijendijk, p. 19. This is because of the discovery of a 'Declaration of Church Property' document dated to 304 AD, and the fact that North Church Street and South Church Street were some of the streets that were assigned guards in the early 300s.

from the 100s AD,[97] and the earliest Christian hymn to contain both lyrics and musical notation dating from the 200s AD.[98] So it is certain that literacy was strong among a sizable number of the Egyptian Christians.

Literacy in Roman-occupied Britain

The main Roman invasion of Britain occurred in 43 AD. Conquest of this and associated territories didn't always go in the Romans' favour: a large part of what is now called Scotland had to be abandoned by the Roman military in the late 80s AD. The Romans made their presence felt in a very enduring way, including the construction of many sites that are visited by tourists today. These include Hadrian's Wall, completed in about 128 AD, and the complex of bathing facilities built at Bath.

Britain itself wasn't the main focus of my investigations; instead it was the invaders who came to dwell there. These military men and their associates came from tribes that were newly incorporated into the Roman Empire. Their cultures had not been heavily influenced by long-standing associations with Roman and Greek civilisations so their degree of literacy, and what they actually wrote, 'illuminate[s] a stratum of society below the social and literary elite, operating in an area very far from the centre of the empire or the already literate Greek east'.[99]

The regions that provided these armed forces were Batavia, located in the Rhine delta now known as the Netherlands, and Tungria, an area west of the Rhine River in and around what is now called Belgium.

---

97 A Luijendijk, p. 18, n. 81, referring to P.Oxy. 64.4404 and P.Oxy. 50.3523. See also PM Head, 'Some recently published NT papyri from Oxyrhynchus: An overview and preliminary assessment', *Tyndale Bulletin*, 2000, vol. 51, pp. 1–16.
98 E Pöhlmann & ML West, *Documents of Ancient Greek Music: The Extant Melodies and Fragments Edited and Transcribed with Commentary*, Clarendon Press, Oxford, 2001. This refers to the papyrus fragment P.Oxy 1786 praising 'the Father, the Son and the Holy Spirit ...'
99 AK Bowman, 'The Roman imperial army: letters and literacy on the northern frontier', in AK Bowman & G Woolf (eds), *Literacy and Power in the Ancient World*, Cambridge University Press, Cambridge, UK, 1994, p. 111.

Britain appears to have been devoid of any significant quantities of literature before the Roman invasion.[100]

The invading army established various forts, including one called Vindolanda on the northern frontier of Roman conquest, located in a land where the indigenous people may not have had a very literate society. Thin slivers of wood written on with ink have been found preserved in this fort, which is astonishing considering that they date from 92 to 130 AD! They were rescued from the ditches and ruins of rooms and streets associated with the fort. Over 1400 of these leaf tablets, which are only 1–3-mm thick, were unearthed between 1985 and 1994.[101] They were generally 20 cm by 9 cm in size, and scored down the middle so that they could be folded. Several leaves were able to be tied together using holes and thread, so that a concertinaed notebook was produced.[102] These tablets may have been called *pugillares*, but also *sectiles* or *laminae*.[103]

As if the large number of leaf tablets discovered wasn't amazing in itself, their numbers are small in comparison to the great store of literature that would have been kept in the official record-office of the fort.[104] The preserved tablets were used to record personal letters and administrative documents, and sometimes were written on both sides.[105] Some were written in Vindolanda, and others came from various towns. Just as in modern times, we read how thoughtful people in these other places sent their battle-hardened men socks and underwear.[106] One of the personal letters reflects the seemingly eternal and ubiquitous phenomenon of women wishing their husbands were better communicators:

> *I want you to know that I am in very good health, as I hope you are in turn, you neglectful man, who have sent me not even one letter.*

---

100 AK Bowman, 'The Roman imperial army: letters and literacy on the northern frontier', p. 111.
101 AK Bowman, *Life and Letters on the Roman Frontier: Vindolanda and its People*, pp. 12–15. They were first discovered in 1973.
102 A Birley, *Garrison Life at Vindolanda: A Band of Brothers*, Tempus Publishing, Charleston, US, 2002, p. 33.
103 A Birley, p. 33.
104 AK Bowman, *Life and Letters on the Roman Frontier*, p. 16.
105 AK Bowman, *Life and Letters on the Roman Frontier*, pp. 16, 85.
106 A Birley, p. 100.

> *But I think I am behaving in a more considerate fashion in writing to you.*[107]

Several hundred different people wrote the various tablets, some of whom had good writing ability despite presumably coming from 'soldiers in the lower ranks'.[108] The evidence from the wooden leaves at Vindolanda illustrate that the ability to write Latin well was:

> *widespread ... among the officer class in northern Britain, extending to their wives and their slaves ... into the non-officer class, perhaps even the ranks and then the traders with military connections.*[109]

Literacy was so extensive that it is likely that it included those individuals who did not own property.[110]

It is not only from Vindolanda that we know that reading and writing were not limited to the upper classes in the major cities of the Roman Empire. Evidence for these skills has been found even among the poor who lived outside the cities in Western Europe. This was highlighted by the discovery of a clay tablet dating to the second century AD found in the countryside at Montenach in the north of France. On it was a memo written by a labourer who worked for a bricklayer![111] It appears to consist of reminders of who he would be working with, and the type of work needed, for several days.[112]

What is also of interest are the efforts made by some Roman conquerors to educate the vanquished. Agricola, a Roman general who became governor over Britain, was quite active in this way. Shortly after his arrival in 77 AD:

> *... Agricola gave private encouragement and public aid to the building of temples, courts of justice and dwelling-houses, praising*

---

107 AK Bowman, *Life and Letters on the Roman Frontier*, p. 94.
108 AK Bowman, *Life and Letters on the Roman Frontier*, p. 88.
109 AK Bowman, *Life and Letters on the Roman Frontier*, p. 96.
110 AK Bowman, *Life and Letters on the Roman Frontier*, p. 96.
111 N Horsfall, 'Statistics or states of mind?', in M Beard et al. (eds), *Literacy in the Roman World*, *Journal of Roman Archaeology*, Supplementary Series no. 3, Ann Arbor, Michigan, 1991, p. 59.
112 B Milns, personal communication, 01/04/12.

the energetic, and reproving the indolent ... He likewise provided a liberal education for the sons of the chiefs ...[113]

The affordability of reading and writing

The evidence in the above sections reveals the presence of many literate people, and shows that writing short communications was an affordable activity. But were books and writing materials affordable to the masses? Answering this is not straightforward; even today, books and writing materials vary in price enormously. Books can sell from less than two dollars to several hundred dollars or more! This variation sometimes depends on genre, with the dearer books being typically of a more specialist nature. Likewise, pens can range from simple biros costing a dollar to those costing considerably more. The cost of literature also varies from country to country and over time. Due to these many variables, the information in the sections below is largely confined to one narrow time period, close to the beginnings of the Christian movement when it was particularly flourishing.

The cost of books

Books came in two basic forms, either as rolls (scrolls) or in the modern-day format called a codex. The codex was about 25% cheaper to produce than the roll.[114] The cost of published works certainly diminished over time, at least during one extended period of Roman rule. One popular material used to make publications was papyrus, which was formed from the six-metre (20-foot) stems of a plant that grew prolifically along the Nile River.[115] A cheap length of papyrus copy sold for six to ten sesterces (a type of Roman coin) in about

---

113 Cornelius Tacitus, *The Life of Gnaeus Julius Agricola*, trans. AJ Church & WJ Brodribb, 1876, para. 21, accessed from www.perseus.tufts.edu/hopper/text?doc=Perseus%3Atext%3A1999.02.0081%3Achapter%3D21 on 29/01/2013.
114 HY Gamble, pp. 54–5.
115 K Aland & B Aland, *The Text of the New Testament: An Introduction to the Critical Editions and to the Theory and Practice of Modern Textual Criticism*, trans. EF Rhodes, WB Eerdmans Publishing Company, Michigan, 1995, p.75.

86 AD.[116] A 'slender little book' of epigrams (small poems) written by Martial, sold for two to four sesterces.[117] His writings frequently included immoral depictions and sexually explicit coarse language. The knowledge that sex sells was quite apparent to him and enabled him to have an audience that included centurions from as far afield as Bulgaria and Romania (as they are now called) to Britain.[118] To put this amount of money in perspective is not easy; however, at around the same time, a jar of wine could be bought for five sesterces,[119] and olive oil sold for about two to three sesterces per litre. Graffiti written in 79 AD on the wall of a room in Herculaneum revealed that two men could spend 105.5 sesterces on 'an evening of festivity' with girls.[120] A soldier in the Roman army had his pay increased from 900 to 1200 sesterces per year during the reign of Domitian (r. 81–96 AD).[121] By contrast, among the wealthy upper echelon of society were the equestrian staff officers. To hold such a position, they needed to have property worth a minimum of 400,000 sesterces. In about 100 AD there were probably about 60 of these men involved in the occupation of Britain.[122]

The wooden leaf tablets at Vindolanda mentioned earlier were also very economical. As leaf tablets have been found in other towns, and as many of the tablets in Vindolanda came from other places, it appears that this type of writing material was 'in everyday use and circulation'.[123] One very long account was written:

> *on several leaves which were joined together in a concertina format, offering us a completely unique example of a wooden notebook. It is this kind of notebook which is probably denoted by the Latin word* pugillaria *used frequently in the writings of the*

---

116 Martial, book 1, epigram 66. The dates of the epigrams are given in the Introduction on pp. 3–4.
117 Martial, book 13, epigram 2, p. 175.
118 Martial, book 11, epigram 3, p. 5.
119 Martial, book 12, epigram 76, p. 155.
120 JJ Deiss, *Herculaneum: Italy's Buried Treasure*, J Paul Getty Museum, Malibu, California, 1989, p. 146.
121 B Campbell, *War and Society in Imperial Rome 31 BC – AD 284*, Routledge, London, 2002, p. 84.
122 AK Bowman, *Life and Letters on the Roman Frontier*, p. 54.
123 AK Bowman, *Life and Letters on the Roman Frontier*, p. 16. See also p. 84.

> *contemporary poets Martial and Juvenal. This unique concertina format ... could have been a medium not only for notebooks but also for early literary works ...*[124]

At the other end of the spectrum, very expensive books also existed. Christians from around the time of the fourth century started using parchment, produced from the skin of animals. A group of books from the New Testament would require about 50 to 60 hides of sheep or goats![125] No wonder Christians continued to use papyrus-based books as late as the eighth century. Christians appear to have been among the forerunners in using papyrus in the form of a modern book. There are several possible reasons for the Christians preference of a codex, one being that it allowed easier access to particular phrases in their holy books compared to scrolls.[126]

Of course in order to sell books, bookshops had to exist:

> *Bookshops in Athens were mentioned by the early writers of comedies in about 430 BC ... In Rome there were bookshops at least as early as Cicero's [b. 106 BC] ... time ... On their entrances and pillars hung lists of available books marked with names of authors and titles, especially the latest. Apparently they also had display cabinets containing specimen extracts from the newest books to excite the curiosity of the public ... In the harbour at Brindisi [in Italy about 480 kilometres from Rome], Gellius [c. b. 125 AD] bought a whole heap of old Greek tomes for a song ... There were also first-class bookshops in the provinces. Pliny the Younger wonders at the bookshops in Lyons [in France about 750 kilometres from Rome] and is overjoyed that his books are sold there. Sidonius Apollinaris is able to tell of great purchases made by a friend of his at a Rheims [in France about 650 kilometres from Rome] bookshop.*[127]

---

124 AK Bowman, *Life and Letters on the Roman Frontier*, pp. 84–5.
125 K Aland & B Aland, pp. 76–7.
126 RL Fox, 'Literacy and power in early Christianity', in AK Bowman & G Woolf (eds), *Literacy and Power in the Ancient World*, Cambridge University Press, Cambridge, UK, 1996, p. 142.
127 HL Pinner, pp. 46–8.

The cost of writing

Just as books were affordable so too were writing materials. The discovery of the vast quantity of leaf tablets in Vindolanda (mentioned above) led one scholar to remark:

> *These leaf tablets must have been cheap (or free) and easy to make. They completely undermine the argument that writing materials were only available to the well-to-do.*[128]

Previous to the Vindolanda discovery, it was thought that the typical Roman wooden writing tablet consisted of a scooped-out depression that was filled with beeswax and inscribed using a metal stylus. When the message was no longer needed, the wax surface would be reworked. Fortunately, the stylus sometimes left an impression in the wood below the wax, allowing us to read letters on them even to this day.[129] Thousands of these tablets (*tabellae ceratae* but also sometimes called *pugillares*) have been found throughout the Roman Empire.[130] Over 250 wooden-based wax tablets have been recovered from Vindolanda, but the majority of the tablets were of the leaf kind.[131] It seems likely that the wax type were more expensive but still relatively inexpensive. As early as the sixth century BC, wooden-based wax tablets were designed in such a way that two could be bound together with string to protect the writing on the inside surfaces. These *tabulae ansatae* notebooks 'were common in Roman times ...'[132]

Wealthier individuals were able to use more luxurious material. A wax tablet made of ivory instead of wood was discovered in Tuscany, Italy, dating as far back as the seventh century BC.[133]

---

128 A Bowman, 'Literacy in the Roman Empire: mass and mode', in M Beard et al. (eds), *Literacy in the Roman World*, University of Michigan Press, Ann Arbor, Michigan, 1991, p. 35.
129 As such impressions represent numerous messages superimposed upon each other, it is generally impossible to read anything substantial. A Birley, p. 31.
130 A Birley, pp. 31–2.
131 A Birley, p. 31.
132 T Cornel, 'The Tyranny of the evidence: a discussion of the possible uses of literacy in Etruria and Latium in the archaic age', in M Beard et al. (eds), *Literacy in the Roman World,* Ann Arbor, Michigan, 1991, p.23.
133 T Cornel, pp. 23–4. The discovery was made near Banditella in the district of Marsiliana, about 140 km north of Rome.

Conclusion

These facts about the prevalence of functional literary indicators (such as curse tables and epitaphs), the variety of literary genres available, the geographical dispersion of books, and the prevalence of graffiti, together with the affordability of books and writing materials, has convinced me that literacy was not at all rare in the societies surrounding the lands in which Jesus lived. I am also convinced that literacy wasn't confined to the elite classes of society. Having determined this, my next task was to see if Jesus' world was more or less literate than other parts of the Greco–Roman Empire.

3

Literacy in Jesus' world

The previous chapter has shown how extensive literacy was in the Greco–Roman world. It's time to focus on Judea and the surrounding countries where Jesus lived and taught. Are they likely to be more or less literate than their neighbours? As Jesus and many of his first followers were Jews, it's necessary to examine literacy within the Jewish society, particularly those living in and around Judea and Galilee, as well as within the fledgling Christian community.

When speaking of the Jewish society in Judea and Galilee during Roman occupation, I don't mean to imply that this society lived in total isolation and wasn't influenced by the cultures surrounding it. In fact, Jerusalem was a centre of Greek language learning in the first century AD,[1] and many Jews in the region knew the Greek language.[2] Jesus may well have been one of those who could speak Greek as well as the other common language of Aramaic.[3] Cities that were dominated by Greeks, such as Caesarea Maritima and Scythopolis,

---

1 G Mussies, 'Greek in Palestine and the Diaspora', in S Safrai & M Stern (eds), *The Jewish People in the First Century: Historical Geography, Political History, Social, Cultural and Religious Life and Institutions*, vol. 2, Van Gorcum & Comp., BV, Assen, The Netherlands, 1976, p. 1054.
2 G Mussies, p. 1056.
3 G Mussies, p. 1056. See also A Millard, *Reading and Writing in the Time of Jesus*, Sheffield Academic Press, Sheffield, UK, 2001, pp. 140–7.

still had large Jewish minorities.[4] Many Jews had Greek names,[5] including two of Jesus' closest disciples (Andrew and Philip). The first Christian church in Jerusalem included Jews so greatly influenced by Greek culture that they were called Grecian Jews (Acts 6:1).[6] Nevertheless, it is important to examine the Jewish society as a separate group in order to confirm its levels of literacy. If they had a significant degree of literacy, then this makes it more likely that they had a reasonable understanding of the normal ways in which the world worked. Such an understanding would imply that many of those who converted to Christianity did so only after weighing the evidence in a rational manner. After exploring this aspect of Jewish literacy, I will turn to considering whether the early Christian community as a whole, irrespective of what they were before their conversion, has left indications of their level of literacy.

Reading and writing in Jewish society

I will use five different angles to gain an insight into Jewish literacy: the teaching of reading and writing to Jewish children and adults and the importance of literacy in religious practices, the profession of the scribe, the conclusions we can draw from the Dead Sea Scrolls, the advanced literacy required to produce the huge number of business documents unearthed, and the prevalence of graffiti.

Reading and writing as part of Jewish expectations and practices

At least as early as the first century AD, the majority of Jewish children received education at schools. Josephus, a famous Jewish historian

---

4   G Mussies, pp. 1058–9.
5   S Safrai & M Stern (eds), *The Jewish People in the First Century: Historical Geography, Political History, Social, Cultural and Religious Life and Institutions*, vol. 1, Van Gorcum & Comp., BV, Assen, The Netherlands, 1974, p. 256.
6   The text in Acts is often translated as Hellenistic Jews. This is because Greeks in general were often referred to as Hellenes, being named after Hellen, who was the legendary father of the Greeks.

and general, records that Jews were taught to bring 'children up in learning and to exercise them in the laws'.[7] Before its destruction in 70 AD, Jerusalem alone had 480 synagogues, each with a 'house of learning'. Even in a small village such as Nazareth, the local synagogue had a sacred scroll that was read aloud (Luke 4:16–20). If a town didn't employ a teacher of the written law, it was regarded as a sin that would lead to the town's destruction.[8] In these synagogue-based schools they were taught the alphabet and how to read seven days a week.[9]

Compared to reading, the ability to write well was less widespread as it was a professional skill taught separately.[10] However, a certain proficiency at writing was still quite common. Many adult Jews continued in regular study and many would write various holy scriptures onto their doors, gates, arms and foreheads.[11] Being able to write at a basic level was such a fundamental aspect of being a Jew that new converts were taught to write the Hebrew alphabet.[12] The Jews even had laws on who was responsible for mistakes when a child was being taught to write scripture. If the child was holding the pen while the adult was guiding his hand, then the child was held liable.[13]

---

[7] Josephus, *Against Apion*, 2.204. James Dunn notes that Josephus referred to the children here as being 'taught to read (learn their letters, *grammata paideuein*)', in JDG Dunn, 'Did Jesus attend the synagogue', p. 221, in JH Charlesworth (ed.), *Jesus and Archeology*, William B Eerdmans Publishing Company, Cambridge, UK, 2006, pp. 206–22.

[8] S Safrai, 'Education and the study of the Torah', in S Safrai & M Stern (eds), *The Jewish People in the First Century: Historical Geography, Political History, Social, Cultural and Religious Life and Institutions*, vol. 2, Van Gorcum & Comp., BV, Assen, The Netherlands, 1976, p. 950.

[9] S Safrai, 'Education and the study of the Torah', pp. 947, 954.

[10] S Safrai, 'Education and the study of the Torah', p. 952.

[11] EP Sanders, *Judaism: Practices and Belief: 63 BCE – 66 CE*, SCM Press, London, 1992, pp. 196–7. Sanders was Arts and Sciences Professor of Religion at Duke University, North Carolina, from 1990 to 2005.

[12] 'Hillel and Shammai', Shabbat 30b–31a, www.ajula.edu/Media/Images/SCM/ContentUnit/2720_9_6106.pdf, accessed 21/01/12. Hillel was a prominent Jewish teacher from about 30 BC to 10 AD.

[13] J Neusner, *Judaisms' Story of Creation: Scripture, Halakhah, Aggadah*, Brill, Leiden, The Netherlands, p. 62.

Jews were also well acquainted with the value of writing as a means of helping memorisation. The Jewish philosopher Philo (c. 20 BC – 50 AD) wrote that:

> while a man is reading, the notions of what he is reading fleet away, being carried off by the rapidity of his utterance; but if he is writing they are stamped upon his heart at leisure, and they take up their abode in the heart of each individual as his mind dwells upon each particular ...[14]

That large numbers of Jews could read is also apparent from practices conducted in the ancient synagogues. Synagogues were meeting places that had a vital role in the community, and in Jesus' time they existed in large numbers throughout Israel. Jewish adults and children would meet at least every Sabbath to listen to readings from the scriptures. The privilege to read to the gathering was not restricted to a handful of specialists, as various people were invited to do so. Ideally, seven individuals would be asked to perform the Sabbath day's readings.[15]

Scribes

Jewish priests and those belonging to the tribe of Levi were often scribes. Scribes carried out activities such as making copies of texts, composing legal documents and acting as experts in interpreting the law.[16] One professor noted:

> The ancient world required scribes in vast numbers ... We shall not be able to arrive at definite numbers, but we may assume that there were some thousands of scribes in Jewish Palestine in our period [63 BC to 66 AD]: legal advisors in each locality, people who could draft documents, and legal experts and copyists in the employ of the temple. At the time of Herod, according to Josephus,

---

14 Philo of Alexandria, *The Special Laws*, IV, XXXII, (160), www.earlychristianwritings.com/yonge/book30.html, accessed 20/10/2012.
15 S Safrai, 'The synagogue', in S Safrai & M Stern (eds), *The Jewish People in the First Century: Historical Geography, Political History, Social, Cultural and Religious Life and Institutions*, vol. 2, Van Gorcum & Comp., BV, Assen, The Netherlands, 1976, pp. 908, 909, 915, 929, 930.
16 EP Sanders, pp.170–1.

there were about 6,000 Pharisees.[17] *We have seen that there were 18,000 to 20,000 priests and Levites ... [It is likely] that many ordinary priests and many of the Levites put their learning to good use and served as scribes and legal experts.*[18]

One particular Jewish priest called Zechariah is described as writing a short sentence shortly before Jesus' birth (Luke 1:5, 63). He had to communicate using writing as he had been mute for several months. Although people expressed surprise at *what* he wrote, none were surprised that Zechariah *could* write.

Dead Sea Scrolls

Further evidence of Jewish literacy comes from the famous Dead Sea Scrolls, which were written in the years between 200 BC and 68 AD. They were found scattered among 11 different caves between the years 1947 and 1956. The remains of over 800 scrolls have been found, and although the vast majority are written in Hebrew, some are in Greek and Aramaic.[19] About 200 of these scrolls are copies, or parts of copies, of the Hebrew Bible (the Old Testament portion of the Christian Bible); another 200 or so relate to the community that wrote them; and the remaining scrolls consist of other Jewish literature.[20] One of the scrolls found is titled the *Manual of Discipline*. This states: 'The general members of the community are to keep awake for a third of all the nights of the year reading book(s), studying the Law and worshipping together'.[21]

Many scholars believe that the people who produced this wealth of literature were a religious offshoot of Judaism called the Essenes. The

---

17 Pharisees were a respected Jewish religious group, who aimed at a level of purity above the ordinary. Although only some were priests, all were scholars and experts in the law. EP Sanders, p. 26.
18 EP Sanders, pp. 179, 181–2.
19 PR Davies, GJ Brooke & PR Callaway, *The Complete World of the Dead Sea Scrolls*, Thames & Hudson, London, 2002, p. 7.
20 PR Davies, GJ Brooke & PR Callaway, p. 77.
21 Cited by LB Yaghjian, 'Ancient reading' in R Rohrbaugh (ed.), *The Social Sciences and New Testament Interpretation*, Hendrickson Publishers, Peabody, US, 1996, p. 221. This copy of the Manual of Discipline is referred to as 1QS 6:7–8. The Manual of Discipline is also called the Rules scroll (PR Davies, GJ Brooke & PR Callaway, p. 82).

Essenes worked and moved outside of their main headquarters, thus influencing others. Their membership was certainly not confined to the wealthier segments of the general Jewish society.

Documentation everywhere

Anyone involved in business transactions, such as buying and selling property, knows the importance of keeping adequate records. It is highly likely that a dispute will arise if there has been inadequate documentation. This same principle was part and parcel of daily life in the ancient world. Such administrative concerns required more than the basic ability to read and write a name and a date. This type of advanced literacy amongst the Jews was prominent even outside of the major cities, as 'even in a backwater town legal paperwork flourished ...' complete with necessary clerks and copyists.[22] An example comes from the discovery of the Cave of Letters, located in the valley of the Nahal Hever brook near the Dead Sea. The contents of the cave included archives from residents of the town of En-gedi. One of the archives included: 'thirty-five documents, mostly legal, belonging to a woman called Babata',[23] who lived in the cave along with dozens of children. The documents range in date from 93 to 132 AD and reflect how Roman, Jewish and Nabatean[24] laws impacted on this Jewish woman's estate. They are written in Greek, Nabatean and Aramaic, with handwriting skills varying from excellent to poor.[25] Many of these official documents were duplicates, indicated by words such as the following written on them: 'Verified exact copy of one item from the minutes of the council of Petra the metropolis, minutes displayed in the temple of Aphrodite in Petra...'[26]

---

22 EP Sanders, pp.179–80. See also Yigael Yadin, *Bar-Kokhba: The Rediscovery of the Legendary Hero of the Second Jewish Revolt against Rome*, Random House, New York, 1971, chapter 16.
23 EP Sanders, p. 179.
24 Nabataea was a region at the southern end of the Dead Sea and became part of the Roman province of Arabia. Nabataeans obtained significant wealth as traders, with routes between Petra in Jordan and Sinai in Egypt. K Gutwein, 'Uncovering Subeita', in *Archaeological Diggings*, 15(3), 2008, pp. 50–3.
25 B Isaac, *The Near East Under Roman Rule: Selected papers*, Brill, Leiden, The Netherlands, 1998, p. 160.
26 B Isaac, p. 164.

When the remains of documents from all of the caves along the Nahal Hever brook are examined, there are over 60 written in Aramaic or Hebrew alone. About half of these documents are deeds of sale and the remainder consists of receipts, accounts and the like.[27] The writing was carried out by a large number of people, at least some of whom were not professional scribes.[28] Some of the deeds of sale have signatures belonging to the purchaser and the seller, as well as up to five signatures from witnesses.[29]

Other people groups in Judea and Galilee have left behind remarkable evidence of being literate societies. In a town called Kadesh, only some 32 kilometres from Capernaum, in the region of Upper Galilee, an archive room was discovered in 1999.[30] The room, which was part of an administrative building about 1800 square metres in size, had been destroyed by fire.[31] Inside were about 1800 clay bullae, which were blobs of clay used to seal and identify papyrus documents of an official nature. These bullae were in use in about 150 BC. The fire baked and preserved the clay seals but destroyed the documents. The bullae indicate that the documents mostly pertained to Greco–Roman, and to a much lesser extent Phoenician, cultures. The archaeologists who made the discovery were excavating what they believed was only a small agriculturally based village and/or a garrison, given the very limited references in historical literature of that period.[32] Therefore even in towns with almost no known significance as far as historical references are concerned, evidence exists that numerous people were able to read and write. As an aside, in the city of Seleucia, located in present-day Iraq, a total of 24,000 clay bullae were discovered from the Hellenistic period (about 323–146 BC)![33]

---

27 HM Cotton & A Yardeni, *Aramaic, Hebrew and Greek Documentary Texts from Nahal Hever and Other Sites: With an Appendix Containing Alleged Qumran Texts*, Clarendon Press, Oxford, 1997, p. 9.
28 HM Cotton & A Yardeni, p. 9.
29 HM Cotton & A Yardeni, p. 17.
30 PM Head, 'A further note on', *Reading and Writing in the Time of Jesus Evangelical Quarterly*, 75(4), 2003, pp. 343–5.
31 H Watzman, 'Phoenician resilience', *Archaeology*, 53(6), 2000, www.archaeology.org/0011/newsbriefs/phoenician.html, accessed 15/07/2009.
32 S Herbert & A Berlin, 'Tel Kadesh, 1997–1999', *Israel Archaeological Journal*, 50, 2000, p. 118–23, cited by PM Head, pp. 343–5.
33 A Millard, *Reading and Writing in the Time of Jesus*, Sheffield Academic Press, Sheffield, UK, 2001, p. 41.

The farmers' need for literacy

Another archaeological discovery indicating the widespread nature of literacy is that of ostraca from the region of Idumea, lying on the southern border of Judea. These ostraca — typically broken bits of pottery used to write on[34] — were first written between the years c. 365 and 312 BC. What is particularly interesting is that they come from an ancient town whose:

> *economic reality ... relates mainly to the cultivation of fields and orchards. Most of the documents deal with raw wheat and barley, or with their products ...fruit trees, vines and olives ... Our ostraca do not contain any administrative or professional titles ... This feature clearly reflects a clan-tribal organisation ... a rural population living on agriculture ...*[35]

Many of the ostraca were composed by 'local rural writers'.[36] Many of them were dockets with all the necessary details that a modern-day receipt might have: personal names; the day, month and year of the reign of a particular ruler; and the type and amount of the product being exchanged.[37]

There is also no hint of this society being overly simplistic in its vocabulary of written words. Consider their use of units of measurement. Just as societies today have several units of measurement for a person's weight, such as pounds and stones (or grams and kilograms), so too did they. The units of measurement included three different units for wheat and barley (*kor*, *seah* and *qab*). Straw was measured in another two units and wood in yet two others. Sub-units such as a quarter and an eighth are also to be found, and so some quantities are measured as being five and three-quarters of a seah.[38] Olives are sometimes specified by the name of their cultivar and other times by their final product, such as olives from which oil for lighting was extracted.[39] The type of barley

---

34 Refer to chapter 4 'Literacy in the ancient world' for more details on ostraca.
35 I Ephal & J Naveh, *Aramaic Ostraca of the Fourth Century BC from Idumaea*, Magnes Press, The Hebrew University, Jerusalem, 1996, pp. 10–11, 15, 16.
36 I Ephal & J Naveh, p. 16.
37 I Ephal & J Naveh, p. 11.
38 I Ephal & J Naveh, p. 11.
39 I Ephal & J Naveh, p. 13.

was sometimes specified and fine flour was distinguished from normal flour.[40] Amounts of money are also detailed, and labourers[41] and tax collectors[42] rate a mention. About 150 personal names were written on the ostraca, each with the name of the king ruling at that time. It seems that many of the individuals in this agriculturally based community were able to read and write relevant words, numbers, dates and units of measurement. They were able to create detailed receipts based on combinations of all of these. Apart from being composed as dockets, some ostraca were also used for more serious legal purposes, such as registrations of fields.[43] One also contained a plea for the release of 'the daughter of Haggai'.[44]

Graffiti in graveyards and houses

Just as graffiti in today's society sometimes reflects the passion two people have for each other at a particular meeting point, so too in the ancient world of Judea. One such piece of amorous graffiti was found in a tomb! The tomb with its Greek inscription belonged to a town that thrived between 221 and 40 BC.[45] Other graffiti reflects the imminent death of its authors. During the first major rebellion of the Jews against the Romans, in the years 66–70 AD, refugees hiding in a cave wrote on the walls in their Aramaic language 'two alphabets, a name, a call for peace and a message, 'Joezer has been taken, the [enemy] guards have entered!'[46]

The region neighbouring Judea to the east of the Jordan River, called Transjordan, also shows how incredibly prevalent literacy was in some seemingly unlikely contexts:

> [T]he Arab tribes in Transjordan scratched graffiti on rocks and boulders ... Dated to the first centuries of the present era, thousands of these have been catalogued, thousands are yet to be

---

40 I Ephal & J Naveh, p. 11.
41 I Ephal & J Naveh, p. 54.
42 I Ephal & J Naveh, p. 84.
43 I Ephal & J Naveh, p. 13.
44 I Ephal & J Naveh, p. 88.
45 A Millard, pp. 104–5.
46 A Millard, p. 99.

> *studied ... Limited in content to epitaphs, prayers and brief reports of an individual's activities, these are remarkable relics of people who are best described as 'literate shepherds'.*[47]

The literacy of this region is relevant as many Transjordanians[48] followed Jesus (Matthew 4:24–5, Mark 3:7–10). They in turn would have spread the good news to their countrymen. Jesus cast out many demons from a man who subsequently travelled through Transjordan to tell others about his encounter with Jesus (Mark 5:18–20).

What I found particularly surprising was discovering how frequently graffiti was written inside houses! For example, consider the archaeological remains of the town of Dura-Europos, located on the River Euphrates in present-day Syria. This town has been described as 'a fairly ordinary town in the Roman Near East ...'[49] Yet graffiti is found on all types of building throughout the town, including 'sanctuaries, shops, houses and fortifications'.[50] The sheer number of houses with graffiti reveals that the ability to write was very common. Of the roughly 130 houses that have been excavated so far, over a third of them (36%) had graffiti on their inside walls. As many of the walls are no longer preserved to their full height, the real number would be much higher.[51] Implements used for writing, such as wooden wax tablets and inkwells, were discovered in houses both large and small, not just those of the elite.[52] Of the total number of graffiti discovered, over 1200 are made up of words and a further 200 are pictorial in nature. The languages represented include Greek, Latin and the Semitic languages (this language group includes Arabic, Hebrew and Aramaic).[53] Some are even bilingual. The vast majority of the graffiti appears to belong to the 100s and 200s AD, although some is certainly earlier.[54] All this is conclusive evidence that the ability to read and

---

47 A Millard, p. 101.
48 English Bibles typically refer to the region as 'across the Jordan'.
49 JA Baird, 'The graffiti of Dura-Europos: a contextual approach', in JA Baird & C Taylor (eds), *Ancient Graffiti in Context*, Routledge, New York, 2011, p. 52.
50 JA Baird, p. 52.
51 JA Baird, p. 61.
52 JA Baird, p. 52.
53 JA Baird, pp. 52–3, 60.
54 JA Baird, p. 53.

write was common amongst the various people groups of this town, which was abandoned in about 256 AD.[55]

Christian literacy

Literacy among Christians in the first few hundred years or so reflected the fact that they were converts from the Jewish, Greek and other communities in their regions. Certainly their conversions didn't result in their levels of literacy diminishing. In fact, it is likely that by becoming Christians, their proficiency in reading and writing increased. Jesus told his followers to: 'Love the Lord your God with all your heart, and with all your soul and with all your mind' (Matthew 22:37). The Greek word used for mind in this verse is *dianoia*, and it encompassed a person's intellectual abilities and understanding.[56] Certainly literacy was a prominent skill in the early Christian communities. As early as 65 AD, leaders within local churches were to devote themselves to the public reading of scripture (1 Timothy 4:13). The letters of Paul to the Christian communities in Thessalonica and Galatia were written between 48 and 50 AD, and the rest of his many letters before 65 AD.[57] The New Testament Gospels and most of the remaining sections were written by 65 AD.[58] If Jesus was crucified in 33 AD, it follows that within 35 years of the crucifixion of Jesus, nearly all of the key Christian scriptures still used today had already been committed to papyrus. These were avidly read and believed by the Christian community. Evidence for this trust is found in the way Christian leaders referred authoritatively to these scriptures when writing letters to their followers. References to 25 of the 27 books of the New Testament can be found in the letters of

---

55 JA Baird, p. 61.
56 S Zodhiates, *The Hebrew-Greek Key Study Bible: King James Version: The Old Testament: the New Testament*, Word Bible Publishers, Iowa Falls, US, 1984, pp. 1177, 1680.
57 P Barnett, *Is the New Testament History*, Aquila Press, Sydney South, 2004, p. 33. See also J McDowell & B Wilson, *Evidence for the Historical Jesus: A Compelling Case for His Life and His Claims*, Harvest House Publishers, Eugene, US, 1998, pp. 161–6.
58 P Barnett, pp. 34–5. See also J McDowell & B Wilson, *Evidence for the Historical Jesus: A Compelling Case for His Life and His Claims*, Harvest House Publishers, Eugene, US, 1998, pp. 148–9.

leaders such as Polycarp, Ignatius and Clement.[59] These letters were written no later than 110 AD. Clement's letter, which refers to content from 11 of the New Testament books, may have been composed before 70 AD.[60] This information testifies to the importance of reading and writing among the Christian world. In the following sections, I will outline more corroborating evidence regarding significant literacy levels amongst the emerging Christian community.

Availability of writing materials

The New Testament makes us aware that writing materials were readily available. As mentioned earlier in this chapter, a priest called Zechariah needed to write a short sentence and asked accordingly for a writing tablet (Luke 1:63). This event happened during the circumcising and naming of his son. Often this ceremony took place in the parents' home.[61] It is apparent from Luke's account that it was quick and easy for Zechariah's associates to find such a tablet.

Paul, who was one of the most prominent first Christian leaders, requested that his scrolls and *membrana* be brought to him whilst he was in prison (2 Timothy 4:13). *Membrana* in the first century AD were notebooks made out of animal skin (parchment).[62] The disciple John described how he wrote with 'ink and paper (papyrus)' (2 John 12 and 3 John 13). Later we read that he was commanded to write words and phrases that were revealed to him (Revelation 14:13, 21:5 and 19:9).

Surviving Christian manuscripts and letters

Large numbers of letters, books and liturgies have been discovered that were written by Christians. At Oxyrhynchus in Egypt, Christian

---

59 P Barnett, pp. 35–7.
60 TJ Herron, *Clement and the Early Church of Rome: On the Dating of Clement's First Epistle to the Corinthians* [Kindle ebook], Emmaus Road Publishing, Steubenville, US, 2008.
61 'Circumcision', *Jewish Encyclopedia*, 1906, www.jewishencyclopedia.com/articles/4391-circumcision, accessed 27/02/2012. The article states that from about 589 AD (the Geonic period) the ceremony had moved from the house to the synagogue.
62 J Murphy-O'Connor, *Paul the Letter-Writer: His World, His Options, His Skills*, The Liturgical Press St. John's Abbey, Collegeville, US, 1995, p. 36.

literary manuscripts have been found going back as far as the 100s AD[63] and letters written by Christians to about 250 AD.[64] Even five lines of a Christian hymn to the Trinity in the late 200s AD have been discovered, complete with musical notation![65]

Examples of second-century Christian literature include arguments against heretics, such as the now totally lost work composed by Agrippa Castor.[66] One of the surviving works belonging to this category is *Against Heresies* written by Irenaeus. This consists of five books, with around 194,520 words in total,[67] making it equivalent to more than three large novels.

One famous letter was written by Clement, a leader in the church in Rome, to the Christian community in Corinth. It was composed sometime before 96 AD, with convincing evidence indicating it was before 70 AD.[68] The letter reveals important aspects about the Corinthians' level of literacy and ability to concentrate. I found its length surprising: 12,500 words[69] — longer than the Gospel of Mark.[70] It's reasonable to assume that the writer expected many of the recipients to individually read it and re-read it, in addition to it being read aloud to others who were not as literate. Reading it to others would take more than 1 hour and 45 minutes, meaning the illiterate had to have a good

---

63 A Luijendijk, *Greetings in the Lord: Early Christian and the Oxyrhynchus Papyri*, Harvard Theological Studies, Cambridge, US, 2008, p. 18.
64 A Luijendijk, p. 11.
65 E Pöhlmann & ML West, *Documents of Ancient Greek Music: The Extant Melodies and Fragments Edited and Transcribed with Commentary*, Clarendon Press, Oxford, 2001, pp. 190–4. The manuscript is labelled as Pap.Oxy.1786.
66 M Green, *The Books the Church Suppressed: Fiction and Truth in the Da Vinci Code*, Monarch Books, Oxford, 2005, pp. 89, 140.
67 Using a word processing program word count, I found there were about 12,968 words in the first 10 chapters of Book 1, which is a little less than a third of Book 1. Therefore, 12,968 x 3 x 5= 194,520.
68 TJ Herron, *Clement and the Early Church of Rome: On the Dating of Clement's First Epistle to the Corinthians* [Kindle ebook], Emmaus Road Publishing, Steubenville, US, 2008.
69 Based on a word count from the following English translation: Clement of Rome, *First Epistle*, www.earlychristianwritings.com/text/1clement-roberts. html, accessed 18/02/2012.
70 F Just, *New Testament Statistics*, http://catholic-resources.org/Bible/NT-Statistics-Greek.htm, accessed 18/12/2012.

concentration span or be able to recall what was read to them over one or more sessions.

Christian libraries

Christian communities also had their own libraries. In 303 AD the Christians in the northern African city of Cirta had a room designated as a library in the house where they were meeting. This library had at least 37 items. Unfortunately, officers serving the Roman Emperor Diocletian started confiscating such Christian book collections in February of 303 AD. Diocletian had ordered that all Christian books be handed over and burnt in his efforts to stifle the growing Christian community.[71] This indicates that he:

> *took it for granted that every Christian community, wherever it might be, had a collection of books and knew that those books were essential to its viability. Thus ... congregational libraries were commonplace by the late third century, and ... this fact was well known to non-Christians.*[72]

Cirta was only one of the places in the African province of Numidia that faced the brunt of Diocletian's edict. A 'large number of Christian bishops' in Numidia, as well as leaders in other provinces, were in possession of Christian literature as revealed by Diocletian's agents.[73]

Christianity among the well educated

The above information establishes that there was a considerable amount of Christian literature, and that many Christian communities included those who could read and write. Next I wanted to know whether any of these early literate Christians were educated beyond an elementary level. This would help verify whether Christianity flourished even amongst educated critical thinkers.

---

71   LD Bruce, 'A note on Christian libraries during the "Great Persecution" 303–305 A.D.', *The Journal of Library History*, 15(2), 1980, pp. 127–37.
72   HY Gamble, *Books and Readers in the Early Church: A History of Early Christian Texts*, Yale University Press, London, 1995, p. 150.
73   LD Bruce, pp. 127–37.

The New Testament provides background information on only a few of those who converted to Christianity in the years shortly after Jesus' resurrection. One of these was certainly very well educated, as he was in charge of the treasury of the queen of the Ethiopians (Acts 8:27). Another one of the early converts, Apollos from Alexandria, is described as *aner logios* (Acts 18:24). These Greek words 'could mean that he was eloquent or educated, since the two were bound together'.[74] He also knew the Old Testament extremely well and so was clearly a scholarly man.

Evidence from pagan writers demonstrates that at least some Christians were from the well-educated parts of society. A very famous Roman governor called Pliny described Christianity as if it was a disease. He wrote the following to the Roman Emperor in about 111 AD:

> *[I have] hastened to consult you ... especially because of the number [of Christians] indicted, for there are many of all ages, every rank, and both sexes who are summoned and will be summoned to confront danger. The infection of this superstition [Christianity] has extended not merely through the cities, but also through the villages and country areas ...*[75]

Some of the Christian documents from the first and second centuries reveal a number of well-educated converts, such as Aristides and Justin Martyr. Aristides was a philosopher from Athens who, after becoming a Christian, wrote a defence of Christianity to be given to the Roman Emperor Hadrian (r. 117–138 AD). It seems that Aristides died towards the end of Hadrian's reign.

Aristides argued very extensively in favour of Christianity, his book being over 6500 words long. One of his subjects was the worshipping of

---

74 Duane Litfin, *St. Paul's Theology of Proclamation: 1 Corinthians 1–4 and Greco-Roman Rhetoric*, SNTSMS 79, Cambridge University Press, Cambridge, 1994, p. 123, cited in DE Garland, *1 Corinthians*, BECNT, Grand Rapids, Baker, 2003.
75 Pliny the Younger, *Complete Letters: Translated with an Introduction and Notes*, book 10, epistle 96, section 9, trans. PG Walsh, Oxford University Press, New York, 2009, p. 279. By permission of Oxford University Press. Pliny is discussed in greater detail in chapter 18.

idols, objects that merely represent parts of the created world. He noted that after creating their idols, the worshippers would then guard them against robbers. He concluded that this was ludicrous as surely the:

> *guard is greater than that which is guarded, and that every one who creates is greater than that which is created. If it be, then, that their gods are too feeble to see to their own safety, how will they take thought for the safety of men?*[76]

Aristides provided logical reasons for not worshipping elements such as earth water and fire. He pointed out that the multitude of gods worshipped by the Greeks clearly were not gods. Surely real gods would not have had the experiences that the Greek pagan writers described, such as becoming insane, being killed by lightning, kidnapped by men, or marrying their own mothers, sisters and daughters.[77]

Justin Martyr was another Greek-educated philosopher who became a Christian. He studied in Alexandria and Ephesus, and followed several different philosophers over time, such as Pythagoras and Plato. He was martyred in about 165 AD. He composed a book that is over 21,000 words long to the Roman Emperor Antoninus Pius (r. 138–161 AD) and his sons. Written in about 140 AD, it presented many teachings about Christianity.[78] Justin argued that although the concept of Jesus being resurrected might seem ridiculous, it should not be immediately dismissed. Even the emperor believed that every person was created in their mother's womb from a 'small drop of human seed', despite this being so hard to imagine given the complexity of our bodies.[79] Justin contended that with God's power surely the resurrection is possible.

I did come across an argument in the literature that maintained that early Christian communities were not interested in producing literature. This

---

76 Aristides, *The Apology of Aristides*, trans. JA Peck, Syriac version, section III, http://preachersinstitute.com/2010/04/15/the-apology-of-aristides-syriac-version, accessed 25/02/12. A Syriac language version was discovered in 1889 on Mt Sinai.
77 Aristides, section XIII.
78 Justin Martyr, *The First Apology*. Word count based on the English translation.
79 Justin Martyr, *The First Apology*.

was supposedly so because they expected Jesus to return from heaven in the very near future. This theoretical idea[80] later lost its force with the discovery of the beliefs and practices of another Jewish religious community that also expected the imminent demise of the world. The Essenes thrived at the same time and in the same country as the budding Christian movement. This same group is that which produced and stored the enormous amount of literature referred to earlier as the Dead Sea Scrolls. This indicates that beliefs in the nearness of the collapse of the world could go hand in hand with writing abundantly. Sadly this community appears to have been destroyed in about 70 AD.

Conclusion

The findings of my research presented in this chapter and the previous one certainly point to a reasonable degree of literacy amongst the masses where Christianity was born during the first century AD. Also, early Christians included those who were educated beyond the basic abilities of reading and writing. Consequently, there was no parallel gross and universal ignorance about the world that allegedly allowed Christianity to flourish more than it would otherwise. In the next chapter, I'll look deeper into how literacy, or the lack thereof, relates to gullibility. In parts III and IV I will explore how such a cross-cultural level of literacy may also make it plausible that Christians used writing as a means to help capture and preserve the words of Jesus.

---

80 HY Gamble, p. 20. Gamble notes that the theory began with Martin Dibelius (d. 1947).

4

Illiteracy and gullibility, miracles and reasoning

The previous chapters have established that literacy was not confined to a privileged few in the ancient Greco–Roman world. However, I was still intrigued about whether people could learn and function in society at a high level even if they were illiterate. Many people I have met believed that the vast majority of the Greco–Roman population at the time of Jesus was illiterate and, therefore, unable to learn and discern much about the way the real world functioned. This, in turn, would make them prone to believing stories about Jesus without checking that they were actually true. Some modern-day people approach the issue of gullibility quite differently and wonder if the alleged miracles performed by Jesus and his disciples were nothing but hoaxes that caused otherwise critical-thinking people to become gullible and start following Jesus.

In part, the belief that illiteracy and gullibility are tightly linked in the ancient world stems from a broader view that all of the people of that era were quite ignorant about how the real world functioned and what it looked like. It is believed by many today that this ancient naivety was associated with an inability to be discerning and rational about all subject matters. Perhaps these views are so prevalent, at least in Australia, because many have been given only a minimal exposure to ancient history during their schooling.

The previous two chapters established that literacy and literature in the ancient world was widespread, and the following example serves as a reminder of the mathematical reasoning ability of people who lived more than 2000 years ago. The North African–born Eratosthenes (276–194 BC) set out to measure the circumference of the Earth using an ingenious system of measurements. He calculated the circumference as being 250,000 stadia (an ancient unit of linear measurement), and one detailed estimate of the value of Eratosthenes's stadion indicates that his result differs by only 2% compared to the present-day value.[1] (In fact, compare Eratosthenes's 39,211,200 metres with NASA's equatorial 40,075,036 metres.[2]) Eratosthenes's mathematical methodology[3] reveals the advanced state of geometric mathematics that existed at that time. Based on this example, and the evidence presented in the earlier chapters, it seems reasonable to conclude that at least some segments of the Greco–Roman population were quite knowledgeable and had the capacity for clear thinking similar to today's people. Interestingly, this knowledge of the shape of the real world was not confined to an intellectual elite. Even illiterate people were made aware of the basic discoveries. For example, Crates of Mallos had constructed a globe model of the Earth in about 150 BC,[4] and it was thought that such globes needed to be at least three

---

1   L Russo, 'Ptolemy's longitudes and Eratosthenes' measurement of the Earth's circumference', *Mathematics and Mechanics of Complex Systems*, vol. 1, no. 1, 2013. Refer to www.academia.edu/2585114/PTOLEMYS_LONGITUDES_AND_ERATOSTHENES_MEASUREMENT_OF_THE_EARTHS_CIRCUMFERENCE, accessed 17/07/2013.
2   P Butterworth & D Palmer, *Ask an Astrophysicist: Speed of the Earth's Rotation*, NASA Goddard Space Flight Centre, http://imagine.gsfc.nasa.gov/docs/ask_astro/answers/970401c.html, accessed 11/07/2013. NASA elsewhere states that the equatorial circumference is 40,030,200 metres. Refer to
    NASA, *Solar System Exploration — Earth: Facts and Figures*, http://solarsystem.nasa.gov/planets/profile.cfm?Display=Facts&Object=Earth, accessed 17/07/2013.
3   Institute of Mathematical Geography, *Eratosthenes's Measurement of the Circumference of the Earth*, www-personal.umich.edu/~copyrght/image/books/Spatial Synthesis/Eratosthenes/, accessed 17/07/2013.
4   JB Harley & D Woodward, 'Greek cartography in the early Roman world', in JB Harley & D Woodward (eds), *The History of Cartography*, Vol. 1: *Cartography in Prehistoric, Ancient, and Medieval Europe and the Mediterranean*, The University of Chicago Press, Chicago, 1987, pp. 162–3.

metres (10 feet) in diameter to display adequately the inhabited parts of the Earth.[5] It has been said that:

> Three-dimensional models of the universe as well as globes and maps were used in schools and sometimes displayed in public places.[6]

As informative as this example is regarding the state of mathematics among a few, and the wider community knowledge about the shape of the world, it does not answer the question of whether illiteracy per se leads to increased gullibility. This is because although literacy was distributed widely among the various social groupings in the ancient Greco–Roman world, a large proportion of the populace would have been illiterate in varying degrees.

Learning without reading

It seems that in the first century AD it was understood by at least some in Roman society that most of its citizens were born with the innate ability to think rationally and learn rapidly. This optimistic attitude (albeit directed to males) is made clear in the following quote from one of the most influential educators of that time, named Quintilian (b. c. 35 AD):

> For there is absolutely no foundation for the complaint that but few men have the power to take in the knowledge that is imparted to them, and that the majority are so slow of understanding that education is a waste of time and labour. On the contrary, you will find that most are quick to reason and ready to learn. Reasoning comes as naturally to man as flying to birds, speed to horses and ferocity to beasts of prey: our minds are endowed by

---

5 Strabo, *Geography*, book 2, ch. 5, s. 10, in trans. HL Jones, Loeb Classical Library, Harvard University Press and Heinemann, 1917–32, p. 449, http://penelope.uchicago.edu/Thayer/E/Roman/Texts/Strabo/2E1*.html, accessed 10/08/2013.

6 JB Harley & D Woodward, 'The growth of an empirical cartography in Hellenistic Greece', in JB Harley & D Woodward (eds), *The History of Cartography, Vol. 1: Cartography in Prehistoric, Ancient, and Medieval Europe and the Mediterranean*, The University of Chicago Press, Chicago, 1987, p. 157. Refer also to pp. 158–60 in their book.

> *nature with such activity and sagacity that the soul is believed to proceed from heaven. Those who are dull and unteachable are as abnormal as prodigious births and monstrosities, and are but few in number.*[7]

Although Quintilian does not specifically refer to illiterate people, it can be reasonably assumed that he strongly believed that illiterate and literate people alike had the ability to reason — that is, think logically — quickly. Assuming Quintilian's judgment is correct, then illiteracy itself is not responsible for gullibility, although the question remains as to how an illiterate individual could gain a substantial amount of general knowledge about the world at large.

Many ancient Greco–Roman documents from Egypt testify to the use of literate friends, relatives and professional scribes who assisted the illiterate in understanding and composing legal documents. This meant that illiterates were able to 'participate in contractual and juridical proceedings as equal partners'.[8] Illiterate people were also able to keep abreast of many aspects of their society through the reading out loud of texts, in much the same way as an illiterate person today could listen to newsreaders and gain much the same basic knowledge as a person reading the newspapers:

> *In Greco–Roman society the illiterate had access to literacy in a variety of public settings. Recitations of poetry and prose works, dramatic performances in theatres and at festivals, declamations in high rhetorical style, street corner philosophical diatribes, the posting and reading of official decrees, the routine traffic of legal and commercial documents, all brought the fruits of literacy before the general population … Besides … many illiterates had recourse to professional scribes for the composition of letters and contracts*

---

[7] Quintilian, *Institutio Oratoria*,1.1.1–2, http://perseus.uchicago.edu/perseus-cgi/citequery3.pl?dbname=LatinAugust2012&getid=1&query=Quint.%201.1.3, accessed 04/08/2013.

[8] TJ Kraus, '"Uneducated", "Ignorant", or even "Illiterate"? Aspects and background for an understanding of ΑΓΡΑΜΜΑΤΟΙ (and ΙΔΙΩΤΑΙ) in Acts 4:13', *New Testament Studies,* vol. 45, 1999, pp. 434–49. Quote from p. 435. Recall from the previous chapter that there may well have been thousands of scribes in Judea during the first century AD.

> ... *[The illiterates were not] barred from the practical benefits of literacy nor from an acquaintance with the substance of texts.*[9]

Early Christian communities made the reading aloud of scriptures a regular part of their weekly meetings. This would have assisted the literate and illiterate to learn. The Jews had already adopted such a practice before this time.

Christian beliefs, miracles and gullibility

The other belief that I mentioned earlier, in relation to miracles inducing gullibility, also warranted investigation. This belief posits that the miracles performed by Jesus and his followers were simply clever deceptions. These hoaxes then caused otherwise discerning people to become gullible, which resulted in the rapid growth of Christian communities. Gullibility can be described as a state in which people can be easily duped. Theoretically, people may become so awestruck by a miracle, or seeming miracle, that they suspend their normal thought processes and uncritically accept what is being spoken to them or asked of them. Leaving aside the question of whether the miracles were authentic, I wanted to consider whether the alleged miracles always induced a profound level of gullibility among large numbers of the first Christians.

Jesus' miracles

When examining the New Testament records of the reactions of some of Jesus' first and most loyal disciples — the inner group of 12 — it soon became apparent that they did not permanently suspend their ability to think critically. This is evident even after they had followed Jesus for years and observed many of his miracles. For example, these first disciples would not believe the eyewitness accounts from the women who visited Jesus' tomb after he had been crucified and found it empty. The women relayed to these disciples that two angels appeared to them and explained that Jesus had come back to life. But the disciples didn't believe the

---

9 HY Gamble, *Books and Readers in the Early Church: A History of Early Christian Texts*, Yale University Press, London, 1995, p. 8.

women 'because their words seemed to them like nonsense' (Luke 24:11). Their disbelief is even more surprising when one considers that Jesus had told them many times that he would come back to life (Matthew 27:63, Mark 8:31). The reason for the disciples' disbelief cannot be explained as them simply being critical of women's testimony in general for the text explicitly states that they simply could not make sense of the story. It is likely that they could not accept the message because they had reasoned that it would be impossible for anyone to come back to life after such a gruesome and protracted period of torture and killing. Thus their critical-thought processes were still well and truly intact.

This level of ongoing questioning, despite many direct observations of what the Bible texts report as miraculous, was not confined to the inner group of disciples. One of the Gospels records that other disciples who had witnessed Jesus performing a miracle still deserted him in large numbers because of his teachings (John 6:66). Their desertion wasn't based on suddenly disbelieving the miracles they had seen, but rather in consciously deciding his teachings were too demanding. Jesus' miracles weren't so overpowering as to cause people to then become gullible to other aspects of his teachings.

Even those who were the beneficiaries of life-changing miracles did not necessarily become followers of Jesus, let alone cease to think critically. In fact, at one stage Jesus healed 10 lepers and only one of these bothered to show any appreciation (Luke 17:11–19). This report counters the idea that many people at that time were very gullible and that all it took for them to become a follower of Jesus was to witness one of the reported miracles.

In order to get an understanding of how crowds responded to Jesus' miracles, I looked at one particular occasion just before Jesus visited Jerusalem but after he had miraculously fed over 5000 people:

> *Among the crowds there was widespread whispering about him. Some said, 'He is a good man.' Others replied, 'No, he deceives the people.' (John 7:12)*

This substantiates that there were plenty of people who were unconvinced despite the miracles of Jesus. In other words, while in some recorded events throngs of people surrounded Jesus, this did not always happen. There was not one single type of crowd mentality that arose wherever Jesus went. Reading through the Gospels, I found one example of a crowd mentality that was quite relevant to my research into the effect of miracles on critical thinking. At one time a miracle performed by Jesus did act as an initial drawcard for a group of people in a town in the region of Samaria (John 4:1–42). The miracle itself was not visually spectacular; rather it involved Jesus telling a woman all about her personal life when he had had no way of knowing those details. A group from the town decided to believe in Jesus based on this woman's testimony (John 4:39). Jesus stayed on in the town for two more days to teach them. At the end of these two days, it is clearly stated that their belief was no longer based on the initial miracle. They said to the Samaritan woman:

> *'We no longer believe just because of what you said; now we have heard for ourselves, and we know that this man really is the Savior of the World.' (John 4:42)*

This event indicates that even when people came to believe in Jesus in the first instance because of a miracle, it was his teachings that were especially convincing.

Miracles performed by early disciples

The New Testament also records occasions when miracles accompanied some of the early disciples, and one of these events is particularly relevant to this discussion on gullibility. Shortly after Jesus' crucifixion, a crowd of people began following two of the disciples after witnessing the healing of a man who had been lame from birth (Acts 14:8–18). This crowd in the city of Lystra (in present-day Turkey) wanted to worship Paul and Barnabas because they thought that both of them were classical Greek gods that had come down to Earth. If the idea that the rapid growth in the numbers of new Christian converts was partly based on the disciples seizing the moment and duping crowds when they were most vulnerable, then we would expect the disciples to have embraced the crowd in Lystra and then tried to persuade them to follow Jesus. Instead the two disciples tore their robes and ran amongst the crowd shouting at them to stop trying to worship them. It might even be expected that many in this crowd of seemingly gullible people would become Christian converts. However, the reality is that the crowd were soon convinced by the mere words of antagonistic Jewish leaders to abandon their worshipping of Paul and Barnabas. The crowds promptly changed their attitude with great gusto, even trying to kill Paul. So, in this case, the persuasive words of the Jewish leaders had a more convincing and longer-lasting influence on the masses than the miracles that accompanied the Christian leaders.

Conclusion

This chapter has shown that illiterate individuals in the ancient Greco–Roman world, just as in today's world, were able to reason and learn, and were therefore not necessarily exceedingly gullible. Illiterate people were no doubt able to use their skills of reasoning and learning to decide whether the stories about Jesus were actually true. This chapter has also documented that the miracles performed by Jesus and his disciples did not always cause otherwise critical-thinking people to become gullible.

Part II

From Jesus' mouth to the disciples' hands

Part II explores in two chapters whether it was possible for Jesus' actions and teachings to be recorded accurately by the early disciples. It analyses the idea that the disciples casually followed Jesus around the countryside and tried to recall what he said and what he did only after he had died. With these half-hearted remembrances, they then began to travel the highways and byways spreading their stories.

Chapter 5 examines the likelihood that Jesus was a teacher who was diligent in teaching his disciples, and that they in turn were equally dedicated to preserving what he said and did.

Chapter 6 will illustrate how Jesus taught using various techniques that would have greatly aided the accurate retention of all that he said. It will also look at why it is that the same account, when described in more than one Gospel, has variations.

5

Jesus the teacher

If Jesus wasn't an author, how do we know what he said?

I am sure many have pondered why Jesus didn't write any of the New Testament books. At first it may seem that if Jesus had actually written his teachings down, this would have been more ideal than having the messages written by those who followed him. Some people I have met believe we can't know with any degree of certainty what Jesus actually taught because he didn't author any of the New Testament books. Others have gone so far as to say that if Jesus was a charismatic teacher, he would not have given any thought to his teachings being preserved in writing.[1]

Even though Jesus didn't compose a book of his teachings, he used techniques to make his lessons memorable. He taught using stories and images to help get his meaning across, and these in turn continue to carry the concepts through time and across language barriers. For example, in John 15:5, Jesus said:

> *I am the vine; you are the branches. If you remain in me and I in you, you will bear much fruit ...*

No matter what time period or culture you come from, most people reading these words will create a mental picture of a vine, and then

---

1 WH Kelber, *The Oral and the Written Gospel: The Hermeneutics of Speaking and Writing in the Synoptic Tradition, Mark, Paul, and Q*, Fortress Press, Philadelphia, 1983, p. 19.

realise that a vine is nothing but branches continually intertwined and that every branch depends on the vine. They get the message that Jesus expects a close relationship with his followers. They will also understand these words to mean that unless they do have this intimate relationship with Jesus they will not be fruitful. Providing they read the words in context, they will not start believing that the fruit being talked about refers to grapes or passionfruit. Jesus' words in this case create an immediate and vivid understanding, but also leave the reader pondering their application.

When researching this chapter and the next, I wanted to know what evidence there was that Jesus intended his message to be preserved in a very precise way. Did Jesus' disciples have the ability to read and write? If they did, what evidence was there that they used written language to record Jesus' teachings? Were they capable of capturing what their master said in an almost word-by-word fashion or did they have the prowess to capture only the essence of his message?

Before further discussion of Jesus as a teacher, I will digress to cover a couple of concerns that people have frequently made. These matters relate to translation and interpretation. The first concern is that because translations appear to distort the original meaning, then the accuracy of the original documents is irrelevant. The second issue is whether the recorded words of Jesus' can be interpreted to mean just about anything. If they can, then there is no value in them.

Making an accurate translation

The ability to capture someone else's oral presentation depends on several factors, including language translation. After all, Jesus didn't speak the modern language versions of English or French.[2] I have met many who say because Jesus' words have to be translated into today's languages, we can't be sure what he actually said. There is an element of truth to this. For instance, even if I correctly translate another language's word for boat as 'boat' in my language, I may still

---

2   Modern English didn't develop until around 1500, and French began in about the 1200s.

conjure up an image of a boat that is totally different to the one in the original language. However, most people are aware of such pitfalls and make subconscious corrections on the fly so that, for example, when they read a book about the Inuit in Greenland fishing from their boats 200 years ago, they don't immediately imagine a type of sailing ship such as a schooner or an aircraft carrier. Good translators also accommodate where necessary. This is especially needed where idioms are used. Even English speakers have trouble with English idioms that have been derived from other parts of the world. I wonder how many present-day New Yorkers or Londoners would understand the Australian idiom 'stone the crows'? Fortunately modern Bibles are translated by groups of scholarly experts, and since our modern languages continue to change, they will never be out of work.

Interpretation

The other issue concerns the matter of interpretation. Many consider that Jesus' words have been interpreted in so many contrasting ways that it is pointless trying to discover the original meaning by reading them yourself. However, most of these contrasting interpretations do not affect the core teachings of Jesus. A few alternate views (one is discussed at the end of this paragraph) have come into being only because of the gross deceitfulness of shysters. Imagine someone proclaiming that the soccer rule book allows a player to pick up the ball and throw it anytime the player wishes during the game. No reasonable person would conclude that the rule book could be fairly interpreted that way. The 'interpreter' would be lampooned and regarded as deliberately misconstruing the throw-in rule used to restart the game when the ball leaves the field. An example of deliberately misconstruing the Christian 'rule book' comes from the mendacious, charismatic leader David Berg. He taught that when Jesus commanded Christians to love others, it meant to have sex with them. His cult encouraged wives to commit adultery so as to obey his teaching. However, no one needs to be duped by such a man because merely reading more of what Jesus had to say would soon dispel such a deliberate misrepresentation of Jesus' words. In fact in the same chapter that Jesus tells his disciples to love their enemies, he also tells them that adultery is evil (Matthew 5:27–44).

Apart from the need to read the context of any passage in a book, it is important to be prepared to go a little deeper. For example, some older English books contain words that are no longer part of modern English vocabulary. Usually a certain measure of understanding can be gained from the context but to get the best out of such a book, a dictionary is useful. In the same way, reading the words of Jesus with tools such as a Greek dictionary will soon reveal that the English word 'love' is a translation of the various Greek words for love and that these various Greek words convey different aspects of love. (Examples are given at the end of this chapter in the second appendix, titled 'Examples of various Greek words for "love"'.)

Did Jesus motivate his disciples to preserve what he taught?

One of the popular images I have come across is that of Jesus being constantly on the move with his disciples following him around as if they were nothing more than illiterate groupies belonging to an ancient fan club. They went where he went only because they wanted to be near the centre of the action. As mere passive observers of their hero, the disciples were not preparing their hearts or minds to take an active leading role in future developments. This view holds that it was only after Jesus was crucified that they tried to recall what Jesus had taught. However, this popular image seems to have very little to do with historical reality. Instead, I came across several lines of evidence that indicate that the disciples were highly motivated by Jesus before his crucifixion to accurately preserve what he taught.[3]

Jesus the teacher

Because of the spectacular nature of Jesus' miracles, many people think of Jesus primarily as a healer. But Jesus was also famous in his

---

3 Many of these lines of evidence have been proposed earlier to contend that Jesus' followers would have carefully preserved accurate information about him. See C Blomberg, *The Historical Reliability of the Gospels*, 1st edn, Inter-Varsity Press, Illinois, 1987, pp. 27–8, summarising R Riesner, *Jesus als Lehrer* (Doctoral Dissertation), Mohr Tubingen, Germany, 1981. Professor Rainer Riesner is from the University of Dortland, Germany.

own lifetime for being a teacher. Jesus' activities included visiting 'all the towns and villages, teaching in their synagogues, preaching the good news of the kingdom' (Matthew 9:35).[4] Jesus taught in a variety of settings, not just in the synagogues. He taught in the courts of the temple in Jerusalem (Mark 14:49), as well as outdoors in the countryside (Matthew 13:1–3). I was surprised to learn that Jesus is called a 'teacher' over 40 times in the New Testament.[5] In the light of all these examples of teaching, it is not surprising to learn that he referred to himself a teacher (Matthew 23:8).

One of the reasons Jesus assigned 12 men to be his special group of followers was so that he could send them out to preach (Mark 3:14). Jesus made it abundantly clear to his disciples that he expected them to pass on his teachings. He commanded, 'What I tell you in the dark, speak in the daylight; what is whispered in your ear, proclaim from the roofs' (Matthew 10:27).

Not only did Jesus teach them what to preach, but they received practice at doing this before he was crucified (Mark 6:7–12, 30; Luke 10:1–17). Occasionally the role of Jesus as a teacher was made particularly clear. He instructed the disciples to 'learn the parable' (Mark 13:28), and he told them: 'If you hold to my teaching, you are really my disciples. Then you will know the truth, and the truth will set you free' (John 8:31–2).

The active role Jesus had as teacher shouldn't be taken to indicate that the disciples were mere passive receptors of all that he said. They are noted as spontaneously striving to learn. When Jesus made reference to himself rising from the dead, the disciples 'seized upon that statement, discussing with one another what rising from the dead meant' (Mark 9:10, NASB). Similarly they requested that Jesus teach them to pray (Luke 11:1).

Jesus' teaching ability and style certainly amplified his mission to teach. He is not portrayed as being merely another teacher, who

---

4   See also Matthew 4:23 and Luke 4:44.
5   Dr Blomberg states that '... Mark actually refers to Jesus as a teacher and to his teaching activity proportionately more often than either Matthew or Luke'. C Blomberg, *The Historical Reliability of the Gospels*, 2nd edn, Inter-Varsity Press, Downers Grove, Illinois, 2007, p. 57, n. 22.

differed from the others only in the content of what he taught or by being very knowledgeable. Rather Jesus spoke as someone who was in a position of great authority (Mark 1:22). Jesus made it clear that he was a prophet (Matthew 13:57), and the Jews regarded prophets as those who proclaimed the very words of God. He asserted that his teachings had at least the same level of authority as the Ten Commandments that the Jews revered. For example, consider how Jesus introduced his further application of the commandment on adultery. He said:

> *You have heard that it was said, 'You shall not commit adultery.' But I tell you that anyone who looks at a woman lustfully has already committed adultery with her in his heart (Matthew 5:27–8).*

Jesus deliberately contrasts 'you have heard that it was said' with 'but I tell you'. Given that the Jews regarded the Ten Commandments as being part of the authoritative word of God (Exodus 20:2–17), Jesus' claim that his extended application of the command was more important than the teaching of the religious leaders' understanding would have been very startling to his audience. Jesus' fostering of this teacher–pupil relationship would have resulted in the disciples aiming to preserve their teacher's messages.

Jesus the movement founder

Perhaps Jesus' most striking claim was that he was the Messiah whom the Jews were expecting (John 4:25–6, 11:25–7). Jesus didn't just use words to get this message across. His actions said it loud and clear. Choosing 12 disciples, publicly forgiving sins and overturning the tables in the national temple in Jerusalem would have all signalled that he was establishing a new movement. This is because his Jewish audience all knew they were descended from a family of 12 brothers, that the temple was where one went for forgiveness of sins, and that overturning the tables was demonstrating his superiority over the present authorities. The goal of his new movement was '... to secure a new and true temple for Israel ... a temple made up of people ...'[6]

---

6   N Perrin, *Lost in Transmission? What We Can Know About the Words of Jesus*, Thomas Nelson, Nashville, US, 2007, p. 91.

The disciples' understanding that they were living in the dawn of an awesome new beginning would have compelled them to awaken others to what was happening. Their desire would naturally have been to preserve their master's words so that the foundation of the new era was stable.

Jesus claimed to be God the Son

According to the New Testament, not only did Jesus claim to be an authoritative teacher, he even claimed to have the authority of the creator of the universe. The New Testament narrates how he specifically performed some miracles to show that he was God. For example, to show that he had the power to forgive sins (an invisible quality that belongs to God alone[7]) he demonstrated that he could easily heal a man who was paralysed (Mark 2:1–12).[8] Similarly, his miracle of walking on the water and calming the waves (Matthew 14:22–33) would have brought to the minds of his disciples the Old Testament passage that God alone 'tramples down the waves of the sea' (Job 9:8, NASB). Jesus said that whoever had seen him had seen the Father (John 14:9), and that people should pray to him and he will answer them (John 14:14). He allowed his disciples to call him Lord and God (John 20:28).[9] These amazing claims and signs would have provided a strong incentive among Jesus' disciples to carefully preserve what he taught and did.

Jesus' teaching methods

Jesus used many different techniques — discussed in the next chapter — to help his listeners remember what he was saying. The very use of these techniques indicates that teaching was a great priority of his

---

7 Micah 7:18: 'Who is a God like you, who pardons sin…'. Psalm 79:9 clearly links God the Saviour to also saving people from their sins and not just from a human oppressor: 'Help us, God our Savior, for the glory of your name; deliver us and forgive us our sins for your name's sake'. Isaiah 43:11: 'apart from me [God] there is no savior'. Mark 2:7: 'Who can forgive sins but God alone?'
8 Anyone can forgive another who has wronged them, but logically only God can forgive someone who has wronged Him.
9 This designation of Jesus as 'My Lord and my God' is almost identical to the call for help to God in Psalm 35:23.

and that he wanted his disciples to remember what he said. Jesus is also recorded as foretelling how he was going to die (Mark 10:33–4; Luke 18:31–3)[10] and when he was going to die (Matthew 26:1–2). Knowing these facts about his death ahead of time, he would have been intentional about the survival of his message. To achieve this, he could easily have encouraged his disciples to use all the strategies common in his society, such as the taking of written notes, as discussed below, and memorisation, which is considered in the next chapter.

All of the above lines of evidence indicate that Jesus was intent on having the disciples preserve his teachings, and that they would have been greatly impacted by him, even before his crucifixion. As a result, the disciples did not follow Jesus in a part-time, easy-going way. They lived and breathed him. As one scholar put it:

> *Here were disciples whose lives had been transformed by Jesus, who had responded to Jesus' call to follow him and abandoned livelihoods and even families in order to live out their discipleship. This was no casual, dilettante affair, where they remembered Jesus as one today might remember a great parliamentarian or actor. Jesus' words meant life for them, his life-style was a model for their own living. Of course they remembered what he said and did. The impact of Jesus' sayings and doings was such that they shaped their lives as lives of discipleship. What they witnessed entered into them and became part of them.*[11]

The disciples were so impacted by Jesus that they were willing to face execution in their efforts to persuade others to follow him. The disciple James was killed under the authority of King Herod (Acts 12:1–2) sometime during or before 44 AD. Another James, the brother of Jesus, was stoned in 62 AD according to the Jewish historian Josephus.[12] A document originally written during the closing decades of the first

---

10 See also John 3:14 and John 12:32–3.
11 JDG Dunn, 'Social memory and the oral Jesus tradition', in *Memory in the Bible and Antiquity: The Fifth Durham-Tubingen Research Symposium (Durham, September 2004)*, Mohr Siebeck, Tubingen, Germany, 2007, p. 187.
12 Josephus, *The Antiquities of the Jews*, book 20, ch. 9.

century AD speaks of the martyrdom of the disciple Peter, as well as the apostle Paul.[13]

Were Jesus' disciples capable of taking notes?

Having found strong reasons for believing that the disciples and Jesus would have acted to preserve his teachings, it is time to examine whether or not they were capable of doing so accurately. I will first examine the evidence for note-taking and shorthand in the Greco–Roman world, then in Jewish society in particular, and finally at evidence for the existence of notes about Jesus' life from the Bible itself.

Note-taking and shorthand in the Greco–Roman world

Sir Frederic Kenyon has pointed out that it was common in the Greco–Roman world of the first century for notebooks to be used in schools, and that these were also regularly used for short letters.[14] In ancient schools, just as in modern ones, students made outline notes. These notes were then shared by the pupils and sometimes expanded on so as to form published books.[15] Rapid note-taking was sometimes achieved through the use of shorthand, a method of rapid writing by means of abbreviations and symbols. Evidence has been found that it was common for scribes and clerks to have been trained in shorthand, and this ability was certainly present during the time of Jesus. In fact, a contract used to outline how payments should be made during the training of shorthand has been discovered dating back to 155 AD. It was found in nearby Egypt,

---

13 Clement of Rome, *Letter of Clement to the Corinthians*, ch. 5:4–5, www.earlychristianwritings.com/text/1clement-roberts.html, accessed 16/05 2012.
For information pointing to a date at or before 70 AD, see TJ Herron, *Clement and the Early Church of Rome: On the Dating of Clement's First Epistle to the Corinthians* [Kindle ebook], Emmaus Road Publishing, Steubenville, US, 2008.
14 FG Kenyon, *Books and Readers in Ancient Greece and Rome*, 2nd edn, Clarendon Press, Oxford, 1951, pp. 90–2.
15 B Gerhardsson, *Memory and Manuscript: Oral Tradition and Written Transmission in Rabbinic Judaism and Early Christianity*, trans. EJ Sharpe, CWK Gleerup, Uppsala, Sweden, 1961, pp. 157–63.

at Oxyrhynchus.[16] The Romans even made a sport of the art of shorthand. Emperor Titus (r. 79–81 AD) was so adept at it that he engaged in friendly competitions with his scribes.[17] A small sample of Latin shorthand found among the leaf tablets of a Roman fort has been dated to somewhere between 92 and 130 AD.[18] The famous Roman philosopher and lawyer Cicero (106 to 43 BC) made great use of those skilled in shorthand:

> *in various parts of the senate-house, several of the most expert and rapid writers, whom he had taught to make figures comprising numerous words in a few short strokes; as up to that time they had not used those we call shorthand writers …*[19]

Latin was not the only language that incorporated the use of shorthand. Greek shorthand, consisting of 'abbreviated or speedy writing',[20] existed before 322 BC, However, there is some controversy as to whether true shorthand, involving signs for syllables and frequently used words, existed for the Greek language during the first two centuries AD.[21]

Note-taking and shorthand in Jewish society

The research from my earlier chapters indicates that it is very reasonable to believe that Jesus' disciples were able to write. One professor, having amassed and analysed the evidence for reading and writing throughout Palestine, noted:

---

16 G Milligan, *The New Testament Documents: Their Origin and Early History*, MacMillan and Co., London, 1913, pp. 241–7, cited by RH Gundry, *The Use of the Old Testament in St. Matthew's Gospel: With Special Reference to the Messianic Hope*, EJ Brill, Leiden, The Netherlands, 1967, p. 182.
17 Suetonius, 'Titus', *The Twelve Caesars*, ch. 3. Cited by G Milligan, p. 247.
18 AK Bowman, *Life and Letters on the Roman Frontier: Vindolanda and its People*, Routledge, New York, pp. 18, 91, 159, plate III.
19 Plutarch, 'Cato the younger', *Parallel Lives of the Noble Greeks and Romans*, trans. AH Clough, p. xxiii, as cited by G Milligan, p. 246. Plutarch (46–120 AD) was a priest, biographer and magistrate. Originally a Greek, he became a Roman citizen.
20 A Millard, *Reading and Writing in the Time of Jesus*, Sheffield Academic Press, Sheffield, UK, 2001, p. 175.
21 A Millard, pp. 175–6.

> *The evidence indicates the presence of some people, not [just the] professional scribes, who could use writing in their daily business throughout Palestine, even in rural regions, able to make notes of a preacher's words if they wished.*[22]

The Jewish rabbis had a form of note-taking which they used when passing on their traditions. These traditions were derived from their holy scriptures, which Christians today call the Old Testament. At first, these teachers relied on their skills at deliberate memorisation 'with precision and accuracy ...'[23] As the traditions became significantly larger, they deliberately created specific phrases that acted as anchors to aid in the less rigid recall of what was to follow. These phrases were later 'reduced to writing and formed the shorthand notes, by which much of the *tannaitic* [Jewish] tradition was preserved during the centuries before it was completely ... put into writing'.[24] This final written form was completed by the third century AD.[25] The use of shorthand notes among the Jews for these particular texts, therefore, goes back as far as Jesus' lifetime.

It is important to emphasise that the purpose of any notes made by Jesus' disciples was probably not to make them so comprehensive that a total stranger could pick them up and read them as one reads an edited textbook. It is more likely that one of the purposes for their notes would include assistance in memorisation. Many of us today use writing as one way to help visualise what we are committing to memory. We make the patterns of a speech easier to remember by visualising them through writing. While writing, we may also speak the patterns out loud, or in our heads, further reinforcing the memory. The disciples may have used writing as such an aid to memorisation, a method that had been recommended by earlier Jews.[26] Therefore, any notes that the disciples made could served

---

22 A Millard, pp. 181–2.
23 L Finkelstein, 'The transmission of early rabbinic teaching', *Hebrew Union College Annual*, 16, 1941, pp. 115–35.
24 L Finkelstein, p. 115.
25 S Safrai (ed.), *The Literature of the Sages: First Part: Oral Torah, Halakha, Mishna, Tosefta, Talmud, External Tractates*, Fortress Press, Philadelphia, 1987, p. 47.
26 Refer to chapter 5 'Literacy in Jesus' world', pp. 2–3 (Philo's quote).

two functions: to jog their memory in broad terms about the actions and lessons of Jesus and to aid the memorisation of the words they heard.

Having looked briefly at the strong evidence for note-taking in Jewish society, and the broader Greco–Roman world, it is understandable that one scholar was able to write confidently:

> *Almost all teachers in the Jewish and Graeco–Roman worlds gathered disciples around them in order to perpetuate their teachings and lifestyle ... If he [Jesus] envisaged his disciples ... continuing his ministry ... then he certainly would have been concerned that they preserve his message and mission intact.*[27]

The Gospel of Luke based on earlier writings

Having discovered that it is reasonable to accept that the disciples lived in a culture and time period where note-taking existed, does the New Testament reveal that the disciples did make written notes? One indication that Jesus' teachings were put into written form at a very early date comes from Luke, one of the New Testament Gospel authors. He wrote in about 60 AD:[28] 'Many have undertaken to draw up an account of the things that have been fulfilled among us ...' (Luke 1:1). He refers to these previous accounts as being *diēgēsis* (διήγησις), which in this context:

> *means a narrative, whether written or oral. Although it was not exclusive to historiography, it regularly appears to mark a historical narrative ... The author [Luke] thus considered his predecessors to have written narratives and proposes to write one himself.*[29]

---

27 C Blomberg, *The Historical Reliability of the Gospels*, 1st edn, Inter-Varsity Press, Illinois, 1987, p. 27–8, summarising R Riesner, *Jesus als Lehrer* (Doctoral Dissertation), Mohr Tubingen, Germany, 1981.

28 NL Geisler & F Turek, *I Don't Have Enough Faith to be an Atheist*, Crossway Books, Illinois, 2004, pp. 239–41.

29 GE Sterling, *Historiography and Self-definition: Josephos, Luke-Acts and Apologetic Historiography*, EJ Brill, Leiden, The Netherlands, 1992, pp. 341–3.

One scholar commented that the words of Luke 1:1 clearly indicate that Luke claimed to have used many previous writers and thus Luke expects his work to be the apex of previous literary activity.[30] Luke further explains that the source material for these narratives has been 'handed down to us by those who from the first were eyewitnesses and servants of the word' (Luke 1:2).

A chief note-taker?

The New Testament does contain another indication of the existence of notes made by the disciples. This evidence is based on a detailed study of similarities and differences between the four different Gospel accounts. It seems to some scholars that one disciple was appointed as chief note-taker.

One New Testament scholar, Dr Gundry, has provided extensive evidence that there was one major set of notes that all the other Gospel writers utilised to varying extents when composing their own Gospels.[31] He considered that one disciple, possibly Matthew, was specifically given the task to take down these authoritative notes.

Dr Gundry has concluded that the first three Gospel writers 'were content to present by and large the same outline of Jesus' life and ministry'.[32] Yet the author of John's Gospel wrote that he presented only a portion of all that Jesus did (John 21:25), and this is clearly true for the other Gospel writers. So a good explanation for their harmony is that there was 'a single authoritative, apostolic source behind the bulk of synoptic tradition [what they wrote about Jesus]'.[33] The other disciples may then have shared the notes made by Matthew, expanding them into their own Gospel accounts.[34] The various authors of these Gospel accounts had different intended audiences, and they differed in what they wished to emphasise.[35]

---

30 CJ Hemer, *The Book of Acts in the Setting of Hellenistic History*, ed. CH Gempf, JCB Mohr (Paul Siebeck) Tubingen, 1989, p. 353
31 RH Gundry, pp. 181–2.
32 RH Gundry, p. 183.
33 RH Gundry, p. 183.
34 RH Gundry, p. 184.
35 Refer also to chapter 8 'Jesus' teaching methods'.

Further investigating Matthew as the chief note-taker

Why is it that Matthew is considered as a candidate for the role of chief note-taker? Being a tax collector (Matthew 10:3), Matthew would have been an ideal candidate for the chief note-taker as he was well educated. In fact, 'the Roman tax system at the beginning of the first century C.E. was quite elaborate. With a series of national, regional, and local layers, it was comparable to those existing today in most Western countries'.[36] Dr Gundry stated that Matthew's 'employment and post near Capernaum on the Great West Road would have required and given a good command of Greek and instilled the habit of jotting down information …'[37] Matthew may also have occupied a special position within the Jewish religious system (i.e. a Levite, as suggested by his alternate name being Levi). It is likely that he passed through the first two basic levels of Jewish education — the House of Reading (called Beth Sepher) and the House of Learning (called Beth Talmud) — and progressed into the next level — the House of Interpretation (or Beth Midrash).[38] Evidence for this level of education arises from Matthew's use of certain standardised techniques to establish that Jesus met the criterion that the long-awaited Messiah was to come from the town of Nazareth.[39]

Matthew's educational background would have given him 'an acquaintance with the Old Testament in its Semitic [Hebrew] as well as Greek forms …'[40] This would help explain some of the patterns we see in the gospels, such as their use of either the Hebrew or Greek forms of the Old Testament. This is because 'the looseness and informality of such notes made it possible for Hebrew, Aramaic, and Greek all to appear in [the Gospels]'.[41]

---

36 JJ Rousseau & R Arav, *Jesus and His World: An Archaeological and Cultural Dictionary*, Fortress Press, Minneapolis, US, 1995, p. 277. A Jewish farmer may have paid 32% tax to the Romans and 12% to Jewish authorities (pp. 275–9).
37 RH Gundry, p. 183.
38 WHU Anderson, 'Jewish education around the time of the New Testament (100 BCE – 100 CE)', *Journal of Beliefs and Values*, 18(2), 1997, pp. 217–26 (p. 219).
39 WHU Anderson, p. 223.
40 RH Gundry, p. 183.
41 RH Gundry, p. 183.

Not all scholars agree with Dr Gundry's concept of there being a chief note-taker amongst Jesus' disciples. There are many excellent books dealing with the issue of sources of information for the Gospel writers.[42] I only wish to lightly touch on sources for two of the Gospel writers: Luke and Mark.

Where did Luke and Mark source their information?

As two of the four Gospels (Luke and Mark) were written by followers who weren't part of Jesus' inner circle (i.e. not one of the Twelve Apostles), I wanted to know how possible it was that these two authors had reliable sources of information about Jesus.

One of these writers, Luke, not only wrote a very large Gospel but also wrote the book of Acts, which is full of historical details. This is especially intriguing as Luke's Gospel includes many details that the other Gospels don't have. While certainly the written Gospel accounts made by the disciples Matthew and John were used by Luke to write his own Gospel, these were most likely not the only information about Jesus to which Luke had access. It has been argued quite adequately:

> *that Luke obtained part of his material by interviewing participants [i.e. those who interacted with Jesus and the disciples], and that he sometimes edited older traditions by re-interviewing such surviving participants as may have been accessible to him ...*[43]

The Gospel of Mark creates a similar question, as it too wasn't written by a disciple. Yet it has all the hallmarks of being the account of someone who was in close contact with at least one of Jesus' disciples. Some of the earliest Christian authors wrote that the disciple Peter passed on his teachings to Mark who wrote them down.[44]

---

42 The following is a good example: R Bauckham, *Jesus and the Eyewitnesses*, William B. Eerdmans Publishing Company, Grand Rapids, Michigan, US, 2006.
43 CJ Hemer, p. 351. Hemer aimed to show the feasibility of his position, and realised that although it was not possible to prove his case, it was plausible (p. 353). He gave an extensive list of scholars who had come to similar conclusions (p. 352, n. 81).
44 For more details see: PR Eddy & GA Boyd, *The Jesus Legend: A Case for the Historical Reliability of the Synoptic Jesus Tradition*, Baker Academic, Grand Rapids, Michigan, US, 2007, pp. 390–6.

But weren't the disciples uneducated?

I came across one interesting objection to the idea that Jesus' disciples were capable of taking notes. The argument is that the New Testament itself speaks of all of the disciples being illiterate, and stems from the words of a passage in Acts 4:1–17. The account reports how the Jewish rulers, elders and teachers of the law (grammateis, γραμματεις) arrested Peter and John. During the interrogation, Peter delivers a short speech, quoting from the Jewish scriptures and accusing these authorities of crucifying Jesus. The words of Acts 4:13 narrate the reaction from these Jewish leaders:

> *When they saw the courage of Peter and John and realized that they were unschooled (agrammatoi, γράμματοι), ordinary men, they were astonished and they took note that these men had been with Jesus.*

Some people today consider that the description of Peter and John as unschooled (agrammatos, γράμματος) indicates that they were illiterate. However, this term was used to contrast someone to a professional scribe (grammateus, γραμματεύς).[45] Among the Jews, such a scribe was a person who had received a formal religious education.[46] This schooling also had to be one that had received their stamp of approval. Naturally, the Jewish ruling elite didn't consider the 'schooling' delivered by Jesus as being acceptable.

Two recent scholars have pointed out that: 'The term *agrammatoi* need imply nothing more than that these two never received a formal education — a fact that is hardly surprising since they were

---

45 CK Barrett, *A Critical and Exegetical Commentary on The Acts of the Apostles*, vol. 2, International Critical Commentary series, T & T Clark, Edinburgh pp. 233–4. See also CA Evans.
46 'Only once in the NT is γραμματεύς used ... in the ordinary Greek sense of "clerk" ... The normal Jewish use, however, is very common. According to this use ... γραμματεύς is a translation of ... [a Hebrew word] which means a "man learned in the Torah," a "rabbi," an "ordained theologian."' J Jeremias, 'γραμματεύς' [this is the dictionary heading] in *Theological Dictionary of the New Testament*, vol. 1, Wm Eerdmans Publishing Company, Grand Rapids, Michigan, US, 1964, p. 740.

fishermen'.⁴⁷ As fishermen, they may have been quite adept at running businesses, keeping abreast of market trends, analysing contracts etc. This is because successful fishermen were part of the upper 10% of wage earners, being on a par with tax collectors and carpenters.⁴⁸

What is also interesting is that illiteracy in the ancient world did not mean that someone was illiterate in all languages. Priests who could read a type of Egyptian script called hieratic were still accused of being illiterate.⁴⁹

Finally, the contention that all the disciples are described in Acts 4:13 as illiterate is exaggerated as only two of the 12 close disciples are mentioned. As discussed above, at least one disciple (Matthew) was highly educated.

Conclusion

The information I gathered for this chapter gave me great confidence in knowing that Jesus strove to teach his disciples and that they were motivated to diligently learn. Further, at least some of his disciples were highly likely to have had the ability and desire to use written means to assist in their recall of Jesus' life and lessons. What I still wanted to discover was their capability to capture in a fairly precise manner what Jesus actually said, even if they didn't always use note-taking skills. I will examine this in the next chapter.

Appendix 1
But why didn't Jesus write his own message?

It is very interesting to speculate as to why Jesus didn't make a written record of his own life and teachings, rather than rely on the disciples. One explanation is that Jesus foreknew that if he did there would be a very strong tendency for people to venerate the actual books rather than worship him and come into relationship with him. Such forms

---

47 PR Eddy & GA Boyd, pp. 249–50. See also TJ Kraus, '"Uneducated", "ignorant", or even "illiterate"? Aspects and background for an understanding of ΑΓΡΑΜΜΑΤΟΙ (and ΙΔΙΩΤΑΙ) in Acts 4.13', *New Testament Studies*, 45, 1999, pp. 434–49.
48 CS Keener, p. 101.
49 TJ Kraus, p. 441.

of veneration easily slip into the arena of superstition. Even today, despite Jesus not having penned any words, this problem does exist to some extent. Those who have little knowledge of Jesus' teachings have been misled into believing that the Bible is a type of good luck charm. George Foreman, a two-time World Heavyweight boxing champion, wrote:

> *In 1974, before I went to Africa to fight Muhammad Ali, a friend gave me a Bible to take along on my trip. He said, 'George, keep this with you for good luck.' ... I was always looking for luck, so I carried that Bible with me ... I never even opened it ... I thought I'd get power simply from owning it; I didn't realize that I needed to read it and believe what it says. Since then, I've come to understand that the Bible is my road map, not my good luck charm.*[50]

Another explanation for Jesus' apparent lack of literary output is that he knew that some of the most important teachings and events would happen when he wouldn't be in a position to write. Such times as his arrest, trials, torture culminating in crucifixion, and resurrection are the main ones. The words he spoke during these times, and the associated events, no doubt became etched into the disciples' minds, impressions that would enable them to compose Gospels that portray these details quite accurately.

Being a prominent teacher of the Jewish scriptures, it is not surprising that Jesus is recorded as being able to read. One of the clearest illustrations of this is when he visited the town of Nazareth:

> *He stood up to read [in the synagogue], and the scroll of the prophet Isaiah was handed to him. Unrolling it, he found the place where it is written: 'The Spirit of the Lord is on me, because he has anointed me to preach good news to the poor. He has sent me to proclaim freedom for the prisoners, and recovery of sight for the blind, to release the oppressed, to proclaim the year of the Lord's favor.' Then he rolled up the scroll, gave it back to the attendant and sat down. (Luke 4:16–20)*

---

50 G Foreman & K Abraham, *God in My Corner: A Spiritual Memoir*, Thomas Nelson, Nashville, Tennessee, US, 2007, p. 91.

Appendix 2
Examples of various Greek words for 'love'

One of these Greek words is *eros*, from which we derive our English word erotic. At its core, it refers to feelings of desire for entities that range from sexual to divine. Eros is created by an attraction produced in the soul by the object of our love having a certain character, such as beauty.[51] In the New Testament, there is nothing inherently evil about such objects of desire.

Another Greek word for love is *agape*, which the New Testament describes as that form of love whereby one desires to meet the needs of another by identifying with that person, having first an appreciation of the fact that we ourselves are receivers of Jesus' amazing grace.[52] The New Testament often speaks of God's agape love, even saying: 'We love because he first loved us.' (1 John 4:19).[53]

English readers of the word 'love' will certainly be correct in identifying the concept of desire lying behind both words, but an understanding of New Testament Greek, and the context, heightens the understanding.

---

51 E Brunner, *Faith, Hope, and Love*, Lutterworth Press, London, 1957, p. 63.
52 C Grant, 'For the love of God: agape', *The Journal of Religious Ethics*, 24(1), 1996, pp. 3–21.
53 See also 1 John 4:7–12, John 15:10–14, 2 Thessalonians 3:5.

6

Jesus' teaching methods

The last chapter discussed the likelihood that Jesus' disciples made use of notes to help them remember all that Jesus said and did. But if they didn't have extensive notes, how reasonable is it that they could memorise Jesus' teachings? Did Jesus himself encourage memorisation? For instance did he deliberately present his teachings in such a way that they could be easily remembered?

Could the disciples have memorised Jesus' teachings?

It is now uncommon for Australian school children (and probably children from other Western-based cultures) to commit to memory large portions of text. Yet many ordinary Australians once took great pride in their ability to memorise word-for-word quite lengthy poems.[1] Perhaps one of the most popular Australian poems was *The Man from Snowy River* by AB 'Banjo' Paterson. Individual Australians recall having learnt by heart *The Man from Snowy River*, together with other poems, in primary school (i.e. before the age of 13 years) as late as the 1950s. This poem consists of 980 words and 113 lines. Another

---

1 S McInerney, 'By heart', *New Springtime: A Journal of Faith, Culture and Society*, Australian Catholic Students Association, March, 2009, www.newspringtime.org.au/content/view/90/1/, accessed 20/06/2009. Dr McInerney, in March 2009, was Lecturer in Literature at Campion College Australia. See also the Australian Bush Poets Association website, www.abpa.org.au/, accessed 17/04/2010.

poem that was often recited from memory was *The Hound of Heaven* by Francis Thompson, which consisted of 1183 words and 182 lines.

These examples indicate that memory can retain information with great accuracy. But how possible is it that those Australian school children who learnt by heart several large poems could similarly memorise all the words spoken by Jesus? I found that the number of words spoken by Jesus, as recorded only in the Gospel of Mark, amounts to 3992.[2] Given that some Australians memorised more than one poem, and just two of the poems together consisted of 2163 words, it seems that many of us have the potential to memorise all of Jesus' words. However, what deductions can we make about the disciples' capacity to memorise and what evidence is there that people in Jesus' day and age actually took the effort to remember the words of their teachers.

Deductions about the disciples' capacity to memorise

Theoretically, people of 2000 years ago had the capacity to remember as well as we have today. There are no scientific reasons to believe that the normal human capacity to memorise was greater or less than today. However, there are situational reasons for accepting that the disciples' task of memorising Jesus' words was easier than that of the Australian pupils learning large poems. Whereas the school children may have learnt from a teacher possessing reasonable motivation, the disciples learnt from one who no doubt had much greater motivations. Whereas the school children had many other subjects to learn, the disciples had all their attention focused on the one subject master. Whereas Australian pupils learnt their poems indirectly from the poet, using anthologies and performers, the disciples learnt directly from a living teacher, probably with the aid of their written notes. The Australian pupil–teacher relationship would certainly never have been of the same order of magnitude as that between the disciples and Jesus. Australian teachers had only school hours during school days in which to teach poetry. Jesus had many hours each day and many more days of the year to instruct his disciples.

---

2   N Perrin, *Lost in Translation? What We Can Know About the Words of Jesus*, Thomas Nelson, Nashville, US, 2007, p. 197.

The disciples may have had another advantage over Australians learning poetry — the advantage of being a well-bonded group. The ability to memorise material can be enhanced when students work together. Groups can accelerate learning and help keep memories alive. Consider how rapidly people can learn another language when totally immersed in a foreign culture. This is very relevant as the disciples didn't follow Jesus as disconnected individuals. They had the advantage of being a group knitted together by Jesus and constantly being worked into the one tapestry. The Gospel of John records how the disciples, after Jesus had been crucified and resurrected, 'talked and discussed' with each other 'everything that had happened' (Luke 24:15). Even groups that are large and loosely knit, such as the modern society in Israel, can collectively retain a vast amount of information. This is highlighted by the publication out of Bethlehem in 1985 of two volumes of proverbs titled: *The Proverb Says: Encyclopedia of Current Proverbs and Wisdom Sayings*. The work includes 6000 proverbs, over 4000 of which:

> *are popular and colloquial in nature and were collected orally ... We are here observing a community that can create (over the centuries) and sustain in current usage up to 6,000 wisdom sayings ... One of the major ways Middle Eastern people express their values is through the creating and preserving of Wisdom sayings ...*[3]

Memorisation in the ancient world

Moving on from the above reasonable deductions about the disciples' ability to memorise Jesus' words, it is fascinating to discover the actual prominence given to memorisation in the ancient world:

> *Memorizing large parts of texts or even whole texts was a common performance in the ancient world, and is attested through various school exercises or public performances ...*[4]

---

3   KE Bailey, 'Informal controlled oral tradition and the synoptic gospels', *Asia Journal of Theology*, 5, 1991, pp. 34–54 (quote from p. 41.)
4   C Jacob, 'Athenaeus the librarian', in D Braund & J Wilkins (eds), *Athenaeus and His World: Reading Greek Culture in the Roman Empire*, University of Exeter Press, Exeter, UK, 2000, p. 109.

Xenophon (c. 430 to 354 BC), in his book *The Banquet (Symposium 3.6)*, describes a man called Niceratus who is asked by his fellow dinner guests about that knowledge which makes him proud. He replied that he could recite from memory all of the *Iliad* and *Odyssey*. (The *Iliad* alone was an epic poem of about 175,000 words.[5]) Those listening downplayed Niceratus' ability, saying that there were many others who could perform the same feat and that what really constituted an admirable feat of memorisation was much more than just the size of the text:

A striking feature of mnemonic performances is the ability to excerpt a few lines from a continuous text and even to move forward or backward in this 'book of memory', from any starting point.[6]

Such memorisation also formed the basis of entertaining games. Individual players would have to recite verses from a poet that started and finished with the same letter of the alphabet. Other times it would be of verses wherein the first syllable and the last syllable together formed a certain word.[7] The ability to learn entire texts, and to move about these texts in one's mind, was imparted to slaves. A man called Calvisius Sabinus paid large sums of money to purchase slaves who had learnt the works of a famous author, such as Homer or Hesiod. These slaves were called 'living books', and they were used to provide quotes during Sabinus' conversations with his dinner guests.[8]

The Jews of the first centuries AD are also known to have cherished the art of memorisation. This is very relevant as Jesus' disciples were Jews. Jewish school children had to learn the first five books of their scripture, namely the Torah. Large portions of it had to be memorised,[9] not just for the short term but for life.[10]

The Jews weren't the only ones in the Middle East who had a culture of valuing memorisation. Professor Kenneth Bailey provides several examples of prodigious memorisation in other Middle Eastern societies,

---

5   See chapter 1 'Writing history and creating libraries'.
6   C Jacob, p. 110.
7   C Jacob, p. 110.
8   Seneca, *Ad Lucilium*, 3.27.5, cited by C Jacob, p. 109.
9   B Gerhardsson, *Memory and Manuscript: Oral Tradition and Written Transmission in Rabbinic Judaism and Early Christianity*, trans. EJ Sharpe, CWK Gleerup, Uppsala, Sweden, 1961 pp. 62–3.
10 B Gerhardsson, p. 64.

often including the memorisation of the Islamic scriptures called the Qur'an (also written as Quran). Although not all Arabic versions of the Quran are identical,[11] it contains over 6200 numbered verses.[12] He relays how various individuals had committed to memory a work consisting of 'a collection of one thousand couplets of Arabic verse, each of which defines some aspect of Arabic grammar'.[13] He then recounts how:

> *It was my privilege to study in Cairo in the [nineteen] fifties under a venerable Islamic scholar, Shaykh Sayyed, who had both of these works [the Qur'an and the collection of a thousand couplets] fully committed to memory with total recall at the age of 75. I would bring to him a couplet of Arabic poetry and ask him if it was in the Qur'an. He would close his eyes for a few seconds, mentally flip through the entire Qur'an, and then give his answer. Similarly, any point of grammar evoked the quotation of one of the one-thousand couplets ...[14]*

Did Jesus cast his message in ways designed to aid memorisation?

Based on the above information, it is certainly well within reason to conclude that the 12 disciples were able to memorise all the words of Jesus recorded in the New Testament. The above comparison between the learning of poetry and Jesus' words has much merit, as it appears that many of Jesus' teachings were deliberately formulated to make memorisation as easy as possible. Just as many poems have a rhythm or rhyme that makes their memorisation easier, it has been found that:

> *The gospels ... phrase over 90% of his [Jesus'] sayings in forms which would have been easy to remember, using figures and styles of speech much like those found in Hebrew poetry.[15]*

---

11 S Green, 'The different Arabic versions of the Qur'an: part 2: the current situation, *Answering Islam*, www.answering-islam.org/Green/seven.htm, accessed 23/11/2012.
12 S Green, 'Comparing the Bible and the Qur'an (How to do it accurately)', *Answering Islam*, www.answering-islam.org/Green/compare.htm, accessed 23/11/2012.
13 KE Bailey, p. 38.
14 KE Bailey, p. 38.
15 C Blomberg, *The Historical Reliability of the Gospels*, 1st edn, Inter-Varsity Press, Illinois, 1987, pp. 27–8, summarising R Riesner, *Jesus als Lehrer* (Doctoral Dissertation), Mohr Tubingen, Germany, 1981.

Techniques used to aid people's memory are called mnemonic devices, and Jesus used a large variety of these. Although many of these are apparent in our Greek New Testament texts, even more of them are revealed when the Greek texts are translated back into Aramaic, which is the language that Jesus probably used the most.[16] These include parables, hyperbole, 'puns, metaphors and similes, proverbs, riddles, and parabolic actions [i.e. actions that convey a message] ...'[17] Most of all he used poetry. These aspects fully show the extent to which Jesus went in training his disciples to remember his teachings. The following is a brief look at a few of the mnemonic devices used by Jesus.

Parables

Jesus was a master at telling parables. There are 41 parables in the first three Gospels alone.[18] Although the rabbis of the first two centuries AD made use of parables, their parables had a different purpose. They did not use parables to teach new truths but to explain scripture or their various laws.[19] In contrast, Jesus used parables to convey new truths. Jesus' parables were anchored in the realities of the daily life of his society, making them even easier to remember. It's easy to imagine that every time his disciples saw workers in a vineyard, they would remember his parable about similar employees complaining about their rates of pay (Matthew 20:1–16). Or every time they saw fishermen with their nets sorting out their catch, they would remember the corresponding parable (Matthew 13:47–48). As one scholar said about them:

> *His parables take us ... into the midst of throbbing everyday life. Their nearness to life, their simplicity and clarity, the masterly*

---

16 AM Berlin & JA Overman, 'Introduction', in AM Berlin & JA Overman (eds), *The First Jewish Revolt: Archaeology, History, and Ideology*, Routledge, London, 2002, p. 9. They state that the active spoken language of Jews in Judea was Aramaic. More specifically it has been said that Jesus spoke a Galilean version of western Aramaic (J Jeremias, *New Testament Theology: The Proclamation of Jesus*, vol.1, trans. J Bowden, SCM Press, London, 1971, p. 4.
17 RH Stein, *The Synoptic Problem: An Introduction*, Baker Book House, Grand Rapids, Michigan, US, 1988, p. 200.
18 J Jeremias, p. 30.
19 S Kistemaker, *The Parables of Jesus*, Baker Book House, Grand Rapids, Michigan, US, 1980, pp. xvi–xvii.

brevity with which they were told, the seriousness of their appeal to conscience, their loving understanding of the outcasts of religion — all this is without analogy.[20]

Actions speak louder than words

Perhaps the most striking technique Jesus used to ingrain his teachings into the minds of his disciples was his use of parabolic actions. These are actions that teach in their own right and so do not always require an explanation. Perhaps the clearest of these is Jesus' decision to have 12 disciples. This was to reflect that the nation of Israel originally consisted of 12 tribes descended from 12 sons. By his action, Jesus was saying that he was establishing a new Israel. That this message was recognised by the disciples is shown by their urgency at appointing another disciple as a substitute for Judas, who had betrayed Jesus shortly before his crucifixion.[21]

The link between actions and teachings is sometimes made particularly clear in the Gospels. One Gospel contains an account of Jesus miraculously feeding thousands of people with only five loaves of bread and two fish (John 6:1–15). The day after this miracle Jesus makes a striking declaration to the crowd: 'I am the bread of life. He who comes to me will never go hungry, and he who believes in me will never go thirsty' (John 6:35).

Poetry

Poetry is a very useful mnemonic device, as is evident by the ease with which people remember songs and long ballads. The types of poetry that Jesus used are called parallelisms, which exist in many forms. Nearly 190 different examples of parallelism can be found in Jesus' teachings.[22] Parallelisms occur when a thought is echoed or repeated in the next line of the poem, whilst also maintaining the same rhythm. These poems are

---

20 J Jeremias, p. 30.
21 Acts 1:12–26.
22 RH Stein, *The Synoptic Problem: An Introduction*, p. 200; citing RH Stein, *The Method and Message of Jesus' Teachings*, Westminster, Philadelphia, US, 1978, pp. 27–32.

built on the basis of rhythm being more important than rhyme, and they are classified into five different forms.[23] A synonymous parallelism is when the thought is repeated almost identically, whereas an antithetical parallelism is when the second line of verse is in contrast to the first. Of the following four examples, the first represents synonymous parallelism and the remaining examples are of antithetical parallelism:

> Ask and it will be given to you;
> Search and you will find;
> Knock and the door will be opened to you.[24]

> A good tree cannot bear bad fruit,
> And a bad tree cannot bear good fruit.[25]

> Whoever finds their life will lose it,
> And whoever loses their life for my sake will find it.[26]

> Whoever can be trusted with very little
> Can also be trusted with much,
> And whoever is dishonest with very little
> Will also be dishonest with much.[27]

Antithetic parallelisms spoken by Jesus are extremely prolific in the Gospels. One scholar found 138 examples of antithetic parallelisms in the first three Gospels alone.[28] Jesus used this form of speech in a very consistent and particular manner, namely placing the emphasis on the second line. This is in contrast to the Old Testament where the second line 'serves, on the whole, to illuminate and to deepen the first by an opposed statement ...'[29] This consistency would have further assisted correct memorisation of Jesus' exact words. Sometimes Jesus incorporated several mnemonic devices in the one lesson, as shown in the following parable that also uses antithetical parallelism:

---

23 The three forms of parallelism not discussed here are synthetic, chiasmic, and step. RH Stein, p. 200.
24 Matthew 7:7
25 Matthew 7:18
26 Matthew 10:39
27 Luke 16:10
28 J Jeremias, pp. 14–16.
29 J Jeremias, p. 18.

> Enter through the narrow gate.
> For wide is the gate and broad is the road
> That leads to destruction,
> And many enter through it.
> But small is the gate and narrow the road
> That leads to life,
> And only a few find it.[30]

Sometimes Jesus' poetry involved rhythm only, without making use of parallelisms. Jesus' teachings incorporated several types of rhythm, including those with two, three and four beats. He took advantage of the mood, invoking abilities of rhythm to match the essence of what he was saying. For example, the briefness of two-beat rhythm requires abruptness of thought and word, creating a feeling of urgency and importance. Jesus used this form often when he 'wanted to impress upon his hearers *central ideas* of his message'.[31] Jesus spoke the following rhyme found in Matthew 10:8 without using joining words (conjunctions):[32]

Asthenountas therapeuete	Heal sick
Nekrous egeirete	Raise dead
Leprous katharizete	Cleanse lepers
Daimonia ekballete	Expel demons

Miscellaneous techniques

In addition to the above mnemonic techniques, Jesus used several others, such as alliteration, assonance and antitheses.[33] The latter occur when contrasts are made between two aspects, but in a manner that is not as symmetrical as antithetic parallelisms. A typical antithesis can be found in Mark 10:45:

> *For even the Son of Man did not come to be served, but to serve ...*

---

30 Matthew 7:13–14
31 J Jeremias, p. 22. Emphasis in the original.
32 J Jeremias, p. 21. It also rhymes in Aramaic. I have shown the English equivalent words and transliteration from the Greek. The omitting of conjunctions is called an asyndeton.
33 J Jeremias, pp. 14, 27–9.

Having discovered these aspects of Jesus as a consummate teacher, it seems certain that the first disciples were expected to memorise the words and stories of Jesus. It has been proposed by one scholar that they had a system in place similar to the rigid:

> *patterns of memorization and paraphrase dominant in rabbinic circles in the centuries immediately following the birth of Christianity. According to [Professor] Riesenfeld, Jesus probably had his disciples memorize his most significant teachings and perhaps even certain narratives about what he did. Thus there is every reason to believe that they were reliably preserved. Riesenfeld's student, Birger Gerhardsson ... has documented how widespread and prodigious the practice of memorization was in ancient rabbinic circles (many rabbis had the entire Old Testament and much of the oral law committed to memory!).*[34]

Why do the Gospels differ from each other?

The above discussion on the great accuracy possible in memorising Jesus' teachings and encounters, and the previous chapter's investigation into the likelihood that written notes were utilised, create confidence that the Gospels are a faithful record of Jesus' life and teachings. However, undermining this impression is the question of why it is that the four written Gospel accounts often record the same story or lesson but with minor differences. The similarities are enormous, but differences are certainly present. Why are there any differences between the Gospels at all?

What I found was that the vast bulk of differences could easily be envisaged as growing out of the influence of five principles at work in the minds of the Gospel authors:

---

34 C Blomberg, pp. 25–6. Blomberg refers to several texts, including: H Riesenfeld, *The Gospel Tradition*, Fortress Press, Philadelphia, US, 1970, pp. 1–29; B Gerhardsson, *Tradition and Transmission in Early Christianity*, Gleerup, Lund, Sweden, 1964; and B Gerhardsson, *The Origins of the Gospel Tradition*, Fortress Press, Philadelphia, US, 1979.

- flexibility in describing background material
- flexibility in Jesus' non-essential words
- variation inherent in Jesus' teachings
- variations in Aramaic to Greek translations
- the freedom to select but not to fabricate.

These principles may not have been in the forefront of their minds, but rather operated at a subconscious level. I have called these principles frameworks of understanding. Just as the framework of a house under construction brings awareness of how the house will form, so too these frameworks create an understanding of how the differences were born.

Flexibility in describing background material

The first framework is that the disciples committed to memory Jesus' *essential teachings* perfectly accurately, though the background information was allowed to be remembered in a more flexible form. For example, the Gospels record that a paralysed man was brought to Jesus on a mat. The initial description of the mat varies between the Gospels. In Matthew 9:2 and Luke 5:18 the Greek word for mat is κλίνη (*kline*), whilst in Mark 2:4 it is κράβαττος (*krabattos*).[35] Both these forms are suitable words for mat, though Mark's word is a slang expression and is akin to 'pad'.[36]

Another example concerns the time when Jesus walked to the wilderness where he was tempted. Luke's Gospel records that Jesus was led [ἤγετο ēgeto] by the Spirit (Luke 4:1), Matthew notes that Jesus was led up [ἀνήχθη anēchthe] by the Spirit (Matthew 4:1, NASB), and Mark speaks of how the Spirit drove [ἐκβάλλει ekballei] Jesus into the

---

35 WD Mounce, *Interlinear for the Rest of Us: The Reverse Interlinear for New Testament Word Studies*, Zondervan, Grand Rapids, Michigan, US, 2006.

36 These examples are taken from Stein, who explains the variations being due to Matthew and Luke using 'a refinement of [Greek] style'; RH Stein, *The Synoptic Problem: An Introduction*, p. 53.

wild (Mark 1:12, NASB).[37] It is, of course, quite reasonable to expect that background information, which merely provides a setting for Jesus' words, although uniform in its basic content, wasn't regarded as having to be remembered precisely.

Flexibility in Jesus' non-essential words

The second framework is that the disciples committed to memory Jesus' e*ssential words* in a precise word-for-word fashion. However, those words of Jesus that supply the broad brushstrokes of the picture were remembered in a more flexible form. Consider the account of the paralysed man mentioned above. In Matthew 9:2 we read that Jesus told a paralysed man: 'Take heart, son; your sins are forgiven'. However Luke 5:20 records that Jesus said: 'Friend, your sins are forgiven'. This difference may be due to the disciples being taught to remember in a word-for-word fashion the essential element of the conversation ('your sins are forgiven'), whilst being granted freedom to recall the less important aspect ('Take heart, son' versus 'Friend') more loosely. However, even the existence of some words of Jesus being recalled loosely does not necessarily imply that these words were totally fabricated. During his short time with him, Jesus may have conversed more with the paralysed man than what is recorded. If so, it is quite conceivable that at different stages in the conversation Jesus addressed the man both as 'friend' and as 'son'.

The reports about the healing of the paralysed man provide another example of the disciples memorising the essential words of Jesus. Depending on the Gospel, Jesus is recorded as saying:

> *Which is easier: to say, 'Your sins are forgiven,' or to say, 'Get up and walk'? But I want you to know that the Son of Man has authority on earth to forgive sins. So he said to the paralyzed man, 'Get up, take your mat* [kline] *and go home.'(Matthew 9:5–6)*

> *Which is easier: to say to this paralyzed man, 'Your sins are forgiven,' or to say, 'Get up, take your mat and walk'? But I want*

---

37 Again, these examples with their English translation are taken from Stein, who explains the variations being due to Matthew and Luke using 'a refinement of [Greek] style'. RH Stein, *The Synoptic Problem: An Introduction*, 1987, p. 53.

> you to know that the Son of Man has authority on earth to forgive sins. So he said to the man, 'I tell you, get up, take your mat [krabattos] and go home.' (Mark 2:9–11)

> Which is easier: to say, 'Your sins are forgiven,' or to say, 'Get up and walk'? But I want you to know that the Son of Man has authority on earth to forgive sins. So he said to the paralyzed man, 'I tell you, get up, take your mat [klinidion] and go home.' (Luke 5:23–4)

Not only is the essential message in the three different accounts the same, but so too are the essential words. The main areas of variation are with the non-essential words, such as the use of the various Greek words for mat and 'paralytic' verses 'paralysed' man.

Variation inherent in Jesus' teachings

The third framework is that Jesus varied the presentation of his messages. It is easy to appreciate that Jesus, as a teacher, would have repeated many of his lessons to his disciples. Constant repetition and memorisation were the principal techniques used by all educators at that time:[38]

> A teacher would typically check whether his teachings were being remembered by requiring his pupils to repeat them back to him, and might well drill them in what he regarded as the most important axioms, maxims and rules he was endeavouring to inculcate.[39]

Some of this memorisation may have been based on a word-for-word format. This is especially likely with those teachings that were in a poetic form, or some other mnemonic structure, that required the words to remain the same. However, some of his teaching was in forms that allowed a certain degree of flexibility without detracting from conveying the essentials. Parables could easily have been retold by Jesus in such a way that the same basic story may have been

---

38 JDG Dunn, 'Social memory and the oral Jesus tradition', in *Memory in the Bible and Antiquity: The Fifth Durham-Tubingen Research Symposium (Durham, September 2004)*, Mohr Siebech, Tubingen, Germany, 2007, p. 185.
39 JDG Dunn, p. 186.

taught but with various alterations from time to time. This can be seen in the two similar parables Jesus gave that spoke about investing (Matthew 25:14–30, Luke 19:11–27). The general plot is of servants receiving money to invest whilst the master went away. Matthew's account speaks of three servants receiving five, two and one *talent(s)* respectively. A talent denoted a very large sum of money. Luke's Gospel has a vaguely similar parable, with ten servants receiving ten *minas* each. A mina was worth only a sixtieth of a talent. However, when the servants report back to their masters what they did with the money, the reports are from three servants in both cases, with one of these being disreputable. In Matthew's account the lazy servant hid the money in the ground, whilst in Luke's the money was put in some cloth. Both Gospels record the master as saying that the servant was wicked (ponēros) and should have at least deposited the money in a bank so that it could earn interest. Therefore, when the same basic parable is recorded differently from one Gospel to the next, some of this difference may be due to the writers choosing different versions that were taught by Jesus. Regardless of the version, the essential message is identical.

Variations in Aramaic to Greek translations

The fourth framework is that some differences between the Gospels arose due to matters concerning translation. If we recall that Jesus mostly spoke in Aramaic, then it is understandable that different Gospel writers may have chosen slightly different ways of translating the words of Jesus that provide non-essential background information. For example the Gospels recount how Jesus brought back to life the daughter of a ruler. Luke 8:54 tells it this way:

> *But he took her by the hand and said, 'My child, get up!'*

Mark, on the other hand, decided to record some of the actual Aramaic words Jesus said, and it is retold in Mark 5:41 as:

> *He took her by the hand and said to her, 'Talitha koum' (which means, 'Little girl, I say to you, get up!')*

The above also serves as an example of how the different Gospel writers had different styles: Mark tended to preserve Aramaic words whereas the others let them drop.[40]

This variation in preservation of the actual Aramaic words that Jesus spoke also relates to how they preserved the Aramaic poetic and other structures found in Jesus' speech. Close examination of the first three Gospels indicates that Luke deviated from the original antithetical poetic form that the others used about 6 out of 17 times, probably because it made the Greek text seem very unattractive to him.[41] However, his alterations do not change the essence of what was being taught. Hence in Luke 12:4 the text reads:

... do not be afraid of those
Who kill the body
And after that can do no more.

But in Matthew 10:28 we have the more poetic structure carried over:

Do not be afraid of those
Who kill the body
But cannot kill the soul.

Sometimes Jesus may have varied his use of Aramaic terms. For example, the prayer that Jesus taught his disciples has the following words as recorded in Matthew 6:12–13:

And forgive us our debts,
As we also have forgiven our debtors.
And lead us not into temptation,
But deliver us from evil. (NASB)

Whereas in Luke 11:4 the prayer has these words:

And forgive us our sins
For we ourselves also forgive everyone who is indebted to us.
And lead us not into temptation. (NASB)

---

40 RH Stein, *The Synoptic Problem: An Introduction*, pp. 55–8. Stein provides seven such examples.
41 J Jeremias, p. 17, notes 3 & 4.

In the first line of the above quotes, Matthew uses the Greek word for debt (*opheilēma*) instead of the more expected Greek word for sin (*hamartia*). The word 'debt' reflects the original Aramaic language in which Jesus spoke the prayer. It has been found that in other ancient Aramaic literature the Aramaic word for debt is used as a substitute for sin when translating Old Testament texts.[42] However, it is also reasonable to speculate that Jesus fluctuated in his use of the words for sin. Certainly Jesus would have repeated this prayer many times as he prayed with his disciples and others over the years. Sometimes he may have varied the content of the prayer with the addition, or subtraction, of a few words. Sometimes he may have prayed using Aramaic language and other times in Greek. Jesus was most likely fluent in at least these two languages.[43]

Freedom to select, but not freedom to fabricate

The fifth framework accounts for variations caused by the selection choices of the Gospel writers. Reading the Gospels also makes it clear that what each writer chose to record varied. This factor would also create small variations between the Gospels in the retelling of the same event. Consider the following three examples.

In the retelling of the encounter Jesus had with the man who was paralysed and presented to him on a mat, Mark and Luke record how the man had to be lowered down through the roof in order to get past the crowd, whereas Matthew skips over this and simply records that the man was brought to Jesus on his mat.[44]

A similar example can be found when reading how Jesus delivered a man from a mob of demons, and then sent the demons into a herd of pigs. Two of the Gospel writers (Mark 5:1–20 and Luke 8:26–39) refer to Jesus dealing with one possessed man, whilst one other Gospel writer (Matthew 8:28–34) speaks of two such men. This

---

42 RH Stein, *The Synoptic Problem: An Introduction*, p. 98. It has also been stated that: 'The Aramaic ôbâ means both *debts* [failure to fulfil obligations] and *sins* [committing evil actions]' (KE Bailey, *Jesus Through Middle Eastern Eyes*, IVP Academic, Downers Grove, Illinois, US, 2008, p. 252).
43 RH Stein, *The Synoptic Problem: An Introduction*, p. 208
44 Matthew 1:1–2; Mark 2:1–4; Luke 5:18–19.

minor difference isn't contradictory, as Mark and Luke do not say that there was only one man. However, it is easy to envisage that Mark and Luke may have had reasons for not bothering to mention the other man. One of the men may well have been much more part of the action than the other, and may have done all of the speaking. Perhaps they considered that the essential elements of the story could be more easily conveyed using just one man and perhaps they wanted their readers to concentrate on other aspects of the account. It is likely that at the end of the encounter Jesus dealt with the two previously afflicted men in different ways, only one of which was important enough for Mark and Luke to include in their story. Matthew doesn't describe what happened to either of the men after the demons were expelled.

The disciples didn't just bring their intellects to Jesus; they also brought their personalities and individual life histories. Jesus didn't proceed to turn them into identities that merely regurgitated the deeds and teachings of their master. Consequently, what greatly resonated within one disciple would have been less engrossing for another. When they relayed to their listeners and readers what Jesus instructed them to teach, they would also have imparted variously those other aspects that had impacted them the most.[45] Perhaps this is one of the reasons why Matthew largely focused on Jesus being the Son of David, Mark on Jesus as the suffering servant, Luke on Jesus as the compassionate teacher, and John on Jesus as God in human flesh.[46] Each of these facets of Jesus is apparent in each of the Gospels, but they are not equally highlighted from one Gospel to the next.

Why four Gospels instead of one?

The various influences that the Gospel writers have had on the grand story of Jesus does raise the question as to why we have four Gospels stemming from the original single group of 12 disciples. Surely it would have been preferable if they could have agreed with one another enough so as to produce just one Gospel! The reality is that the Gospel writers wrote with different readers in mind, and this was one of the

---

45 JDG Dunn, pp. 188–91.
46 C Blomberg, p. 74.

factors that created a need for different accounts. For example, Matthew appears to have written his Gospel primarily for those knowledgeable in the teachings of the Old Testament, while Mark directed his Gospel writing to those who were quite unfamiliar with Jewish customs.

The Gospel writers also had a variety of sources of information about Jesus. How heavily they used one source or another also would have affected the finished written account. Matthew and John, having been disciples of Jesus from the beginning, would have been able to draw on their own memories and lessons learnt while students of Jesus. They also could have accessed any written notes made by themselves and their colleagues. Mark wrote his Gospel having learnt it from the disciple Peter, who in turn may have used the notes made by one or more other disciples.[47] Luke explicitly states that he used the accounts of others who were directly associated with Jesus and the first disciples (Luke 1:1–2). Luke may well have been handed written notes from many of the first 12 disciples when he spent about two years staying with them in Jerusalem.[48] In essence, each Gospel writer added their portrait to the collective art gallery in order to help viewers have a more three-dimensional understanding of the colossal figure of Jesus, the God-man.

One way to view the divergences arising from having four different Gospel accounts is to consider the following analogy:

If four photographers were asked by a travel magazine to submit their best three unedited photographs of the eastern face of a particular mountain, it would be unlikely that all four would supply identical pictures. One photographer may have considered that autumn was the best season to capture the true essence of the mountain, and consequently supplied photographs from that season. The other photographers may have preferred other seasons. Some of the photographers may have focused their lenses on a waterfall cascading down a tree-lined slope, while others focused theirs above the snow line. Whatever their preferences,

---

[47] Peter was 'present for certain events (usually with James and John) when the rest were not ... [making] it credible that Matthew would want to consult Mark for at least some information' (C Blomberg, p. 45).

[48] Luke appears to have stayed in Jerusalem for the entire period between the years 57 AD and 59 AD (R Riesner, *Paul's Early Period: Chronology, Mission Strategy, Theology*, William B Eerdmans Publishing Company, Grand Rapids, Michigan, US, 1998, pp. 322–5.

each photographer still provided unedited and accurate images of the eastern face. In this scenario it would be very unreasonable for the travel magazine's editor to say that in exercising personal judgements the photographers deliberately attempted to present a false picture of the mountain's terrain. As Dr Perrin, a professor of the New Testament noted:

> ... *even the most realistic representation requires selectivity and personal judgement ... And yet there is remarkable continuity in how the ... [four Gospel writers] present Jesus. Any discussion of the differences between the Gospels, in order to be fair-minded, must be set against the basic recognition that Matthew, Mark, Luke, and John are far more similar in what they purport than they are different.*[49]

Dr Perrin goes on to note how the early Christian writer Irenaeus (130–202 AD) extolled the virtues of having four accounts of Jesus' life and teachings:

> *Irenaeus is more or less saying that no one gospel has the bottom line on the person of Jesus Christ. Each evangelist writes a truthful account so far as a factual account of Jesus' life goes. And each evangelist offers a self-contained account that stands on its own two feet, and each gospel can be used, if properly read, to refute various heresies. But no one gospel gives an exhaustive account of Jesus Christ ... Together the four gospels create the framework for the truth and mark off its boundaries ...*[50]

Conclusion

Bearing in mind the nuances of language translation and other factors, it seems very reasonable to conclude that we do have a direct link to Jesus' teachings. When we read the words of Jesus in the New Testament today, we are also hearing him speak the thoughts and words he spoke all those years ago. One professor expressed his confidence in the New Testament eloquently:

---

49 N Perrin, p. 105.
50 N Perrin, pp. 121–2.

> there is every reason to believe that many of the sayings and actions of Jesus would have been very carefully safeguarded in the first decades of the church's history, not so slavishly as to hamper freedom to paraphrase, explain, abbreviate and rearrange, but faithfully enough to produce reliable accounts of those facets of Christ's ministry selected for preservation.[51]

Knowing that there were more than adequate reasons for believing that the disciples recorded accurately what Jesus said, my next question was: How is it possible to be confident that this material has been copied accurately over many hundreds of years?

Appendix
Did Jesus discourage memorisation amongst his disciples?

It is pertinent to point out that the New Testament doesn't specifically record Jesus saying 'Memorise this'. But this isn't surprising as it is normal for authors not to state that which they expect their readers to know or be able to infer. It was so common for a teacher in Jesus' culture to expect some degree of memorisation that the New Testament writers would have considered that it 'did not need mentioning'.[52] As shown in the previous chapter, Jesus was widely regarded as a teacher.

There is one verse in the New Testament that some may understand as implying that Jesus downplayed the need for the disciples to memorise his teachings:

> All this I have spoken while still with you. But the Advocate, the Holy Spirit, whom the Father will send in my name, will teach you all things and will remind you of everything I have said to you. Peace I leave with you; my peace I give you. I do not give as the world gives. Do not let your hearts be troubled and do not be afraid. (John 14:25–7)

---

51 C Blomberg, pp. 30-1
52 R Bauckham, *Jesus and the Eyewitnesses: The Gospels as Eyewitness Testimony*, William B Eerdmans Publishing Company, Grand Rapids, Michigan, US, 2006, p. 284.

It seems to some that by telling the disciples that the Holy Spirit will remind them of everything Jesus had said that Jesus was implying that they didn't need to put effort into remembering it in the first instance. However, this is only an inference, or an extrapolation. It is reasonable to understand that Jesus was reassuring the disciples that they would not need to solely rely on their previous efforts to retain Jesus' teachings.

The immediate context of Jesus' statement is one of reassurance, rather than of encouragement to complacency in enshrining his words. The passage above ends with Jesus offering peace and instructing the disciples to take heart. A few sentences before the passage, Jesus told the disciples that he is:

going to the Father ... And I will ask the Father, and he will give you another advocate to help you and be with you forever – the Spirit of truth ... I will not leave you as orphans. (John 14:12,16–18)

Other considerations also indicate that Jesus did not intend the words of John 14:26 to be an excuse for not retaining his words:

- In the same breath that Jesus told the disciples that the Holy Spirit will remind them of words, he also declares that the Holy Spirit will teach them 'all things'. If it is correct to infer that Jesus was encouraging the disciples to be lackadaisical about remembering, then it would also be correct that Jesus was not diligent about being a teacher. The idea of Jesus being a half-hearted teacher goes against the tenor of the Gospels: Jesus was very renown for being a teacher, as shown in my previous chapter.
- The next time John records Jesus' teaching about the Holy Spirit, the context is reassurance that during persecution and execution they will be able to stay loyal to Jesus:

When the Advocate comes, whom I will send to you from the Father – the Spirit of truth who goes out from the Father – he will testify about me. And you also must testify, for you have been with me from the beginning. All this I have told you so that you will not fall away. They will put you out of the synagogue; in fact, the time is coming when anyone who kills you will think they are offering a service to God (John 15:26 to 16:2).

- When other Gospel writers record Jesus' teaching about the Holy Spirit, it is also in a context of reassurance during persecution:

    On account of me you will stand before governors and kings as witnesses to them. And the gospel must be preached to all nations. Whenever you are arrested and brought to trial, do not worry beforehand about what to say. Just say whatever is given to you at the time, for it is not you speaking, but the Holy Spirit. Brother will betray brother to death ... Everyone will hate you because of me, but the one who stands firm to the end will be saved. (Mark 13:9–13)

    On my account you will be brought before governors and kings, as witnesses to them and to the gentiles. But when they arrest you, do not worry about what to say or how to say it. At that time you will be given what to say, for it will not be you speaking but the Spirit of your Father speaking through you. Brother will betray brother to death ... You will be hated by everyone because of me, but the one who stands firm to the end will be saved. (Matthew 10:18–22)

In these passages it can be seen that the Holy Spirit will provide the disciples with the correct words when they are being brought to trial. There is no indication that Jesus expected the Holy Spirit to do the work of providing words every day and on every occasion.

Part III

Accuracy in copying of the New Testament

Part III responds to the claim that because the New Testament was copied many times over the centuries, with copies being made of copies, it is impossible to be certain of the original content of the New Testament books.

Chapter 7 reveals that complete manuscripts, and large partial copies, of the New Testament exist dating back to within a few hundred years of the originals. Modern-day New Testament scholars make use of these early copies — as well as later copies — when attempting to capture the wording of the original copies of the New Testament books.

Based on an investigation into several ancient Greek manuscripts, chapter 8 illustrates that Christian scribes were able to make very accurate copies of the New Testament.

From an examination of a broad range of dozens of ancient Greek manuscripts, chapter 9 discovers the reasons why some ancient scribes deliberately introduced variations into the wording of the New Testament.

Although the vast bulk of variations introduced by ancient scribes had no real impact on the content of the New Testament, there are three sections of the New Testament where a large number of words are included in some manuscripts but not others. These three prominent variations are investigated in chapter 10.

Chapter 11 directly compares the English translations of two very different Greek New Testament text types in order to gauge the extent of the divergences. It also compares these manuscripts with a modern English New Testament.

7

Ancient copies of the New Testament: from Egypt to the Vatican

Some people are alarmed when they hear that the original handwritten books and letters composed by the New Testament writers ceased to exist many hundreds of years ago. When I further explain that the originals were copied, and then these copies were in turn copied over and over again, they become concerned. They quickly surmise that if the printing press wasn't invented until c. 1450, then surely this process of copying resulted in many changes, intentional or otherwise.

From the above line of thinking, many questions arise: Just how extensive were the changes in the copying process? Have these alterations significantly affected the teachings of Jesus? Is it reasonable to assume that Jesus' words are basically the same as what was written in the original accounts? Or has the message of these originals (which are called autographs) become greatly distorted and corrupted? Certainly these are all very reasonable thoughts and ones that spurred me on to do extensive research.

It's possible to investigate these questions using several different avenues. The first way I approached the topic was to learn about the oldest New Testament copies in Greek. Greek is the original language of the New Testament.[1] This approach was based on the idea that the

---

1   K Aland & B Aland, *The Text of the New Testament: An Introduction to the Critical Editions and to the Theory and Practice of Modern Textual Criticism*, trans. EF Rhodes, William B Eerdmans Publishing Company, Grand Rapids, US, 1989, p. 52.

older the copy then the closer in wording it would be to the original manuscripts. I later discovered that this isn't necessarily true all the time, but as a general rule it has some merit. So this chapter aims to provide an overview of what ancient copies have been found so far.

The second approach to the question was then to explore the differences that exist between the various copies. This is the basis of the subsequent chapters.

I have divided this chapter into two broad sections: the first looking at the oldest copies that cover nearly the entire New Testament, and the second looking at those that contain only partial amounts of the New Testament.

Ancient extensive copies: Codices Sinaiticus, Vaticanus, Alexandrinus and Bezae

When going back in time to discover very old manuscripts, the first startling discovery is that complete, and virtually complete, copies have been found that are about 1700 years old. Many people are quite surprised to learn that these copies, made so close to when the books of the New Testament were first penned, still exist. The Gospels were completed sometime before 66 AD, with many believing that the latest date for their completion was by the late 50s AD.[2] The majority of the remaining New Testament books were written between 48 AD and 66 AD. Although two very small New Testament books[3] are of uncertain date, the evidence points strongly to the entire New Testament being written before the 90s AD.[4] Given that our earliest sizeable copies of the New Testament date from 200 AD, then it is amazing that they haven't perished, or simply become lost, over this time period. After all, these days most people have difficulty finding hard copies of their own documents only a few years later! Even a

---

[2] J McDowell & B Wilson, *Evidence for the Historical Jesus: A Compelling Case for his Life and his Claims*, Harvest House Publishers, Eugene, Oregon, US, 1993, pp. 148–9.
[3] 2 John and Jude.
[4] P Barnett, *Is the New Testament History?*, rev. edn, Aquila Press, Sydney South, 2004, pp. 30–9.

time capsule buried in a small town of less than 7000 people as late as 1985 was lost by 2010.[5]

Each one of the extensive copies of the New Testament is called a codex, meaning that they are in the form of a modern book with pages that can be turned. The following are some interesting details concerning their discovery, publication and contents. Details about their contents are included, as this is needed to appreciate correctly the variations between the various copies. I have focused on Codex Sinaiticus as it has a fascinating history.

Codex Sinaiticus

The oldest complete copy of the New Testament that survives to this day is one called the Codex Sinaiticus, which was written in about 350 AD. How this codex was discovered makes very interesting reading. It all started in 1839 when a young 24-year-old man set out to 'reconstruct, if possible, the exact text [of the New Testament], as it came from the pen of the sacred writers ...' At first he attempted to do this by making a 'fresh examination of the original documents [used to make the various copies of the Greek New Testament known at that time].[6]

On a shoestring budget, without 'sufficient means to pay even for my travelling suit', Constantine von Tischendorf went to the libraries of Paris to examine the various known Greek manuscripts.[7] After a while he took his research to a whole new level, because he realised that:

> *The literary treasures which I have sought to explore have been drawn in most cases from the convents of the East, where, for ages, the pens of industrious monks have copied the sacred writings, and collected manuscripts of all kinds. It therefore occurred to me whether it was not probable that in some recess*

---

5 ML Vincent, 'Kimberly misplaces its place in history', *The Post-Crescent*, 20 December 2010, p. A.1.
6 C Tischendorf, *Codex Sinaiticus: The Ancient Biblical Manuscript Now in the British Museum: Tischendorf's Story and Argument Related by Himself*, English trans., The Lutterworth Press, London, 1934, pp. 16–17.
7 C Tischendorf, p. 17.

> *of Greek or Coptic, Syrian or Armenian monasteries, there might be some precious manuscripts slumbering for ages in dust and darkness ...*[8]
>
> *It was in April, 1844, that I embarked ... for Egypt. The desire which I felt to discover some precious remains of any manuscripts, more especially Biblical, of a date which would carry us back to the early times of Christianity, was realised beyond my expectations. It was at the foot of Mt Sinai, in the Convent of St Catherine, that I discovered the pearl of all my researches. In visiting the library of the monastery, in the month of May, 1844, I perceived in the middle of the great hall a large and wide basket full of old parchments; and the librarian, who was a man of information, told me that two heaps of papers like these, mouldered by time, had been already committed to the flames.*[9]

Unfortunately the monks, having noticed Tischendorf's great excitement, only allowed him to take a third of the 129 pages that he rescued. These pages were originally a part of a very ancient copy of the Old Testament written in Greek.[10] Tischendorf returned home to Germany, but kept the location of his discovery a secret so that no other treasure seekers would go to the monastery.[11] It was not until January 1859, and this time with the support of the Russian government,[12] that Tischendorf obtained many more pages of the Old Testament portion, and something even more amazing. For it was during his last night at the monastery that the steward of the monastery pulled down from a shelf above his room's doorway:

> *a bulky kind of volume, wrapped up in a red cloth ... I unrolled the cover, and discovered, to my great surprise, not only those very fragments which, fifteen years before, I had taken out of the basket,*

---

8   C Tischendorf, pp. 21–2.
9   C Tischendorf, p. 23.
10 C Tischendorf, pp. 23–4.
11 C Tischendorf, p. 26.
12 C Tischendorf, p. 26: 'People were astonished that a foreigner and a Protestant should presume to ask the support of the Emperor of the Greek and Orthodox Church for a mission to the East'.

but also other parts of the Old Testament, and the New Testament complete ...[13]

Eventually Tischendorf was able to bring this invaluable treasure to Russia, and there present it to the Russian emperor, who had funded his expedition since 1858.[14] In 1862 Tischendorf published a lavish reproduction (technically called a facsimile) of the codex, and several popular plain editions followed soon after. The codex was therefore now readily available to the public. Surprisingly as late as 1975 further portions of the Old Testament from the codex were discovered.[15]

Who wrote it and how?

One last point that needs to be made is that the codex was written by at least three different scribes:

These three hands are extraordinarily alike, and the scribes must have received their training in some large writing establishment with a definite tradition of its own.[16]

I say at least three, as some scholars believe that there were four, designating them as A, B1, B2 and D.[17] Scribe A wrote the vast bulk of

---

13 C Tischendorf, p. 27. Some have questioned Tischendorf's account, so I have added the following excerpt from HJM Milne & TC Skeat, *The Codex Sinaiticus and Codex Alexandrinus: With Seven Illustrations*, The Trustees of the British Museum, London, 1955, p. 6, n. 2: 'The shelf was also used for the storage of spare coffee-cups kept for the entertainment of visitors to the monastery; this picturesque detail was related to a Russian scholar, V. N. Beneshivitch, in 1908 by the Steward Polycarp, who added that the manuscript itself had come to light among some "rubbish" which his predecessor in office had been clearing out and burning in the bread ovens!'
14 C Tischendorf, pp. 25–31.
15 K Aland & B Aland, p. 107, and Chart 6: The textual contents of New Testament uncial manuscripts, pp. D to K.
16 HJM Milne & TC Skeat, *The Codex Sinaiticus and Codex Alexandrinus: With Seven Illustrations*, The Trustees of the British Museum, London, 1955, p. 15.
17 DC Parker, *Codex Sinaiticus: The Story of the World's Oldest Bible*, The British Library, London, 2010, pp. 48–51.

Echoes of Jesus

the New Testament, with scribe D responsible for the remainder. As far as the Gospels are concerned, scribe D copied Matthew 16:9 to 18:12 and 24:36 to 26:6, and Mark 14:54 to Luke 1:56.[18]

One of the ways the scribes can be distinguished from one another is their ability to spell. One scribe was nearly faultless, whilst another who wrote most of the New Testament was a poor speller. However, a third scribe was so bad that 'it is indeed a puzzle to understand how he can ever have been chosen to work on a manuscript of this class'.[19] Nearly all of the spelling mistakes were phonetic. (An example of a phonetic misspelling in English would be to write 'enuff' instead of 'enough'.) The fact that such spelling mistakes were made indicates that the codex was probably made by dictating to the scribes. These phonetic misspellings account for many of the variations we find between various copies of the New Testament, but I will write more about these variations in the next chapter.

The scribes didn't just write the words as they were being dictated, they also made minor corrections, ones that could be done without pausing as they went along.[20] Later, when a section being read had been completed, the scribe then had opportunity to make further corrections as it was read a second time. In this way it sometimes became apparent to the first scribe that the reader had skipped lines or sentences during the first reading. These corrections were often made in the margins. Sometimes one of the other two scribes corrected the work of the first scribe. There even appears to be variations included in the manuscript because these variations may have existed in the copy that was being read in the first instance. Over the centuries after it was completed, more corrections were made in different hands yet again. The various handwriting styles used means that any one particular correction can be named according to who wrote it. The result of these and other factors is a book whose 'pages swarm with corrections in various scripts ...'[21]

---

18 DC Parker, p. 49.
19 HJM Milne & TC Skeat, p. 15.
20 HJM Milne & TC Skeat, pp. 16–18.
21 HJM Milne & TC Skeat, p. 110.

State of preservation

I originally thought that any document that had managed to survive for more than 1600 years would be so degraded that individual letters and words would be faint and difficult to discern. It is easy to imagine that the form of writing material used, namely treated animal skins, would have deteriorated enormously. The treated goat and sheep skins used to make Codex Sinaiticus, variously called vellum or parchment, was quite thin. So it's surprising to discover that Codex Sinaiticus, like several of these old New Testament copies, was quite readable. The following two paragraphs describe the condition of the Codex Sinaiticus:

> *After more than 1600 years, it is clear that the quality of the writing medium originally used by the scribes was truly exceptional, as is the quality of the parchment. The ingredients appear to be well balanced creating a smooth and thin fluid perfect for writing on parchment. The recipe and the manufacturing technique seem to be exquisite too, revealing high craftsmanship and skilled experience for producing good quality inks ...*[22]

> *Apart from a small percentage of folios [i.e. pages] with heavy ink corrosion, most of the folios appeared to have survived the rigours of 16 centuries with an unexpected lack of damage, suffering in the main only from small tears and losses along the head, tail, fore-edge and spine folds. Much of this damage is more likely attributable to mechanical damage than physical deterioration.*[23]

Codex Vaticanus

Another very old, extensive copy of the New Testament is the Codex Vaticanus. It was written sometime in the 300s AD, and perhaps

---

22 S Mazzarino, 'Report on the different inks used in Codex Sinaiticus and assessment of their condition', *Codex Sinaiticus*,http://codexsinaiticus.org/en/project/conservation_ink.aspx, accessed 22/08/2010.

23 G Moorhead, 'Parchment assessment of the Codex Sinaiticus', *Codex Sinaiticus*, May 2009, http://codexsinaiticus.org/en/project/conservation_parchment.aspx, accessed 22/08/2010.

is slightly older than Codex Sinaiticus.[24] The origins of it are still enshrined in mystery, as is the location of where it was housed for over a thousand years. The Roman Catholic Church has held it in the Vatican since at least 1475. It became available to the wider academic community only in 1857,[25] as prior to that the Roman Catholic Church would not let others study it.[26] Unfortunately it is completely missing a few of the smaller New Testament books, namely 1 and 2 Timothy, Titus, Philemon and Revelation. A portion of Hebrews is also absent.[27] Because this codex contains nearly all of the Old Testament in Greek,[28] it is also important for those studying the Old Testament.

Codex Alexandrinus

This codex was written sometime in the 400s AD.[29] In about the 1300s this Greek manuscript made its way from Alexandria in Egypt to Constantinople (modern-day Istanbul).[30] It was gifted to the English King Charles I in 1627, and was placed in the Royal Library. A terrible fire engulfed the library in 1731, with many rare books being destroyed. Fortunately the codex was saved by the heroic actions of 'the Librarian, the famous Dr Bentley, [who] was observed in his nightgown and great wig carrying a volume of the codex under his arm to safety'.[31] The New Testament portion

---

24 FG Kenyon, *Our Bible and the Ancient Manuscripts*, rev. AW Adams, Eyre & Spottiswoode, London, 1958, p. 204.
25 K Aland & B Aland, p. 107.
26 NL Geisler & WE Nix, *A General Introduction to the Bible: Revised and Expanded*, Moody Press, Chicago, US, 1986, p. 391; and GL Robinson, *Where Did We Get Out Bible?*, Doubleday, Doran, New York, 1928, p. 111.
27 K Aland & B Aland, p. 109 and Chart 6: The textual contents of New Testament uncial manuscripts, pp. D to K.
28 K Aland & B Aland, p. 109. The major parts missing from the Old Testament, due to the original pages being lost, are Genesis 1:1 to 46:28 and Psalms 105:27 to 137:6.
29 K Aland & B Aland, p. 107.
30 HJM Milne & TC Skeat, p. 33.
31 HJM Milne & TC Skeat, p. 31.

of it was published in 1786 by the assistant librarian of the British Museum, CG Woide.[32]

It is possible that only two scribes wrote this codex.[33] The ink is faded unevenly in different parts, and the vellum itself now has a 'limp, dead appearance in marked contrast to the vellum of the Codex Sinaiticus'.[34] All of the 27 books contained in the New Testament are present in this codex. However, only three of the 28 chapters of Matthew's Gospel are present, as the codex is now missing Matthew 1:1 to 25:6. The only other portions that have been lost are John 6:50 to 8:52 and 2 Corinthians 4:13 to 12:6.[35]

Codex Bezae Cantabrigiensis

This is the oldest New Testament manuscript written in two languages, namely Greek and Latin. The Greek is written on the left-hand page and the Latin on the right. It was written sometime around 400 AD, being found in 1562 by Theodore de Beze, who then passed it on to the University of Cambridge in 1581. The university produced a photographic copy of it in 1899.[36] De Beze discovered it in a monastery in France, and it may well have been written there or in Italy. It is a quite peculiar bilingual publication, as the Latin was translated from a different Greek manuscript to the Greek on the facing page.[37]

I have listed it in this section dealing with extensive copies of the New Testament, even though the Greek portion of the manuscript now contains only the Gospels and Acts. Although the vellum is of a very high quality, the Greek portion is now missing:

---

32 HJM Milne & TC Skeat, p. 40.
33 HJM Milne & TC Skeat, pp. 38–40.
34 HJM Milne & TC Skeat, p. 37.
35 K Aland & B Aland, p. 109 and Chart 6: The textual contents of New Testament uncial manuscripts, pp. D to K.
36 JF Fenlon, 'Codex Bezae', *The Catholic Encyclopedia*, vol. 4, Robert Appleton Company, New York, www.newadvent.org/cathen/04083a.htm, accessed 4/02/2011.
37 J Rius-Camps & J Read-Heimerdinger, *The Message of Acts in Codex Bezae: A Comparison with the Alexandrian Tradition, vol. 1: Acts 1.1–5.42*, Jerusalem, T & T Clark International, New York, US, 2004, p. 6.

- parts of Matthew chapters 1, 6 and 9, and all of chapters 7 and 8
- the last portion of Mark 16
- parts of John chapters 1 and 3, and all of John chapter 2
- parts of Acts chapters 8, 10, 21 and 22, and all of Acts chapters 9, 23 to 28.[38]

This codex is the 'most controversial' of all the New Testament extensive copies because its wording of many passages in the New Testament is often quite different to many of the other famous copies. To help comprehend how various manuscripts relate to each other, it is useful to know a little about text types. When the wording of several manuscripts have a large number of similarities, these copies are said to share the same text type. Codex Vaticanus and Codex Sinaiticus are said to have text types called Alexandrian,[39] whilst the Gospel portion of Codex Alexandrinus is called Byzantine.[40] Codex Bezae is sometimes called the main representative of a text type called Western.[41] However, this Western type is not really a type as this group of texts is largely characterised by the fact they 'do not share a common text. Their chief characteristic is that they differ to the AT [Alexandrian text]'.[42] More will be said about Codex Bezae, and the relevance of text types, in the next few chapters.

Ancient partial copies

Whilst the ages of the above extensive copies are staggering enough, similarly old and even older partial copies of the New Testament have

---

38 NL Geisler & WE Nix, pp. 395–6. For all of the above facts, except where indicated.
39 KD Clarke, *Textual Optimism: A Critique of the United Bible Societies' Greek New Testament,* Sheffield Academic Press, Sheffield, UK, 1997, p. 40. The modern Alexandrian grouping includes the old category called Neutral. The term 'Neutral' was coined as it referred to the belief that this text type represents a series of copies that were 'almost uncorrupted from the autographs ...' (HJM Milne & TC Skeat, p. 23).
40 KD Clarke, pp. 40–1.
41 K Aland & B Aland, p. 103.
42 J Rius-Camps & J Read-Heimerdinger, p. 5.

been unearthed. These were all discovered after the four extensive copies of the New Testament mentioned above. Generally the oldest ones have been written on papyrus, an ancient form of paper made from reeds growing on the edges of the River Nile.

So far 61 of these partial copies written on papyrus and dating from before 400 AD have been found.[43] A further five copies from the same period have been found written on parchment or vellum,[44] making a total of 66 ancient partial copies. One of these copies on vellum, called 0189, dates from the late 100s to early 200s AD.[45]

Chester Beatty Papyri

Some of the most important partial copies are part of the collection now called the Chester Beatty Biblical Papyri. The 12 codices were probably found in northern Egypt in the ruins of a town called Aphroditopolous (modern-day Atfih).[46] Most likely they belonged to the library of a Christian community or a Christian individual. They are now on display in Dublin Castle, Ireland. These were such an exciting find that *The Times* of London featured an announcement of them by Sir Frederic Kenyon in November 1931.[47]

---

43 PW Comfort, *Early Manuscripts and Modern Translations of the New Testament*, Tyndale House Publishers, Wheaton, US, 1990 pp. vii–viii. One hundred New Testament papyrus documents have been found since 1868 and 1990, some written as late as the 600s AD (pp. 16–17). More are expected to be published (p. 18).
44 PW Comfort, pp. viii, 71–3. Their names and contents are: 0162, part of John 2; 0171, parts of Matthew 10 and Luke 22; 0189, part of Acts 5; 0212, parts of one chapter from each of the gospels; 0220, part of Romans 4.
45 PW Comfort, p. 72.
46 CH Roberts, Manuscript, *Society, and Belief in Early Christian Egypt*, Oxford University Press, London, 1979. Chapter 7 stated that: 'Carl Schmidt was told in 1934 that the Chester Beatty Papyri had been found in a pitcher in the ruins of a church or monastery near Atfih (Aphroditopolis)'. Others have suggested that they were composed in a town about 200 km further south. See EG Turner, *Greek Papyri: An Introduction*, Princeton University Press, Princeton, US, 1968, pp. 52–3.
47 G Stanton, 'Early Christian preference for the Codex', in C Horton (ed.), *The Earliest Gospels: The Origin and Transmission of the Earliest Christian Gospels*, T & T Clark International, London, 2004, p. 40.

Of these 12 manuscripts, the three important New Testament ones are known as P45, P46 and P47. They are not imaginatively named; the P indicates that they were all written on papyrus. Normally they are formatted using superscripts (e.g. P^{45}), but this can create some confusion with footnoted references. To avoid the misleading similarity, the superscript convention has been dropped except where it is used in quotations and titles of publications.

P45 consists of the four Gospels and the book of Acts, albeit with many large gaps due to holes.[48] It was written sometime between 200 and 250 AD.[49]

P46 doesn't contain any of the same books as P45, but has nine other New Testament books.[50] It may date from the late 100s [51] or early 200s AD.[52]

P47 has portions of the last book of the New Testament, called Revelation, and was composed between 250 and 300 AD.[53]

Before these three partial copies were discovered, the earliest Greek New Testament manuscripts known to exist were dated to the 300s and 400s AD.[54] This is why there was such incredible excitement about the discovery of these Chester Beatty copies.

---

48 For a detailed listing of which portions of the New Testament have been preserved in these and other ancient copies of the New Testament, see the excellent book by PW Comfort, *Early Manuscripts and Modern Translations of the New Testament,* Tyndale House Publishers, Wheaton, US, 1990.
49 LW Hurtado, 'P^{45} and the textual history of the gospel of Mark', in C Horton (ed.), *The Earliest Gospels: The Origin and Transmission of the Earliest Christian Gospels,* T & T Clark International, London, 2004, p. 133.
50 These nine books are Romans, 1 and 2 Corinthians, Galatians, Ephesians, Philippians, Colossians, 1 Thessalonians and Hebrews.
51 BW Griffin, *The Paleographic dating of P-46,* paper delivered to the Society of Biblical Literature: New Testament Textual Criticism Section, New Orleans, November, 1996.
52 K Aland & B Aland, p. 99.
53 PW Comfort, p. 52.
54 LW Hurtado, 'P^{45} and the textual history of the gospel of Mark', p. 133. The previously earliest ones were codices Sinaiticus, Vaticanus and Washingtonianus.

Three different scribes composed these documents, and the three of them differed in their degree of skill. It has been suggested that the writers were 'experienced writers of documents. They aim for a high degree of "regularity and clarity" ... [but] they have not been trained to copy literary texts ... "[I]n none can be traced the work of the professional calligrapher or the rapid, informal hand of the private scholar"'.[55]

The purpose of the copies was 'for reading in worship services, and possibly also for private devotions'.[56] They were not being made simply to adorn bookshelves and to collect dust. When looking at them further, it has been said that we should do so by:

> *assuming that the copyists of the early papyri were both willing and able to make accurate copies, as much as is generally expected of anyone transcribing documents. Just as scribes do not make changes arbitrarily, the same principles applies to their copying of books, and especially of sacred books. And further, they might even be expected to be even more painstaking because of the special honour of their task. And yet errors creep in, errors completely consonant with their scribal function.*[57]

State of preservation

The ink of the Chester Beatty Biblical Papyri has lasted surprisingly well, as one scholar stated: 'The ink is dark brown and has faded little. There has been little rubbing of the surface, so that almost every letter is still legible'.[58] Unfortunately the pages themselves sometimes have defects such as holes (called lacunae) in them. In other places, the

---

55 B Aland, 'The significance of the Chester Beatty Papyri in early church history', in C Horton (ed.), *The Earliest Gospels: The Origin and Transmission of the Earliest Christian Gospels,* T & T Clark International, London, 2004, p. 109, citing CH Roberts, *Manuscripts, Society and Belief in Early Christian Egypt,* Oxford University Press, London, 1979, pp. 14–15.
56 B Aland, p. 109.
57 B Aland, p. 109.
58 Advanced Papyrological Information System, 'P.Mich.inv. 6238; Recto', University of Michigan, US, http://quod.lib.umich.edu/a/apis/x-3561/6238_42.tif, accessed 22/08/2010.

pages have been deliberately torn in two by the local Egyptian dealers who were selling them onto the highest bidders, their reasoning being that the more pieces, the greater the profit. The prices became incredibly high, with the millionaire Beatty eventually paying as much as £100 per page.[59]

Bodmer Papyri

Another famous group of ancient partial copies of the New Testament are called the Bodmer Papyri, which can now be viewed in Geneva. These came from Egypt and were originally composed between 175 and 300 AD.[60] The most important ones are called P66, P72 and P75.

P66 contains nearly all of the first 15 chapters of the Gospel of John, and small portions of a few other chapters. It was composed sometime around 175 to 200 AD.[61]

P72 has survived so well that it preserves all of the books of 1 and 2 Peter and Jude. It was written in the late 200s or early 300s AD.[62]

P75 has very large portions of the Gospel of Luke from the third chapter onwards, as well as most of the first 15 chapters of John. P75 consists of 'twenty-seven almost perfectly preserved sheets ... together with a part of their binding'.[63] It was completed around 200 AD.[64]

The oldest portion of the New Testament discovered so far is called P52, which was most likely composed somewhere between 100 and 125 AD. Being quite small, only about six verses from the Gospel of John are written on it.

---

59 C Horton, 'The Chester Beatty Biblical Papyri: A find of the greatest importance', in C Horton (ed.), *The Earliest Gospels: The Origin and Transmission of the Earliest Christian Gospels,* T & T Clark International, London, 2004, pp. 155–6.
60 PW Comfort, pp. 60–4.
61 PW Comfort, pp. 60–4.
62 PW Comfort, pp. 60–4.
63 K Aland & B Aland, p. 87
64 PW Comfort, p. 73.

Conclusion: Reconstructing the autographs

The descriptions of these extensive and partial copies of the Greek New Testament make it clear that it is possible to go a long way back in time. Back far enough, in fact, to see the words of the New Testament 1800 years ago. So far back that some of these copies are edging towards the time when the autographs were originally written, and perhaps were still in circulation. Having determined this, I now wanted to know just how much these various copies differed from each other. If they all differed from each other in ways that greatly affected the accounts of Jesus' life and teachings, then this would make it difficult for anyone to be certain of them. These aspects are discussed in the next few chapters.

8
Making copies without photocopiers

Some of the very important, ancient handwritten copies (manuscripts) of the Greek New Testament were discussed in the previous chapter. But these are just a small fraction of the total — over 5000 — that have been discovered. Because the New Testament is such a large document, even the best-trained copying professional (scribe) will make the occasional mistake. Therefore, each of these thousands of copies differ from each other somewhere in the text. If only they had photocopiers back then.

Some scholars have calculated that there are over 400,000 variations between all the New Testament manuscripts.[1] This is enough to make anyone think that the original wording must surely have been lost in the maze. I will delve into the intricacies of the causes and impacts of these variations later in this chapter and in subsequent chapters.

First, however, it is important to determine the degree of similarity between the texts. If even the so-called similar ones are similar only in a general sense, then the task of recovering the original wording will be very daunting.

To answer this question, I began by exploring how accurately scribes could make successive copies of New Testament manuscripts over several generations. Fortunately this enquiry was relatively easy as there are two manuscripts, separated by about 150 years, which represent the work of several copyists using a similar master copy or

---

1   JH Greenlee, The Text of the New Testament: From Manuscript to Modern Edition, Hendrickson Publishers, Massachusetts, 2008, p. 38.

template. Both of these, P75 (P[75])[2] and Codex Vaticanus, were briefly described in the previous chapter.

How accurately could Christian communities make copies of the New Testament?

What makes P75 and Codex Vaticanus useful for my purposes is that one wasn't directly copied from the other, which means that there was an even greater chance that variations would creep in. However, the texts are close enough in their content to make it certain that they stem from the same template.

So how close are they? They are, in fact, amazingly similar. The text of Codex Vaticanus has such a close appearance to P75 that one could be forgiven at first sight for thinking that it was copied directly from P75. However, it wasn't. In the words of Professor EJ Epp,[3] it is a 'striking and highly significant fact that the texts of P75 and Codex Vaticanus (B) are almost identical ...'[4] Similarly Dr Phillip Comfort[5] concluded that the Codex Vaticanus was 'simply a copy (with some modifications)' of an earlier document that was very similar to P75.[6]

A deeper comparison of P75 and Codex Vaticanus

The above statements are very clear and strong. However, I still wanted to go beyond reading the conclusions made by others. This is because

---

2   Papyrus manuscripts are often formatted using superscripts (e.g. P[45]). To avoid the misleading similarity with footnote references, the superscript convention has been dropped except where it is used in quotations and titles of publications.
3   In 1989 EJ Epp was Professor of Biblical Literature. WL Petersen (ed.), 'Contributors', *Gospel Traditions in the Second Century: Origins, Recensions, Text, and Transmission*, University of Notre Dame Press, London, 1989, p. ix.
4   EJ Epp, 'The significance of the papyri for determining the nature of the New Testament text in the second century: A dynamic view of textual transmission', in EJ Epp & GD Fee, *Studies in the Theory and Method of New Testament Textual Criticism*, William B Eerdmans Publishing Company, Grand Rapids, Michigan, US, 1993, p. 289.
5   Dr Comfort is Senior Editor of Bible Reference at Tyndale House Publishers and Adjunct Professor of Religion at Coastal Carolina University.
6   PW Comfort, Early Manuscripts and Modern Translations of the New Testament, Tyndale House Publishers, Wheaton, US, 1990, p. 21.

it is vitally important to know one way or the other whether at least some Christian communities could and did make very accurate copies over several generations. So I began to search for details that allowed a closer look at the accuracy of copying. In particular, I was looking at how well Jesus' quoted words were copied.

Professor Fee examined Luke chapter 10, which in our English Bibles consists of 980 words.[7] A huge percentage of these (74%, or 722 words) are words spoken by Jesus. Among the 980 words, Fee found that there were 'only twelve disagreements between P75 and B [Codex Vaticanus] ...'[8] Only six of these relate to words spoken by Jesus (namely 10:18, 10:19, 10:24, 10:31 and two in 10:42). They are all inconsequential in the way they relate to Jesus' teaching. For example, in Luke 10:18, the disagreement is simply a matter of word order. Codex Vaticanus reads 'I saw Satan out of the heaven as lightning falling', whereas the older P75 has the words 'I saw Satan as lightning falling out of heaven'.[9] Both manuscripts still convey that Jesus saw Satan falling out of the heaven as lightning. Similarly, the two variations in Luke 10:41–2 are also insignificant. Codex Vaticanus has the verses worded this way:

> *Martha, Martha ... you are worried and upset about many things, but few things are needed — or only one. Mary has chosen what is better, and it will not be taken from her.*[10]

Whilst P75 has the following:

> *Martha, Martha ... you are worried and upset about many things, but only one thing is needed. Mary has chosen what is better, and it will not be taken from her.*[11]

---

7 My calculation is based on the NASB.
8 GD Fee, 'P75, P66, and Origen: The myth of early textual recension in Alexandria', in EJ Epp & GD Fee, Studies in the Theory and Method of New Testament Textual Criticism, 1993, pp. 247–73 (quote from p. 255).
9 GD Fee, 'P75, P66, and Origen: The myth of early textual recension in Alexandria', p. 253.
10 PW Comfort, p. 95. Codex Vaticanus and Codex Sinaiticus read identically. I have constructed this English translation by combining the NIV with Dr Comfort's translation.
11 PW Comfort, p. 95. P75 and P45 read identically. I have constructed this English translation by combining the NIV with Dr Comfort's translation.

Professor Fee went on to say that in the first 18 verses of Luke chapter 10 there were no variations at all.[12] To put this into sharper focus, the first 18 verses of this chapter consist of 373 words in total, of which 85% (or 317 words) are spoken by Jesus.[13]

This examination of Luke chapter 10 strongly illustrates that these particular words of Jesus were well preserved over time. There is no logical reason to believe that any of Jesus' other words would have been preserved with any less a degree of accuracy. Even the backdrop to Jesus' words (i.e. details concerning his location and interactions with others) are reproduced quite adequately over time. We can conclude from this that at least some Christian copyists, generation after generation, conducted their task with great diligence and success.

I say 'at least some' as it is evident that not all manuscripts were copied with incredible diligence in all places. At this point, it is useful to group together manuscripts to make the task of analysing copying accuracy more manageable. One way of grouping them is to place together those that have the same wording when variations are present. This categorising results in the formation of text types. Some of the more famous include the Alexandrian and Western text types.[14] At least three text types are considered to have existed by around 200 AD, namely those that are similar in character and quality to Codex Vaticanus and P75, P45, and Codex Bezae.[15] It is important to note that although these text types existed so early, that does not necessarily mean that the manuscripts used to typify these text types also existed at that time.

What appears to have happened is that some text types were copied over time more faithfully than others. The scribes who copied some text types, such as the Western type, appear to have worked with less

---

12 GD Fee, 'P75, P66, and Origen: The myth of early textual recension in Alexandria', pp. 253–4.
13 I based my calculations on an English translation, namely NASB. I have assumed that similar results would be found if the calculations were based on Greek.
14 The naming of these text types can be misleading. The gospel portion of Codex Alexandrinus is not regarded as being part of the Alexandrian text type.
15 EJ Epp, 'The significance of the papyri for determining the nature of the New Testament text in the second century: A dynamic view of textual transmission', pp. 274–98, esp. p. 295.

care for making perfect word-for-word manuscripts.[16] Later I will explore how the New Testament teachings may have been impacted by the workmanship of these scribes. But first I want to explore further the relationship between P75 and Codex Vaticanus.

The relationship in time and space between P75 and Codex Vaticanus

Seeing that Codex Vaticanus wasn't copied directly from P75, how is it they ended up being so similar? What appears likely[17] is that there once existed a manuscript that I will call the Master. The Master was copied and this copy became what we call P75. However, the Master was used as a template more than once, and one of these copies was itself copied — perhaps several times — with the copy we have now being called Codex Vaticanus.

What I find tantalising is the possibility that the Master (the common ancestor) may have been a copy of an autograph (the original manuscript), or an autograph itself. Just as today we can find manuscripts that are 1800 years old, it is possible that some autographs survived for 200 years and were copied during this time. Whether there were none or several copies between the autographs and the Master can only be speculated.

P75 and Codex Vaticanus aren't the only manuscripts that share this high degree of faithfulness in copying. Rather they are part of a group of manuscripts from ancient Egypt that have a high degree of similarity. The text type they represent is often called Alexandrian. Professor Fee considers that: 'P75, P46, P72, B [i.e. Codex Vaticanus], and to a lesser degree P66 ... [look] very much like a good, but not

---

16 GD Fee, 'Codex Sinaiticus in the gospel of John', p. 243.
17 GD Fee, 'P^{75}, P^{66}, and Origen: The myth of early textual recension in Alexandria', p. 261. The alternative but less likely explanation is that the Master was copied, producing P75, and in turn a copy of a copy of P75 became Codex Vaticanus. Professor Fee wrote: 'they are related through a common ancestor (step-brothers or uncle-nephew), or B [Codex Vaticanus] is a direct descendant (grandson or great-grandson) with slight corruption through the intermediate source(s). A careful analysis of the disagreements ... suggests a common ancestor as the most plausible' (p. 261).

perfect, preservation of the original texts themselves'.[18] As out of this group, only P75 and Codex Vaticanus contain the Gospels, or a portion of the Gospels, their importance can be readily appreciated.

Certainly not all scholars believe that an autograph was the Master for P75, as sometimes other text types appear to better represent what is generally presumed to be the wording found in the autograph. However, overall the text type shared by P75 and Codex Vaticanus helps us get a very close look at what the New Testament autographs actually stated. Dr Comfort's judgement is that these two manuscripts are 'probably the best representatives of the autographs.'[19]

Even if the Master wasn't itself an autograph, Professor Epp considers there is strong evidence to show that it had itself been a faithful copy of an even earlier template. This conclusion is based partly on the fact that P75 and Codex Vaticanus often share certain types of variation, yet these same types are not found in the majority of other manuscripts.[20] After much consideration of detailed data, it has been concluded that P75 and Codex Vaticanus 'seem to represent a "relatively pure" form of preservation of a "relatively pure" line of descent from the original text'.[21]

The ability of Christian communities to make accurate copies didn't grind to a halt with Codex Vaticanus. For centuries after Codex Vaticanus had been written, copies were still being made in such a way as to reliably preserve this same type of text. These include Codex L from the eighth century and Codex 33 from the ninth century.[22]

---

18 GD Fee, 'The use of Greek patristic citations in New Testament textual criticism: The state of the question', in EJ Epp & GD Fee, Studies in the Theory and Method of New Testament Textual Criticism, William B Eerdmans Publishing Company, Grand Rapids, Michigan, US, 1993, pp. 344–59, quote from p. 358.
19 PW Comfort, p. 21.
20 GD Fee, 'P^{75}, P^{66}, and Origen: The myth of early textual recension in Alexandria', p. 261.
21 GD Fee, 'P^{75}, P^{66}, and Origen: The myth of early textual recension in Alexandria', p. 272.
22 EJ Epp, 'Decision points in past, present, and future New Testament textual criticism', in EJ Epp & GD Fee, Studies in the Theory and Method of New Testament Textual Criticism, William B Eerdmans Publishing Company, Grand Rapids, Michigan, US, 1993, p. 38. Epp cites Codex L in the eighth century and Codex 33 in the ninth century.

What do the ancient, less-accurate copies of the New Testament teach?

Not all scribes were as accurate as those involved in the making of P75 and Codex Vaticanus. So the question arises: did the less-precise scribes produce manuscripts with a different set of Christian teachings, either deliberately or inadvertently? I will focus my investigation on two papyrus copies produced by such scribes, namely P45 and P46. These date from around 200 to 250 AD, and have been broadly described in the previous chapter.

Minor errors and deliberate changes found in P45

By examining all the variations found in P45, or any other text, certain tendencies or patterns emerge. These patterns create an insight into the scribe's approach to the task of copying. The approach may have been one of carelessness, or a deliberate attempt at distorting the original messages, or some other factor. The following examples of variations found in P45 reveal some interesting observations about the scribe's approach.

I came across the following variation early on in my research, as well as a suggested explanation for how it arose. The New Testament text is from Matthew 26:1, and it states:

And it happened when Jesus had finished all these sayings, he said to his disciples ...[23]

---

23 B Aland, 'The significance of the Chester Beatty Papyri in early church history', in C Horton (ed.), The Earliest Gospels: The Origin and Transmission of the Earliest Christian Gospels, T & T Clark International, London, 2004, p. 111, Aland's English translation of the Greek found in such manuscripts as the Codex Sinaiticus, and many others, that have been compiled into the modern critical Greek text. See for example http://codexsinaiticus.org/en/manuscript.aspx?book=33&chapter=26&lid=en&side=r&zoomSlider=0, accessed 02/03/2013.

Whereas P45 reads:

> *And it happened when he
> had finished these sayings, Jesus, all of them,
> he said to his disciples ...*[24]

This mistake is certainly not earth shattering, but does shed light on how the scribe worked and how he would rectify his mistakes. It would seem that the copyist knew the original sense of the passage, and started by aiming to reproduce it faithfully, but without looking back to the original for each and every word. This would explain why the copyist wrote 'he' instead of 'Jesus' in the first line. Then, having nearly completed the clause, the scribe observed that he had omitted the word 'Jesus', and that 'these sayings' were qualified as being 'all' the sayings. So then these aspects were added, albeit awkwardly, so that the end result is a copy that states all of the original information.

What I find interesting about the next few variations is that the scribe appears to have deliberately, but perhaps almost automatically, omitted certain words. The result is still a faithful reproduction of the meaning, but not of every single word. These omissions are of redundant words. Redundant words are words such as 'coloured' in the following sentence: 'She wore a red coloured dress'. 'Coloured' is redundant as red is a colour. The following example of omissions comes from the account describing how Jesus miraculously fed a large crowd. Jesus' disciples had just told him that the only food available for the crowd was five loaves and two fish (Mark 6:38). Jesus organised the crowd into groups of hundreds and fifties, and then:

> *Taking the five loaves and the two fish and looking up to heaven, he gave thanks ... (Mark 6:41).*

The P45 version leaves out the words 'five' and 'two' in Mark 6:41, which doesn't alter the account as verse 38 has already made it known that there were five loaves and two fish.

Another case of a word being omitted is found in Luke 11:14–19. This portrays Jesus' response to critics who accused him of using

---

[24] B Aland, p. 111. A footnote states that the P45 translation was based on reconstructions of fragments, n. 15.

demonic powers to make a show of driving out demons from afflicted individuals. In Luke 11:19 the word 'demons' (τα δαιμονια) is omitted by the scribe, which doesn't change the meaning of the passage as the verses before it (14–18) mention five times that it was demons being driven out.[25]

Because of such changes the scribe of P45 can be said to have indulged in 'deliberate pruning' and 'intentional changes'.[26] However, as can be seen from above, these changes do not affect the meaning or accuracy of the text in any significant way, but do improve its readability.

One scholar summarised the skills and attitude of the copyist of P45 in this way:

> *The nature and method of copying in P^{45} is both intelligent and liberal: intelligent because the sense of the exemplar [original] is quickly grasped and in essence precisely reproduced; and liberal, because involved expressions and repetitious words are simplified or dropped ... We may conclude that P^{45} represents the kind of manuscript one might expect from an experienced transcriber of documents ... Superfluous elements and repetitious meanings are dropped, parallels are restored, conjunctions are inserted and intended meanings are clarified. But it must be stated clearly that here again there is no question of scholarly or stylistic revision, but only of such half-conscious changes as transcribers of documents make in seeing that exemplars [originals] are reproduced accurately, but also clearly and intelligibly ...*[27]

Others have stated that the scribe who made P45 was only:

> *'rather rarely' subject to accidental copying errors of sight, and seems on the whole to have been a careful and rather competent*

---

25 JK Elliott, 'Singular readings in the gospel text of P45', in C Horton (ed.), The Earliest Gospels: The Origin and Transmission of the Earliest Christian Gospels, T & T Clark International, London, 2004, p. 125.

26 LW Hurtado, 'P45 and the textual history of the gospel of Mark', in C Horton (ed.), The Earliest Gospels: The Origin and Transmission of the Earliest Christian Gospels, T & T Clark International, London, 2004, p. 146 & p. 147 respectively.

27 B Aland, pp. 112–13.

worker, who copied by sense units and not (as in the case of some scribes) mechanically letter by letter or word by word.[28]

Are there any ethical teachings affected by the variations?

The scribe of P45 appears to have generally succeeded in being accurate in terms of conveying the correct meaning of the original New Testament. However, there is one error in P45 that, at first sight, appears to have a large impact on the New Testament teaching of how a Christian should behave. If this codex had become the sole textual source for all future copies of this part of the New Testament, what would have been the outcome? I will start my investigations by coming to an understanding of the context.

What is the context?

After Jesus was resurrected from the dead, many non-Jewish people (who are collectively called Gentiles) became Christians. Two famous early Christian leaders called Paul and Barnabas were travelling through various cities such as Derbe, Lystra, Iconium and a very prominent city called Antioch (in Syria). The New Testament speaks of these new Christians forming churches and having leaders (elders) appointed by Paul and Barnabas (Acts 14:21–8). These two leaders stayed a long time with these new believers. Some Jews who had become Christians went from Jerusalem to Antioch and unfortunately tried to persuade the Gentile Christians that they had to become circumcised or they weren't really saved from hell after all (Acts 15:1). These particular Jewish Christians taught this idea despite Jesus' teachings that believing in him was all that was needed to 'do the works God requires' (John 6:28–9 and Mark 10:45). They didn't even have the authority of the well-established church in Jerusalem (Acts 15:24). Paul and Barnabas argued strongly against these teachers, and went to the apostles and elders in the church in Jerusalem to report what was happening. Even in the meeting in Jerusalem there were some Jewish Christians (perhaps

---

28   LW Hurtado, p. 146. 'Rather rarely' being cited from JR Royse, 'Scribal habits in early Greek New Testament papyri', PhD thesis, Graduate Theological Union, Berkeley, US, 1981 pp. 156–7.

the same ones) arguing for the practice of circumcision (Acts 15:5). However, Peter (one of the original 12 disciples of Jesus) explained that all Christians are saved by faith (i.e. believing that Jesus can take their punishment) and not by actions, and that this is possible because of the grace given by Jesus (Acts 15:8–10). Peter concludes by saying:

> *It is my judgement, therefore, that we should not make it difficult for the Gentiles who are turning to God. Instead we should write to them, telling them to abstain from food polluted by idols, from sexual immorality, from the meat of strangled animals and from blood. For the law of Moses has been preached in every city from the earliest times and is read in the synagogues on every Sabbath. (Acts 15:19–21)*

In the Greek manuscripts, the last sentence simply uses 'Moses' as an abbreviation for the laws (commandments) given by God to Moses who was the leader of the Jews many hundreds of years earlier. These commands were read to all Jews (both Christian and non-Christian) who came together each week in the Jewish meeting places called synagogues. Peter is therefore explaining that the reason for giving these particular prohibitions is because the Gentile Christians should show sensitivity to their Jewish Christian brothers. Apparently some, if not many, Jewish Christians continued to follow many of the food prohibitions given by Moses after becoming Christians. Certainly it wasn't necessary for them as Christians to abstain from eating certain foods in order to please God, as Jesus and Peter had taught that food by itself doesn't make a person sinful (Mark 7:17–23 and Acts 10:9–16).

After listening to Peter, the apostles and elders and the whole church[29] agreed with him and wrote a letter accordingly. The contents of this letter are given in Acts 15:23–9, with the last verse saying:

> *You are to abstain from food sacrificed to idols, from blood, from the meat of strangled animals and from sexual immorality. You will do well to avoid these things. Farewell. (Acts 15:29)*

From the context, it is apparent that the instructions in the letter are not telling the Gentiles what they must not do in order to be saved from

---

29 The 'whole church' indicates that those who formerly insisted on circumcision were now convinced otherwise.

hell by Jesus. Rather the instructions are what they in particular should avoid so that they do not unnecessarily disturb their Jewish Christian neighbours. Therefore, the passage does not concern the important issue of how Jesus can rescue people. (As an aside, the following verses speak of all that is necessary in order to be saved by Jesus: Ephesians 2:8–9, Galatians 3:3, John 3:14–18 and John 6:28–45.)

What are the variations?

Here again is the last part of Acts 15:20:

> *Instead we should write to them, telling them to abstain from food polluted by idols, from sexual immorality, from the meat of strangled animals and from blood.*

Many of the ancient Greek manuscripts (such as P74 and the codices called Sinaiticus, Alexandrinus, Vaticanus and Ephraimi Syri Rescriptus) have the words of the texts as shown above (though, of course, in Greek).[30] So there is little doubt that the general sense of the text of P45 is correct. What is surprising is that P45 omits 'and sexual immorality'. The likely explanation for the variation here is that the scribe left the words out due to an accidental oversight, as suggested by others.[31]

After pausing to take in all of the above, it seems reasonable to draw the following conclusion: if all of the original P45 manuscript were to have survived today, it would contain a copy of the Gospels and Acts that adequately conveys the Christian message found within its pages. This is despite minor errors, deliberate changes and the omission of sexual immorality in one section.

I began this particular discussion on the impact of variations on Jesus' teachings by asking the following: if this codex had become the sole textual source for all future copies of this part of the New

---

30 J Delobel, 'Textual criticism and exegesis: Siamese twins?', in B Aland & J Delobel (eds), *New Testament Criticism, Exegesis, and Early Church History: A Discussion of Methods*, Kok Pharos Publishing House, Kampen, The Netherlands, 1994, p. 108.

31 J Delobel, p. 109, n. 35.

Testament, what would have been the impact on Christian teachings? Given that the context of the passage makes it clear that the passage was not intended to be an exhaustive list of all actions Christians should avoid, the impact would be very minimal. Elsewhere in the New Testament there are many verses teaching Christians to avoid sexual misconduct. For instance, Jesus condemns such immorality in Matthew 15:19, Mark 7:21, Mark 10:11–12, Mark 10:19, Luke 16:18 and Luke 18:20.[32] Therefore, even if all surviving subsequent copies of Acts 15:20 were derived from P45, Christians throughout the centuries would still know that sexual immorality was to be avoided.

Minor errors caused by copyists: a look at P46

There is a third and final ancient papyrus manuscript that I felt compelled to explore. Possibly dating back to as early as the late 100s AD,[33] the age of P46 alone arouses quite a degree of curiosity. P46 has a reputation for having more errors than either P75 or P45. Looking at the less-than-ideally copied manuscript, a worse-case scenario can be developed. However, while it is not impossible that individuals may have maliciously tried to create misleading copies of the New Testament, it is more likely that the errors were caused by scribes with reasonable intentions but with less-than-perfect skills. Nonetheless, I was interested in whether such scribes could make copies of the New Testament that still adequately conveyed the main gist of Christian teachings. The handwriting of P46 is of very good quality, being described as 'graceful and flowing, almost calligraphic'.[34] Yet despite this appearance of beauty, the workmanship has plenty of blemishes in terms of making an accurate copy. It is precisely because it has a reputation for making many errors that it is particularly intriguing.

---

32 None of these gospel references are regarded as having serious question marks about their textual integrity. This is based on the fact that the following very famous textual commentary designed to discuss significant variations does not contain any discussion on these verses: BM Metzger, *A Textual Commentary on the Greek New Testament: A Companion Volume to the United Bible Societies' Greek New Testament*, 4th rev. ed., German Bible Society, Stuttgart, Germany,1994.
33 Refer to the previous chapter for more details.
34 B Aland, p. 115.

Some of these errors are due to changes in the order of words. In Galatians 1:3 the word order of the Greek standard text results in the English translation being:

Greetings to you and peace from God our Father and Lord Jesus Christ.[35]

Whereas in P46 the word order of the Greek text results in the English translation being:

Greetings to you and peace from God the Father and our Lord Jesus Christ.[36]

Is this alteration due to the scribe of P46 having an aversion to calling God 'our Father'? Or is it due to a certain degree of carelessness? These questions are answered by looking at other verses copied by the scribe. In Ephesians 1:2 the scribe does write the Greek in such a way that it translates as:

Grace to you and peace from God our father and the Lord Jesus Christ.[37] *(Translators' version)*

So it becomes apparent that the scribe is not averse to calling God 'our father' but is sometimes careless. This is reinforced by looking again at the opening lines of Ephesians 1:2–3. The standard texts read as follows:

Grace to you and peace from
God our Father and the Lord Jesus Christ.
Blessed be the God and Father of our Lord Jesus Christ,
who has blessed us with every spiritual blessing in the heavenly places in Christ ... (NASB)

---

35 PW Comfort, p. 149. I have constructed this English translation by combining the NASB with Dr Comfort's translation.
36 PW Comfort, p. 149. I have constructed this English translation by combining the NASB with Dr Comfort's translation.
37 F Stratikis & G Schwendner (trans), 'Supplemental transcriptions and translations: The Book of Enoch; Melito: Homily on the Passion; The Epistles of Paul' (supplemental booklet), in K Beam & T Gagos (eds), The Evolution of the English Bible: From Papyri to King James, The University of Michigan Press, Ann Arbor, US, 1997, p. 146.

When the scribe of P46 came to this section, he omitted some words, causing it to appear as follows:

> *Grace to you and peace from*
> *God our father and the Lord Jesus Christ.*
> *who blesses us with every spiritual blessing in Christ in heavenly things.*[38] *(Translators' version)*

It's easy to conclude that the omission is most likely due to a lapse of concentration. The scribe's eyes have skipped from the first time the master copy has the words 'Lord Jesus Christ' to the second time these same words are repeated.

In contrast to the above, the cause of some omissions is not easily fathomable. Why did the scribe leave out the following italicised words of Paul: 'Even if I am untrained in speech, I am not in knowledge. *We have made this perfectly clear to you in every way*' (2 Corinthians 11:6, Translators' version and footnote).[39] Did the scribe deliberately leave them out as they seemed too terse? This is unlikely as he has not omitted the following sarcastic words of Paul found just a few lines later: 'For you bear with fools gladly, since you are wise' (2 Corinthians 11:19, Translators' version).[40]

Scholars have concluded that none of the many variations present in P46 show evidence of the scribe trying to alter the basic facts of the accounts in the New Testament. For this reason it can be said that:

> *[P^{46}] represents a rough and inadequate copy of a good exemplar ... [it] is not a text intentionally altered by the scribe.*[41]

Are there any doctrinal teachings affected by variations?

Given that there appears to have been no intentional effort by P46 to alter Christian doctrines, has this nevertheless happened inadvertently?

---

38 F Stratikis & G Schwendner (trans), p. 146.
39 F Stratikis & G Schwendner (trans), p. 139.
40 F Stratikis & G Schwendner (trans), p. 140.
41 B Aland, p. 116.

The doctrines I am interested in here are ones concerning the nature of God, Jesus, and what happens after death.

My search found one variation that has this misleading potential. As I analysed this error in 1 Corinthians 15:51, I also wanted to better appreciate how an error can be discerned as an error and not what was actually written by the original author. In this case, this discernment is based on what is termed 'internal evidence', or evidence from the context.

The verse in question is found in a lesson given by Paul when he wrote to the Christians in the town of Corinth. He wrote that after death, all Christians will be given new bodies that will live forever. However, as some Christians will still be alive when Jesus returns in the future, these Christians will not die but instead be suddenly transformed into new bodies as if they had died. The following passage is from a present-day New Testament Greek interlinear version[42] of Paul's teaching in 1 Corinthians 15:51:

Listen, I tell you a mystery:

We will not all sleep [die], but we will all be changed —

ἰδοὺ μυστήριον ὑμῖν λέγω πάντες οὐ κοιμηθησομεθα πάντες δὲ ἀλλαγησόμεθα

However, the scribe of P46 wrote this same verse as:[43]

Listen, I tell you a mystery:

We will not all sleep, but we will not all be changed.

ἰδοὺ μυστήριον ὑμῖν λέγω πάντες οὐ κοιμηθησομεθα οὐ πάντες δὲ ἀλλαγησόμεθα

This variation certainly is alarming as it is completely the opposite of what was originally taught, assuming of course that the verse we have

---

42 WD Mounce, *Interlinear for the Rest of Us: The Reverse Interlinear for New Testament Word Studies*, Zondervan, Grand Rapids, Michigan, US, 2005, p. 526.
43 B Aland, p. 115. I have modernised and slightly altered Aland's original quote: 'We shall not all die, but we shall not all be changed'. The Greek word translated die and sleep is the same in P46 and the Greek interlinear.

in our Bibles, which is based on the readings found in Codex Vaticanus and others, actually is the original. The dilemma about which is the correct verse is solved by looking at the immediate context of the passage in P46 itself. From this vantage point, it is possible to discern that the scribe of P46 should have written 'we will all be changed'. This is because immediately after verse 51, P46 has these words of Paul in verses 52 and 53.[44]

For the trumpet will sound,

the dead will be raised imperishable,
οι νεκροι εγερθησονται αφθαρτοι

And we will be changed
και ημεις αλλαγησομεθα

For the perishable [body] must clothe itself with the imperishable,
δει γαρ το φθαρτον τουτο ενδυσασθαι αφθαρσιαν

and the mortal with immortality.

Therefore, even in an imaginary isolated Christian community that had only P46, they would still learn that all Christians will one day have new eternally living bodies. As for discerning what the original text of Paul's letter stated, the immediate context of P46 points to the copyist having made a mistake in verse 51. Other surviving ancient manuscripts, such as Codex Sinaiticus[45] and Codex Vaticanus,[46] also verify this. Early Christian scribes appear to have detected the error in verse 51, as evidenced by a dot being placed in the margin of P46 at this point.[47]

---

44 The translation was found using the New Testament Transcripts Prototype, http://nttranscripts.uni-muenster.de/AnaServer?NTtranscripts+0+start.anv, accessed 23/01/2011.

45 You can view the actual verse in Codex Sinaiticus by http://codexsinaiticus. org/en/manuscript.aspx?book=38&chapter=15&lid=en&side=r&verse= 51&zoomSlider=0, accessed 22/08/2010.

46 Again, the translation for the Codex Vaticanus can be found using the New Testament Transcripts Prototype, http://nttranscripts.uni-muenster.de/ AnaServer?NT transcripts+0+start.anv, accessed 23/01/2011.

47 B Aland, p. 115.

Conclusion

It is evident from the above discussion of several ancient manuscripts that scribes differed in their ability to make accurate successive copies, with some being extremely competent in their skill and others having lesser skills. However, even the manuscripts written by the less-accurate scribes still faithfully convey the teachings of the originals written by the New Testament authors. The lack of photocopiers doesn't seem to have caused an insurmountable difficulty. Those scribes that made deliberate changes did so to improve the readability of their workmanship, rather than to mislead their readers. These facts create a very favourable confidence in the copying process.

But could this confidence be somewhat excessive given we have explored only a few of the ancient handwritten copies? This is the question that motivated the research lying behind the next chapter.

9

Deliberate changes and their cumulative impact on Jesus' words

The previous chapter considered the impressive accuracy of copying found in several ancient Greek manuscripts. Given that there were dozens of manuscripts dated from before 400 AD,[1] I now wanted to obtain a broader view. Had there been an extensive degree of faithfulness among these other copies? The following pages are devoted to this wider exploration of variations in copies of the New Testament. Three prominent variants that arise from this study are further examined in the next chapter as they are complex in nature.

To get an overview of the possible impact of many of the variations, one scholar counted the number of words Jesus spoke in the Gospel of Mark and then looked at how many of these words were affected by variations found in the ancient copies. His analysis indicates that the early copyists were quite scrupulous about their work. He wrote:

> *By my count in Mark 1:1–16:8 there are 3,992 words attributed to Jesus, and only 28 of these (.7 percent) are subject to any serious question [about what were the original words]. But these involve questions such as the presence of the article "the," whether a given command was given in the present or the perfect ("Stand up!" versus "Having stood up!"), or whether a given noun*

---

1 Refer to chapter 7 'Ancient copies of the New Testament', in particular the section titled 'Ancient partial copies' on p. 140.

takes a certain grammatical ending (which effects no change in meaning).[2]

Another analysis counted all the variations found in early manuscripts of Mark, whether in Greek or not, no matter how unlikely the variations were to represent the original text. It discovered that of the 11,270 words in the entire Greek Gospel of Mark, there are only 575 that are in question, resulting in a word-for-word accuracy of 94.9%.[3]

The above evaluations create a favourable impression of the fidelity of copying the words of Jesus for the book of Mark. Does this hold true for the other Gospels? I started my research by looking for the causes of variations. The previous chapter examined the causes of variations in three important papyrus manuscripts. Now I wish to take a broader view by looking at causes found in many other copies and, in particular, those causes that have been termed 'deliberate'.

What were the causes of variations among the many manuscripts?

To understand why variations arose in the first place, it is helpful to first describe the types of variation. The following is one common way of categorising them:[4]

(a) the adding or omitting of words, phrases, sentences or large sections

(b) the substitution of some words, tenses and numbers

(c) changes in the order of words or phrases

(d) any combination of the first three in a single variant

(e) shifting (i.e. transposing) a large section of text from one place to another

---

2   N Perrin, *Lost in Translation? What We Can Know About the Words of Jesus*, Thomas Nelson, Nashville, US, 2007, p. 197.
3   Bible Query – Early Manuscripts of Mark: April 29, 2012 version, www.biblequery.org/mkmss.htm, accessed 18/08/2012. Copyright © 1997–2012 Christian Debater™, PO Box 144441, Austin, Tx 78714. (512) 218-8022. www.BibleQuery.org.
4   GD Fee, 'The Majority text and the original text of the New Testament', in EJ Epp & GD Fee, *Studies in the Theory and Method of New Testament Textual Criticism*, 1993, pp. 183–208 (quote p. 195).

(f) major rewriting of a sentence or paragraph.

The benefit of this form of classification is that it covers all possible forms of variation.[5] The previous chapter gave examples of some of these categories, as found in P75, P45 and P46. Of the above types of change, it has been said that the first three may or may not have arisen deliberately. That is, these three sometimes have arisen because of the carelessness of the scribe, other times the copyist made the change deliberately. The next two types often appear to have been deliberately made, and the last type is always based on the scribe's clear intention — that is, the scribe's deliberate choice.[6]

Changes made deliberately by copyists

I found it alarming to realise that many changes made by copyists were done deliberately. This is because I had always assumed that a deliberate change would detract from the original author's intention. However, writing this book has helped me appreciate that this is not always the case. At various points, my editors made suggested changes to what I had written. The majority of the time these changes resulted in a clarification of the original or an improvement in style. Similarly, it appears that many scribes made deliberate changes to the original text for very benign reasons, such as improving the flow of sentences. By examining many variations in the ancient Greek New Testament manuscripts, it is evident that these scribes were not maliciously trying to alter important doctrines or radically change the recorded events. Perhaps this is because scribes 'were not engaged in studying the text but simply copying it'.[7]

Professor Fee summed it up by saying:

> *If one were to take any five to 10 verses from anywhere in the NT [New Testament] and collate all the available textual evidence, [i.e. collect all the variations from all the manuscripts] the vast majority of variants among the MSS [manuscripts] belong to categories (a), (b), and (c), and of these the substantial majority*

---

5 GD Fee, p. 195. Fee actually wrote: 'Apart from careless errors, most of which could be placed in the above categories, these are the only kinds of variation to a text that are possible'.
6 GD Fee, p. 195.
7 JH Greenlee, *The Text of the New Testament: From Manuscript to Modern Edition*, Hendrickson Publishers, Massachusetts, 2008, p. 75.

simply do not fit in any meaningful way the concept of theologically motivated alteration.[8]

To illustrate the above, Professor Fee looked at the first five verses of John chapter 13, none of which contain any of the words of Jesus.

It was just before the Passover Feast. Jesus knew that the time had come for him to leave this world and go to the Father. Having loved his own who were in the world, he now showed them the full extent of his love. The evening meal was already being served, and the devil had already prompted Judas Iscariot, son of Simon, to betray Jesus. Jesus knew that the Father had put all things under his power, and that he had come from God and was returning to God; so he got up from the meal, took off his outer clothing, and wrapped a towel around his waist. After that, he poured water into a basin, and began to wash his disciples' feet, drying them with the towel that was wrapped around him. (John 13:1–5, NIV 1984)

Professor Fee then thoroughly searched numerous ancient Greek manuscripts. He focused on all those instances where a section of Greek text had been found to have two or more variations, and each variation is found in at least two ancient Greek copies.[9] These 'double-double' changes are called variation units. Fee found a total of 27 variation units in this way and noted that:

fourteen are add/omit; ten are substitutions; two are word order; and one is a combination of add/omit and substitution. Many of these are probably not deliberate at all ... But many were almost certainly deliberate.[10]

---

8 GD Fee, p. 195.
9 EJ Epp, 'Toward the clarification of the term "textual variant"', in EJ Epp & GD Fee, *Studies in the Theory and Method of New Testament Textual Criticism*, 1993, p. 49. Fee examined all the ancient partial copies written on papyrus as well as a large number of later manuscripts as collated by Tischendorf and also by von Soden. Tischendorf's collation included 64 uncials, a large number of minuscules; von Soden included many more. Refer to K Aland & B Aland, The *Text of the New Testament: An Introduction to the Critical Editions and to the Theory and Practice of Modern Textual Criticism*, trans. EF Rhodes, William B Eerdmans Publishing Company, Grand Rapids, 1989, pp. 13–23.
10 GD Fee, p. 195.

I want to now look at these deliberate changes more closely. What are the impacts to the basic messages of the Gospels from these intentional changes made by copyists? These deliberate changes have been categorised as either simple or complex.

Deliberate and simple changes

Professor Fee illustrated a deliberate but simple case of variation by pointing to verse 2 of John chapter 13 wherein a word, serve, is found either spelt γενομενου or spelt γινομενου. Depending on which word is used, the passage describes Jesus as washing his disciples' feet either after or during the evening meal. Yet, although Fee considered this change had been deliberately made (and possibly even theologically motivated), he certainly didn't regard it as a 'malicious' act of distortion.[11]

Another simple case of a deliberate change can be found by comparing two verses found in Codex Vaticanus with the same two verses found in Codex Sinaiticus. In Codex Vaticanus we read in Matthew 14:24 that the ship containing the disciples was 'many stadia from the land' (a stadia was about 156 metres long).[12] This same event is also recorded in Mark's Gospel, but there the boat is described as being in the 'midst of the sea' (Mark 6:47) of the same codex.[13] There is no significant difference between these two descriptions of where the boat was, and the difference certainly doesn't have any theological relevance. However, the wording of these passages is a little different when we examine Codex Sinaiticus. In this codex, both passages from Matthew and Mark state that the ship was in the 'midst of the sea'.[14] To explain this, it is

---

11 GD Fee, p. 195.
12 The Sea of Galilee (also called Lake Tiberias) is about 13 km wide. The length of a stadia appears to have varied in the ancient world.
13 H Heinfetter, *A Literal Translation of the New Testament of our Lord and Saviour Jesus Christ, On Definite Rules of Translation, From the Text of the Vatican Manuscript*, Evan Evans London, 1863, sixth edition, digital copy available online at http://archive.org/details/aliteraltransla00unkngoog.
14 HT Anderson, *The New Testament: Translated from the Sinaitic Manuscript Discovered by Constantine Tischendorf at Mt. Sinai*, The Standard Publishing Company, Cincinnati, US, 1918, digital copy available at http://archive.org/stream/newtestamenttran00ande#page/n5/mode/2up, accessed 23/01/2013.

conjectured that when the scribe of Codex Sinaiticus started to copy the passage in Matthew, he recalled the slightly different description in Mark, and chose to use it to better harmonise both Gospels.[15] This type of intentional change, called a harmonisation, does occur frequently in the Gospels of various manuscripts. The harmonising action of the scribe in this case is unlikely to be motivated by an attempt to cover up an inconsistency found between the original Gospel accounts. This is because although they used different means of stating where the boat was, none of the descriptions are contradictory.

Of course, the question springs to mind as to how to know whether differences between the Gospels represent a harmonisation or whether in fact the Gospels originally were worded identically. This question is usually resolved by assuming that if the passages in Matthew and Mark were originally identical, then there is no clear reason why a scribe would deliberately make them different. However, if they were different in the originals, then it is easy to imagine some scribes wanting to harmonise the passages.[16] So by comparing various manuscripts, and keeping this and other principles in mind, it is generally easy to be confident about the wording of the original autograph. Although it is unfortunate that it is only *generally* easy, and not *always* easy, the impact on the meaning is usually negligible. An illustration of when it is not an easy matter to determine the original is shown in the following section.

Deliberate and complex changes

As an example of a complex intentional change, Professor Fee looked at the last portion of verse 2 from John chapter 13:

> *During supper, when the devil had already put it into the heart of Judas Iscariot, Simon's son, to betray him ... (ESV 2001)*

Fee notes that there are at least seven different alternatives of word order among the various manuscripts, but these result only in essentially two choices of reading, one being as written above and the other being:

---

15 JH Greenlee, p. 60.
16 JH Greenlee, p. 60.

During supper, when the devil had already put it into the heart that he might betray him, Judas Iscariot, Simon's son ...[17]

So despite there being several changes in the order of the words, the meaning has remained unchanged. Fee emphasises that these variations were deliberate, but certainly not with malicious intent or to teach some peculiar doctrine. After all, both readings teach the same facts. It seems very unlikely that anyone would purposely re-write the first reading into the second, when the second reads very awkwardly in the Greek, just as it is in the English. Fee believes that the variation arose from John, who wrote the Gospel, having written in the first instance the second version, but then added 'Judas Iscariot, Simon's son' so as to clarify whose heart was affected by the devil. Then later 'copyists simply helped him out further by changing the word order ...'[18] and the form of the words to make it grammatically correct.

Variations in the content of all of the Gospels

The above analysis dealing with John chapter 13 leads to the conclusion that the modern-day New Testament is a very good representation of the autographs. But is the same conclusion reached when an analysis of all the chapters in all four Gospels is conducted? At this point I am thankful for the detailed study produced by Dr Philip Comfort.

Dr Comfort's research was made possible due to the difference in time between the discoveries of the ancient, extensive Greek New Testament manuscripts and the even older, partial copies of the Greek New Testament. The most famous of these have been described in a previous chapter.[19] The extensive New Testament manuscripts were made known to the world in the 1800s, and were heavily relied upon to produce an English translation called the

---

17 GD Fee, p. 196.
18 GD Fee, p. 196. The later copyists also changed the form of the words so that the grammar would be correct.
19 See chapter 7 'Ancient copies of the New Testament: from Egypt to the Vatican'.

American Standard Version (ASV). Published in 1901, the ASV was produced mostly using the Greek texts found in Codex Sinaiticus and Codex Vaticanus.[20]

By contrast, the older 66 partial New Testament documents were mostly discovered in the 1900s, and were used in varying degrees to form several more modern English versions. These more modern English translations were published between 1941 and 1986,[21] the most recent English translation being the New Jerusalem Bible. Because of this difference in timing, Dr Comfort was able to discern what impact the variations found in the 66 ancient partial copies had on the various English translations since the publication of the ASV.[22] The ASV, therefore, served as his yardstick, or benchmark.

So, in effect, Dr Comfort indirectly examined how consistently the words of the New Testament were being written in different places, between the years 125 AD (the date of one of the earliest partial copies called P52) and 350 AD (the approximate dates of Codex Sinaiticus and Codex Vaticanus).

As many of the variations found between the ancient manuscripts are of no importance, Dr Comfort chose only those that had some impact on the translation of the Greek into English. In practical terms, this meant that Dr Comfort examined all the variations in the ancient partial copies, provided that at least one English translation had mentioned the variation, even if only in a footnote.[23]

---

20 PW Comfort, *Early Manuscripts and Modern Translations of the New Testament*, Tyndale House Publishers, Wheaton, US, 1990, pp. 202–207. Comfort states that he used the American Standard Version as 'it reflects the text current at the beginning of this [20th] century (a text heavily influenced by [Codex Sinaiticus and Codex Vaticanus]...' (p. 189).
21 PW Comfort, pp. 26–7. Dr Comfort examined seven English translations, namely: American Standard Version, 1901; Revised Standard Version, 1946; New American Standard Bible, 1971; New International Version, 1973; New English Bible, 1970; Today's English Version, 1969; New Jerusalem Bible, 1986. A few select comparisons were also made using the New Revised Standard Version, 1990.
22 PW Comfort, pp. 202–213.
23 PW Comfort, pp. 24–5. For an example of only one variant being cited, see pp. 114–15, 206.

This last criterion immediately aroused my curiosity. How often were footnotes used in the different English translations? Dr Comfort addressed this question by pointing out that many Bible publishers have extensively used such footnotes. The Revised Standard Version of 1946 incorporated 239 of these footnotes, whilst the New Jerusalem Bible has 602. The reason for the New Jerusalem Bible having so many is that it aimed to 'provide as many alternate readings as possible — even if they [the translators] thought the readings in the margins could not be the original reading'.[24]

Getting back to Dr Comfort's research, it is now possible to analyse his findings. Did he discover a very different set of teachings about Jesus that had been hidden in the ancient partial copies of the Greek New Testament? Did the later extensive copies of the New Testament show that the scribes had substantially changed the original?

The types of variation Dr Comfort found included additions and omissions, changed word order and altered spellings. As I am particularly interested in the impact these may have had on Jesus' words, and in order to save space, I am presenting here only the changes Dr Comfort recommended regarding the words spoken by Jesus, and those that I consider are the most important in terms of their possible impact on Christian teachings.[25] His research revealed that many variations affected the English wording, but not the English meaning, indicating that the scribes had performed their work very faithfully.

In the presentation of these relevant Gospel verses, I will indicate in square brackets the source, or sources, of each version of the New Testament passage being considered. These versions have been described in chapter 7, and brief explanations are also provided in the glossary.[26] Each pair of verses being analysed will be followed by a discussion on the impact on Jesus' teaching. The discussion will

---

24 PW Comfort, pp. 25–7.
25 A few prominent variants are covered in the next chapter.
26 The glossary can be found at the beginning of this book in the section titled 'Abbreviations, symbols, glossary and distances'. D is used as an abbreviation for Codex Bezae.

explore whether there would be any material change in the teachings of Jesus if either version was regarded as the original.

Regarding the book of Matthew[27]

Matthew 5:22 [Sinaiticus, Vaticanus, P67]
But I tell you that anyone who is angry with his brother will be subject to judgement.

Matthew 5:22 [Bezae]
But I tell you that anyone who is angry with his brother without cause will be subject to judgement.

The first reading teaches that being angry with a brother will lead to some form of judgment. The second teaches that only such anger that is also without cause will result in judgement. How then should a Christian behave? As Jesus is the ultimate example that every Christian aspires to, then it is his example that should provide a wider perspective. Jesus certainly was angry at times (Mark 3:5, John 2:13–18), therefore, there must be times when it is appropriate for Christians to be angry.

Regarding the book of Mark[28]

Mark 9:29 [Sinaiticus, Vaticanus]
This kind [of demon] can only be driven out by prayer.

Mark 9:29 [Alexandrinus, and seemingly by P45]
This kind [of demon] can only be driven out by prayer and fasting.

Even if the original words of Jesus had included the need for fasting, and these words had been lost for all time in this passage, it wouldn't result in Christians changing their behaviour. This is because Jesus' encouragement of fasting can be found elsewhere (Mathew 4:2, 6:16–18). Other passages in the New Testament also encourage fasting (Acts 13:2, 14:23).

---

27 PW Comfort, p. 80.
28 PW Comfort, pp. 87–8.

Regarding the book of Luke[29]

Luke 22:19b–20 [Sinaiticus, Vaticanus, Alexandrinus, P75]
And he [Jesus] took bread, gave thanks and broke it, and gave it to them, saying,

'This is my body given for you; do this in remembrance of me.' In the same way, after the supper he took the cup, saying, 'This cup is the new covenant in my blood, which is poured out for you.'

Luke 22:19b–20 [Bezae]
And he [Jesus] took bread, gave thanks and broke it, and gave it to them, saying,
'This is my body.'

The context of this passage is the annual Jewish feast called the Passover. Jewish families sacrificed lambs during the Passover. It was particularly significant as Jesus was called the lamb of God (John 1:36), and this was the last time Jesus was to celebrate it before his crucifixion. The breaking of the bread is a tradition performed in Christian denominations even to this day. The Roman Catholic Church calls it the Eucharist and gives it enormous significance. Some Christian denominations call it communion and regard it as having only symbolic importance. It is celebrated weekly by some and monthly by others.

The second reading differs to the first in that there is no command given to Jesus' disciples to break the bread and share it. Nowhere else in the book of Luke is this commandment to break the bread given during the Passover, nor is it given in the other Gospels. So would Christians celebrate it less often if the only version we had was the second version? Possibly. Would they still celebrate it at all if we had only the second version? Definitely. It was such a dramatic and passionate scene it is hard to believe it would have been ignored when they commemorated Jesus' sacrifice. Moreover, just before the words about the bread, Luke records:

And He [Jesus] said to them, 'I have earnestly desired to eat this Passover with you before I suffer; for I say to you, I shall never again eat it until it is fulfilled in the kingdom of God.' And when He

---

29 PW Comfort, pp. 99–100.

had taken a cup and given thanks, He said, 'Take this and share it amongst yourselves ...' (Luke 22:15–17)

The other way the second reading differs to the first is that there is no mention of a cup of a new covenant (agreement) being poured out for others. However, Matthew 26:27–8 and Mark 14:23–4 do record these sentiments, and of course the earlier words in Luke still mention the existence of a cup. So even if only the second reading survived in Luke's Gospel, this particular Christian re-enactment would still continue.

Luke 23:34 [Sinaiticus, Alexandrinus]
Jesus said, 'Father, forgive them, for they do not know what they are doing.'

Luke 23:34 [Vaticanus, Bezae, P75]
These copies omit the entire verse. Dr Comfort recommends placing it in a footnote.[30]

Jesus spoke these very famous words when he was on the crucifix. He was referring to his torturers when he asked his Father to forgive them. I was quite startled at the notion that these words might not have been in the original Gospel of Luke. However, a moment's reflection helped me realise that even if these words were to be omitted from our present-day Gospels, it would not affect any Christian doctrine. This is because Jesus often emphasised the need for his followers to be very forgiving. Consider the following examples:

- Jesus taught that Christians are to forgive those who sin against them:

    For if you forgive other people when they sin against you, your heavenly Father will also forgive you. (Matthew 6:14)

    Even if they sin against you seven times in a day and seven times come back to you saying 'I repent,' you must forgive them. (Luke 17:4)

- Jesus even used a parable to emphasise how important it is for his followers to forgive, concluding with the words:

---

30 PW Comfort, pp. 101, 205.

> *This is how my heavenly Father will treat each of you unless you forgive your brother or sister from your heart. (Matthew 18:35)*

- Even more relevant to the statement in Luke are Jesus' words to his followers that they should love their enemies and pray for their persecutors (Matthew 5:44). Needless to say that it would be impossible to pray for someone if you hadn't granted him or her forgiveness.

The words 'Father, forgive them, for they do not know what they are doing', may, of course, have been real words spoken by Jesus. The question I am concerned with here is not so much whether they are authentic, but whether Luke wrote them into his Gospel.

Regarding the book of John[31]

John 9:35 [Alexandrinus]
Jesus heard that they had thrown him out, and when he found him, he said: 'Do you believe in the Son of God?'

John 9:35 [Sinaiticus, Vaticanus, Bezae, P66, P75]
Jesus heard that they had thrown him out, and when he found him, he said: 'Do you believe in the Son of Man?'[32]

Jesus certainly did refer to himself as the Son of Man elsewhere in John's Gospel (John 1:51; 3:13 and 14; 5:27; 6:27, 53, 62; 12:23, 34; 13:31) so the alternate reading of 'Son of Man' is not some novel idea created by a scribe. Similarly Jesus did designate himself as the 'Son of God' in each of the four Gospels.

What is of interest here is whether these changes reflect a systematic attempt by a scribe or scribes to consistently change Jesus' designation. Did the scribes of P66 or P75 deliberately alter Jesus' teaching about who he was by referring to him as the Son of Man instead of the Son of God? I discovered that there is no evidence for such actions. The scribes of Vaticanus, Sinaiticus, D, P66 and P75 that referred to the

---

31 PW Comfort, p. 118.
32 PW Comfort, pp. 101, 206.

'Son of Man' in John 9:35, also used the expression 'Son of God' elsewhere in John's Gospel.[33]

The above list of variations found in the Gospels can be regarded as inconsequential. Yet textual critics like Dr Comfort regard them all as *significant*. The question arises though, 'significant for what?'[34] Obviously what is significant to a textual critic is not necessarily significant to someone trying to establish what Jesus actually taught. In trying to find the reason for this ambiguity, I note that scholars such as Dr Comfort regard as significant any variant that 'substantially changes the meaning of the text; this usually excludes variations of word order and spelling ...'[35] However, earlier in his book Dr Comfort stated:

> *No matter what differences in wording may have existed in these early MSS [manuscripts] ... the early Christians who had these MSS read the same basic message about the Lord Jesus Christ, the Son of God, who died on the cross for the remission of sins and rose again to give life to all who believe in him.*[36]

So although academics might rightly regard all of the variations listed above as ones that *substantially* change the text, that does not mean that they *substantially* alter the New Testament doctrines of who Jesus is, why and how he died, and what people must do to get right with God. Even Jesus' teachings on how we should conduct our daily lives appear to have remained largely intact.

---

33 Vaticanus has Jesus as the Son of God in John 1:34. Sinaiticus, D, P66 and P75 use the phrase in John 5:25. Sourced from www.bibletranslation.ws/trans/johnwgrk.pdf, accessed 19/06/2011 and based on the presence of footnote. Alexandrinus also uses the phrase 'Son of God'.
34 EJ Epp, 'Toward the clarification of the term "textual variant"', p. 48.
35 PW Comfort, pp. 24–5. The sentence finished with 'grammatical aberrations, and variant readings supported only by a few and/or very late MSS [manuscripts]'.
36 PW Comfort, p. xvii.

Conclusion

This investigation has focused on the accuracy of copying in dozens of manuscripts dated from before 400 AD.[37] It reveals that these manuscripts exhibit a high degree of similarity; the scribes who wrote them clearly made very accurate copies of their master manuscripts. The changes they made during the copying process were sometimes deliberate, but such changes have practically no impact on the teachings of the New Testament. This is a similar finding to that of the previous chapter, which looked at only a few ancient manuscripts. What remains to consider are three prominent variations between the ancient copies of the Greek New Testament. What I was keen to discern was what impact these variations could have on Christian teaching, particularly on those teachings that have impacts on the way Christians should conduct their lives.

---

37 Refer to chapter 7 'Ancient copies of the New Testament', in particular the section titled 'Ancient partial copies' on p. 140.

10

Prominent variations and their impacts on Christian living

While the previous chapter looked at several minor variations between the ancient manuscripts of the Greek New Testament, this chapter will examine in detail three prominent variations. They are prominent because one involves the ever-present unfortunate reality of divorce, while the remaining two involve a significant number of words.

A variation impacting Christians considering marriage after divorce

This passage from Matthew's Gospel concerns Jesus' teachings about divorce. The immediate context is Jesus' vivid portrayal of marriage. He states in Matthew 19:4–6 that God designed people such that a man and a woman become 'one flesh' when they are married: 'So they are no longer two, but one flesh. Therefore what God has joined together, let no one separate' (Matthew 19:6). Clearly Jesus is conveying that God considers marriage as the creation of a new single entity. After declaring this, Jesus responds to a question about divorce. Codex Sinaiticus[1] records this in Matthew 19:9 using the following words:

> *I tell you that anyone who divorces his wife, except for marital unfaithfulness, and marries another woman commits adultery.*

---

1 You can view the actual verse in Codex Sinaiticus by visiting www.codexsinaiticus.org/en/manuscript.aspx?book=33&chapter=19&lid=en&side=r& verse=9&zoomSlider=0, accessed 25/01/2013.

Surprisingly, the scribe who wrote Matthew 19:9 in Codex Vaticanus[2] recorded it this way:

> *I tell you who divorces his wife, except on the grounds of marital unfaithfulness, causes her to be an adulterer, and the one who marries a divorced woman commits adultery.*[3]

Looking at these two passages in parallel reveals elements in common, as well as differences. Both codices instruct that there is only one valid reason to seek a divorce, namely adultery. This teaching was particularly important to those who were listening to Jesus in the first century. At that time some religious authorities were teaching that only adultery was a sufficient reason for divorce, whilst others were saying that adultery and any other reason for disgruntlement were adequate reasons.

Codex Sinaiticus' version teaches that if a man divorces his wife without the legitimate grounds of adultery, and then remarries, he would be committing adultery with the new wife. The implication is that as the husband should never have obtained the divorce in the first instance, the first marriage commitment is still binding in God's eyes. Therefore if the man enters into a second marriage, although this is humanly legal, it is not acknowledged by God and is therefore adulterous.

By contrast, Codex Vaticanus' version does not directly teach anything about the husband remarrying, but does speak about the former wife

---

2   To view the manuscript, visit http://images.csntm.org/Manuscripts/GA_03/GA03_015b.jpg. This has pencilled in verse numbers. Try also http://archive.org/stream/CodexVaticanusbFacSimile/Codex-Vaticanus-NT#page/n25/mode/2up. Both accessed 25/01/2013.

3   DA Hagner, *Word Biblical Commentary*, vol. 33b: Matthew 14–28, Thomas Nelson, Nashville, Tennessee, US 1995, p. 545. See also BM Metzger, *A Textual Commentary on the Greek New Testament: Second Edition: A Companion Volume to the United Bible Societies' Greek New Testament (Fourth Revised Edition)*, 2007, pp. 38–9. Metzger notes that the words 'causes her to be an adulterer' applies when that woman remarries. See also the digital copy of H Heinfetter, *A Literal Translation of the New Testament of our Lord and Saviour Jesus Christ, On Definite Rules of Translation, From the Text of the Vatican Manuscript*, 6th edn, Evan Evans London, 1863, available at http://books.google.com.au/books?id=PYsEAAAAQAAJ&pg=PA9&source=gbs_toc_r&redir_esc=y#v=onepage&q&f=false, accessed 25/01/2013.

remarrying. The emphasis is on how the husband who divorces a faithful wife causes this wife to be an adulterer. No details are offered as to how the man can be regarded as causing her to be an adulterer. One explanation is that a divorced woman in that culture could 'easily find herself trapped in prostitution'[4] in order to survive. Another is that the divorced woman would eventually remarry, but as the first marriage commitment is still recognised by God, she would then be in effect involved in adultery with the new husband. As such this new husband would also then be guilty of adultery. On the other hand, it can be seen by way of implication that the husband who divorces a wife on the legitimate ground of adultery is therefore able to marry again.

Intriguingly, the rendering of the divorce statement given in Codex Vaticanus causes it to become almost a mirror image of Matthew 5:32. Matthew 5:32 is the first record in Matthew's Gospel of Jesus' teaching on divorce. In both Codex Sinaiticus and Codex Vaticanus, Matthew 5:31–2 reads as follows:

> *It has been said, 'Anyone who divorces his wife must give her a certificate of divorce.' But I tell you that anyone who divorces his wife, except for marital unfaithfulness, causes her to become an adulteress [μοιχευθηναι], and anyone who marries the divorced woman commits adultery [μοχαται].*[5]

Considering all of the above, trying to understand what Jesus originally said in Matthew 19:9 creates several possibilities. If Codex Sinaiticus has the correct wording in Matthew 19:9, then perhaps the scribe of Codex Vaticanus deliberately changed the original wording to be similar to that found in Matthew 5:32 so as to harmonise the two sayings. Many scholars favour this view.[6] This is possible as the same scribe wrote both statements, and may well have remembered the words of Matthew 5:32 when writing Matthew 19:9. If this is correct then although the scribe of Codex Vaticanus has made a deliberate

---

4   RH Mounce, *New International Bible Commentary: Matthew*, Hendrickson Publishers, Massachusetts, 1991, p. 181.
5   You can view the actual verses in Codex Sinaiticus by visiting www.codexsinaiticus.org/en/manuscript.aspx?book=33&chapter=5&lid=en&side=r&verse=32&zoomSlider=0, accessed 4/08/12.
6   For example, BM Metzger, pp. 38–9.

change, it does not introduce any new teachings. The scribe has, however, deleted the emphasis on the evilness of the man remarrying if his first wife had been faithful.

Alternatively, if Codex Vaticanus preserves the original words of Matthew 19:9, it is possible that the scribe of Codex Sinaiticus deliberately changed the wording to leave out the emphasis on the morality of the faithful wife remarrying. However, this is extremely unlikely as the scribe who wrote Matthew 19:9 in Codex Sinaiticus also wrote Matthew 5:32.[7] If the scribe wanted to deliberately change the emphasis of Jesus teaching in Matthew 19:9, there is no explanation for why the scribe didn't similarly change the teaching in Matthew 5:32. Unlikely or not, in this scenario, some of the original teaching has been lost from Matthew chapter 19, but none has been lost from Matthew's Gospel, as it is still present in Matthew 5:32.

The other possible explanation for the differences between the codices is that an accidental error occurred by the scribes of both codices. If the original words of Matthew 19:9 were in fact very similar to Matthew 5:32, then perhaps the scribe of Codex Sinaiticus made an error arising from their eye skipping from the end of one line to the end of the next line, leaving out the intervening words. This is conceivable if one line of the Greek text originally ended with the word adulteress (μοιχευθηναι), and the next line ended with the word adultery (μοχαται). The scribe of Codex Vaticanus would also have had to be responsible for changes,[8] as the Greek of Matthew 19:9 reads differently to the Greek of Matthew 5:32. In this third scenario, the scribe of Codex Sinaiticus has accidentally added the emphasis on the evilness of the man remarrying if his first wife had been faithful.

Examination of the two versions of Matthew 19:9, as well as Matthew 5:31–2, reveals a strong common lesson delivered by Jesus. From this foundation, a simple flow of logic produces all the other elements

---

7   DC Parker, *Codex Sinaiticus: The Story of the World's Oldest Bible*, The British Library, London, 2010, pp. 48–51. Scribe A wrote both of these; see chapter 7 for more details.

8   The explanation involving errors by both scribes is derived from J Smelser, *Matthew 19:1–12*, corrected and revised, July 12, 2008, www.diktuon.com/smelser_j/mt19unicode.html, accessed 25/01/2013.

found in these sections of scripture, without any contradictions. This is demonstrated as follows: all these passages record Jesus making it clear how wrong it is for a husband to instigate a divorce unless his wife had been committing adultery. Jesus' message is a strong but brief rejection of the then prevailing attitudes to divorce, whereby a certificate of divorce was important. The custom was that if the husband issued a certificate, the husband was acting correctly. Jesus countered this by saying that the issuing of a certificate did not validate the action of divorce, unless the wife had committed adultery. It logically flows from this that if a man divorces a faithful wife then he has not acted morally, and therefore his divorce is not valid in God's eyes. If that man then remarries he, in effect, commits adultery with his next wife. Matthew 19:9 in Codex Sinaiticus makes this plain.[9] Similarly, another logical consequence of Jesus' basic teaching is that if a woman is divorced despite being faithful, then she is not really divorced in God's eyes, and so she is committing adultery when she remarries, as does her second husband.[10]. This is made plain in Matthew 19:9 in Codex Vaticanus and Mark 5:31–2 in both codices.

Summing up, the variation between the codices describes different but complementary impacts of the issue of remarriage after divorce on grounds other than adultery, as taught by Jesus in Matthew 5:31–2. The Codex Vaticanus describes the impact on the divorced wife while the Codex Sinaiticus describes the impact on the divorcing husband. There is only confusion if the relevant passages are taken in isolation or not looked at in terms of a logical outworking of God's view of marriage as being permanent.

Variations to the ending for Mark's Gospel

I found one other section in the New Testament that has variations that may affect how Christians should live. This concerns quite exotic activities, such as the drinking of poisons and the handling of snakes. It is also of great interest because it is one of only two

---

9   RH Mounce, p. 181. Mounce states this deduction when commenting on Matthew 19:7–10.
10 RH Mounce, p. 47. Mounce states this deduction when commenting on Matthew 5:31–32.

variations in the New Testament that involves a large number of words as a block of text. It is found in the last chapter of Mark's Gospel. This ending has created a lot of intrigue for centuries. All major English translations of the New Testament preface the section that begins in chapter 16, verse 9 with words such as the following: 'The most early manuscripts and other ancient witnesses do not have Mark 16:9–20'.[11]

In brief, the verses in question describe the resurrected Jesus appearing first to Mary Magdalene. Mary then tells various disciples, who do not believe her account of events. Jesus then appears to two of these others, who then relay their encounter to the remaining disciples. Once again the account was not believed. Finally Jesus appears to all 11 disciples at the same time and chastises them for their lack of faith and disbelief towards the others. After this we read:

> *He said to them, 'Go into all the world and preach the good news to all creation. Whoever believes and is baptized will be saved, but whoever does not believe will be condemned. And these signs will accompany those who believe: In my name they will drive out demons; they will speak in new tongues; they will pick up snakes with their hands; and when they drink deadly poison it will not hurt them at all; they will place their hands on sick people, and they will get well.'*
>
> *After the Lord Jesus had spoken to them, he was taken up to heaven and he sat at the right hand of God. Then the disciples went out and preached everywhere, and the Lord worked with them and confirmed his word by the signs that accompanied it. (Mark 16:15–20, NIV 1984)*

The tenacity of the scribes

The ancient copies of the Greek New Testament present a mixed picture. The two extensive copies of the New Testament, Codex Vaticanus and

---

11 *The NIV Study Bible*, Zondervan Bible Publishers, Grand Rapids, Michigan, 1985, p. 1530.

Codex Sinaiticus, do not contain these verses.[12] The longer ending in Mark presented above is found in Codex Alexandrinus (400s AD), Codex Bezae (c. 400 AD) and other manuscripts from this and later time periods. In fact, it is present in 99 per cent of all Greek manuscripts.[13] The manuscript P45, which dates to about 200 AD, is missing all of Mark chapters 13 to 16 due to mutilation, so it is impossible to know whether it contained the longer ending. Many of the manuscripts that contain the longer ending do have an interesting characteristic:

> *A considerable number of manuscripts add Mark 16:9–20 either with critical notations, or with a marginal comment questioning its originality, even as late as the sixteenth century! This is a striking example of what is called tenacity in the New Testament textual tradition ... Any reading that occurred once would continue to be preserved faithfully.*[14]

In other words, when a scribe copied a portion of the New Testament that was regarded as being *possibly* original, it would be tenaciously included rather than deleted. Often the scribe would alert the reader to the dubiousness of the words using marginal notes, but the words would remain nevertheless.

This tenacity becomes even more obvious when the full scope of variations to the end of Mark's Gospel is realised. There is one manuscript dating from around 400 AD, written in Latin, that has a shorter and very different ending to the longer ending. The content simply conveys that the women reported to Peter and his colleagues and then jumps to stating that Jesus sent the disciples east and west to proclaim the message of eternal salvation. Apart from this one manuscript, no other manuscript preserves this as the one and only ending to Mark's Gospel. The situation becomes even more interesting from the 600s AD onwards. From that point 'a whole group'[15] of

---

12 K Aland & B Aland, *The Text of the New Testament: An Introduction to the Critical Editions and to the Theory and Practice of Modern Textual Criticism*, trans. EF Rhodes, William B Eerdmans Publishing Company, Grand Rapids, US, 1989, p. 292. Information on the Greek manuscripts found in this entire paragraph comes from this source.
13 K Aland & B Aland, p. 292.
14 K Aland & B Aland, p. 292–3.
15 K Aland & B Aland, p. 293.

manuscripts preserve both endings! So the scribes diligently preserved both endings for centuries, ensuring that 'Any reading that occurred once would continue to be preserved faithfully'.[16]

The tenacity of scribes to preserve what they have in front of them, and only what is in front of them, is shown by the fact that as late as the 1100s AD, a manuscript can be found that finishes at Mark 16:8, in the same way as Codex Vaticanus and Codex Sinaiticus.[17]

What is puzzling is whether the original author penned any of the words found after Mark 16:8, and how is it that different manuscripts have different endings. At present the available evidence only allows for speculation, of which there has been plenty.[18] Here are a few of the more popular ones:

- Scenario 1: Mark finished a draft of his Gospel at verse 8, which was then copied. At a later date he completed a final edition that finished at verse 20, which was also copied. Mark is therefore the author of verses 9 to 20.

- Scenario 2: The last page of the original Gospel was lost shortly after the Gospel was completed. Unknown individuals then composed verses 9 to 20 as it seemed to them that verse 8 was an unsatisfactory way to finish the Gospel. Therefore Mark did not write any of the words after verse 8.

- Scenario 3: Mark finished his Gospel at verse 20, but due to various factors, the scribes of several manuscripts, such as Codex Sinaiticus and Codex Vaticanus, accidentally left these verses out. In this case, scribes may have played no part, as the loss may have been due to

---

16 K Aland & B Aland, p. 293.
17 K Aland & B Aland, p. 292.
18 In favour of the long ending being from Mark, and with very readable detailed arguments, is J Snapp, *The Authenticity of Mark 16:9–20*, May 16, 2012. A digital copy of this book is available from james.snapp@gmail.com. Obtained from the author on 20/08/12. Also see http://lavistachurchofchrist.org/LVarticles/AuthenticityOfMark16920.html, accessed 19/08/12.
   In favour of verse 8 being the earliest ending is BM Metzger, pp. 102–107. For a variety of viewpoints see DA Black (ed.), *Perspectives on the Ending of Mark: 4 Views*, Broadman & Holman Publishers, Nashville, US, 2008.

fire or other accidental causes destroying the original before it could be copied.

What I am particularly interested is how the teachings of Jesus are affected by this passage being regarded as genuine or not. In other words, if certain scribes did add either the short or long endings, have they added new teachings to the Gospel? Alternatively, if other scribes were responsible for leaving out these various endings from certain manuscripts, have some new teachings been neglected that would alter our view of Jesus or how Christians should live.

Are new teachings found in the short ending?

The short ending, typically placed after verse 8, reads as follows:

> *And they [Mary Magdalene, Mary the mother of James, and Salome] promptly reported all these instructions to Peter and his companions. And after that, Jesus Himself sent out through them from east to west the sacred and imperishable proclamation of eternal salvation. (Mark 16:8, NASB footnoted alternate reading)*

Verse 7 of this same chapter already teaches that these women were to report to Peter, so this short ending only confirms that they did as instructed. Concerning Jesus sending out the disciples, Mark 13:9–10 records Jesus' prophecy that the disciples would go to various nations and preach the Gospel. It is apparent that nothing significantly new is found in the short ending.

Are new teachings found in the long ending?

We will examine these verses by breaking them up into three groups.

Who is saved and who condemned?

> *He said to them, 'Go into all the world and preach the good news to all creation. Whoever believes and is baptized will be saved, but whoever does not believe will be condemned.' (Mark 16:15–16, NIV 1984)*

This passage is teaching that belief and baptism are necessary in order to be saved. As baptism demonstrates to others that you have believed in Jesus, it has a close parallel to a statement found earlier in Mark's Gospel:

> 'Whoever acknowledges me before others, I will also acknowledge before my Father in heaven. But whoever disowns me before others, I will disown before my Father in heaven.' (Matthew 10:32, NIV)

In a similar fashion Matthew 28:19 records Jesus instructing his disciples to make disciples and to baptise them. John 4:2 tells of Jesus' disciples baptising people before Jesus' crucifixion. It is clear that Jesus does expect baptism to be the normal course of action to follow after a person becomes a believer. However, it is also evident that some have no opportunity to be baptised after believing, and yet Jesus still saves them (Luke 23:43, Acts 10:45–7). Taking all of the above into consideration, it is reasonable to conclude that there is nothing new in this portion of the longer ending.

Can all Christians expect to be protected from dangerous activities?

> And these signs will accompany those who believe: In my name they will drive out demons; they will speak in new tongues; they will pick up snakes with their hands; and when they drink deadly poison it will not hurt them at all; they will place their hands on sick people, and they will get well.' (Mark 16:17–18, NIV 1984)

At least one group in the United States have used these verses to encourage snake handling and drinking poison, unfortunately with deadly results.[19] Not only is this act extremely rare, it is not practising what Jesus is teaching. The passage does not teach that all Christians *must* drive out demons, speak in tongues and do deadly acts in order to be saved. It does not even teach that Christians *should* do these various activities. In other words, it contains a description of what will happen, rather than an imperative of what must happen. It simply

---

19   K Barth, 'Snake-handling pastor dies of rattler's bite', *Wired World*, 10 June, 2012 http://karlscrowd.blogspot.com.au/2012/06/snake-handling-pastor-dies-of-rattlers.html, accessed 18/08/12.

states that certain signs will accompany believers. Some of these signs are recorded in the New Testament. In the book of Acts, we read how Paul was accidentally bitten by a poisonous snake and yet lived (Acts 28:3–5). The disciples did cast out demons (Luke 10:17, Acts 19:11–16) and believers did at times speak in tongues (Acts 2:4). It is apparent that whether or not this portion of the long ending is included, no new teachings are evident.

As an aside, apart from Paul's encounter, there is only one other place where Christians encounter snakes. The first is when 72 disciples report back to Jesus about their successful missionary adventure. In particular, they tell of the demons that submitted to the power of Jesus' name. Jesus responds by saying:

> *'I saw Satan fall like lightning from heaven. I have given you authority to trample on snakes and scorpions and to overcome all the power of the enemy; nothing will harm you. However, do not rejoice that the spirits submit to you, but rejoice that your names are written in heaven.' (Luke 10:18–20, NIV)*

As the disciples never spoke about stepping on snakes and scorpions, it is likely that Jesus was referring metaphorically to evil spirits when talking of snakes and scorpions, especially as Jesus equates these venomous creatures to spirits that had been brought under submission.

The New Testament as a whole clearly shows that normal Christians did not go about purposefully seeking out snakes, poisons and demons. Jesus even clearly teaches that it is wrong to purposefully engage in deadly acts. In Luke 4:5–7 we read of Satan telling Jesus that if he (Jesus) really is the Son of God he would jump off a tall height. Jesus rejected this proposal by saying it was against the clear teaching of God to purposefully engage in a deadly act in order to test God.

Jesus sits at the right hand of God

> *After the Lord Jesus had spoken to them, he was taken up to heaven and he sat at the right hand of God. Then the disciples went out and preached everywhere, and the Lord worked with them and confirmed his word by the signs that accompanied it. (Mark 16:19–20, NIV 1984)*

One other teaching found in the long ending of Mark is that after Jesus was taken up to heaven for the last time, he sat at the right hand of God. This is spoken of in Mark 14:62, as well as in Matthew 26:64 and Luke 22:69, so is certainly not new.

From the above three points regarding the ending of Mark's Gospel, it can be seen that whether the alternate endings are regarded as authentic or not, no new teaching is gained or lost. At this point it seems that of all the variations found in the various New Testament manuscripts, only those concerning remarriage would appear to have an effect on how people should live out their lives if they wished to follow Jesus. Yet there is one more variation that warrants attention. Not so much because its presence may affect how Christians should behave, but because it involves a large number of words. Together with the different endings for Mark's Gospel, it is the only other part of the New Testament that has a variation involving several sentences. Looking closely at this variation reveals that it is not always easy to know whether one manuscript has added words or another has deleted them.

Another variation involving a large number of words: Jesus and the woman caught in adultery

In John 7:53 to 8:11 there is an account of Jesus being presented with a woman caught in adultery. Those who brought her were Pharisees, a group that were part of the religious hierarchy of Judaism. They hoped to ensnare Jesus with their questioning about the woman. Jesus' first response to their question was to stoop and write on the ground:

> *But when they persisted in asking Him, He straightened up, and said to them, 'He who is without sin among you, let him be the first to throw a stone at her.' Again He stooped down and wrote on the ground. When they heard it, they began to go out one by one, beginning with the older ones, and He was left alone, and the woman, where she was, in the center of the court. Straightening up, Jesus said to her, 'Woman, where are they? Did no one condemn you?' She said, 'No one, Lord.' And Jesus said, 'I do not condemn you, either. Go. From now on sin no more.' (John 8:7–11, NASB)*

It seems highly unlikely that this account was in the original autograph, as it is absent from a large number of Greek manuscripts containing the Gospel of John,[20] including: P66, P75, Codex Sinaiticus, Codex Vaticanus, Codex Washingtonianus (400s AD), and Codex Borgianus (400s AD).[21] The passage is also absent from many other languages' translations made from the ancient Greek manuscripts. For example, it is not found in the Coptic language manuscripts that represent dialects such as Sahidic and sub-Achmimic. The earliest Greek New Testament copy to include it is Codex Bezae, dated to around 400 AD. The next codex to include it, Codex Fuldensis, is dated to 546 AD. Many of the scribes who did include the incident in their copies have the passage marked in such a way to indicate 'they were aware that it lacked satisfactory credentials'.[22]

However, even though many ancient Greek manuscripts have survived over the centuries, no doubt many hundreds of others have perished. So is it possible that many of these lost manuscripts did have this passage about the adulterous woman? There is one way to determine whether this passage was incorporated into any of these lost documents, namely by reading the large number of documents composed by early Christian leaders. One of these, Jerome (c. 347–420 AD), wrote the following:

> ... in the Gospel according to John in many manuscripts, both Greek and Latin, is found the story of the adulterous woman who was accused before the Lord.[23]

Due to these and other reasons, there is some doubt, and has been for many centuries, about whether this famous passage was part of the original autograph written by John. What I find particularly relevant is how the ancient scribes have dealt with this question. It seems clear that when making copies of the New Testament, at least some scribes were more inclined to leave out a passage that was doubtful rather

---

20 BM Metzger, pp. 187–8. Metzger notes that it is 'highly probable' that the account is also absent from Codex Alexandrinus (p. 187).
21 The dates for these two manuscripts are based on K Aland & B Aland, p. 113.
22 BM Metzger, pp. 189. See also footnote 1 on p. 188.
23 Jerome, *The Gospel of John: Part of The Holy Bible,* trans. DR Palmer, December 2010 edn, p. 51 citing Jerome PL 23:553, which most likely refers to Migne, Patrologiae Cursus Completus, Series Latina, vol. 23, col. 579.

than include it. Others, however, acted in the opposite manner but still made it transparent to the reader that doubt did exist.

Similarly, at least some of the scribes that did not include it have marked the text to show that there were alternate readings at this point. Even today, English translations of the Bible have indicated with footnotes or other similar devices that 'John 7:53 – 8:11 is not found in most of the old mss [i.e. manuscripts]'.[24]

An important aspect related to this short narrative is whether its presence or absence affects the way Christians are instructed to live. As Jesus teaches that adultery is sinful both in this passage and elsewhere in the New Testament (Matthew 15:19, Mark 7:22, Luke 18:20), how Christians should live is not affected by its inclusion or exclusion. There are other issues that also would remain unchanged irrespective of whether the account is included in the Gospels: Jesus indicates that the Pharisees were sinful people both in this passage and elsewhere (Matthew 12:24–34, 15:1–9); Jesus teaches that he has not come to condemn others both in this passage and elsewhere (John 12:47); and both this passage and elsewhere (Matthew 9:34, Luke 11:53–4, John 7:32) teach that the Pharisees detested Jesus and would barrage him with questions trying to trap him. The Gospels' message about Jesus remains quite the same whether the event is included or excluded.

Conclusion

It seems that there is one variation that may have some effect on how Christians should behave in a particular situation, namely when facing divorce and remarriage, although reading through all of Jesus' teachings on the subject should resolve that issue. The existence of the other two variations does not result in uncertainty about what Christians should believe or how they should live. It is evident at this stage of research that a fair-minded and scholarly appraisal of variations in the New Testament copies can discern which variants represent the words of the original texts. However, what if scholarly experts have been mistaken in deciding which copies are faithful representatives of the autographs?

---

24 *New American Standard Bible: Text Edition*, Thomas Nelson Publishers, Nashville, US, 1977, p. 744.

11

Boundaries of divergence between ancient manuscripts and an English New Testament

Having looked at the differences between the ancient manuscripts and discovering that these differences, whether minor or significant, caused no changes to the teachings that explain how a Christian ought to live, I now considered this question: Imagine if, by some great stretch of the imagination, many of the world's experts were incorrectly labelling variations in one ancient manuscript as errors, and instead these errors actually contained the correct original wording. How different would the Christian message be? For example, the Codex Bezae is often considered the 'most controversial' of the ancient manuscripts because it is often quite different to the other manuscripts. But what if Codex Bezae was really the most accurate of the manuscripts and the others contained the errors? If it turned out that the Christian message was still quite similar regardless of whether or not the variations were considered to be errors, then the findings would carry significant implications. That is, that the Christian message found in modern English versions can be confidently considered as presenting the core teachings of the original Greek New Testament.

Comparing the Codex Vaticanus and the Codex Bezae

My investigation benefited greatly from an excellent detailed comparison between Codex Vaticanus, belonging to the Alexandrian text type, and Codex Bezae from the Western text type.[1] This comparison, by Emeritus Professor Rius-Camps and Dr Read-Heimerdinger, includes an English translation of the New Testament book of Acts based on the two codices. These two codices certainly differ significantly from each other, which made them ideal. A basic statistical approach made the extent of these differences very apparent. The following statistics[2] are based on comparing the surviving portion of Codex Bezae with the corresponding passages in Codex Vaticanus:

- Codex Bezae is 6.6% longer than Codex Vaticanus.

- There are 1448 words present in Codex Bezae which are not found in Codex Vaticanus.

- There are 579 words absent in Codex Bezae that are present in Codex Vaticanus.

Having chosen two different text types, the next step was to find a way to compare identical New Testament passages found in each ancient Greek codex. A straightforward way to visualise any potential differences between them is to align the words from selected portions of the New Testament into parallel lines of text. To make this comparison meaningful for as many people as possible, English translations of the two codices are used. A third line of text is then added to the two parallel lines, this being from the New American Standard Bible. Like many modern English versions, it is derived from an enormous pool of ancient Greek manuscripts, but it also has the advantage of translating the Greek manuscripts using a method called formal equivalence. The result is:

> *that there is a grammatical formal equivalence: if the Greek has a participle, the English has a participle; if the Greek has a*

---

1   J Rius-Camps & J Read-Heimerdinger, *The Message of Acts in Codex Bezae: A Comparison with the Alexandrian Tradition, vol. 1: Acts 1.1–5.42: Jerusalem*, T & T Clark International, New York, 2004. Codex Bezae refers to D05, and Codex Vaticanus B03.

2   J Rius-Camps & J Read-Heimerdinger, p. 15.

conjunction, the English has a conjunction; and if the Greek has ten words, the English tries to have ten words.[3]

My process resulted in sets of three parallel lines of text for any given portion of the New Testament being studied. The first line in each set is from Codex Bezae,[4] the second (italicised) is from the Codex Vaticanus,[5] and the third is from the New American Standard Bible. Using the New Testament book of Acts, the first part of verse 22 in chapter 2 looks like this:

(2:22)　Men of Israel, hear these words: Jesus the Nazorene,
(2:22)　Men of Israel, listen to these words: Jesus the Nazorene,
(2:22)　'Men of Israel, listen to these words: Jesus the Nazarene,

The next task is to choose which portions of the New Testament to compare. The requirement for this investigation is that the chosen New Testament passages must contain at least some of the main teachings of Christianity. But how to decide what are the main teachings of Christianity? A study of doctrinal statements from some of the major denominations reveals a common group of foundational Christian teachings based on passages from the New Testament.[6] I have selected a few of the core doctrines, which, fortuitously can all be found in the first few chapters of the book of Acts.

The following pages present groups of verses from Acts that teach these doctrines, with the verses being laid out in sets of three lines as described earlier. At the beginning of each group is a listed summary of the doctrines being taught, followed by background information.

3　WD Mounce, *Greek for the Rest of Us: Mastering Bible Study Without Mastering Biblical Languages*, Zondervan, Grand Rapids, Michigan, US, 2003, p. 24. The other method of translating aims to reproduce the same meaning as in the Greek texts, but will use English grammatical forms that do not necessarily reflect that of the Greek.
4　J Rius-Camps & J Read-Heimerdinger, pp. 47–246.
5　J Rius-Camps & J Read-Heimerdinger, pp. 47–246.
6　Refer to appendix 1 at the end of this chapter, titled 'Foundational teachings of mainstream Christianity'.

Comparing verses on Jesus, the crucifixion and forgiveness

Jesus is Lord and Christ.	Acts 2:16–21, 36–8
Jesus was crucified.	Acts 2:36
The crucifixion resulted in Jesus' death.	Acts 2:22–3
God had planned that Jesus would be crucified.	Acts 2:22–3
Jesus died so that people can be forgiven.	Acts 2:38
After conversion, believers receive the Holy Spirit.	Acts 2:38

This group of verses convey some of the words of a speech delivered by the disciple Peter to a crowd in Jerusalem. Peter quotes from a book in the Hebrew scriptures authored by the prophet Joel.

(2:16) Rather this is what was spoken through the prophet:
(2:16) Rather this is what was spoken through the prophet Joel:
(2:16) but this is what was spoken of through the prophet Joel:

(2:17) 'It shall be in the last days, says the Lord,
(2:17) 'And it shall be after that, says God,
(2:17) 'And it shall be in the last days,' God says,

> I will pour out from my spirit onto all flesh ...
> *I will pour out from my spirit onto all flesh ...*
> 'That I will pour forth of My Spirit on all mankind ...

(2:19) and I will give wonders in heaven above and signs on earth below;
(2:19) And I will give wonders in heaven above and signs on earth below,
(2:19) 'And I will grant wonders in the sky above and signs on the earth below,

> [Codex Bezae is blank at this point]
> *blood and fire and clouds of smoke;*
> Blood, and fire, and vapor of smoke.

(2:20)   the sun turns into darkness and the moon into blood
(2:20)   the sun shall be turned into darkness and the moon into blood
(2:20)   'The sun will be turned into darkness and the moon into blood,

    before the great day of the Lord comes
    before the great and glorious day of the Lord comes
    Before the great and glorious day of the Lord shall come.

(2:21)   and it shall be that anyone who calls on the
(2:21)   and it will be that everyone that calls on the
(2:21)   'And it shall be that everyone who calls on the

    name of the Lord shall be rescued.'
    name of the Lord will be rescued.'
    name of the Lord will be saved.'

(2:22)   Men of Israel, hear these words: Jesus the Nazorene,
(2:22)   Men of Israel, listen to these words: Jesus the Nazorene,
(2:22)   'Men of Israel, listen to these words: Jesus the Nazarene,

    a man from God, proved among us by powerful deeds
    a man attested among you by God with powerful deeds
    a man attested to you by God with miracles

    and wonders and signs, all of which God did through him
    and wonders and signs that God did through him
    and wonders and signs which God performed through Him

    in the midst of you, just as you know.
    In the midst of you, just as you know.
    in your midst, just as you yourselves know —

(2:23)   this man who was given up by the deliberate plan and
(2:23)   this man who was given up in line with the deliberate plan and
(2:23)   this Man, delivered over by the predetermined plan and

    foreknowledge of God you held in your power
    foreknowledge of God,
    foreknowledge of God,

through the hands of men outside the law and you nailed him and killed him.
> *through the hands of men outside the law you nailed and killed him.*

you nailed to a cross by the hands of godless men and put Him to death.

(2:36) Accordingly, let all the house of Israel know with certainty
(2:36) Accordingly, let all the house of Israel know with certainty
(2:36) Therefore let all the house of Israel know for certain

that God appointed as both Lord and Messiah this Jesus whom you crucified.'
> *that God appointed him both Lord and Messiah, this Jesus whom you crucified.'*

that God has made Him both Lord and Christ — this Jesus whom you crucified.'

(2:37) Then all of those who had come together and had listened
(2:37) When they heard they
(2:37) Now when they heard this,

were cut to the heart, and some of them said to Peter and the apostles,
> *were cut to the heart, and said to Peter and the rest of the apostles,*

they were pierced to the heart, and said to Peter and the rest of the apostles,

'So what shall we do, brethren; show us.'
> *'What are we to do, brethren?'*

'Brethren, what shall we do?'

(2:38) Peter said to them, 'Repent and be baptized, each one of you
(2:38) Peter said to them, 'Repent and be baptized, each one of you
(2:38) Peter said to them, 'Repent, and each of you be baptized

in the name of the Lord Jesus, the Messiah, for the forgiveness of sins
> *upon the name of Jesus, the Messiah, for the forgiveness of your sins*

in the name of Jesus Christ for the forgiveness of your sins;

and you will receive the gift of the Holy Spirit;
and you will receive the gift of the Holy Spirit;
and you will receive the gift of the Holy Spirit.

Comparing verses on the resurrected Jesus

Jesus was resurrected.   Acts 1:3–4, 2:32

The resurrected Jesus went up to heaven.   Acts 1:9–10, 2:33

The resurrected Jesus will return to earth.   Acts 1:11

In this group of verses, the writer of Acts, namely Luke, is addressing his correspondence to a person called Theophilus. Luke writes of how the resurrected Jesus, referred to as 'he', spent 40 days with his disciples before going to heaven. (The 'first book' referred to is the Gospel of Luke.)

(1:1)   In the first book, O Theophilus, I dealt with all the things that Jesus did
(1:1)   *In the first book, O Theophilus, I dealt with all the things that Jesus did*
(1:1)   The first account I composed, Theophilus, about all that Jesus began

    and taught from the beginning
      and taught from the beginning
    to do and teach,

(1:2)   up to the day he was taken up, having given instructions to the apostles
(1:2)   *up to the day when, having given instructions to the apostles*
(1:2)   until the day when He was taken up to heaven, after He had by the

    whom he had chosen through the Holy Spirit
      whom he had chosen through the Holy Spirit, he was taken up.
Holy Spirit given orders to the apostles whom He had chosen.

and to whom he had ordered to preach the gospel.
[Codex Vaticanus is blank at this point.]
[NASB is blank at this point.]

(1:3)   It was to them that he presented himself as alive after his suffering,
(1:3)   It was to them that he presented himself as alive after his suffering,
(1:3)   To these He also presented Himself alive after His suffering,

giving many proofs, for a period of forty days during which he
giving many proofs, over forty days, when he
by many convincing proofs, appearing to them over a period of forty

appeared to them and told them things about the kingdom of God.
appeared to them and told them things about the kingdom of God.
days and speaking of the things concerning the kingdom of God.

(1:4)   While he was sharing a meal with them, he ordered them
(1:4)   While he was sharing a meal, he ordered them
(1:4)   Gathering[7] them together, He commanded them

not to leave Hierosoluma but, on the contrary, but to wait
not to go away from Hierosoluma but, on the contrary, to wait
not to leave Jerusalem, but to wait

for the promise of the Father ...
for the promise of the Father ...
for what the Father had promised ...

(1:9)   And when he had said this,
(1:9)   And when he had said this, as they were watching
(1:9)   And after He had said these things,

a cloud took him up and he was lifted away
he was lifted up and a cloud took him up

---

7   A footnote in the NASB provides the alternatives to 'gathering' as to 'eat with' or 'lodge with'.

He was lifted up while they were looking on, and a cloud received Him

from their sight.
from their sight.
out of their sight.

(1:10) While they were staring into the sky as he was going,
(1:10) While they were staring into the sky, watching him as he was going
(1:10) And as they were gazing intently into the sky while He was going,

behold! two men dressed in white had come to stand beside them.
behold! two men dressed in white had come to stand beside them.
behold, two men in white clothing stood beside them.

(1:11) Finally, they spoke: 'Men from Galilee why are you standing gazing
(1:11) Finally, they spoke: 'Men from Galilee why are you standing looking
(1:11) They also said, 'Men of Galilee, why do you stand looking

into the sky? Jesus himself, who has been taken up from you will come in
into the sky? Jesus himself, who has been taken up from you into the sky,
into the sky? This Jesus, who has been taken up from you into heaven,

just the same way that you saw him going into the sky.'
will come in just the same way as you saw him going into the sky.'
will come in just the same way as you have watched Him go into heaven.'

(2:32) Accordingly, God resurrected this man, Jesus of which we are all witnesses.
(2:32) God resurrected this man Jesus, of which we are all witnesses.
(2:32) This Jesus God raised up again, to which we are all witnesses.

(2:33) Consequently, having been exalted to the right hand of God
(2:33) Consequently, having been exalted to the right hand of God,
(2:33) Therefore having been exalted to the right hand of God,

> and having received the promise of the Holy Spirit from his Father,
> > *and what is more, having received the promise of the Holy Spirit from his Father,*
> and having received from the Father the promise of the Holy Spirit,

> he poured out for you what you both see and hear.
> > *he poured out for you what you both see and hear.*
> He has poured forth this which you both see and hear.

Comparing verses on doctrines relating to who Jesus is and his uniqueness

Jesus is the creator of life.   Acts 3:15

Jesus is God.[8]   Acts 4:12

Only through Jesus can people be rescued.   Acts 4:12

This group of verses are again portions of speeches given by Peter to people in Jerusalem. The first speech (3:15) is addressed to a crowd; the second (4:10–12) to a Jewish religious council. As Peter rebukes the council, he quotes an Old Testament verse about a rejected foundational stone (a building's cornerstone). Peter states that Jesus is this stone, and the council's rejection of Jesus is bringing to pass what the Old Testament verse spoke about.

(3:15) And instead, you killed the author of life whom God
(3:15) And instead, you killed the author of life whom God
(3:15) but put to death the Prince[9] of life, the one whom God

---

8   Refer to appendix 2 'Jesus considered as God, as taught in Acts chapters 2 to 4' at the end of this chapter.
9   A footnote in the NASB provides the alternative to *Prince* as *Author*.

> raised from the dead, to which we are all witnesses.
> *raised from the dead, to which we are witnesses.*
> raised from the dead, (a fact) to which we are witnesses.

(4:10) let it be known to you and all the people of Israel
(4:10) let it be known to you and all the people of Israel
(4:10) let it be known to all of you and to all the people of Israel,

> that by the name of Jesus Christ the Nazorene,
> *that by the name of Jesus Christ the Nazorene,*
> that by the name of Jesus Christ the Nazarene,

> whom you crucified and God raised from the dead, by this name
> *whom you crucified and whom God raised from the dead, by this name*
> whom you crucified, whom God raised from the dead — by this name

> this man is standing before you whole
> *this man is standing before you whole.*
> this man stands here before you in good health.

(4:11) (it is the stone that was treated with contempt by you, the builders,
(4:11) (It is he the stone that was treated with contempt by you, the builders,
(4:11) 'He is the stone which was rejected' by you, 'the builders',

> but that has become the cornerstone),
> *but that has become the cornerstone.)*
> but 'which became the chief corner' stone.

(4:12) and it is by none other for there is no other kind of name
(4:12) And salvation is in no-one else, since neither is there any other name
(4:12) And there is salvation in no one else; for there is no other name

> under heaven that has been given to men by which we must be saved.
> *under heaven given among men by which you must be saved.*

under heaven that has been given among men by which we must be saved.'

Conclusion

Based on comparing the content of each verse shown above, it is apparent that there are no differences between the three texts that impact upon main Christian teachings, which shows that even if variations were incorrectly considered as errors these teachings would not be altered if one text type were chosen over the other. This demonstrates the ability of scribes to make accurate copies of the New Testament. This capability is particularly noteworthy when it is remembered that the above comparison was between two widely different text types, and between versions that are separated in time by over 1700 years.

This research reinforces the conclusions arrived at in the previous chapters: readers of the New Testament can be confident that the words in front of them are an accurate reflection of the words penned by the original authors about 2000 years ago.

Appendix 1
Foundational teachings of mainstream Christianity

The foundational teachings I have selected can be found in doctrinal statements made hundreds of years ago, although each set of doctrines may not directly contain all of the foundational teachings. These doctrinal creeds include:

- the Baptist Confession of Faith from 1689[10]

- the Westminster Confession of Faith from 1647,[11] used by the Anglican and Presbyterian denominations

---

10 1689 Baptist Confession of Faith, rewritten in modern English by Andrew Kerkham, rev. edn, 2001, www.creeds.net/baptists/1689/kerkham/1689.htm, accessed 26/01/2013.
11 A full copy of the Westminster Confession of Faith from 1647 can be found at The Presbyterian Church of Canada website, http://presbyterian.ca/, accessed 14/07/2012.

- the Augsburg Confession of Faith (Lutheran) from 1530[12]
- the Nicene Creed[13] from 325 AD.

Appendix 2
Jesus considered as God, as taught in Acts chapters 2 to 4

To see how the book of Acts clearly teaches that Jesus is God it is first necessary to look at the book of Joel from which it quotes. Joel is a book found in the Old Testament, and Acts 2:17–21 is a speech given by the disciple Peter that directly quotes Joel 2:28–32. Joel 2:32 states:

> *And everyone who calls on the name of the LORD [YHWH] will be saved ...*

YHWH is one of the Hebrew language words for God used in the Old Testament.[14] A famous passage illustrating this is found in Isaiah 44:6.

> *This is what the LORD [YHWH] says – Israel's King and Redeemer, the LORD Almighty: I am the first and I am the last; apart from me there is no God.*

The book of Acts records Peter's quote from Joel using the Greek word *kyrios* instead of the Hebrew word YHWH.[15] So it looks like this:

> *'And it shall be that everyone who calls on the name of the Lord [kyrios] will be saved.' (Acts 2:21, NASB)*

---

12 A full copy of the Augsburg Confession can be found at The Book of Concord website, http://bookofconcord.org/augsburgconfession.php, accessed 16/12/12.

13 A full copy of the Nicene Creed can be found at the Centre for Reformed Theology and Apologetics, www.reformed.org/documents/index.html?mainframe=http://www.reformed.org/documents/nicene.html, accessed 16/12/12.

14 Many English language translations of the Old Testament use LORD instead of YHWH.

15 WD Mounce, *Interlinear for the Rest of us: The Reverse Interlinear for New Testament Word Studies*, Zondervan, Grand Rapids, Michigan, US, 2006, p. 351.

In the same speech, Peter then takes the words of Joel 2:32 as quoted a few sentences earlier in the Greek, which refer to God as kyrios,[16] and applies them to Jesus:

> *'Therefore let all the house of Israel know for certain that God has made Him both Lord [kyrios] and Christ — this Jesus whom you crucified.' (Acts 2:36, NASB)*

In a different speech in the same city, Peter even takes the action of 'saving' carried out by YHWH in Joel 2:32 and applies it to Jesus:

> *And there is salvation in no one else; for there is no other name under heaven that has been given among men by which we must be saved. (Acts 4:12, NASB)*

The first speech of Peter's provides a second indication that Peter was deliberately emphasising that Jesus is God. When Peter starts his quote from Joel, he actually adds the words 'God says' (or 'says the Lord' in the case of Codex Bezae) to the original quote in Joel. This results in Acts 2:17 (NASB) stating that:

> *'And it shall be in the last days,' God says, 'That I will pour forth of My Spirit on all mankind ...*

In that same speech, Peter then takes the action of 'pouring' carried out by YHWH in Joel 2:32, and applies it to Jesus:

> *This Jesus God raised up again, to which we are all witnesses. Therefore having been exalted to the right hand of God, and having received from the Father the promise of the Holy Spirit, He [Jesus] has poured forth this which you both see and hear. (Acts 2:32–3, NASB)*

Another New Testament writer, Paul, gives a similar presentation of Jesus as God in the book of Romans, where he states:

> *That if you confess with your mouth, 'Jesus is Lord [kyrios],' and believe in your heart that God raised him from the dead, you will be saved ... for, 'Everyone who calls on the name of the Lord [kyrios] will be saved.' (Romans 10:9–13, NIV 1984)*

---

16 WD Mounce, p. 352.

Part IV
Evidence from early Christian and non-Christian witnesses

Part IV explores two questions: Firstly, if our earliest copies of significantly large portions of the New Testament are dated from 200 AD onwards, what can we know about the content of the New Testament before this time? Secondly, what evidence is there that the New Testament writers did in fact record the truth about Jesus?

Chapter 12 looks at the teachings of the Christian leader Polycarp in a letter dated to around 110 AD and compares these teachings to those found in the books of the New Testament. This reinforces the claim that at least parts of the New Testament have not been changed. This chapter also attempts to uncover whether two types of bias, excessive disdain and exaggerated glorification, are evident in the New Testament.

Finally, chapter 12 then introduces a series of writings composed by various non-Christians written before 200 AD. The bias of these men was not towards Jesus, although they still would have had a bias of some sort. Their writings make it possible to compare their image of Jesus and the Christians with the picture painted in the New Testament. Two of these writers, Tacitus and Thallus, are looked at briefly.

The remaining chapters delve into various non-Christian authors — Lucian (chapters 13 and 14), Pliny (chapter 15) and Josephus (chapters 16 and 17).

12

Christian beliefs as revealed by Christian and non-Christian writers prior to 200 AD

The evidence from many of the previous chapters strongly indicates that Jesus' disciples could have faithfully recorded his teachings and that their writings then became the basis for the New Testament Gospels. Previous chapters also established that the content of the New Testament has been well preserved over the 18 centuries that have passed since the writing of the earliest partial copies of the New Testament still in existence today. But two questions remain:

1. Firstly, if our earliest copies of significantly large portions of the New Testament are dated from 200 AD onwards, what can we know about the content of the New Testament before this time?

2. Secondly, what evidence is there that the New Testament writers did in fact record the truth about Jesus?

Was the pre-200 AD New Testament the same as today's?

I think it is very reasonable to assume that because the New Testament was copied accurately after 200 AD for many hundreds of years, then it most likely was copied accurately over the 150 years or so before 200 AD. But I wanted to discover if there were any means of being more certain that the teachings of the New Testament before 200 AD were identical to those afterwards.

I discovered that one way of peering into the core teachings of Christianity in the first 200 years was to search through the letters of various Christian leaders from that time period. Surprisingly, copies of several of their letters to various Christian communities have survived and been published. Because these letters provide instructions on following Jesus, they also inform us about the beliefs of Christian leaders during the first 200 years after Christ. If their knowledge about Jesus and his teachings has parallels with the New Testament, then this reinforces the claim that at least these parts of the New Testament have not been changed.

As I have only a limited amount of space in this book, I have selected only one Christian leader, namely Polycarp, who wrote a letter to the Christians in the town of Philippi in about 110 AD. Polycarp's letter is ideal because it clearly states that it was written after Paul had preached in the city.[1] The letter also implies that all the apostles had died.[2] So if there are any parallels between this letter and the words of the New Testament, it must be because Polycarp had sourced them from the New Testament and not the other way round. Because Polycarp was also a disciple of John, one of Jesus' disciples, then Polycarp could be expected to have good knowledge of the Gospels and perhaps even other sayings and actions of Jesus. (John wrote in his Gospel — John 20:30 and 21:25 — that he hadn't been able to write down all of Jesus' actions.)

In order to compare the beliefs of Polycarp with those found in the New Testament, I have reproduced parts of Polycarp's letter and then placed below it corresponding passages from the New Testament. I have also tried to arrange the comparisons into topics.

God regards the poor and those persecuted for righteousness as blessed.

> *Blessed are the poor, and those that are persecuted for righteousness' sake, for theirs is the kingdom of God.*[3]

---

1 *The Epistle of Polycarp to the Philippians*, trans. A Roberts & J Donaldson, ch. 3, digital copy available at www.earlychristianwritings.com/text/polycarp-roberts.html, accessed 10/06/2013.
2 *The Epistle of Polycarp to the Philippians*, ch. 6.
3 *The Epistle of Polycarp to the Philippians*, ch. 2.

[Jesus said] 'Blessed are the poor in spirit, for theirs is the kingdom of heaven ... Blessed are those who are persecuted because of righteousness, for theirs is the kingdom of heaven.' (Matthew 5:3,10)

Praying and avoiding temptation is important as God is all-seeing.

... 'watching unto prayer,' and persevering in fasting; beseeching in our supplications the all-seeing God 'not to lead us into temptation,' as the Lord has said: 'The spirit truly is willing, but the flesh is weak.'[4]

[Jesus said] 'Watch and pray so that you will not fall into temptation. The spirit is willing, but the flesh is weak.' (Matthew 26:41)

'When you fast, do not look somber as the hypocrites do, for they disfigure their faces to show others they are fasting ... But when you fast, put oil on your head and wash your face, so that it will not be obvious to others that you are fasting, but only to your Father, who is unseen; and your Father, who sees what is done in secret, will reward you.' (Matthew 6:16–18)

Christians should pray for their secular rulers and those who hate Christians and those who are enemies of belief in the work of Jesus' crucifixion.

Pray for all the saints. Pray also for kings, and potentates, and princes, and for those that persecute and hate you, and for the enemies of the cross, that your fruit may be manifest to all, and that ye may be perfect in Him.[5]

[Jesus said] 'But I tell you, love your enemies and pray for those who persecute you ...' (Matthew 5:44)

'Bless those who persecute you; bless and do not curse.' (Romans 12:14)

---

4   The Epistle of Polycarp to the Philippians, ch. 7.
5   The Epistle of Polycarp to the Philippians, ch. 12.

Everyone will be asked to give an account of their life when they die.

... 'we must all appear at the judgment-seat of Christ, and must every one give an account of himself.'[6]

... For we will all stand before God's judgment seat ... So then, each of us will give an account of ourselves to God. (Romans 14:10–12)

Remind the people to be subject to rulers and authorities, to be obedient, to be ready to do whatever is good, to slander no one, to be peaceable and considerate, and always to be gentle toward everyone. (Titus 3:1–2)

Christians are to forgive others.

... but being mindful of what the Lord said in His teaching: 'Judge not, that ye be not judged; forgive, and it shall be forgiven unto you; be merciful, that ye may obtain mercy; with what measure ye mete, it shall be measured to you again ...'[7]

'Do not judge, and you will not be judged. Do not condemn, and you will not be condemned. Forgive, and you will be forgiven. Give, and it will be given to you. A good measure, pressed down, shaken together and running over, will be poured into your lap. For with the measure you use, it will be measured to you.' (Luke 6:37–8)

Jesus is the judge of all people.

He comes as the Judge of the living and the dead.[8]

He [Jesus] commanded us to preach to the people and to testify that he is the one whom God appointed as judge of the living and the dead. (Acts 10:42)

---

6 *The Epistle of Polycarp to the Philippians*, ch. 6.
7 *The Epistle of Polycarp to the Philippians*, ch. 2.
8 *The Epistle of Polycarp to the Philippians*, ch. 2.

Jesus had real flesh and blood; he was not just a spirit tricking people that he had a physical body.

'For whosoever does not confess that Jesus Christ has come in the flesh, is antichrist;' ...[9]

I say this because many deceivers, who do not acknowledge Jesus Christ as coming in the flesh, have gone out into the world. Any such person is the deceiver and the antichrist. (2 John 1:7)

People are saved from their sins by believing in Jesus, not by their actions or works. Being saved, they can look forward to resurrection.

... knowing that 'by grace ye are saved, not of works,' but by the will of God through Jesus Christ.[10]... If we please Him in this present world, we shall receive also the future world, according as He has promised to us that He will raise us again from the dead, and that if we live worthily of Him, 'we shall also reign together with Him,' provided only we believe.[11]

Then they [the crowds of people wanting to make Jesus king] asked him, 'What must we do to do the works God requires?' Jesus answered, 'The work of God is this: to believe in the one he has sent.' (John 6:28–9)

But because of his great love for us, God, who is rich in mercy, made us alive with Christ even when we were dead in transgressions — it is by grace you have been saved. And God raised us up with Christ and seated us with him in the heavenly realms in Christ Jesus, in order that in the coming ages he might show the incomparable riches of his grace, expressed in his kindness to us in Christ Jesus. For it is by grace you have been saved, through faith — and this is not from yourselves, it is the gift of God — not by works, so that no one can boast. (Ephesians 2:4–9)

---

9   The Epistle of Polycarp to the Philippians, ch. 7.
10 The Epistle of Polycarp to the Philippians, ch. 1.
11 The Epistle of Polycarp to the Philippians, ch. 5.

> *[Jesus said] 'Do not let your hearts be troubled. You believe in God; believe also in me. My Father's house has many rooms; if that were not so, would I have told you that I am going there to prepare a place for you? And if I go and prepare a place for you, I will come back and take you to be with me that you also may be where I am.' (John 14:1–3)*

Jesus was crucified so that our sins could be forgiven, and we should live in him.

> *Let us then continually persevere in our hope, and the earnest of our righteousness, which is Jesus Christ, 'who bore our sins in His own body on the tree,' 'who did no sin, neither was guile found in His mouth,' but endured all things for us, that we might live in Him.*[12]

> *'He himself bore our sins' in his body on the cross, so that we might die to sins and live for righteousness; 'by his wounds you have been healed.' (1 Peter 2:24)*

> *'He [Jesus] committed no sin, and no deceit [guile]*[13] *was found in his mouth.' (1 Peter 2:22)*

> *[Jesus said] 'For even the Son of Man did not come to be served but to serve, and to give his life as a ransom for many.' (Mark 10:45)*

> *[Jesus said] 'Abide in Me, and I in you. As the branch cannot bear fruit of itself unless it abides in the vine, so neither can you unless you abide in Me ... If anyone does not abide in Me, he is thrown away as a branch and dries up; and they gather them, and cast them into the fire and they are burned.' (John 15:4–6, NASB)*

Loving money is evil.

> *'But the love of money is the root of all evils.'*[14]

---

12 *The Epistle of Polycarp to the Philippians*, ch. 8.
13 See the 21st Century King James version: 'who did no sin, neither was guile found in His mouth'.
14 *The Epistle of Polycarp to the Philippians*, ch. 4.

> For the love of money is a root of all kinds of evil. Some people, eager for money, have wandered from the faith and pierced themselves with many griefs. (1 Timothy 6:10)

The very strong similarities between Polycarp's words and those in the New Testament indicate that his beliefs were the same as those found in the New Testament. In fact it is certain that he was often quoting, or at least strongly alluding to, actual passages found in the New Testament. These clear references to various passages in the New Testament led one historian to state that Polycarp's letter to the Philippians, written in 110 AD, substantiates that 18 of the 25 books that comprise the New Testament were in circulation among various Christian communities at that time.[15]

Having investigated from just one angle whether the New Testament was the same before 200 AD as afterwards, I wanted to use a different approach. But I will do this after briefly examining the second main question that I raised earlier.

Did the New Testament authors record the truth about Jesus?

What evidence is there that the New Testament writers did in fact record the truth about Jesus? Although they had the *ability* to preserve Jesus' teachings, did they in fact carry out this task completely? It has been said that their favourable bias towards Jesus would have unduly affected what they wrote. For example, the original authors may have deleted parts of Jesus' teachings and actions that would have revealed him to be a militant rebel, not merely an authoritative teacher. Alternatively, they may have invented new details purporting that his followers worshipped him, whereas in reality Jesus was only ever greatly admired. A similar question arises even if it is granted that the authors themselves wrote the truth: perhaps those responsible for copying the New Testament books before 200 AD allowed bias to distort their workmanship. These issues have been examined in many different ways, but perhaps the most straightforward method is

---

15   P Barnett, *Is the New Testament History?*, Aquila Press, Sydney South, 2004, pp. 35–6.

to delve into the New Testament itself to see if it has the hallmarks of bias-induced excessive disdain or glorification. It should, however, be noted that simply because an author is biased, doesn't necessarily mean that he or she will allow that bias to distort the truth.

Bias due to partiality causing excessive disdain

This form of bias results in the writer of a historical event expressing excessive denigration of those in opposition to the historian's favoured character or worldview. It manifests in portrayals that always unduly belittle those who were opposed to the movement or hero favoured by the historian.

It seems reasonable to expect that this discrimination would be voiced loudly in the Gospel accounts containing the actions and words of Jesus and the disciples. This is because the first disciples of Jesus were Jews, and the Jews had regarded several other groups with great disdain for centuries. Such longstanding chauvinism is not always quickly dispelled. However, although there are echoes of prejudice, the overall analysis reveals that the authors narrating these encounters do not succumb to bias due to negative partiality.

For example, Chapter 9 of the book of Luke in the New Testament records a time when Jesus sent messengers ahead of himself. The messengers were sent into the land of the Samaritans so that arrangements could be made for the arrival of Jesus and his followers. The Samaritans are recorded as being unwilling to cooperate. The disciples' reaction is a desire to call down curses on the Samaritans, but Jesus rebukes them (Luke 9:51–5).

An examination of the entire account shows no excessive denigration. Nowhere does Luke state that the Samaritans were unjustified in their response to the request for help. In fact, the disciples' only reason for being so angry is the Samaritans refusal to be helpful. The disciples' reaction is very realistic as it reflects Jewish attitudes found in other literature from the same time period. For example, the Jewish historian Josephus declared that Samaritans align themselves with Jews when it suits them, but are quick to distance themselves if the Jews fall on hard times.[16] Later he made the comment that 'the Samaritans, being evil and enviously disposed to the Jews', made life very difficult for the Jews.[17] This seems to have reached a peak when Josephus records that at one stage (about 190 BC) the Samaritans had taken some Jews as slaves and stolen Jewish land.[18]

The centuries-old animosity between the Jews and the Samaritans highlights Luke's control of negative bias due to prejudice. He faithfully records Jesus' disapproval of the disciples' expressed hatred; he does not allow his favourable bias towards Jesus' disciples to twist the truth. Luke could have manipulated the truth by not writing about the disciples' vengefulness, minimising the intensity of Jesus' rebuke or by disparaging the Samaritans to justify the disciples' response.

In other parts of his Gospel, Luke records one of Jesus' most famous parables. Jesus' story not only depicts the courageous and generous actions of a Samaritan, but also contrasts the Samaritan with the uncaring actions of two influential Jewish religious figures (Luke 10:30–7). Later still, Luke records that when Jesus healed 10 men with leprosy, the only one that gave him thanks was a Samaritan (Luke 17:11–19).

Another New Testament author that did not let his Jewish national bias against the Samaritans influence his Gospel was John. This is made very apparent when John recorded that Jesus first declared he was the Messiah (a God-appointed chosen leader) to a Samaritan woman (John 4:26). Equally remarkable is the way John records Jesus' response to Jewish antagonists who asked Jesus:

> *The Jews answered him, 'Are we not right in saying that you are a Samaritan and have a demon?' Jesus answered, 'I do not have a demon, but I honor my father, and you dishonor me.' (John 8:48–9, ESV)*

---

16 Josephus, *The Antiquities of the Jews*, book 9, ch. 14, para. 3§291, in trans. W Whiston, *The Works of Josephus: Complete and Unabridged: New Updated Edition*, Hendrickson Publishers, Peabody, Massachusetts, US, 1987, p. 265.
17 Josephus, *The Antiquities of the Jews*, book 11, ch. 4, para. 9§114, p. 293.
18 Josephus, *The Antiquities of the Jews*, book 12, ch. 4, para. 1§156, p. 318.

Jesus' lack of rebuff to the accusation of being a Samaritan, whilst denying being demon possessed, shouts a very loud message. If John, or even those who copied John's Gospel, had carried over some partiality in their narrating of this conversation, it would be easy to imagine that the accusation of being a Samaritan would have been deleted so that only the accusation of being demon possessed remained.

The above examples of the lack of partiality against the Samaritans cannot be due to the editing out of some imaginary harsh words of Jesus directed at Samaritans, or even due to the Gospel writers inventing stories in favour of the Samaritans. It is unlikely that either of these explanations had transpired, as in other situations Jesus is recorded as showing significant disdain towards certain groups. For example, Jesus is recorded as implying that a Greek woman from the region of Syrian Phoenicia had the status of a dog (Matthew 15:21–8, Mark 7:24–30). Similarly, Luke reports how Jesus repeatedly denigrated a group of respected Jewish religious leaders — the Pharisees — even saying they were 'full of greed and wickedness' (Luke 11:39–44). John records the very surprising words of Jesus to certain Jews who had once believed in Jesus, saying their father was the devil (John 8:31–44). It is not realistic to believe that Jesus' favourable words and actions towards the Samaritans were invented or reveal selective editing by Christian scribes when the same Gospels contain Jesus' other harsh sayings.[19]

Bias due to partiality causing excessive glorification

Bias as a consequence of favouritism may also have a negative effect on a writer's accuracy because it causes excessive glorification of the historian's paragon. Typically, this bias would result in accounts that are devoid of any details that would tarnish the reputation of the historian's hero. As the writers of the New Testament worshipped Jesus as God, then it would seem inevitable that this type of bias would be easily found among its pages.

---

19 But naturally this raises another question: did Jesus exhibit ethnic disdain towards at least one racial group? For a deeper look at Jesus' words to the Syro-Phoenecian woman, refer to KE Bailey, *Jesus Through Middle Eastern Eyes: Cultural Studies in the Gospels*, Inter-Varsity Press, Downers Grove, Illinois, US, 2008, pp. 217–26, and FF Bruce, *The Hard Sayings of Jesus*, Hodder and Stoughton, London, 1985, pp. 110–11.

It certainly is surprising then to discover that the four Gospel writers do not shy away from presenting a 'warts and all' account of Jesus and his disciples. The writer of John's Gospel describes how Jesus was not able to sustain the loyalty of large numbers of his followers (John 6:66) because of the strangeness of his teachings. Matthew's Gospel records that Jesus was not even able to prevent three of his closest disciples from falling asleep when he needed their support (Matthew 26:36–46). Mark wrote in his Gospel how Jesus had not been successful in convincing his own family that he was 'in his right mind' (Mark 3:21). Luke recounts how the disciples argued among themselves as to who would be the greatest (Luke 9:46).

Canvassing Christian beliefs during the first 150 years

I started this chapter with two very important questions, namely:

1. If our earliest copies of significantly large portions of the New Testament are dated from 200 AD onwards, what can we know about the content of the New Testament before this time?

2. What evidence is there that the New Testament writers did in fact record the truth about Jesus?

Having shown that both questions can be examined in different ways, it seems to me that there is one method of inquiry that is simultaneously relevant to these two concerns. If it is granted for a moment that the earliest teachings of Christianity are those that are found in the New Testament, then it is reasonable to believe that this set of teachings would be the most popular during the first 100 years. Any deviant group of teachings that developed later would most likely be believed by only a smaller number of people, at least for a period of time. So if it were possible to travel back in time to the first 150 years after Jesus and canvas the beliefs of Christians from geographically separate places and various social strata, then there would be a good probability that these beliefs would all be regarded as mainstream Christian beliefs. However, if the reverse were true, and the so-called deviant beliefs represented the original teachings of Jesus, then there would be a good chance that such a random survey would reveal that today's mainstream Christianity was not the original set of beliefs.

Similarly, if the original teachings of Jesus were distorted by the unfaithful copying of early scribes, or because the original disciples had allowed their bias to unduly affect the truth, then it would be expected that at least some people would have carried the true version forward from one generation to the next. This is particularly so with major events and depictions, such as the death of Jesus and whether he was a teacher and healer or a militant rebel. If Jesus had not been crucified in Jerusalem under Pontius Pilate, then at least some of his faithful followers would have passed this message on from one generation to the next. Also, various non-Christian Roman officials and historians would soon have become aware that there was a Christian group who erroneously taught that Jesus was crucified under a Roman governor. So, if it were possible to conduct a survey of Christian beliefs in the first 150 years after Jesus, then some of these divergent views of Jesus' teachings would be revealed.

What is particularly exciting to know is that such time travel is possible, albeit in a limited fashion, by exploring the writings of various non-Christians written before 200 AD. Because these authors were not Christians, they were not biased towards Jesus, though they still would have had a bias of their own. Their writings make it possible to compare their image of Jesus and the Christians with the picture painted in the New Testament. If the two pictures differ widely, then it would be reasonable to try to ascertain which is the more untainted image. On the other hand, if the images are more like reflections of each other, then this would be strong evidence that bias had not unduly affected the New Testament writers' portrayal of Jesus.

These non-Christian writers also create a window into mainstream Christian beliefs. If the common understanding of the majority of Christians about Jesus and his teachings was quite different before 200 AD, then it is likely that the non-Christian authors would have reported such a divergent view. This is because these authors had lived in different geographical areas, were from different cultures, and some wrote in different decades to others. They had different sources of information, making it very unlikely that the most popular Christian beliefs would be entirely missing in their writings. These non-Christian writers would also have been delighted to report on any widespread lack of unity between Christian communities.

The remainder of this chapter is devoted to uncovering portraits of early Christianity from two non-Christian authors, namely Tacitus and Thallus. The five subsequent chapters are devoted to examining in much greater depth Christian characterisations made by three other non-Christian authors: Lucian, Pliny the Younger and Josephus.

Tacitus the historian

Cornelius Tacitus lived an impressive life. Born into a wealthy family in about 56 AD,[20] he rose in rank to become a very senior magistrate, a senator and the governor of the province of Asia by 112 AD. In modern times, he is remembered as a brilliant and prolific historian. Although a career as a historian in today's world — at least in some Western democracies — would be regarded as extremely safe, it held many dangers during Tacitus' era. For example, Emperor Domitian (r. 81–96 AD) was so offended at words penned by the historian Hermogenes of Tarsus that he executed Hermogenes and crucified the slaves that copied out the manuscript.

Tacitus' life was lived when the Roman Empire was passing through some very turbulent times, so he had the opportunity when writing about recent history to decry the actions of previous emperors. In his pre-teen years, he witnessed the rule of one of Rome's most infamous emperors, Nero (r. 54–68 AD). Tacitus revealed his talent for vividly painting scenes, and his desire to teach moral standards, when he wrote that:

> *Nero, who polluted himself by every lawful or lawless indulgence, had not omitted a single abomination which could heighten his depravity, till a few days afterwards he stooped to marry himself to one of that filthy herd, by name Pythagoras, with all the forms of regular wedlock. The bridal veil was put over the emperor; people saw the witnesses of the ceremony, the wedding dower, the couch and the nuptial torches; everything in a word was plainly visible, which, even when a woman weds darkness hides.*[21]

---

20 M Grant, *Greek and Latin Authors, 880 BC – 1000 AD*, HW Wilson, New York, 1980, p. 415.
21 Tacitus, *The Annals*, book 15, ch. 37, eds AJ Church & WJ Brodribb, *Complete Works of Tacitus*, Random House, New York, 1942, from the Perseus Digital Library, www.perseus.tufts.edu/hopper/text?doc=Perseus%3Atext%3A1999.02.0078%3Abook%3D15%3Achapter%3D37, accessed 28/04/2013.

Tacitus' capability as a historian can be seen in a number of ways. He was quite an active researcher, sending off letters requesting information from others, such as requesting from Pliny the Younger details concerning the death of Pliny the Elder. Pliny replied by writing:

> *Your request that I should send you an account of my uncle's end, so that you may transmit a more exact relation of it to posterity, deserves my acknowledgements; for if his death is celebrated by your pen, the glory of it, I am aware, will be for ever deathless.*[22]

Pliny's reply raised even more questions in Tacitus' mind, so that he had cause to send another letter asking Pliny for further details.[23] Because Tacitus even used the postal system to hunt down reliable information from the recent past (Pliny the Elder died in 79 AD), it is no further stretch to imagine him arranging conversations with others who were intimately related to historical events.[24] Tacitus wrote in one of his history books, published in about 112 AD, that 'there are many living now whose ancestors suffered punishment, or incurred disgrace, under Tiberius ...'[25] This is particularly relevant to my investigation of Tacitus' remarks about Christianity, as Jesus was crucified during the last few years of Tiberius' reign as emperor (r. 14–37 AD). It raises the possibility that Tacitus communicated directly with the descendants of officials who witnessed notable Christian events such as Jesus' crucifixion. Other sources of information on Christians may have come from various court records, senatorial archives and daily gazettes.[26] It has been said that Tacitus' focus on recent events meant that he had:

---

22 Pliny, *Letters*, book 6, ch. 16, trans. W Melmoth, rev. WML Hutchinson, vol. 1, William Heinemann, London, and The MacMillan Co, New York, 1931, www.archive.org/stream/letterswithengli01plinuoft#page/474/mode/2up, accessed 29/04/2013.
23 Pliny, *Letters*, book 6, ch. 20.
24 R Mellor, *Tacitus*, Routledge, New York, 1993, p. 33.
25 Tacitus, *The Annals of Tacitus*, trans. GG Ramsay, John Murray, London, 1904, book 4, ch. 33, www.archive.org/stream/annalsanenglisht01taciuoft#page/292/mode/2up, accessed 28/04/2013.
26 PR Eddy & GA Boyd, *The Jesus Legend: A Case for the Historical Reliability of the Synoptic Tradition*, Baker Academic, Grand Rapids, Michigan, US, 2007, pp. 179–84.

> *access to a unique wealth of information, in the form of biographies, histories, general's memoirs, and the oral tradition, all of which must have allowed him to check stories about specific events against each other.*[27]

Another way to view his ability as a historian is to note his admission of uncertainty when conflicting historical details became evident. For example, he wrote that permission for troops to sack the Italian town of Cremona might have come from Antonius or Hormus, as Pliny the Elder stated it was Antonius whilst another authority reckoned on Hormus.[28] This type of activity has led some scholars to comment that Tacitus 'investigated the facts painstakingly'.[29] Not that Tacitus was always correct: he once wrote several successive paragraphs on the Jews and the first few, which focused on their ancient origins, have many mistakes.[30] However, among these same paragraphs Tacitus demonstrated that he was keenly aware of the importance of comparing more than just two sources of information. How he achieved this can be seen by reading the very first paragraph of his section on the history of the Jews:

> It is said *that the Jews are refugees from Crete* ... Another tradition *makes them Assyrian refugees* ... Yet another version *assigns to the Jews an illustrious origin as the descendants of the Solymi* ...[31]

Tacitus' depiction of the Jews and their religion became more accurate as he moved from dealing with their ancient beginnings to focusing on their behaviour closer to his own era. He very astutely noted that:

> *The Egyptians worship most of their gods as animals, or in shapes half animal and half human. The Jews acknowledge one god only, of whom they have a purely spiritual conception. They think it*

---

27 R Ash, *Tacitus*, Bristol Classical Press, London, 2006, p. 63.
28 Tacitus, *The Histories*, book 3, para. 28, trans. WH Fyfe, Clarendon Press, Oxford, UK, vol. 2, www.gutenberg.org/files/16927/16927-h/ii.html#BOOK_III, accessed 27/04/2013.
29 R Ash, p. 63.
30 Tacitus, *The Histories*, book 5, paras 2–4, www.gutenberg.org/files/16927/16927-h/ii.html#fnm464, accessed 06/05/2013.
31 Tacitus, *The Histories*, book 5, para. 2, www.gutenberg.org/files/16927/16927-h/ii.html#fnm464, accessed 06/05/2013. Emphasis added.

> *impious to make images of gods in human shape out of perishable materials. Their god is almighty and inimitable, without beginning and without end. They therefore set up no statues in their temples, nor even in their cities, refusing this homage both to their own kings and to the Roman emperors.*[32]

This progression of accuracy when writing about events closer to his own time seems to have been quite deliberate. One scholar wrote that there is:

> *little doubt that Tacitus engaged in serious research ... Tacitus consulted both obvious and obscure sources ... [He] thought that personal research was more important for the history of recent times and he diligently sought eyewitness accounts of important events.*[33]

> *Tacitus, like any writer, had his own set of biases. One writer thought that his contempt of 'all easterners — Greeks, Jews, and Egyptians alike ...' was a reason for his less than usual competence in writing their histories.*[34] *However, his bias against other groups, such as emperors, did not cause him to confuse fact from fiction. Tacitus distinguished: fact from rumor with a scrupulosity rare in any ancient historian ... [he] hated emperors passionately, but with good reason. Hatred is no more or less biased than love; either may inspire great history ... Truth is sometimes the product of painstaking research, but it may also result from moral resolution ... Tacitus wrote with passion: a passion to expose official lies and to replace them with a politically and morally true history of the empire. It is a truth based on factual accuracy ...*[35]

Having established that Tacitus exhibited the hallmarks of being a thorough historian, I now want to examine his words that touch on the beginnings of Christianity.[36]

---

32 Tacitus, *The Histories*, book 5, para. 5, www.gutenberg.org/files/16927/16927-h/ii.html#fnm464, accessed 06/05/2013.
33 R Mellor, pp. 31–2.
34 R Mellor, p. 32.
35 R Mellor, pp. 45–6.
36 For a more thorough examination of Tacitus' words about Jesus Christ than what I have written, refer to JP Holding, 'Nero's scapegoats: Cornelius Tacitus' Annals 15:44 as a reference to Jesus', in JP Holding (ed.), *Shattering the Christ Myth: Did Jesus not Exist?*, Xulon Press, Maitland, Florida, 2008, pp. 55–68.

Tacitus' comments on Christianity

Perhaps the first major persecution of Christians was in 64 AD, when a fire destroyed a large part of Rome. Rumours spread quickly that the Emperor Nero had started it. Tacitus narrated what happened because of these rumours in his series of books titled *Annals of Imperial Rome*. The following excerpt from this series was written in approximately 112 AD:[37]

> *Consequently, to get rid of the report, Nero fastened the guilt and inflicted the most exquisite tortures on a class hated for their abominations, called Christians by the populace. Christus, from whom the name had its origin, suffered the extreme penalty during the reign of Tiberius at the hand of one of our procurators, Pontius Pilatus, and a most mischievous superstition, thus checked for the moment, again broke out not only in Judea, the first source of the evil, but even in Rome, where all things hideous and shameful from every part of the world find their centre and become popular. Accordingly, an arrest was first made of all who pleaded guilty; then, upon their information, an immense multitude was convicted, not so much of the crime of firing the city as of hatred against mankind. Mockery of every sort was added to their deaths. Covered with the skins of beasts, they were torn by dogs and perished, or were nailed to crosses, or were doomed to the flames and burnt, to serve as a nightly illumination, when daylight had expired.*
>
> *Nero offered his gardens for the spectacle and was exhibiting a show in the circus, while he mingled with the people in the dress of a charioteer stood aloft on a cart. Hence, even for criminals who deserved extreme and exemplary punishment, there arose a feeling of compassion; for it was not, as it seemed, for the public good, but to glut one man's cruelty, that they were being destroyed.*[38]

---

37 Tacitus, *The Annals*, book 15, ch. 44, www.perseus.tufts.edu/hopper/text?doc=Perseus%3Atext%3A1999.02.0078%3Abook=15%3Achapter=44, accessed 10/06/2013.

38 F Goodyear, *Tacitus*, Clarendon Press, Oxford, 1970, pp. 25–6 & 43. See also Tacitus, *The Annals*, book 15, ch. 44, www.perseus.tufts.edu/hopper/text?doc=Perseus%3Atext%3A1999.02.0078%3Abook%3D15%3Achapter%3D44, accessed 28/04/2013.

Parallels between Tacitus and the New Testament

Tacitus' portrayal of Christianity mirrors several highlights found within the pages of the New Testament: The leader of the Christian movement was called Christ (Christus in Latin), who was crucified by a Roman governor called Pontius Pilate (Pilatus in Latin) while Tiberius was emperor. Although the Christian religion began in Judea, it spread to Rome, where Christians were persecuted.

How strongly Tacitus' comments reflect the content of the New Testament can be seen from the following passages:

> *In the fifteenth year of the reign of Tiberius Caesar — when Pontius Pilate was governor of Judea ... [John the Baptist] went into all the country around the Jordan ... [He preached] 'I baptize you with water. But one more powerful than I will come ...' When all the people were being baptized, Jesus was baptized too. (Luke 3:1–3, 16, 21)*

> *Wanting to satisfy the crowd, Pilate released [another prisoner called] Barabbas to them. He had Jesus flogged, and handed him over to be crucified. (Mark 15:15)*

> *On one occasion, while he [Jesus] was eating with them [his disciples], he gave them this command: 'Do not leave Jerusalem, but wait for the gift my Father promised ... and you will be my witnesses in Jerusalem, and in all Judea, and Samaria, and to the ends of the earth.' (Acts 1:4–8)*

> *When we got to Rome [having originally started in Jerusalem], Paul [a prominent Christian teacher] was allowed to live by himself, with a soldier to guard him ... For two whole years Paul stayed there ... He proclaimed the kingdom of God and taught about the Lord Jesus Christ — with all boldness and without hindrance! (Acts 28:16, 30–31)*

> *Meanwhile, Saul was still breathing out murderous threats against the Lord's disciples ... [He wanted to go to] the synagogues[39] in Damascus, so that if he found any there who belonged to the*

---

[39] Synagogues were places were Jews met regularly.

Way, whether men or women, he might take them as prisoners to Jerusalem. (Acts 9:1–2)

But other Jews were jealous; so they rounded up some bad characters from the marketplace, formed a mob and started a riot in the city [of Thessalonica] ... they dragged Jason and some other [Christian] believers before the city officials ... (Acts 17:5–7)

This persecution of Christians is mentioned in several places throughout the pages of the New Testament. The two cities mentioned above, namely Damascus and Thessalonica, are more than 1400 kilometres (880 miles) apart.

This short comparison between the writings of the non-Christian Tacitus and the authors of the Gospels reveals that there is strong agreement on some of the essential elements of Christianity, despite some major differences in bias towards Christianity. It seems very reasonable to conclude that these elements have a very credible foundation, and that the bias of the Christian authors has not resulted in them distorting the truth. It is also apparent that Christian beliefs, at least those that have been touched on here, were identical before 200 AD as afterwards.

Thallus the historian

Christians have known this non-Christian historian for over 18 centuries. Initially they referred to his books when buttressing their belief that the Roman gods were not supernatural. One of the earliest Christian writers to do so was Tertullian, whose works date from 196 AD. He was audacious enough to address his book *The Apology* to 'Rulers of the Roman Empire'.[40] His book appealed to Thallus' writings to point out that even this famous Roman historian acknowledged that their first god, namely Saturn, was originally a mere man.[41]

---

40 Tertullian, *The Apology*, trans. S. Thelwall, ch. 10, www.earlychristianwritings.com/text/tertullian01.html, accessed 05/04/2013.
41 Tertullian, *The Apology*, trans. S. Thelwall, ch. 10, www.earlychristianwritings.com/text/tertullian01.html, accessed 05/04/2013. Tertullian strengthened his argument by citing in similar fashion writers such as Diodorus and Cornelius Nepos.

Thallus' three history books were written after 29 AD and possibly as early as 49 AD.[42] They covered the period from the fall of Troy (about 1100 BC) to about the first century after Christ.[43] Fortunately, although none of these three books remain today, we are able to know a little about their contents due to the comments of ancient authors. For example, in the third book of his history, Thallus tried to find a rational explanation for the darkness that fell upon the Earth when Jesus was crucified. This rationale was in itself preserved by an early Christian historian called Julius Africanus (160–240 AD).[44]

In order to understand Africanus' argument against Thallus' explanation, it is necessary to know that the New Testament authors recorded that Jesus was crucified on a special Jewish feast day called the Passover (John 19:13–16). After Jesus had been hanging on the crucifix for some time during that day, the sky went dark from midday until 3.00 pm. During this time Jesus uttered his last words and died (Luke 23:44–6).

With this background knowledge, the following words of Africanus begin to make sense:

> *As to His [Jesus] works severally, and His cures effected upon body and soul, and the mysteries of His doctrine, and the resurrection from the dead, these have been most authoritatively set forth by His disciples and apostles before us. On the whole world there pressed a most fearful darkness; and the rocks were rent by an earthquake, and many places in Judea and other districts were thrown down. This darkness Thallus, in the third book of his History, calls, as appears to me without reason, an eclipse of the sun. For the Hebrews celebrate the passover on the 14th day according to the moon, and the passion of our Saviour falls on the day before the*

---

42 M Goguel, *The Life of Jesus*, trans. O. Wyom, George Allen and Unwin, London, 1954, pp. 91–3.

43 This description is from Eusebius' book *Chronographia*. For a translation of the relevant section, see AA Mosshammer, *The Chronicle of Eusebius and Greek Chronographic Tradition*, Associated University Presses, London, 1979, p. 140. Mosshammer points out that the end date for Thallus' work is uncertain (pp. 144–5).

44 For more on Africanus, refer to the appendix at the end of this chapter.

passover; ... how then should an eclipse be supposed to happen when the moon is almost diametrically opposite the sun?[45]

What did Africanus and Thallus actually say?

A straightforward reading of the above quote reveals that Africanus is focusing on an unusual darkness that was associated with Jesus and an earthquake. Africanus knew that an earthquake accompanied the darkness, though it would seem that Thallus did not.[46] Thallus was certainly aware of a darkness that was associated with Jesus, as Africanus wrote 'This darkness' to link Thallus' explanation of the darkness with the previous sentence about the earthquakes and darkness in Judea. Africanus rebuffs Thallus' suggestion by narrating that the crucifixion took place at the time of the Passover, which is when there is a full moon. Africanus is clearly aware that a solar eclipse is impossible if there is a full moon.

This particular darkness must be the one that occurred during Jesus' crucifixion, as the New Testament records only one occasion when these three elements were together, which was the day of Jesus' crucifixion:

> *From noon until three in the afternoon darkness came over all the land ... And when Jesus had cried out again in a loud voice, he gave up his spirit. At that moment the curtain of the temple was torn in two from top to bottom. The earth shook and the rocks split. (Matthew 27:45–51)*

Given that the New Testament's only mention of an untimely darkness is the one at the time of Jesus' death, there appears to be no doubt

---

45 A Roberts & J Donaldson (eds), *The Ante-Nicene Fathers, Vol. 6: Gregory Thaumaturgus, Dionysius the Great, Julius Africanus, Anatolius and Minor Writers, Methodius, Arnobius*, rev. AC Coxe, WB Eerdmans Publishing Company, Michigan, US, 1978, pp.130–8. This quote of Africanus was taken from a book by Georgius Syncellus, who died c. 814 AD. Syncellus wrote a world chronicle. Refer to AA Mosshamer, *The Chronicle of Eusebius*, Associated University Press, London, 1979. See also Julius Africanus, *Extant Works*, fragment 18, para. 1, www.newadvent.org/fathers/0614.htm, accessed 05/04/2013.

46 Or if Thallus did, his comments did impel Africanus to make a response.

that the darkness for which Thallus is offering an explanation is the darkness related to Jesus' crucifixion.

From Africanus' quote, it is not readily apparent why he considered that an eclipse was a mistaken explanation. After all, as a believer in an all-powerful God he could have favourably considered the possibility that God had miraculously caused a true eclipse to happen. However, Africanus appears to be of the strong opinion that God did not use his powers to alter the positions of the sun and moon, as happens during an eclipse, but rather created the darkness in some other way. This rationale highlights in an inadvertent way that Thallus himself tried to argue against the darkness being the result of Jesus' death, rather than simply record that a darkness had occurred due to an eclipse. This is because of the following train of thought:

1. If Thallus' original words were simply that a darkness — due to an eclipse — occurred in a particular year ...

2. and if only the Christians linked this year as being the same year as when Jesus was crucified ...

3. then it is extremely unlikely that Africanus would have bothered to counter such a seemingly good piece of evidence in favour of the darkness having at least happened, even if the reason why the darkness happened was not accurate.

Certainly Africanus could not have been opposed to Thallus' explanation merely on the basis that God would not have used a natural event. Christians before and after Africanus' time certainly believed God had used various natural phenomena, such as droughts and plagues of locusts,[47] to accomplish his purposes in his timing. The natural causes of eclipses had been discovered long before the lives of Africanus or Thallus. Pliny the Elder (23–79 AD) had even recorded that a Greek scholar called Hipparchus (c. 190–120 BC) had calculated that solar eclipses occurred somewhere on Earth

---

47 For droughts, see Deuteronomy 11:16–17, 1 Kings 8:35 and Nahum 1:3. For locusts, see Exodus 10:12–15.

every seven months.[48] This is the same frequency as determined by modern astronomers.[49]

From where did Thallus learn about the darkness and when did he write?

As I wanted to understand more about the importance of Thallus' comments, I started looking at the sources of his information about the darkness, and how soon he may have penned these words. Some scholars have voiced the opinion that 'a man like Thallus would never have taken the trouble to correct and criticize a miraculous story' that had not been preserved in written accounts.[50] Whatever the source or sources of information, it is 'highly unlikely that a Roman historian would take the claims of a recent and relatively minor religious sect (i.e. the Christians) so seriously that it would warrant a counter explanation — *unless he believed it to be true on other grounds*'.[51]

Because several ancient authors referred to Thallus' publications, and as we know when *they* wrote, then it is possible to establish a rough time frame for dating Thallus' books. I mentioned above that Tertullian wrote a book, dating from 196 AD, which referred to Thallus. About a decade earlier, another Christian called Minucius Felix had made mention of Thallus in his book *Octavius*, which was written in about 185 AD. Thallus' publication must be at least several years earlier than 185 AD in order for Minucius Felix and Tertullian to have had time to come in contact with the book. (As an aside, Felix's story is interesting in itself. He and his friend Octavius were both lawyers who had observed the court trials against Christians. After noting the unfairness

---

48 Pliny the Elder, *The Natural History*, book 2, ch. 10, trans. J Bostock, www.perseus.tufts.edu/hopper/text?doc=Perseus%3Atext%3A1999.02.0137%3Abook%3D2%3Achapter%3D10, accessed 07/04/2013.
49 CSIRO, 'What is a solar eclipse?', www.csiro.au/en/Outcomes/Understanding-the-Universe/Tracking-spacecraft/What-is-a-solar-eclipse.aspx, accessed 07/04/2013.
50 MJ Harris, 'References to Jesus in early classical authors', in D Wenham (ed.), *Gospel Perspectives, Vol. 5: The Jesus Tradition Outside the Gospels*, JSOT Press, Sheffield, UK, 1984, p. 361, n. 14, quoting R Eisler, *The Messiah Jesus and John the Baptist*, trans. AH Krappe, Methuen, London, 1931, p. 298.
51 PR Eddy & GA Boyd, p. 173. Emphasis in the original.

of the trials and the heroic behaviour of the Christians, they too started to follow Jesus. When trying to convince a second friend, Natalis, about Christianity, Octavius appealed to writings of historians such as Thallus to show that the god Saturn was originally only a mortal.[52])

The next clue to the date of Thallus' books comes from a very prolific Christian historian called Eusebius (c. 263–339 AD). Eusebius gave a list of authors that he used to put together a chronology of the Roman Empire. This list included Thallus, describing Thallus' three books as covering the period 'from the fall of Troy to the 167th Olympiad'.[53] This 167th Olympiad is the four-year interval covering the years 112–109 BC. However, many regard this number, 167, as mistaken, probably being due to a copying error. Not just this number, but other Olympiad numbers given in Eusebius' list are also thought to have become corrupted over time.[54] One scholar proposed that Thallus' last Olympiad was originally the 207th, spanning the years 49–52 AD.[55] This theory was based on the idea that the Greek letters for the number 167, which are ρξζ, were originally σζ, where the mistaken repetition of the ξ for the ζ, and the writing of ρ instead of σ, is due to the carelessness of the scribes. It is easier to appreciate how such errors could arise when it is understood that Greek numbers were based on Greek letters. For example, ρ has the value of 100, ξ the value of 60 and ζ equals 7. So if the scribe copying the Greek number ρξζ had glanced at a nearby word having some of these same letters, he or she may then have accidentally incorporated these letters in the number. It is important to appreciate that

---

52 Minucius Felix, *Octavius*, ch. 22, a digital copy can be found at www.earlychristianwritings.com/text/octavius.html, accessed 05/04/2013.
53 MJ Harris, 'References to Jesus in early classical authors', citing *Eusebius' Werke V: Die Chronik aus dem Armenischen übersetzt mit textkritischem Kommentar*, ed. J Karst, Henricks, Leipzig, 1911, p. 125. See also RE Van Voorst, *Jesus Outside the New Testament: An Introduction to the Ancient Evidence*, Wm B Eerdmans Publishing Company, Grand Rapids, Michigan, US, 2000, p. 22.
54 AA Mosshammer, *The Chronicle of Eusebius and Greek Chronographic Tradition*, Associated University Presses, London, 1979, pp. 140–5.
55 M Goguel, *Life of Jesus*, trans. O Wyon, George Allen & Unwin, London, 1954, p. 92, citing R Eisler, ΙΗΣΟΥΣ ΒΑΣΙΛΕΥΣ ΟΥ ΒΑΣΙΛΕΥΣΑΣ, Heidelberg, 1928–1930 (publisher details were not supplied). This theory is based on the idea that the error occurred in the copying of the Greek text, rather than in the Armenian translation of Eusebius' work.

the author of this theory, R Eisler, was not someone who considered that the New Testament provides an accurate account of Jesus' teachings. Instead he considered that the movement that Jesus inspired was 'mainly a political movement', and that the New Testament therefore presents an 'altered picture' of reality.[56] Therefore his theory was not based on a strong desire to present the New Testament as reliable history.

Although the earliest date that Thallus wrote his history cannot be definitely determined, it is clear that he wrote sometime after the death of Jesus, perhaps as early as the 50s AD, but no later than about 180 AD.

It is apparent that Thallus had heard of the darkness during Jesus' crucifixion and, while he did not doubt the existence of the darkness at that time, he sought to give it a natural explanation. His words provide evidence within 100 years after the crucifixion of Jesus that the New Testament's account of the darkness was a real event, and not merely a fabrication due to the bias of the Gospel authors. Thallus' words also make it clear that this particular Christian belief, expressed in the pages of the New Testament was unchanged before and after 200 AD

Conclusion

Just as Tacitus' writings provide support for the trustworthiness of the Gospel authors, so too do Thallus' words. Despite the fact that Tacitus and Thallus had biases that were opposite to those of the New Testament authors, they both describe events that are in agreement with the New Testament's portrayal of these same events. These similarities are important not only because they show that the bias of the New Testament authors did not have a negative impact on their reliability as authors, but also because these events form a part of the fabric of Christian belief. These beliefs include the following:

1. There existed a leader of the Christian movement called Christ; he was not merely a mythical being.

2. A Roman governor called Pontius Pilate crucified Christ while Tiberius was emperor. Clearly Christ was not just a spiritual essence without flesh and blood.

---

56 M Goguel, p. 54.

3. A darkness came upon the earth when Jesus was crucified.

4. The Christian religion began in Judea.

The belief that Jesus was a real person is so foundational that the New Testament states that anyone who does not believe that Jesus came in the flesh is a deceiver (2 John 1:7). These beliefs also have an importance for Christians as the New Testament greatly emphasises that the truthfulness of its claims about spiritual matters hinges upon the reality of its historical claims.

Finally, the words of Tacitus and Thallus, together with those from the Christian leader Polycarp, provide strong evidence that important Christian beliefs from before 200 AD are the same as those found in copies of the New Testament dated after 200 AD.

Appendix
Sextus Julius Africanus

Given that Thallus' comment about the darkness is about such a unique event, and as it is preserved only by Africanus, I wanted to learn more about Africanus, particularly his sources of information, his attention to detail and his reasons for writing.

A historian with access to many historical publications

Africanus had completed a five-volume history of the world in 221 AD. Portions of all five books still exist today, but only as fragments. One of his aims was to juxtapose a notable event from Hebrew history with Greek or Persian actions. To do this he would sometimes make use of the four-yearly Greek Olympiads.[57]

---

57 We know much about Africanus' motivation because an extensive portion of one his works was quoted by Eusebius (c. 263–339 AD). See Eusebius, *Preparation for the Gospel*, book 10, ch. 10, a digital copy is available at www.earlychristianwritings.com/fathers/eusebius_pe_10_book10.html, accessed 05/04/2013. It has been discovered that Eusebius 'carefully copied his sources' (G Sterling, *Historiography and Self-definition: Josephus, Luke-Acts and Apologetic Historiography*, EJ Brill, New York, 1992, p. 142.

To achieve this goal he sourced a very impressive array of historical texts. Sometimes he would mention several of these in the one paragraph, so as to reinforce the veracity of his statements. For example, he links the 55th Olympic festival to Cyrus becoming king of Persia, citing the publications of the historians Diodorus, Thallus, Castor, Polybius and Phlegon.[58] Elsewhere Africanus refers to Polemo's *Greek History*, Herodotus' second book, Ptolemy, Philochorus, Apion's *Against the Jews* and the fourth book of Apion's *History*, and Theopompus' *Tricarenus*. Africanus also appears to have had a copy of, or at least excerpts from, a book by a Jewish historian and chronographer called Justus ben Pistus of Tiberius.[59] Africanus' scholarly approach is also reflected by the fact that he was in charge of the library at the Pantheon in Rome during the reign of the Roman emperor Alexander Severus (r. 222–235 AD).[60]

The type of information that Africanus obtained from Thallus, such as linking an Olympiad with a Persian king, reveals another important fact, namely that he knew details from Thallus' writings that were not related to Jesus' crucifixion. This strongly suggests that he possessed Thallus' three volumes of history, not just an isolated quote from one of Thallus' books regarding the darkness during Jesus' crucifixion. This also would imply that he knew firsthand the context of Thallus' remarks about the crucifixion.

A discerning historian

Africanus was also able to discriminate between various historians, pointing out that some were more accurate than others:

> *For both the historians of Athens, Hellanicus and Philochorus who wrote* The Attic Histories, *and the writers on Syrian history, Castor and Thallus, and the writer on universal history, Diodorus*

---

58 Eusebius, *Preparation for the Gospel*, book 10, ch. 10, www.earlychristianwritings.com/fathers/eusebius_pe_10_book10.html, accessed 05/04/2013.

59 S Bowman, 'Josephus in Byzantium', in LH Feldman & G Hata (eds), *Josephus, Judaism, and Christianity*, Wayne State University Press, Detroit, 1987, p. 365.

60 F Granger, 'Julius Africanus and the Library of the Pantheon', *Journal of Theological Studies*, (1933) os XXXIV (134), pp. 157–161.

> *the author of the* Bibliotheca, *and Alexander Polyhistor, and some of our own historians recorded these events more accurately even than all the Attic writers.*[61]

A historian who paid attention to detail

Africanus was well aware of the different calendars being used in his time, commenting on how the Hebrews measure the course of the year by the moon:

> *...according to the Hebrew numeration, as they measure the years by the course of the moon; so that, as is easy to show, their year consists of 354 days, while the solar year has 365 1/4 days. For the latter exceeds the period of twelve months, according to the moon's course, by 11 1/4 days. Hence the Greeks and the Jews insert three intercalary months every 8 years.*[62]

Another example of his attention to detail is apparent when reading his letter to a colleague called Origen. In this letter he proves that a certain story was not part of the Old Testament when written in the original Hebrew language, but instead was added to a later Greek language version of the Old Testament. Africanus' argument is based on the fact that the story contains a play on words in the Greek language, not just once but twice. Because the Old Testament books were originally written in Hebrew, then this pun would not have had any meaning or relevance, so the story must have been first penned in Greek.[63]

Africanus was a prolific writer who was able to source information from many different areas of knowledge. He wrote a large encyclopaedia

---

61 Eusebius, *Preparation for the Gospel*, ch. 10, book 10, www.earlychristianwritings.com/fathers/eusebius_pe_10_book10.html, accessed 05/04/2013.
62 Julius Africanus, *Extant Works*, fragment 16, para. 3, www.newadvent.org/fathers/0614.htm, accessed 05/04/2013.
63 Africanus, 'A letter to Origen from Africanus about the history of Susanna', in AC Coxe (ed.), *Ante-Nicene Fathers, Vol. 4: Fathers of the Third Century: Tertullian, Part Fourth, Minucius Felix; Commondian; Origen, Parts First and Second*, T & T Clark, Edinburgh, Wm B Eerdmans Publishing Company, Grand Rapids, Michigan, US, www.ccel.org/ccel/schaff/anf04.vi.vi.html, accessed 14/06/2013. The story of Susanna is usually placed among the apocrypha.

dedicated to the Emperor Severus, which covered a very diverse range of subjects such as medicine, magic and naval warfare. It certainly appears strange to a modern reader that he called this work *Embroidered Girdles*.

Conclusion

Africanus certainly reveals himself as a meticulous researcher, who knew his sources of information well. It is easy to see why Eusebius (a famous Christian historian) said that the five history books of Africanus were '… very laboriously and accurately achieved'. Africanus appears to have thoroughly read Thallus' writings, ensuring he would have correctly understood the context regarding the unnatural darkness. All of this evidence strongly supports Africanus as a reliable recorder of details from Thallus' publication.

13

Lucian and his view on Christianity

This chapter will examine over 20 points of agreement between the writings of Lucian (c. 120–180 AD) — one of the most colourful, independent witnesses of early Christianity — and the Bible.

Lucian was a writer of Greek satire and was popular among his contemporaries. He was born in Samosata, which was the capital of the kingdom of Commagene[1] until the Romans took control in 72 AD. The town is now called Samsat and lies in south-eastern Turkey on the Euphrates River. Lucian appears to have spent some years studying Greek authors, improving his understanding of the Greek language and, later, becoming a lawyer. After this he was a successful travelling lecturer and held for a time a well-paid teaching position in Gaul (a region encompassing France and neighbouring countries). At the age of 40 he spent time in Athens. Later he obtained a senior post in the imperial administration in Egypt. He had friends in high places, including a Roman consular and the governor of a region in Turkey called Cappadocia.[2] That Lucian travelled widely is also evident from his visits to towns such as Rome, Corinth and Olympia and the regions of Ionia and Pontus.

About 70 of his books have survived to the present, and he appears to have enjoyed a reasonable amount of fame during his life.[3] He had a rich imagination and a bright and agile wit. Some of his works have

---

1 CP Jones, *Culture and Society in Lucian*, Harvard University Press, London, 1986, p. 6.
2 CP Jones, p. 19. The consular was Sisenna Rutilianus.
3 CP Jones, p. 19.

amusing titles, such as *Praise of a Fly*, *The Illiterate Book-Buyer* and *The Cross-Examination of Zeus*. One title is reminiscent of modern-day quirky humour; although it is called *True Story*, Lucian from the outset declares it to be entirely untrue. Apparently it was a mockery of the then very popular books of travellers' tales. I think of this book as the ancestor of science fiction, as within the pages of *A True Story* (also called *The True History*), Lucian visits various places in the heavens, including the moon and a city between the constellations of Pleiades and Hyades![4] The book also tells of his fantastic sea adventure, during which his ship was swallowed by a sea monster 240 kilometres (150 miles) long, complete with a large island in its stomach that had hills, trees and sea birds.[5]

Lucian's religious and philosophical beliefs

As a pagan, Lucian's attitude towards Christians has been described as 'neutral and sometimes sympathetic — or condescending'.[6] He mocked all religious beliefs in general, including men's hopes and fears for what lies beyond death. This is well illustrated in one of his books titled *Of Mourning*. He first narrates that many people put a coin in the mouth of the deceased so that the ferryman of the underworld will take the departed across the lake that separates the living from the dead. Lucian then asks how they know which currency of coin to use, and comments that it would be much better if they did not supply any payment because then the ferryman would refuse to transport the corpse and they would return to the living![7]

Lucian ridiculed not only religious ideas but also various philosophies. His fictitious dialogue entitled *Hermotimus* was named after a character

---

4   Pleiades and Hyades are clusters of stars about 150 and 425 light years from Earth, respectively.
5   Lucian, *A True Story*, para. 31, in *Lucian*, vol. 1, trans. AM Harmon, William Heinemann, London, & Harvard University Press, Cambridge, Massachusetts, US, 1962, pp. 284–7, www.archive.org/stream/lucianha01luciuoft#page/286/mode/2up, accessed 12/03/2013.
6   B Baldwin, *Studies in Lucian*, Hakkert, Toronto, 1973, p. 102.
7   Lucian, *Of Mourning*, para. 10, in *The Works of Lucian of Samosata*, vol. 3, trans. HW Fowler & FG Fowler, The Clarendon Press, Oxford, 1905, p. 214, www.archive.org/stream/worksoflucianofs03luciuoft#page/214/mode/2up, accessed 29/01/2013.

who was a pupil of one of the philosophical schools called Stoicism for more than 20 years. In this dialogue, Hermotimus is persuaded to cease his studies after a long debate with Lycinus (Lucian's stage name). Hermotimus is so radically turned around that he concludes: 'Henceforth, if I meet a philosopher on my walks (and it will not be with my will), I shall turn aside and avoid him as I would a mad dog'.[8] The book is in fact a sustained attack on all philosophical schools, with the conclusion being 'that the pursuit of it [philosophy] is hopeless for mortal man'.[9]

Lucian also found worldly wealth and pride pointless. He frequently drew ideas from literature of the past and humorous illustrations of the life and customs of his own time. He did not hold any consistent philosophical position, and his principal aim was often to amuse. Sometimes his humour focused on various aspects of society that he thought were contemptible, other times on exposing frauds.[10]

Lucian's contemptuous attitude towards religion, coupled with the fact that Christianity was not a dominant religion in his world, explains why he didn't produce an account that solely dealt with describing Christian customs and beliefs. In fact, Lucian would have never mentioned Christians at all if they hadn't been in the background when he was exposing certain imposters.

The Passing of Peregrinus

Given that it would not have been in Lucian's character to extol the virtues of any religion, let alone Christianity, it is interesting to

---

8   Lucian, *Hermotimus, or the Rival Philosophies*, para. 86, in *The Works of Lucian of Samosata*, vol. 2, trans. HW Fowler & FG Fowler, The Clarendon Press, Oxford, 1905, p. 90, www.archive.org/stream/ worksoflucianofs02luciuoft#page/90/mode/2up, 29/01/2013.
9   HW Fowler & FG Fowler (trans.), 'Introduction', in *The Works of Lucian of Samosata*, vol. 1, p. xii, www.archive.org/stream/ worksoflucianofs01luciuoft#page/xii/mode/2up, accessed 29/01/2013.
10 M Grant, *Greek and Latin Authors, 800 B.C. – A.D. 1000*, HW Wilson, New York, 1980, pp. 260–2. See also AM Harmon (trans.), 'Introduction', in *Lucian*, vol. 1, William Heinemann, London, & Harvard University Press, Cambridge, Massachusetts, US, 1962, www.archive.org/stream/lucianha01luciuoft#page/ n11/mode/2up, accessed 8/02/2013.

examine those writings that mention Christianity and compare them with statements about early Christianity from other authors with divergent biases.

The book of Lucian's that refers the most to Christianity is *The Passing of Peregrinus*, which concerns a charlatan named Peregrinus, whom Lucian met once while sailing.[11] One scholar described this book as:

> *An account of the life and death of a Cynic philosopher [Peregrinus] who for a time in his early life went over to Christianity, practising it to the point of imprisonment under a very tolerant administration, and after returning to Cynicism became in his old age so enamoured of Indic ideas and precedents that he cremated himself at Olympia, just after the games of AD 165 ... Lucian believes himself to be exposing a sham, whose zeal was not at all for truth but only for applause and renown ... Lucian not only knew the man but knew others who knew him ...*[12]

The description of Peregrinus as a Cynic philosopher doesn't simply mean that he was cynical in the modern sense of the word. In ancient times, Cynic philosophers were popularly known as dog philosophers, probably because of their outlandish actions and appearance. The outward characteristics that united them were built on the concepts of radical freedom of speech, self-sufficiency and indifference. They tried to alert society of its pathetic slavery to social conventions. Hence they would dress barefoot in ragged dirty clothes while using disgusting language to verbally abuse their listeners and perform vile acts in public. Their self-sufficiency amounted to nothing more than begging.[13]

---

11 Lucian, *The Passing of Peregrinus*, para. 43, in *Lucian*, vol. 5, trans. AM Harmon, William Heinemann, London, & Harvard University Press, Cambridge, Massachusetts, US, 1962, p. 49, www.archive.org/stream/lucianhar05luciuoft#page/n5/mode/2up. Lucian wrote much of the story of Peregrinus as if he heard it from an anonymous male speaker. The translator's footnote (n. 2) on pp. 8–9 states that it is 'beyond doubt' that Lucian is using artistic means to refer to himself, and expects his readers to understand that this is so.

12 AM Harmon (trans.), *Lucian*, vol. 5, William Heinemann, London, & Harvard University Press, Cambridge, Massachusetts, US, 1962, p. 1, www.archive.org/stream/lucianhar05luciuoft#page/x/mode/2up, accessed 12/03/2013.

13 PR Eddy, 'Jesus as Diogenes? Reflections on the Cynic Jesus thesis', *Journal of Biblical Literature*, 115(3), 1996, pp. 449–69.

Peregrinus certainly was a dubious character who was said to have been caught in adultery and later strangled his father. He ended his life in a very public manner through self-immolation. Lucian actually laughed when Peregrinus threw himself into the flames, as just before he leapt into the pyre, Peregrinus said: 'Spirits of my mother and my father, receive me with favour'.[14] Lucian also refers to him (though not by name) in *The Runaways* (*De Fugitives*), wherein Zeus and the personification of Philosophy discuss his burning.[15]

It seems that Lucian's motive for choosing Peregrinus lied in the fact that Peregrinus was not merely a small-time con artist, but someone who had 'philosophical, political, and religious pretensions'.[16] Peregrinus founded a new cult with a co-conspirator, Theagenes. It was well within Lucian's nature to publicly ridicule Peregrinus and to use a pamphlet to counter the growth of the new cult.[17]

The following is the portion of *The Passing of Peregrinus* that discusses the Christians and their 'instigator':

> *It was then that he [Peregrinus] learned the wondrous lore of the Christians, by association with their priests and scribes in Palestine. And — how else could it be? — in a trice he made them all look like children; for he was prophet, cult-leader, head of the synagogue, and everything, all by himself. He interpreted and explained some of their books and even composed many, and they revered him as a god, made use of him as a lawgiver, and set him down as a protector, next after that other [Christ], to be sure, whom they still worship [sebousi, σέβουσι]; the man who was crucified in Palestine because he introduced this new cult into the world.*
>
> *Then at length Proteus [Peregrinus' alternative name] was apprehended for this and thrown into prison, which itself gave him no little reputation as an asset for his future career and the charlatanism and notoriety-seeking that he was enamoured of.*

---

14 Lucian, *The Passing of Peregrinus*, para. 36, p. 41.
15 Lucian, *The Runaways*, para. 7, in *Lucian*, vol 5, trans. AM Harmon, William Heinemann, London, & Harvard University Press, Cambridge, Massachusetts, US, 1962, pp. 63–5, www.archive.org/stream/lucianhar05luciuoft#page/n5/mode/2up.
16 CP Jones, p. 132.
17 CP Jones, pp. 130–2.

> *Well, when he had been imprisoned, the Christians, regarding the incident as a calamity, left nothing undone in their effort to rescue him. Then, as this was impossible, every other form of attention was shown him, not in any casual way but with assiduity; and from the very break of day aged widows and orphaned children could be seen waiting near the prison, while their officials even slept inside with him after bribing the guards. Then elaborate meals were brought in and sacred books (logoi hieroi, λόγοι ἱεροί) of theirs were read aloud, and excellent Peregrinus — for he still went by that name — was called by them 'the new Socrates.'*
>
> *Indeed, people came even from the cities in Asia, sent by the Christians at their common expense, to succour [assist] and defend and encourage the hero. They show incredible speed whenever any such public action is taken; for in no time they lavish their all. So it was then in the case of Peregrinus; much money came to him from them by reason of his imprisonment and he procured not a little revenue from it. The poor wretches have convinced themselves, first and foremost, that they are going to be immortal and live for all time, in consequence of which they despise death and even willingly give themselves into custody, most of them. Furthermore, their first lawgiver persuaded them that they are all brothers of one another after they have transgressed once for all by denying the Greek gods and by worshipping [proskynosin, προσκυνῶσιν] the crucified sophist himself and living under his laws. Therefore they despise all things indiscriminately and consider them common property, receiving such doctrines traditionally without any definite evidence. So if any charlatan and trickster, able to profit by occasions, comes among them, he quickly acquires sudden wealth by imposing upon simple folk.*[18]

Peregrinus was eventually freed by the governor of Syria, and once again lived off the generosity of the Christians for a time. However, '... after he had transgressed in some way even against them — he was seen, I think, eating some of the food that is forbidden them — they no longer accepted him ...'[19]

---

18 Lucian, *The Passing of Peregrinus*, para. 11–13, pp. 13-15.
19 Lucian, *The Passing of Peregrinus*, para. 16, p. 19. The relationship between Christians and food is discussed later.

Two portraits of Christianity

Whilst scrutinising the above passage, I tried to picture the details of Lucians' portrait of Christians. If his was the only description of Christianity to have ever survived from antiquity, and if Christianity died out during Lucian's lifetime, what could be learnt about their customs and beliefs? As Lucian's picture emerged, I sought to examine any similarities and differences between his portrait and that provided by the text of the New Testament. In this way I found more than 20 identical brushstrokes between the two pictures. This harmony provides evidence that the New Testament's comments about Jesus and the early Christian community can be trusted. Some of these identical features are discussed below, each being named by a short summarising statement drawn from *The Passing of Peregrinus*. Matching excerpts from the New Testament and brief comments follow each summary.

Jesus was a lawgiver

One particular Pharisee, who was an expert in the Jewish law, asked Jesus:

> *'Teacher, which is the greatest commandment in the Law?'*
>
> *Jesus replied: '"Love the Lord your God with all your heart and with all your soul and with all your mind." This is the first and greatest commandment. And the second is like it: "Love your neighbor as yourself." All the Law and the Prophets hang on these two commandments.' (Matthew 22:36–40)*

Jesus also gave new laws that went further than the classical Jewish laws. It is recorded in Matthew 5:27–8 that Jesus said:

> *'You have heard that it was said, "You shall not commit adultery." But I tell you that anyone who looks at a woman lustfully has already committed adultery with her in his heart.'*

Jesus' message was regarded as 'the perfect law that gives freedom' (James 1:25). Paul in the New Testament writes of the 'law of Christ' being met when Christians carry each other's burdens (Galatians 6:2).[20]

Jesus was crucified

Lucian apparently wanted to emphasise this fact by stating it twice. All four Gospels record this event: Matthew 27, Mark 15, Luke 23 and John 18:28 to 19:42. The highlighting of this fact by Lucian may reflect that the intent of the first Christians was to 'preach Christ crucified' at the heart of their message (1 Corinthians 1:22–4). Lucian's statement is all the more pertinent when it is realised that Roman authorities weren't restricted to killing criminals by crucifixion; decapitation and burning being other commonly used methods.[21] Those guilty of sacrificing a man or obtaining omens from his blood were to be thrown to the beasts, and actual magicians were to be burnt alive.[22] Herod the tetrarch (a Roman puppet king) had John the Baptist beheaded.[23]

Jesus was crucified in Palestine

The Biblical references given above not only describe how Jesus died, but also where the deadly torture took place. What is startling is the New Testament's record that Jesus predicted these two aspects:

> *Now as Jesus was going up to Jerusalem, he took the twelve disciples aside and said to them: 'We are going up to Jerusalem,*

---

20 Ignatius also spoke of the 'law of Jesus Christ' in *Epistle to the Magnesians*, ch. 2, in A Roberts & J Donaldson (eds), *Ante-Nicene Fathers*, vol. 1, *The Apostolic Fathers, Justin Martyr, Irenaeus*, rev. AC Coxe, Hendrickson Publishers, Massachusetts, US, 2004. A digital copy is available at www.ccel.org/ccel/schaff/anf01.toc.html, accessed 29/01/2013.
21 B Chilton & CA Evans, *Studying the Historical Jesus: Evaluations of the State of Current Research*, EJ Brill, Leiden, The Netherlands, 1994, p. 410.
22 JB Rivers, 'Magic, religion, and law: the case of the Lex Cornelia de sicariis et veneficiis', in C Ando & J Rupke (eds), *Religion and Law in Classical and Christian Rome*, Franz Steiner, Verlag, Germany, 2006, pp. 47–67. Those found guilty of arranging someone to be transfixed were to be crucified or thrown to the beasts. Rivers was citing sections of *The Opinions of Paulus*, attributed to the jurist Julius Paulus, who flourished in the second and third centuries AD. His work was a summary of Roman law.
23 Matthew 14:1–12.

and the Son of Man [Jesus himself] will be betrayed to the chief priests and the teachers of the law. They will condemn him to death and will turn him over to the Gentiles [non-Jewish people, in this case the Roman rulers] to be mocked and flogged and crucified. On the third day he will be raised to life.' (Matthew 20:17–20, NIV 1984)

During Jesus' lifetime, Jerusalem was in the Roman province of Judea, but the province had been renamed Syria Palaestina in about 135 AD by Emperor Hadrian.[24,25] As Lucian wrote the story about Peregrinus about 30 years after this, he naturally used the more up-to-date name for the region.

Certainly Judea wasn't the only place where crucifixions were carried out. Tiberius — who was the emperor when Jesus was crucified — had ordered crucifixions even in Rome.[26] A 213-kilometre (115-mile) road between Rome and Capua, called the Appian Way, was used to crucify a slave every 32 metres (35 yards). These 6000 crucifixions marked the end of the slave revolt led by Sparticus.[27]

Jesus was crucified because of his relationship to the new cult

The Bible states that the Jews wanted Jesus crucified because he called himself the Christ, the Son of God (Luke 22:66–70). Christ was a term that carried the connotation of 'King of Israel'. Jesus deliberately acted out the role of a king shortly before his crucifixion (Matthew 21:4–6). Due to the Jewish crowd's anger towards Jesus, the Roman governor agreed to their demand for crucifixion (Mark 15:13–15, Luke 23:1–23). This governor may also have ordered the crucifixion because he

---

24 IJ Davidson, *The Birth of the Church: From Jesus to Constantine, A.D. 30 – 312*, Baker Books, Michigan, US, p. 146.
25 EM Smallwood, *The Jews Under Roman Rule: From Pompey to Diocletian: A Study in Political Relations*, EJ Brill, Leiden, The Netherlands, 1981, p. 1.
26 Josephus, *The Antiquities of the Jews*, book 18, ch. 3, s. 4, pp. 480–1.
27 Appian, *The Civil Wars*, book 1, para. 120, trans. John Carter, Penguin Books, London, 1996, p. 67. The interval of 32 metres is based on the assumption that the 6,000 were spread out evenly along the length of The Appian Way (refer to n. 189 for book 1, p. 366).

was concerned about the kingship claims of Jesus arousing the ire of his superiors. The governor, Pontius Pilate, commanded that a sign be placed at the top of the crucifix calling Jesus the 'King of the Jews' (Matthew 27:37).

Rome was certainly in the business of crushing any potential political adversaries. Finding a man who was considered by his followers as a king, and who was in the middle of significant public disturbances, was more than enough reason for the local Roman governor to sentence him to death. Jesus stated that he had come to offer his life to take the punishment of many (Mark 10:45), and acceptance of Jesus' forgiveness is the hallmark of being one of his followers. Jesus considered his ransoming action to be an implicit part of him being the Christ, and that his kingdom was from a different world (John 18:33–40). So from all these perspectives Jesus was crucified because of his new cult.

Jesus began the new cult of Christians

The New Testament describes how the term 'Christian' was first applied to Greek converts in the city of Antioch (Acts 11:19–26). They had become followers of Jesus after his crucifixion.

Jesus was a sophist

Originally the word 'sophist' (sophisten, σοφιστην) came from the Greek word *sophia*, meaning wisdom. In the Roman Empire, sophists were those who practiced rhetoric. Rhetoric refers to the art of impressive speaking or writing.[28] When Jesus taught, people were 'amazed at his teaching, because he taught as one who had authority, not as the teachers of the law' (Mark 1:22).

It is unlikely that Lucian was trying to give a compliment here to Jesus, even though Lucian himself was once a sophist. As Lucian described

---

28 HW Fowler & FG Fowler (trans.), *The Works of Lucian of* Samosata, vol. 1, p. 238, also defined 'sophist' this way: 'At Athens this word denoted in particular a paid teacher of grammar, rhetoric, politics, mathematics, etc. Lucian sometimes uses it also for "philosopher," and perhaps sometimes in the modern sense of a quibbler.'

the one worshipped by Christians as a 'crucified sophist', he may well have been sarcastic, as a crucified person symbolised a person deserving of terrible punishment. Ridicule is even more likely given Lucian's contempt of religion and philosophy, as discussed earlier. Lucian may have heard that Christians referred to the wisdom of Jesus (1 Corinthians 1:30, Colossians 2:3), and the great impact of his talks. But Lucian's cynical mind would have assumed that Jesus' wisdom was simply another form of philosophy or religion, and his preconceived notions did not allow such wisdom therefore to be good.[29]

Jesus was worshipped

Before going further, it is necessary to note that words often exist in several inflected forms. This simply means that the basic word changes form depending on the way an author or speaker wishes to make it function. For example, depending on the rules of English grammar, the noun 'teacher' may be inflected to become 'teacher's' to indicate ownership, and 'natal' may be qualified by writing 'ante-natal' or 'pre-natal'. When reading the following paragraphs in this section, keep in mind that although the basic Greek word may be, for example, *sebō*, it will be inflected depending on the rules of Greek grammar.

Lucian uses two different basic words to describe the worship given to Jesus: *proskyneō* and *sebō*. When Lucian wished his readers to understand that a creature was worshipped in the same way that a god was worshipped, he used those particularly poignant words. For example, Lucian narrated how the goddess Philosophy reported to her father — Zeus — that a multitude of people 'held me [Philosophy] in honour, respecting, admiring, and all but worshipping [proskyneontes, προσκυνουντες] me'.[30] In another book, Lucian writes of how the

---

29 Although the term sophist came to eventually have negative connotations, it did not necessarily have them at the time, Lucian wrote. The term had '... become a quasi-professional designation, analogous to "professor" or "doctor." Under Hadrian [r. 117–138 AD] and the Antonines [collectively r. 138–180 AD] the Sophists reached a high degree of dignity and influence' (p. 189), from R Jebb, 'Lucian', in *Essays and Addresses*, Cambridge University Press, Cambridge, UK, 1907, pp 164-192.. Sir Richard Jebb was Professor of Greek at Glasgow University and Regius Professor of Greek at Cambridge University.
30 Lucian, *The Runaways*, vol. 5, para. 3, p. 59.

Greek gods must be annoyed that the Egyptian animal gods — such as ibises, monkeys and billy-goats — were also being worshipped. One of the story's main characters asks Zeus and the other assembled Greek gods:

> 'How can you endure it, Gods, to see them worshipped [proskynoumena, προσκυνουμενα] as much as you, or even more?'[31]

The other Greek word used by Lucian to describe the worshipping of the divine is sebō. In his book *On Sacrifices*, he wrote:

> *That is the way the gods live, and as a result, the practices of men in the matter of divine worship are harmonious and consistent with all that. First they fenced off groves, dedicated mountains, consecrated birds and assigned plants to each god. Then they divided them up, and now worship (sebousi, σβουσι) them by nations and claim them as fellow-countrymen; the Delphians claim Apollo ...*[32]

Several other examples of how sebō functions to describe divine worship are given in the appendix at the end of this chapter. It is important to try to ascertain whether Lucian intended his readers to understand that Jesus was merely honoured by his followers in the same manner as they would honour a distinguished person or was actually worshipped by them. Part of this importance is due to the fact that in recent times some claim that Jesus was never worshipped by the disciples and early Christians but simply held in high esteem.[33] The

---

31 Lucian, *The Parliament of the Gods*, in *Lucian*, vol. 5, para. 10, trans. AM Harmon, William Heinemann, London, & Harvard University Press, Cambridge, Massachusetts, US, 1962, p. 431.

32 Lucian, *On Sacrifices*, in *Lucian*, vol. 3, para. 10, line 6, trans. AM Harmon, William Heinemann, London, & Harvard University Press, Cambridge, Massachusetts, US, 1962, (Greek text, p. 164, English text p. 165), www.archive.org/stream/lucianhar03luciuoft#page/n7/mode/2up.

33 Although the Jehovah's Witnesses' *1945 Yearbook* states that the purpose of their Watch Tower Bible and Tract Society was 'for public Christian worship of Almighty God and Christ Jesus ...', their *1969 Yearbook* deleted the last three words. For the 1945 publication, see p. 32 at http://wtarchive.svhelden.info/archive/en/yearbooks/yb1945_E.pdf, accessed 5/1/2013. For the 1969 publication, see www.mmoutreachinc.com/jehovahs_witnesses/charterscans/wt_chartscans.html, accessed 05/01/2013.

difficulty is that all words have a range of meanings and are subject to context, as with examples of hyperbole. For example, Christians today can be said to worship Jesus as God the Son, but an ardent husband may be described, albeit in an exaggerated fashion, as 'worshiping the ground his wife walks on'. Context is therefore always important — as is seeking patterns in the way a particular author, or group of authors, uses a certain word.

The New Testament gives an example of Jesus being worshipped after He had been crucified and resurrected:

> *While he [Jesus] was blessing them [the disciples], he left them and was taken up into heaven. Then they worshipped [proskynesantes, προσκυνήσαντες] him and returned to Jerusalem with great joy. (Luke 24:51–2)*

This passage is particularly powerful because the author, Luke, chose proskyneō only two other times in his Gospel. These were when he recorded Satan tempting Jesus to worship him (Luke 4:6–8):

> *And he [the devil] said to him 'I will give you all ... [the kingdoms of the world] ... authority and splendor ... If you worship [proskyneses] me, it will all be yours.' Jesus answered, 'It is written: "Worship [proskyneseis] the Lord your God and serve him only."'*

Luke also appears to have deliberately avoided using proskyneō to narrate how people greeted Jesus with the usual customary degree of respect. This is shown by the way that he records two encounters that are also found in the Gospel of Matthew. In both of these encounters, Matthew makes use of proskyneō (Matthew 8:2, 9:18), whereas Luke uses different words (Luke 5:12, 8:41). It seems very likely that Luke deliberately restricts his use of the word proskuneō so that there would be no uncertainty about what he meant by this word when he described the disciples worshipping Jesus.

Other New Testament references to Jesus being worshipped are made transparent when it is recalled that praying to a god is itself an act of worship. Jesus instructed that prayers be addressed to him and that he would answer these prayers (John 14:13–14). The Bible records Christians praying to Jesus (Acts 7:59).

Although the word sebō is not used by any of the New Testament authors in relation to Jesus, several do so to describe the devotion of God-fearing people,[34] or to describe the worshipping of God[35] or the goddess Artemis.[36]

There is also evidence from outside of the New Testament that Christians worshipped Jesus. Justin Martyr (c.100–165 AD) wrote that worshipping Jesus was intrinsic to their faith:

> *But both Him [the most true God, the Father of righteousness], and the Son ... and the prophetic Spirit, we worship and adore [sebometha kai proskunoumen, σεβόμεθα καὶ προσκυνοῦμεν], knowing them in reason and truth ...*[37]

Lucian's recounting of the worship given to Jesus belies his disgust that a man should be regarded in this way as a god. This is borne out by the following excerpt from *The Passing of Peregrinus*, which emphasises that Lucian considered Jesus as a mere man:

> *And set him down as a protector (prostaten, προστατην), next after that other, to be sure, whom they still worship, the man who was crucified in Palestine because he introduced this new cult into the world.*[38]

Following the word 'whom', a note in the English translation states that:

> *The sense of the unemended text here is '[And set him down as a] protector; that great man, to be sure, they still worship,' etc.*

---

34 Acts 13:43, 50; 17:4,17.
35 Matthew 15:9, Mark 7:7; Acts 16:14; Acts 18:7,13.
36 Acts 19:27
37 Justin Martyr, *The First Apology of Justin*, ch. 6, p. 164, in A Roberts & J Donaldson (eds), *Ante-Nicene Fathers*, vol. 1, *The Apostolic Fathers, Justin Martyr, Irenaeus*, rev. AC Coxe, Hendrickson Publishers, Massachusetts, US, 2004. A digital copy is available at www.ccel.org/ccel/schaff/anf01.toc.html, accessed 29/01/2013. See also 'Dialogue with Trypho', ch. 68, pp. 232–3 of the same book.
38 Lucian, *The Passing of Peregrinus*, para. 11, p. 13.

Reinforcing this understanding of prostaten as a human hero, Sir Jebb translated the relevant section as: '... and adopted him as their champion ...'.[39]

In another English translation, the Greek word for protector is rendered 'president', and the phrase under consideration is as follows:

> ... and declared him their president. The Christians, you know, worship a man to this day,—the distinguished personage who introduced their novel rites, and was crucified on that account.[40]

It seems that by calling the instigator of Christianity, 'the distinguished personage' or 'great man', Lucian was emphasising that both the instigator and Peregrinus were mere mortals. Perhaps Lucian uses the Greek word prostaten to reinforce his contempt for the Christians who — as far as he was concerned — worshipped the crucified man as a God. Jebb considers that Lucian is being mildly ironic, intending the reader to understand that Jesus is great only in the eyes of the Christians.[41]

Christian priests were in Palestine

All Christians collectively are regarded as being a royal priesthood (hierateuma, ἱεράτευμα) in the New Testament (1 Peter 2:9). The priesthood of all believers is implicit in the New Testament teaching that all Christians are described as actually being the temple of God

---

39 R Jebb, p. 186. Jebb also states that *prostaten* does not warrant the inference made by others that Peregrinus had held the office of bishop. It is hard to imagine why this inference arose, as the femine form *prostatis* is only used once in the New Testament (Romans 16:2), and not at all in the Septuagint or in the writings of the apostolic fathers. The term 'apostolic fathers' refers to Christian leaders who wrote between c. 150 AD to 250 AD. The masculine form *prostaths* is not present at all in these collections.

40 Lucian, *The Death of Peregrine*, para. 11, in *The Works of Lucian of Samosata*, vol. 4, trans. HW Fowler & FG Fowler, The Clarendon Press, Oxford, 1905 *The Works of Lucian of Samosata*, vol. 3, trans. HW Fowler & FG Fowler, The Clarendon Press, Oxford, 1905, p. 82, www.archive.org/stream/worksoflucianofs04luciuoft#page/82/mode/2up, accessed 03/02/2013. The word 'man' is italicised in the original.

41 R Jebb, pp. 189–90. Jebb writes the phrase a second time as 'the Christians still reverence that person who (to them) is so great'.

(1 Corinthians 3:16, 2 Corinthians 6:16). Normally a Jewish priest would be an intermediary between God's presence in the temple and the common people. However, if the common people become indwelt by God's presence then they in fact function as priests. Even in the early part of the second century, and possibly in the last part of the first century, 'priest' was a label used for Christians by other Christians such as Ignatius of Antioch in Syria.[42] From the late second century the term priest was applied to Christian leaders such as bishops and elders, and it is probably in this sense that Lucian uses the word.[43]

Christians read from sacred books, which were interpreted and explained

Christian holy books were called scripture, and according to the New Testament: 'All scripture is God-breathed and is useful for teaching, rebuking, correcting and training in righteousness' (2 Timothy 3:16). The letter of Paul to the Christians in Colosse states:

> *After this letter has been read to you, see that it is also read in the church of the Laodiceans and that you in turn read the letter from Laodicea (Colossians 4:16).*[44]

And, Justin Martyr wrote:

> *And on the day called Sunday, all who live in cities or in the country gather together in one place, and the memoirs of the apostles or the writings of the prophets are read ...*[45]

---

42 Ignatius, *The Epistle of Ignatius to the Ephesians*, ch. 5. The term 'priests' is used instead of disciples. Later in chapter 9, Ignatius quotes 1 Peter 2:9 to remind the Christians that they are royal priests. The Didache 13:3 (see www.ccel.org/l/lake/fathers/didache.htm for the Greek version) speaks of Christian leaders as high priests (αρχιερεις).
43 IJ Davidson, p. 298.
44 Other scriptural letters were also to be read to all the Christians in the area; refer to 1 Thessalonians 5:27.
45 Justin Martyr, *The First Apology of Justin*, ch. 67.

Not only did the Christians read their holy books,⁴⁶ they extensively quoted from them. A total of 36,289 citations of the New Testament can be found among the writings of the early (c. 150–340 AD) Christians.⁴⁷ Lucian's description of the books read to Peregrinus while he was in prison are noteworthy, as he appears to have never used the description 'sacred books' (logoi hieroi, λόγοι ἱεροὶ) in any of his other writings, despite discussing various religions and their practices in a number of his books. It is probable that Lucian highlighted the reading of holy books, as this was especially evident among Christians compared to the Greco–Roman religions prevalent at that time. These other religions in particular '... maintained strict secrecy about ... [their] teachings and practices, revealing them only to initiates'.⁴⁸ Even today there are religions that haven't committed much or any of their beliefs to writing. The Japanese religion of Shinto has 'no scripture corresponding to the Bible of Christianity ...'. ⁴⁹ (More on the existence of sacred books in pagan religions can be found in the appendix at the end of this book, 'A brief background of first-century Judea').

Christians revered their leaders greatly

The first book of Thessalonians 5:12 states: 'Now we ask you, brothers, to respect those who work hard among you, who are over you in the Lord and who admonish you'. The New Testament declares that deacons are 'worthy of respect' (1 Timothy 3:8).

---

46 Irenaeus, *Fragments from the Lost Writings of Irenaeus*, ch. 52, in A Roberts & J Donaldson (eds), *Ante-Nicene Fathers*, vol. 1, *The Apostolic Fathers, Justin Martyr, Irenaeus*, rev. AC Coxe, Hendrickson Publishers, Massachusetts, US, 2004, p. 576. A digital copy is available at www.ccel.org/ccel/schaff/anf01.toc.html, accessed 29/01/2013.

47 NL Geisler & WE Nix, *A General Introduction to the Bible: Revised and Expanded*, Moody Press, Chicago, US, 1986, pp. 422–31.

48 D Ulansey, 'Mithraism: The cosmic mysteries of Mithras', www.well.com/~davidu/mithras.html, accessed 10/3/2007. This article is a summary of his book *The Origins of the Mithraic Mysteries*, paperback edn, Oxford University Press, New York, 1991.

49 Umeda Yoshimi, 'The role of Shinto in Japanese culture (past, present and future', keynote speech presented at the First International Sun and Tao Conference, Korea University, Republic of Korea, 22–25 October 2009, accessed at www.shinto.org/eng/shinto-e.html, accessed 10/01/2013.

The statement that Christians 'revered him [Peregrinus] as a god' may simply reflect Lucian's view of what he regarded as excessive admiration. It is evident from the Greek verb chosen to describe this esteem, *ēdounto* (ἡδοῦντο),[50] that Lucian did not wish to convey the notion that Pergerinus was actually worshipped as a god. Sir Richard Jebb translated ēdounto as 'regard', and hence wrote the phrase as 'regarded him as a god'.[51] Harmon's Greek version of *The Passing of Peregrinus* supplies a footnote indicating that some manuscripts have *hēgounto* (ἡγουντο) as the Greek verb.[52] The dictionary (lexical) entry for this word (*hēgeomai*, ἡγέομαι) means to 'go before, lead the way'.[53] Although the beings that we freely worship must at least also be respected by us, those we respect are definitely not always those that we worship. This difference is reflected in the writings of an early Christian leader of Rome, Clement, who wrote: 'Let us reverence them that are over us. Let us honour our elders'.[54] Certainly Clement didn't intend his Christian readers to worship their elders.

Lucian's description of Christian leaders — in this case Peregrinus — being held in such high regard mirrors a practice found among early Christians. Apart from the example of Clement's writings, another Christian leader, Ignatius (c. 35–117 AD), wrote to the Christians in Ephesus that: '... we should look upon the bishop even as we would look upon the Lord Himself'.[55] At first sight this seems to be a recommendation for Christians to idolise their bishops. However,

---

50 Definitions of the dictionary (lexical) form, based on the Liddell-Scott-Jones (LSJ) Greek–English lexicon, include 'to stand in awe of' and 'show a sense of regard' (Perseus Digital Library, www.perseus.tufts.edu/hopper/morph?l=h%29dounto&la=greek#lexicon, accessed 3/02/2013).

51 R Jebb, p. 186.

52 Lucian, *The Passing of Peregrinus*, para. 12, n. 2.

53 Definition of the dictionary (lexical) form based on the Liddell-Scott-Jones (LSJ) Greek-English lexicon (Perseus Digital Library, www.perseus.tufts.edu/hopper/morph?l=%28+h%29gounto&la=greek#lexicon, accessed 12/01/2013).

54 Clement, *The First Epistle of Clement to the Corinthians*, trans. Charles H. Hoole, 1885,digital copy available at www.earlychristianwritings.com/text/1clement-hoole.html, accessed 12/01/2013.

55 Ignatius, *The Epistle of Ignatius to the Ephesians*, ch. 6. The Ignatian letter to the Ephesians is part of a group of seven letters that are generally held to be authentic.

upon closer scrutiny it is clear that Ignatius did not expect his readers to worship bishops in a way that they would worship Jesus. Ignatius wrote several lines later that: 'Nor indeed do ye hearken to any one rather than to Jesus Christ, the true Shepherd and Teacher ... there is one Lord ... one God and Father of all, who is over all'.[56]

There are New Testament accounts of those who excessively revered Christians. A God-fearing centurion called Cornelius tried to revere Peter, a disciple of Jesus, by bowing in front of him, but Peter immediately admonished Cornelius (Acts 10:23–6). On another occasion, a non-Christian crowd needed rebuking for worshipping two Christian leaders as the gods Zeus and Hermes. This occurred after they had watched Barnabas and Paul perform a healing miracle (Acts 14:8–10). These two leaders made a very strong response to the crowd's worship:

> ... *they tore their clothes and rushed out into the crowd, shouting: 'Friends, why are you doing this? We too are only human, like you.' (Acts 8:14–15)*

Christian leaders were lawgivers

The New Testament instructs that Christian leaders were to preach, teach and command their flock (1 Timothy 4:11, 5:17). In these ways, such leaders were certainly acting as lawgivers from the point of view of those outside of the Christian faith.

Christians were imprisoned for their faith

The New Testament records how King Herod imprisoned various Christian leaders, including Peter (Acts 12:1–4). It appears that one of Herod's reasons for doing so was because it pleased the Jewish authorities, who were directly opposed to the Christian faith. On another occasion, the book of Acts relates how the magistrates of the city of Philippi (in present-day Greece) imprisoned Paul and Silas (Acts 16:16–40). This was after these Christian men freed a girl from demon possession.

---

56 Ignatius, *The Epistle of Ignatius to the Ephesians*, ch. 6.

Socrates was a name held in esteem by Christians

Socrates had been placed on trial by the Athenians and his main accuser charged:

> *That Socrates is a doer of evil, and corrupter of the youth, and he does not believe in the gods of the state, and has other new divinities of his own.*[57]

Despite believing in the existence of a god, or gods, of some type, he was accused of being a 'complete atheist'.[58] He was given the death sentence in about 399 BC. The Athenian Christian philosopher Athenagoras (c. 133–190 AD)[59] made reference to Socrates in order to establish the principle that the virtue of a person may be great, despite the opinions of the majority of the populace at that time. As other virtuous Greek heroes had also met the brunt of the majority, Athenagoras said that it was the tendency for vice to wage war on virtue. This war — in Athenagoras' argument — thus accounted for the atrocious charges levelled at the Christian community. These charges included cannibalism and sexual immorality.

Justin Martyr[60] also used Socrates as a commendable example. He lauded Socrates for rightfully ascribing certain gods as merely evil spirits.

---

57 Plato, *Apology*, trans. B Jowett, http://classics.mit.edu/Plato/apology.html, accessed 29/12/2012.
58 Plato, *Apology*.
59 Athenagoras, *A Plea for the Christians*, ch. 31, trans. BP Pratten, in A Roberts & J Donaldson (eds), *Ante-Nicene Fathers*, vol. 2, *Fathers of the Second Century, Hermas, Tatian, Athenagoras, Theophilus, and Clement of Alexandria (Entire)*, rev. AC Coxe, Hendrickson Publishers, Massachusetts, US, 2004. A digital copy is available at http://www.ccel.org/ccel/schaff/anf02.i.html, accessed 29/01/2013.
60 Justin Martyr, *The First Apology of Justin*, ch. 5, p. 164. He also refers to Socrates favourably in chapter 46, p. 178. In his *Second Apology*, ch. 10, p. 191–2 Justin notes that Socrates was accused of the same crime as the Christians, namely that of denying godhood to certain gods recognised by the state (thus an atheist) and of introducing new divinities.

Lucian's praising of Peregrinus as the 'new Socrates' may therefore indicate that at least some of Peregrinus' teachings were famous for denigrating various popular gods as being evil or irrelevant. This is corroborated by the likelihood, given the context, that the compliment was given to Peregrinus while he was in prison. It is quite reasonable to assume that Peregrinus' very vocal denunciation of the popular gods resulted in him being imprisoned, similar to the experience of Socrates.

Christians included orphaned children and aged widows

The New Testament speaks of a number of widows whose actions indicated that they were followers of Jesus (1 Timothy 5:9–10). Athenagoras wrote that old uneducated women were also included as part of the Christian community.[61] The Bible states in James 1:27 that: 'Religion that God our Father accepts as pure and faultless is this: to look after orphans and widows in their distress …'. Given that Christians cared for widows and orphans, it is reasonable to assume that some of them became Christians. Not just aged widows, but older women in general were instructed to 'teach what is good' (Titus 2:3). The Christian community was certainly not an exclusive, male chauvinistic group.

Christians believed they would be immortal and live forever

The New Testament strongly asserts the amazing concept that Christians will live forever because of their belief in Jesus:

> *For God so loved the world, that he gave his one and only Son [Jesus], that whoever believes in him shall not perish but have eternal life. (John 3:16)*

> *I [Jesus] tell you the truth, whoever hears my word and believes him who sent me has eternal life and will not be condemned; he has crossed over from death to life. (John 5:24)*

---

61 Athenagoras, *A Plea for the Christians*, ch. 31.

> *We [baptised Christians] were therefore buried with him through baptism into death in order that, just as Christ was raised from the dead through the glory of the Father, we too may live a new life. For if we have been united with him in a death like his, we will certainly also be united with him in a resurrection like his. (Romans 6:4–5)*

Christians denied the Greek gods

Denouncing the existence and relevance of other gods is a direct outworking of believing Jesus' teachings. Jesus taught: 'I am the way, the truth and the life. No one comes to the Father except through me' (John 14:6). Jesus made it abundantly clear that he was God in human flesh;[62] and that all other apparent ways to God were detrimental:

> *Therefore Jesus said again, 'Very truly I tell you, I am the gate for the sheep. All who have come before me are thieves and robbers ... I am the gate, whoever enters through me will be saved.' (John 10:7–9)*

It is only logical that a convert to Christianity could not continue to worship other so-called gods, and it therefore follows that they deny giving authority to these idols (1 Corinthians 12:9). An example of Christian converts ceasing their idol worship is described by Paul. Writing in about 55 AD, he records how some of the first people in Corinth to become Christians had (past tense) been worshippers of other gods (idols):

> *Do you not know that the wicked will not inherit the kingdom of God? Do not be deceived: Neither the sexually immoral nor idolaters nor adulterers nor male prostitutes nor homosexual offenders nor thieves nor the greedy nor drunkards ... will inherit the kingdom of God. And that is what some of you were. But you were washed ... [and] justified in the name of the Lord Jesus Christ.' (1 Corinthians 6:9–11, NIV 1984)[63]*

---

62 Refer to the section titled 'Jesus claimed to be God the Son' in chapter 7. See also RL Reymond, *Jesus, Divine Messiah*, Christian Focus Publications, Fearn, Scotland, 2003.

63 Refer also to Acts 4:12, John 14:6, Matthew 7:13–14 and John 10:7–10.

Justin Martyr wrote:

> ... and in obedience to Him [Jesus Christ], we [Christians] not only deny that they who did such things as these were gods, but assert that they are wicked and impious demons ...[64]

Christians become brothers only after worshipping Jesus

Jesus taught: 'If anyone loves me, he will obey my teaching. My Father will love him, and we will come to him and make our home with him' (John 14:15–24). Loving Jesus is a prerequisite for worship. The New Testament teaches that only when people believe in Jesus are they adopted into God's family (Romans 8:9–17). This privilege is actually referred to in a legal sense as being a 'right':

> Yet to all who did receive him, to those who believed in his name, he gave the right to become children of God — children born not of natural descent, nor of human decision or a husband's will, but born of God. (John 1:12–13)

Christians shared their belongings and were not materialistic

Sharing was a prominent aspect of Christian life (Acts 9:36, 11:29). At one point in time Christians were so ardent in this manner that it was said:

> All the believers were one in heart and mind. No one claimed that any of their possessions was their own, but they shared everything they had ... there were no needy persons among them. For from time to time those who owned land or houses sold them, brought the money from the sales and put it at the apostles' feet, and it was distributed to anyone who had need. (Acts 4:32–5)

Christians had regulations about food

When the Christians finally disowned Peregrinus, it was in regard to him eating incorrect food. The New Testament teaches that food

---

64 Justin Martyr, *The First Apology of Justin*, ch. 5.

sacrificed to idols can be eaten, as the idol is nothing but a man-made creation. However, some less-informed Christians were not aware of this teaching and felt that eating such food was wrong because it would have been first offered to an idol and therefore become unclean. In consideration of these less-informed Christians, other Christians were not meant to eat such food (1 Corinthians 8:4–13).

Christians were simple folk

In about 55 AD, Paul reminded those Christians living in Corinth that before they were rescued by Jesus: 'Not many of you were wise by human standards; not many were influential; not many were of noble birth' (1 Corinthians 1:26). So it seems that the majority of Christians living in that one particular city were of low social standing. However, the New Testament also states that the early Christian community included people of high public standing: a director of public works (Romans 16:23), an Ethiopian treasurer (Acts 8:26–30), a centurion from an Italian regiment (Acts 10:1–48), a person brought up with Herod the tetrarch (Acts 13:1), a governor of Cyprus (Acts 13:6–12) and a Jewish synagogue ruler (Acts 18:8). By the time of Lucian, Christians also included those who had been philosophers, such as Athenagoras. It is quite possible that Lucian's implication that all Christians were simple was a deliberate exaggeration designed to add to the ridicule.

Alexander the Oracle-Monger

This investigation of *The Passing of Peregrinus* has revealed a very rich picture of early Christian community. However, there is one other book of Lucian's that provides a few more fine points.

Lucian mentions Christians in his book *Alexander the Oracle-Monger*. Alexander was called an oracle-monger because he greatly profited from the many oracles (or prophecies) that he gave in response to individual questions from his numerous followers. In this account, Christians and Epicureans[65] opposed the evil impostor, Alexander, while he was in Rome. During this encounter, Alexander

---

65   A group of philosophers following the teaching of Epicurus.

proclaimed that the Christians had overrun the region of Pontus and should be stoned. This brief reference to Christians supports the historical accuracy of the New Testament in two more ways: the New Testament specifically tells of Christians being in Pontus and Rome (Romans 1:7, 1 Peter 1:1–2) and it also speaks of Christians being punished by stoning (Acts 7:54–60, 14:19 and 2 Corinthians 11:25).

Conclusion

Lucian's books provide a portrait of Jesus and the beliefs of early Christians. If the New Testament's portrayal of Christianity had become lost, we could recover many of the same brushstrokes that had been present in the New Testament by reading some of Lucian's work. Lucian's canvas would reveal:

- The instigator of the Christian religion was a lawgiver and impressive speaker.

- He was crucified in Palestine because of his relationship to the new cult.

- Christians read from sacred books, which were interpreted and explained to them by leaders whom they revered greatly.

- These leaders were also lawgivers, and some lived in Palestine.

- Christians were imprisoned for their faith and some were orphaned children and aged widows.

- They believed they would live forever and denied the potency and existence of the Greek gods.

- They so admired the originator of their religion that they worshipped him, and through this act became brothers of one another.

- As a community they were noted for sharing their belongings and not being materialistic.

- They had regulations about food, and many were simple folk.

- Christians could be found in Rome and the region of Pontus, and were sometimes persecuted by stoning.

This depiction of Christians given by Lucian raises many questions. Some scholars have suggested that Lucian never expected his readers to consider the story truthful. Others have speculated about how Lucian learnt about Christianity. The next chapter investigates these and other related matters.

For convenience, all these matching statements from Lucian and other non-Christian writers are presented at the end of this book in the appendix 'Points of agreement between biblical and non-biblical sources'.

Appendix
Examples of sebō being chosen to indicate worship of divinities

As mentioned earlier, many words have a range of meanings, making the context in which a word is used very important. It is also helpful to search for patterns in the way a particular author, or group of authors, has used a certain word. The Greek word sebō has been defined as meaning 'to stand in awe; to venerate; reverence; worship; adore'.[66]

Lucian's book *A True Story* contains a very obvious example of how he uses sebō to describe divine worship:

> *As one enters the city, on the right is the temple of Night, for the gods they worship [nychtoousebousi, Νυκτῶονσέβουσι] most are Night and the Cock, whose sanctuary is built near the harbour. On the left is the palace of Sleep, who rules among them ...*'[67]

Other authors living at about the same time as Lucian also made use of sebō in this manner:

---

66 WD Mounce, *Interlinear for the Rest of Us: The Reverse Interlinear for New Testament Word Studies*, Zondervan, Grand Rapids, Michigan, US, 2005, p. 889.
67 Lucian, *A True Story*, p. 339 (English), 338 (Greek), www.archive.org/stream/lucianha01luciuoft#page/338/mode/2up.

- A book by the Greek historian Appian describes how the inhabitants of Cyzicus (a town in modern-day Turkey) gave their ultimate veneration [*sebousin*] to the goddess Proserpina.[68]

- Philo's (c. 20 BC to 45 AD) writings contain two poignant examples of how sebō can be used to distinguish between honouring and worshipping. In *The Decalogue*, he notes that the Egyptians:

    select the most fierce, and untameable of all wild animals, honouring lions, and crocodiles ... with temples, and sacred precincts, and sacrifices, and assemblies in their honour, and solemn processions, and things of that kind... both which creatures they honour and worship [sebousi kai timosi, σέβουσι καὶ τιμῶσι).[69]

    Similarly, Philo's *On the Virtues* describes:

    the Hebrews [who] ... honour and worship [sebousi kai timosi, σέβουσι καὶ τιμῶσι) the highest and mightiest Cause of all things, as being dedicated to the Creator and Father of the universe as his peculiar people ...[70]

- Pausanias' 10-volume series on Greece, written in the second century AD, speaks of the 'god most worshipped [sebousi]' by the people of Bulon.[71]

---

68 Appian, *The Foreign Wars*, ch. 11, para. 75, in *The Roman History of Appian of Alexandria*, vol. 1, trans. H White, Macmillan Company, New York, 1899: 'It is said that the city of Cyzicus was given by Zeus to Proserpina by way of dowry, and that of all the gods the inhabitants have most veneration for her'. Appian (c. 95 – c.165 AD) also had Roman citizenship.

69 Philo, *The Decalogue*, 78, in *The Works of Philo Judaeus: the Contemporary of Josephus, translated from the Greek*, trans. CD Yonge, HG Bohn, London, 1855 www.archive.org/stream/worksofphilojuda03phil#page/152/mode/2up, accessed 3/2/2013. Note Yonge changed the title of this chapter to 'A treatise concerning the Ten Commandments, which are the heads of the law'.

70 Philo, *On the Virtues*, 34, in *The Works of Philo Judaeus: the Contemporary of Josephus, translated from the Greek*, trans. CD Yonge, HG Bohn, London, 1855, www.archive.org/stream/worksofphilojuda03phil#page/420/mode/2up, accessed 3/2/2013. Note Yonge changed the title of this chapter to 'A treatise on three virtues, that is to say, courage, humanity, and repentance'.

71 Pausanias, *Description of Greece*, book 10, ch. 37, para. 3.

14

Lucian's book about Peregrinus: history or fantasy?

The Passing of Peregrinus has been regarded as belonging to the genre of satire. Some people assume that satire belongs only to the realm of fiction and then deduce that Lucian's depiction of Christians is also entirely fictitious, or at least contains much that is spurious.[1] Others surmise that as Lucian was so adept at writing fantasy, he may have been incapable of writing history. These concerns are worth investigating because, if true, Lucian's witness to Christian beliefs is diminished.

By definition satire does not indicate a lack of truth in a story, but simply that ridicule — including hurtful remarks — is one of the main components.[2] As shown in the previous chapter, Lucian was a very adept writer of fantasy. But his works of fantasy are very easily discerned from his other writings. For example in *The Runaways*, the main characters are all Greek gods, such as Zeus, Apollo and Philosophy, who are clearly portrayed as fictitious.

---

1 For example, see chapter 2 of WR Cassels, *Supernatural Religion*, Watts and Co., London, 1902, p. 165, www.ftarchives.net/cassels/sr/contents.htm, accessed 8/02/2013.
2 HW Fowler & FG Fowler (eds), *The Concise Oxford Dictionary of Current English*, 5th edn, 1964: 'Satire: use of ridicule, irony, sarcasm, etc., in … writing for the ostensible purpose of exposing & discouraging vice or folly.'

Four ways to examine *The Passing of Peregrinus*

The following four questions seem to be worth investigating in order to determine if *The Passing of Peregrinus* is essentially historical:

1. What indications are there that Lucian had the ability to write a historically accurate account?

2. Did Lucian intend his readers to regard the material as being true (apart from the satirical sections of the story)?

3. Was the content true, or at least grounded in truth?

4. Is Lucian's account consistent within itself?

Was Lucian capable of writing a historically accurate account?

Lucian was very particular about the need for truth, accuracy and integrity when writing about historical matters. In fact he wrote a book on *How to Write History*.[3] The following are excerpts from it:

> ... but history cannot admit a lie, even a tiny one ...[4]

> ... we can put up with all these things [poor writers] as far as they are faults of expression ... but to misplace localities even, not just by parasangs [approx. 5 kilometres or 3 miles] but by whole days' marches, what fineness of style does that resemble?[5]

> The historian's sole task is to tell the tale as it happened ... even if he personally hates certain people [that he is writing about] he will think the public interest far more binding, and regard truth as worth more than enmity, and if he has a friend he will nevertheless not spare him if he errs.[6]

---

3   Lucian, *How to Write History*, in *Lucian*, vol. 6, trans. K Kilburn, William Heinemann, London, & Harvard University Press, Cambridge, US, 1959, www.archive.org/stream/luciankilb06luciuoft#page/n17/mode/2up. The study of how history is written is called historiography. Lucian particularly focuses the book (also called *On Writing History*) on the Parthian war, which ceased in 166 AD.
4   Lucian, *How to Write History*, para. 7, p.11.
5   Lucian, *How to Write History*, para. 24, p. 35.
6   Lucian, *How to Write History*, para. 39, p. 55.

> As to the facts themselves, he should not assemble them at random, but only after much laborious and painstaking investigation. He should for preference be an eyewitness, but, if not, listen to those who tell the more impartial story ... When he has collected all or most of the facts ... after arranging them into order, let him give it beauty and enhance it with the charms of expression, figure, and rhythm.[7]

The above points indicate that Lucian knew how to write the genre of history. This awareness infiltrates his various works, even those belonging to what could be called historical satire. One scholar noted that Lucian's ability to write accurate details in his non-fiction writings has been well established:

> It had long been observed that some of his [Lucian's] details were confirmed by other literary witnesses such as the Elder Pliny and Aelian, but the evidence of archaeology has added much more.[8]

Did Lucian intend his readers to regard the work as true?

There are many indicators that Lucian expected his readers to understand that *The Passing of Peregrinus* was a genuine account describing real people and events. These include the following six points:

1. Lucian's penchant for wanting the reader to know what was true and what was not is shown when he discloses any of his doubts. At one point, Lucian was not sure what exactly Peregrinus did to cause a rift in his relationship with the Christians, so he wrote: 'he was seen, I think, eating some of the food that is forbidden them ...'[9]

2. Lucian's account of Peregrinus sometimes cited sources of information, which is a mark of historical writing. This is despite

---

7 Lucian, *How to Write History*, paras 47–8, p. 61.
8 CP Jones, *Culture and Society in Lucian*, Harvard University Press, London, 1986, p. 41.
9 Lucian, *The Passing of Peregrinus*, para. 6, in *Lucian*, vol. 5, trans. AM Harmon, William Heinemann, London, & Harvard University Press, Cambridge, Massachusetts, US, 1962, p. 19, www.archive.org/stream/lucianhar05luciuoft#page/n5/mode/2up.

the fact that citations were not given much priority in ancient times.[10] One of these sources was Onesicritus, a biographer of Alexander the Great. Lucian made use of Onesicritus' work when noting that Peregrinus' stated aim of self 'carbonisation' was to illustrate great fortitude.[11] One of Peregrinus' disciples said that this aim was in line with the Brahmans of India, however, the Hindu Brahmans' style had more of a stoic flare about it as, in the words of Lucian:

> *They do not leap into the fire (so Onesicritus says, Alexander's navigator, who saw Calanus [a Brahman sage] burning), but when they have built their pyre, they stand close beside it motionless and endure being toasted; then, mounting upon it, they cremate themselves decorously, without the slightest alteration of the position in which they are lying.*[12]

3. Lucian indicated when he had heard only some of an oration, thus being only a partial eyewitness (ear-witness?). He noted that during one of Peregrinus' last speeches that 'though I heard but little on account of the number of bystanders ... This much, however, I overheard ...'[13]

4. He was able to admit when he had to rely on someone else's verbal report for his source of information, as seen when recounting the following:

> *Well, a short time before his [Peregrinus'] end, about nine days, it may be, having eaten more than enough, I suppose, he was sick during the night and was taken with a very violent fever. This was told me by Alexander the physician, who had been called in to see him. He said that he found him rolling on the ground, unable to stand the burning, pleading very passionately for a drink of cold water, but that he would not give it to him. Moreover, he told him, he [Alexander] said,*

---

10 'Unfortunately, like most ancient authors, Appian [a historian of Rome] hardly ever mentions an authority ...' (Appian, *The Civil Wars*, book 1, trans. J Carter, Penguin Books, London, 1996, p. xxxii).
11 Lucian, *The Passing of Peregrinus*, para. 23, pp. 26–7.
12 Lucian, *The Passing of Peregrinus*, para. 25, pp. 29–31.
13 Lucian, *The Passing of Peregrinus*, paras 32–3, p. 37.

that Death, if he absolutely wanted him, had come to his door spontaneously, so that it would be well to go along, without asking any favour from the fire; and Proteus [Peregrinus' alternative name] replied: 'But that way would not be so notable, being common to all men.' That is Alexander's story.[14]

5. As noted earlier in this chapter, Lucian regarded accuracy in reporting distances to be a necessary feature in historical accounts. This is reflected when he wrote that Peregrinus' immolation was at Harpina '... quite twenty furlongs [4 kilometres, 2.5 miles] from Olympia as one goes past the hippodrome towards the east'.[15] In the 1800s its ruins were said to 'stand upon a ridge a little northward of the village of Miraka'.[16] Present-day maps show that Miraka village is less than 3 kilometres (about 2 miles) from ancient Olympia (Archia Olympia).[17]

6. Lucian's essential honesty in *The Passing of Peregrinus* is highlighted when he readily admits to the one occasion that he gave a fanciful verbal version of a particular event to various others:

In that business [of turning away those who were too late for the fiery spectacle], I assure you, my friend, I had no end of trouble, telling the story to all while they asked questions and sought exact information. Whenever I noticed a man of taste, I would tell him the facts without embellishment, as I have to you, but for the benefit of the dullards, agog to listen, I would thicken the plot a bit on my own account, saying that when the pyre was kindled and Proteus flung himself bodily in, a great earthquake first took place, accompanied by a bellowing of the ground, and then a vulture, flying up out of the midst of the flames, went off to Heaven, saying, in human

---

14 Lucian, *The Passing of Peregrinus*, paras 44–5, pp. 49–51.
15 Lucian, *The Passing of Peregrinus*, para. 35, pp. 39–41.
16 W Smith (ed.), *Dictionary of Roman and Greek Geography*, vol. 1, James Walton, London, 1869, p. 1031.
17 See the map at the Greek Travel Pages site at www.gtp.gr/LocPage.asp?id=4456, accessed on 25/09/2012.

speech, with a loud voice: 'I am through with the earth; to Olympus I fare.'[18]

Was the content of The Passing of Peregrinus in fact true?

Places mentioned in *The Passing of Peregrinus* were certainly real rather than imaginary. Peregrinus was said to have built his pyre in Harpina. The town's name appears in the literature from authors of that period, namely the second century AD Greek geographer Pausanius[19] and the Greek historian Diodorus Siculus (c. 90–27 BC).[20]

Similarly, the existence of Peregrinus' hometown, Parium, has been verified. The Greek geographer and historian Strabo (c. 64 BC – 23 AD) spoke of Parium (also called Parion) in the present tense as a seacoast town with a harbour.[21] The town's magistrates created enough of a political disturbance to warrant a letter from a consul of the Romans, Julius Gaius, in the middle of the first century BC. He instructed them to cease prohibiting the Jews in the town of Delos from worshipping in their customary fashion.[22]

The ruins of Parium's aqueduct had been photographed before 1923, and in 1818 there were still remains of its walls, which had been made

---

18 Lucian, *The Passing of Peregrinus*, para. 39, p. 45. Sir Richard Jebb states that the story of the vulture rising up from the pyre may have arisen from Lucian having heard of the dove rising from the flames when the Christian Polycarp was martyred a few years before Peregrinus' death. However, Jebb states that there are no other indications from the narrative about Peregrinus that 'warrants the notion that it was meant as a travesty of Christian martyrdoms ...' (R Jebb, 'Lucian', in *Essays and Addresses*, Cambridge University Press, Cambridge, UK, 1907, p. 188). Eagles were associated with the departed souls of emperors and other individuals (CP Jones, p. 129).
19 Pausanius, *Description of Greece*, book 6, ch. 21, s.8, trans. WHS Jones & HA Omerod, Loeb Classical Library Volumes, Harvard University Press, Cambridge, Massachusetts, US, & William Heinemann, London, 1918, www.theoi.com/Text/Pausanias6B.html, accessed 19/02/2013.
20 Diodorus Siculus, *Bibliotheca Historia*, book 4, ch. 73, s. 1.
21 Strabo, *Geographica*, book 13, ch.1, s. 14, in *Strabo on the Troad,* ed. & trans. W Leaf, Cambridge University Press, London, 1923, p. 80.
22 This letter is recorded in Josephus, *The Antiquities of the Jews*, book 14, ch. 10, s. 8. Gaius is referred to here as Caius.

from large blocks of square-cut marble.[23] Archaeologists from Ataturk University have recently unearthed more remains of Parium from about 2000 years ago.[24]

While some modern authors have regarded Peregrinus as being a totally fictitious character,[25] Lucian was not the only one to mention Peregrinus. Several writers of the second century made comments about Peregrinus Proteus, including: Aulus Gellius, Philostratus and the Christian writers Athenagoras, Tatian and Tertullian.[26] Although these sources do not add information concerning Peregrinus' relations with the Christians, when their information intersects with that of Lucian they do corroborate the truth of what he wrote. This indicates that the satirical nature of *The Passing of Peregrinus* doesn't detract from it being accurate history.

Gellius (born c. 125 AD) recounted how he frequently met in Athens:

> *a philosopher named Peregrinus, who was later surnamed Proteus, a man of dignity and fortitude, living in a hut outside of the city … [who said many things] that were in truth helpful and noble.*[27]

Gellius gave one particular piece of philosophy as an example of Peregrinus' philosophy: sinning by a wise man should be prevented by 'love of justice and honesty and from a sense of duty'.[28] However, those who were not so motivated should sin less if they were aware that over

---

23 Strabo, *Geographica*, ch. 1, s. 14, pp. 80–81, including Plate II. It had a circumference of about 4 miles, and lies above the village of Kemer. Troad was a small region bordering the Dardanelles and the Sea of Marmara.
24 *Turkish Press*, 'A number of works of art unearthed in Parion ancient city', 3 August, 2005, reproduced at www.atrium-media.com/rogueclassicism/Posts/00001075.html, accessed 8/02/2013.
25 J Stott, *The Cross of Christ: With Study Guide*, Intervarsity Press, Leicester, UK, 1989, p. 25. No reasons are given by Stott to support his assertion.
26 'There is no doubt that Peregrinus, alias Proteus, is an historical character … Gellus speaks of him from personal knowledge, and the fact that he burned himself … is recorded also by Tatian, by Tertullian, and by Eusebius' (R Jebb, p. 188).
27 Gellius, *The Attic Nights of Aulus Gellius*, vol. 2, book 12, ch. 11, trans. JC Rolfe, William Heinemann, London, 1968, p. 393.
28 Gellius, vol. 2, book 12, ch. 11, p. 395.

time all would be revealed.²⁹ Gellius also mentioned Peregrinus as the philosopher who rebuked a young wealthy Roman 'who stood before him inattentive and constantly yawning'.³⁰ Although Gellius regarded Peregrinus' philosophy more favourably than Lucian, nevertheless they both agree he was a philosopher. It may well be that Peregrinus changed his style of philosophy and began conning the Christians after his meetings with Gellius.

Athenagoras (c. 177 AD) simply noted that the town of Parium honoured Proteus by erecting a statue, which some pagans thought uttered oracles (or prophecies) and that this Proteus threw himself into the fire near Olympia.³¹

Tatian (c. 110–172 AD) also referred to Proteus critically when commenting on the parasitic nature of philosophers:

> *What great and wonderful things have your philosophers effected? They leave uncovered one of their shoulders; they let their hair grow long; they cultivate their beards; their nails are like the claws of wild beasts. Though they say that they want nothing, yet, like Proteus [a text note indicates that the Cynic Peregrinus is meant] they need a currier [a person who works with tanned leather] for their wallet, and a weaver for their mantle, and a wood-cutter for their staff, and the rich [a text note adds: to invite them to banquets] and a cook also for their gluttony.*³²

Finally, Tertullian (c. 145–220 AD) used the fiery deaths of the philosophers Peregrinus, Heraclitus and Empedocles to encourage

---

29 Gellius, vol. 2, book 12, ch. 11, p. 395.
30 Gellius, vol. 2, book 8, ch. 3, p. 143.
31 Athenagoras, *A Plea for the Christians*, ch. 26, trans. BP Pratten, in A Roberts & J Donaldson (eds), *Ante-Nicene Fathers*, vol. 2, *Fathers of the Second Century, Hermas, Tatian, Athenagoras, Theophilus, and Clement of Alexandria (Entire)*, rev. AC Coxe, Hendrickson Publishers, Massachusetts, US, 2004. A digital copy is available at www.ccel.org/ccel/schaff/anf02.v.ii.html, accessed 29/01/2013.
32 Tatian, *Address to the Greeks*, ch. 25, trans. JE Ryland, in A Roberts & J Donaldson (eds), *Ante-Nicene Fathers*, vol. 2, *Fathers of the Second Century, Hermas, Tatian, Athenagoras, Theophilus, and Clement of Alexandria (Entire)*, rev. AC Coxe, Hendrickson Publishers, Massachusetts, US, 2004. A digital copy is available at www.ccel.org/ccel/schaff/anf02.iii.i.html, accessed 8/02/2013. Tatian believed in the deity of Jesus, but not his true humanity.

Christians to face persecution with courage.[33] He went on to say if these men, and the many other examples he gave, were willing to suffer for falsehood, then similarly should Christians be willing to endure persecution for the sake of truth.

Another reason some give for questioning the historicity of the details is that the con artist's name, Peregrinus, may have been chosen by Lucian to indicate that it was a fictitious person. This is based on the fact that *peregrini* were freeborn citizens of provinces taken over by Rome. The term was used as early as 30 BC. Peregrini constituted the vast majority of the empire's inhabitants in the first and second centuries AD. However, there also existed individuals with the name Peregrinus. For example the first bishop of Auxerre in present-day central France was called Peregrinus, and he lived during the late 200s and early 300s AD.[34] The official website of the Russian Orthodox Church Outside Russia, describing Latin saints of the Orthodox Patriarchate of Rome, lists three different individuals by this name that lived in or about the time of the second century AD.[35] There is even an ancient piece of graffiti that has a caricature of one Peregrinus with an enormous nose.[36]

Is Lucian's account consistent within itself?

One scholar, Christopher Jones, regards Lucian's chronology as inconsistent in regard to a particular sequence of events.[37] This relates to Peregrinus' return to his hometown of Parium immediately after leaving jail. Upon arriving there he found that many locals were

---

33 Tertullian, *Ad Martyras*, ch. 4, trans. Rev. S Thelwall. in A Menzies (ed.), *Ante-Nicene Fathers*, vol. 3, *Latin Christianity: Its Founder, Tertullian*, rev. AC Coxe, Hendrickson Publishers, Massachusetts, US, 2004, p. 695. A digital copy is available at www.ccel.org/ccel/schaff/anf03.vi.v.iv.html, accessed 8/02/2013.

34 HGJ Beck, 'Auxerre' in *The New Catholic Encyclopedia*, vol. 1, 2nd edn, Thompson Gale, New York, 2003, p. 927.

35 'Latin Saints of the Orthodox Patriarchate of Rome', from the website of the Russian Orthodox Church Outside Russia, St John's Orthodox Church, www.orthodoxengland.org.uk/s2centy.htm, accessed 12/02/2013.

36 'Graffito', *Online Encyclopedia*, originally appearing in vol. V12, p. 316 of the 1911 *Encyclopedia Britannica*, http://encyclopedia.jrank.org/GOA_GRA/GRAFFITO.html, accessed 29/12/2012. A picture of this is on the Internet at www.vroma.org/images/mcmanus_images/caricature4.gif, accessed 8/02/2013.

37 CP Jones, p. 123.

agitating for him to be charged with the murder of his father. Wanting to improve his popularity with the town, Peregrinus responded by giving away his wealth to the citizens. He announced his donation to the crowd while wearing the typical Cynic fashion of long hair, dirty cloak, staff and wallet slung over shoulder. The assembly then hailed him as a great philosopher and patriot.

This donation of wealth occurred after his imprisonment among the Christians, but before he offended them by his choice of food. Jones considers this sequence unlikely because Peregrinus would then have had to simultaneously pretend to be a Christian and a Cynic philosopher. However, it may simply be that Peregrinus regarded it as prudent to adopt such a guise to help his cause of appeasement, knowing that the Christians would not necessarily be offended by such dress. Perhaps he also considered that generosity per se was regarded highly by Christians. Providing he didn't express anti-Christian sentiments, he probably considered the style quite safe. In this way he was able to continue to profit from the Christian community afterwards, though it seems it was not long before they made him an outcast.

Other areas of interest in Lucian's work

I started this chapter presenting four ways to investigate the historical accuracy of *The Passing of Peregrinus*. From what I have found, there appears no reason to suspect that Lucian was indulging in imaginative fiction. Thinking further, if Peregrinus and the descriptions of early Christianity were only the product of Lucian's creative mind, it seems unbelievable that his descriptions of Christian beliefs and practices could dovetail so well with the content found in the New Testament.

However, there were still three questions that I wanted to explore:

7. Were there any elements of *The Passing of Peregrinus* that disagreed with the New Testament?

8. Who were Lucian's sources of Christian information?

9. Was he referring, as some critics have suggested, to someone other than Jesus as the founder of the faith?

Does Lucian's account contain elements that disagree with the New Testament?

The previous chapter found many points of agreement that strongly indicates the reliability of the New Testament, at least in relation to the matters covered. What is also pertinent is whether there are any comments made by Lucian that run counter to the information given in the New Testament.

Christopher Jones, mentioned above, cites two examples — using his own translation[38] — of what he believes are Lucian's 'misconceptions'. Firstly, that 'the founder [of Christianity] introduced a "novel form of initiation ..."'.[39] As Jones does not elaborate on this point, it can only be assumed that Jones understands this to mean that the founder began a new passage of initiation, perhaps baptism. However, other translations describe the role of the founder in a way that is entirely harmonious with the New Testament's account. Harmon translated the relevant passages as 'the man who was crucified in Palestine because he introduced this new cult into the world'.[40] Similarly, Richard Jebb translated it as 'because he brought this new mystery (τελετὴν) into the world ...'.[41] This is, of course, an entirely correct way to view what the New Testament records about Jesus. Given that Lucian wasn't himself a Christian, he may have misunderstood the role of baptism among Christians and not appreciated that this ceremony pre-dated Jesus' public teaching ministry.

The second misconception Jones refers to concerns the terms Lucian used to describe Peregrinus as a Christian leader. Jones believes that these titles — '*thiasarch* and convenor' — indicate that Lucian was lacking knowledge about the designations Christians used at that time. This at least seems to be Jones' argument as he states that these terms 'have no place in early Christianity',[42] citing another author for

---

38 CP Jones, p. 7, n. 3.
39 CP Jones, p. 122.
40 Lucian, *The Passing of Peregrinus*, para. 11, p. 13.
41 R Jebb, p. 188.
42 CP Jones, p. 122.

support.[43] This argument loses much of its persuasiveness when it is realised that the term *thiasarch* is not found anywhere else in Greek literature.[44] It may well have been used by other writers but, if so, such literature no longer exists. Perhaps *thiasarch* belonged to the normal readers' passive vocabulary (i.e. words they knew but didn't use), though not their active vocabulary (i.e. words they used) during that era? Assuming *thiasarch* was a well-known word, it is more likely that Lucian was simply using terms familiar to his Greek readers. Jebb would seem to support this.[45] Surely Lucian was more interested in describing Christians to those who knew nothing about them rather than to show off his prowess concerning Christian terminology?

Lucian's choice of terms to reflect functions familiar to his readers, rather than using titles specific to the Christian community, was discussed in reference to scribes in the previous chapter. It is therefore quite possible Lucian did have precise knowledge of the terms used by the Christian community, but chose not to use this knowledge in his writings for the sake of clarity to the reader. This response is also relevant to the objection made by Van Voorst concerning Lucian's use of the word 'priest' rather than 'presbyter'. Van Voorst considered that Lucian therefore was not well acquainted with the Christian literature.[46] However, as shown in the previous chapter, 'priest' was a term used by the Christian community at about the time Lucian lived.

There is another instance that some might consider as an example of Lucian making a statement different to that of the New Testament. This concerns the reason given as to why Jesus was crucified. Lucian's

---

43 HD Betz, 'Lukian von Samosata und das Christentum', *Novum Testamentum*, vol. 3, 1959, pp. 226–37. Robert Van Voorst (*Jesus Outside the New Testament*, William B Eerdmans, Grand Rapids, US, 2000) also commented that *thiasarch* was not found in the New Testament.

44 E Kline, personal correspondence on her search of TLG-E AD1 to AD4, 27/12/2007.

45 R Jebb, p. 86. 'Θιασάρχης, συναγωγεύς, προστάτης — they are merely such terms as a pagan writer might naturally employ to describe leadership in a religious community of which the organisation was not accurately known to him.'

46 R Van Voorst, pp. 60–1. Jebb considered that the 'mention of "priests and scribes" … looks like a statement from an anti-Christian, possibly a Jewish source' (R Jebb, p. 186).

reason was that Jesus 'began this new cult'. It is practically universal that the originators of cults typically are their first leaders. It is possible then, that Lucian's reason is equivalent to stating that it was because Jesus was the (first) leader of the cult.

The New Testament narrates that the Jews and Romans crucified Jesus because his followers regarded him as the long-awaited king and Christ of the Jewish religion. Jesus probably would not have been crucified if whilst claiming such titles he was largely ignored. Rather, he was crucified because he claimed such titles *and* persuaded many others that his claims were true. His new religious group consisted of these converted ones. This strongly suggests he was crucified because he was the leader of this new religion, and he was the leader because he began it.

What were Lucian's sources of Christian information?

It is intriguing to conjecture as to how Lucian learnt so much about Christians. It is possible that he met them personally given some of the towns and regions he visited, such as Corinth and Pontus, were known to have vibrant Christian communities. If Lucian used Christian sources for some of his information on Christianity then this would make it very valuable, as he has gone direct to the prime source.

The other possibility is that Lucian learnt all or some of what he knew from his friendships with those who knew Christians. During Lucian's era 'cultured Greeks'[47] had become Christians. Some of these may have been colleagues of Lucian's non-Christian associates, or even Lucian's friends. Lucian's non-Christian contacts included Peregrinus' acquaintances, as Lucian states:

> ... *I have observed his [Peregrinus'] character and kept an eye on his career from the beginning, and have ascertained various particulars from his fellow-citizens and people who cannot have helped knowing him thoroughly.*[48]

---

47 CP Jones, p. 121.
48 Lucian, *The Passing of Peregrinus*, para. 9, p. 11.

One of Lucian's non-Christian sources may have been Peregrinus himself, if the sea voyage they both shared to Greece occurred after Peregrinus' conning of the Christian community.[49]

However, there is another reason for accepting that Lucian investigated Christians using non-Christian contacts or literature. This is because he twice used the word *anaskolopisthenta* (ἀνασκολοπισθέντα) to describe the crucifixion of Jesus, and this word is not found in the New Testament.[50] His choice could not have been based on trying to avoid a word for crucifixion found only in Christian parlance, as he used *stauron* (σταυρὸν) — meaning a stake or a cross[51] — elsewhere in the story,[52] and *stauron* is used elsewhere outside of the New Testament.[53] If his sources were solely Christian, we could expect that Lucian would have predominantly used the term *stauron* into his account when discussing the death of Jesus given *stauron* is used so much in sacred Christian writings concerning Jesus — and thus most likely to be used in Christians' speech. A modern parallel would be a writer of sport in the United Kingdom using the word 'soccer', where normally the word chosen would be 'football'. This would alert the reader to the likelihood that the writer had obtained his information of the sport from outside of the UK football culture.

---

49 Lucian, *The Passing of Peregrinus*, para. 43, p. 49.
50 CA Evans, 'Jesus in non-Christian sources', in B Chilton & CA Evans (eds), *Studying the Historical Jesus: Evaluations of the State of Current Research*, EJ Brill, Leiden, The Netherlands, 1994, pp. 443–78 (esp. p. 462). Evans states that Lucian's lack of using the common New Testament word for crucifixion (*stauron*) indicates he may have used non-Christian sources. The following site was used to check that *anaskolopisthenta*, or inflections of it, are not found in the New Testament: Perseus Digital Library Project, GR Crane (ed.), Tufts University, Massachusetts, US, www.perseus.tufts.edu, accessed 20/04/2007.
51 The lexical form is *stauros* (σταμπός) (Persus Digital Library, Greek Work Study Tool, ed. GR Crane, Tufts University, Massachusetts, US, www.perseus.tufts.edu/hopper/morph?l=stauron&la=greek#lexicon, accessed 19/02/2013).
52 Lucian, *The Passing of Peregrinus*, para. 34, p. 39.
53 Perseus Digital Library, www.perseus.tufts.edu, accessed 20/04/2007. Apart from frequent use — over 40 times in the New Testament for crucifixion (e.g. Matthew, Mark, Luke and some of Paul's letters), *stauros*, or inflections of it, was also used for crucifixion by Polybius (*Histories*, book 1, ch. 86), s. 6) and Flavius Josephus (*The Antiquities of the Jews*, book 11, s. 261 and s. 266; *The Wars of the Jews*, book 5, s. 451 and book 7, s. 202). Polybius also used *anaskolopisthenta* in his *Histories*, book 10, ch. 33, s. 1.

However, Lucian appears to have used *anaskolopisthenta* and *stauron* interchangeably, and scholarly works on Greek language also indicate that the two words are interchangeable. So it may be nothing more than coincidence that Lucian used the former term to refer to the crucifixion of Jesus, as opposed to the common New Testament term. In support of this, at least two different Christian writers from the third and fourth centuries made use of the word *anaskolopistethenta*, or inflections of it, to refer to the crucifixion of Peter.[54] Obviously they were not using the word in a mocking tone. So it may well be that Christians were using this term much earlier but that written records of this have disappeared.

Another reason offered for Lucian's choice of words is that perhaps crucifixion had arisen from a more simple technique of impaling and, by inference, that Lucian preferred this older description. The author who suggested this noted that it was probable that Lucian used the word in 'a mocking tone'.[55]

Whether Lucian obtained his information about Christians directly and/or indirectly, he certainly was very capable of finding reliable sources. As one scholar wrote:

> *Lucian is far from an outsider in his own society. As a youth he had imbibed that higher education which dominated the Greek culture of his day. He travelled widely in the east and west, and was known to educated Greeks and Romans ... It is to be expected that when he talks of contemporary culture and society he does so from the vantage point of a practiced observer: ... a man in touch with his time.*[56]

---

54 Eusebius, *The History of the Church from Christ to Constantine (Historia Ecclesiastica)*, book 2, ch. 25, GA Williamson (trans.), rev. & ed. A Louth, Penguin Books, London, 1989 p. 62; and Eusebe De Cesaree, *Histoire Ecclesiastique Livres I-IV*, ch. 255–6, Les Editions Du Cerf, Paris, 1986, p. 92. Eusebius used ανασχολοπισθηναι. The other writer was Gregorius Nyssenus, a Christian bishop (335–94 AD) in his 'Orationes viii de beatitudinibus', 44.1297.53, para.01340, www.documentacatholicaomnia.eu/04z/z_0330-0395__Gregorius_Nyssenus__Orationes_viii_de_beatitudinibus__MGR.pdf.html, accessed 3/01/2008.
55 JP Meier, *A Marginal Jew: Rethinking the Historical Jesus: The Roots of the Problem and the Person*, vol.1, Anchor Bible Reference Library, New York, 1991, p.102, n. 20. He also states that *anaskolopisthenta* was probably used here scornfully.
56 CP Jones, p. 23.

Could Lucian have been referring to someone other than Jesus as the instigator of Christianity?

Some antagonists to Christianity have pointed out that Jesus is not actually named by Lucian and that the person referred to as having 'introduced this new cult' could have been any one of thousands of individuals who were crucified in Palestine at about that time. This appears to be a very weak argument for at least three reasons.

Firstly, all ancient historical records dealing with the origins of Christianity — be they pagan, Jewish or Christian, irrespective of the bias of the authors — clearly indicate that Jesus of Nazareth was the founder of Christianity. They do not even hint at the possibility that it could have been someone else.

Secondly, Lucian indicates that the founder of the Christian cult was not only a teacher and first lawgiver, but that his followers also worshipped him. There are no historical records indicating that Christians were ever divided in their thinking as to the fact that it was Jesus of Nazareth who they worshipped. Even the non-Christian document called the Gospel of Philip (a strange title as it doesn't present the Gospel and wasn't penned by Philip), written in about 150–250 AD,[57] portrays the Messiah ('Christ' is the Greek translation) as being Jesus of Nazareth[58] and as having a virgin mother called Mary.[59]

Thirdly, as Lucian scorned Christianity, surely he would not have passed up the opportunity to point out that there were actually several crucified teachers-cum-lawgivers from Palestine whose followers worshipped them and who claimed to have started Christianity! How could such a hot topic be ignored when trying to ridicule Christians?

---

57 DL Bock, *The Missing Gospels: Unearthing the Truth Behind Alternative Christianities*, Nelson Books, Nashville, Tennessee, US, 2006, p. 67.
58 *Gospel of Philip*, written sometime after 150 AD: 'The apostles who were before us had these names for him: "Jesus, the Nazorean, Messiah," that is, Jesus the Nazorean, the Christ.'" in W Barnstone (ed.), *The Other Bible: Jewish Pseudepigrapha, Christian Apocrypha, Gnostic Scriptures, Kabbalah, Dead Sea Scrolls*, Harper, San Francisco, 1984, p. 91.
59 W Barnstone (ed.), citing the *Gospel of Philip*: 'Christ, therefore, was born of a virgin to rectify the Fall which occurred in the beginning' (p. 95) and 'Mary is the virgin ...' (p. 89).

If there were other possible instigators, perhaps Lucian would have added words to this effect:

> *This crucified sophist is said by some Christians to have been Jesus of Nazareth, whereas others say it was a different Jesus. Who cares! Both groups are clearly deluded, as why would anyone worship someone who had been tortured to death in such a humiliating fashion.*

Conclusion

Lucian's *The Passing of Peregrinus* has all the hallmarks of being a historically accurate and biting critique. There are many reasons for considering that this satirical account arose after thorough investigation. Its description of Christian beliefs does not differ in any significant way from that given by the authors of the New Testament and other early Christian writers. Lucian may have obtained some of his information about Christians through non-Christian associates, although he could also have had Christian contacts. Although Lucian does not specifically name the crucified instigator of Christianity as Jesus of Nazareth, it is inconceivable that he had someone else in mind. This and the previous chapter have established that Lucian has provided a highly reliable independent source of information about the beliefs and practices of Christians living within 130 years of Jesus' crucifixion.

15

Pliny the Younger

Perhaps one of the saddest portraits of early Christian beliefs is that composed by Gaius Plinius Caecilius Secondus, otherwise known as Pliny the Younger. His father, Lucius Caecilius, was a rich landowner in northern Italy when Pliny was born in 61 or 62 AD, but unfortunately he died when Pliny was still young.[1] Pliny later studied law in Rome, and was mostly cared for by Pliny the Elder until this caring uncle died during the volcanic eruption of Mount Vesuvius in 79 AD. Pliny was a studious youth, having written a Greek tragedy at the age of 14. He describes how he was quietly reading the historian Livy[2] during the great volcanic eruption that killed his uncle. He was a pupil of two famous academics, the Roman Quintilian and the Greek Nicetes Sacerdos.

He began his career as a lawyer, becoming involved in the prosecution of provincial governors charged with extortion, and simultaneously became director of the national treasury from 98 to 100 AD. Sometime between 109 and 111 AD he was sent to the region called Bithynia-Pontus to act as a provincial governor, and this is where he stayed until

---

1 M Grant, *Greek and Latin Authors, 800 B.C. – A.D. 1000*, HW Wilson, New York, 1980, pp. 345–6. This is the source of all subsequent information in the first two paragraphs, unless otherwise referenced.
2 Livy (c. 59 BC - 17 AD) wrote a history of Rome called *From the Founding of the City*.

he died two years later.³ Emperor Trajan (r. 98–117 AD) sent Pliny to the region because of:

> *intense inter-city rivalry ... [and] extravagance of the cities in [constructing] public buildings ... Pliny was sent, not to stop this orgy of construction, but to check its wastefulness.*⁴

Extracts from Pliny's letters describing the investigation of Christians

Pliny was a prolific letter writer,⁵ to the extent that nine books of his letters were published between the years 100 and 109 AD. These letters have been described as:

> *genuine in the sense that they were written communications addressed and dispatched to their recipients, but, each all the same, was a carefully constructed and elaborately posed composition ... intended for publication ...*⁶

When he began his role as governor of Bithynia-Pontus, he sought advice from Emperor Trajan through an exchange of letters written in Latin. Trajan's replies consisted of instructions concerning Pliny's questions, covering aspects of 'military discipline, the banning of social and political clubs, and the control of municipal building operations'.⁷ These letters, and others, were collected and published after Pliny's death into the famous Book 10 of Pliny's letters.⁸ It consists of 68

---

3 RF Clavelle, 'Problems contained in Pliny's letter on the Christians: a critical analysis', PhD thesis, University of Illinois, Urbana-Champaign, Illinois, US, 1971, pp. 1–2
4 AN Sherwin-White, *The Letters of Pliny: A Historical and Social Commentary*, Clarendon Press, Oxford, 1966, pp. 526–7.
5 Pliny, *Letters*, trans. W Melmoth, rev. WML Hutchinson, vol. 1, William Heinemann, London, and The MacMillan Co, New York, 1931, www.archive.org/stream/letterswithengli01plinuoft#page/n7/mode/2up; and Pliny, *Letters*, trans. W Melmoth, rev. WML Hutchinson, vol. 2, William Heinemann, London, and GP Putnam, New York, 1927, www.archive.org/stream/letterswithengli02plinuoft#page/n7/mode/2up; both accessed 19/03/2013.
6 M Grant, p. 346.
7 AN Sherwin-White, p. 543.
8 RF Clavelle, p. 2.

letters from Pliny to Trajan, and 50 from Trajan to Pliny.[9] This 'stylish collection of letters is one of the most elegant and informative witnesses to the culture and education of the time'.[10]

The following exchange of letters between Pliny and Trajan illustrate this elegance.[11] Because the correspondence occurred in about 111 AD, it also serves to reveal aspects of Christian beliefs only 80 years after Jesus' crucifixion.

> *It is a rule, Sir, which I inviolably observe, to refer myself to you in all my doubts; for who is more capable of guiding my uncertainty or informing my ignorance? Having never been present at any trials of the Christians, I am unacquainted with the method and limits to be observed either in examining or punishing them. Whether any difference is to be made on account of age, or no distinction allowed between the youngest and the adult; whether repentance admits to a pardon, or if a man has been once a Christian it avails him nothing to recant; whether the mere profession of Christianity, albeit without crimes, or only the crimes associated therewith are punishable — in all these points I am greatly doubtful.*
>
> *In the meanwhile, the method I have observed towards those who have been denounced to me as Christians is this: I interrogated them whether they were Christians; if they confessed it I repeated the question twice again, adding the threat of capital punishment; if they still persevered, I ordered them to be executed. For whatever the nature of their creed might be, I could at least feel no doubt that contumacy [i.e. stubbornness][12] and inflexible obstinacy deserved chastisement. There were others also possessed with the*

---

9   RF Clavelle, p. 12.
10 J Boardman and J Griffin (eds), 'The use of formal prose', in, *The Oxford Illustrated History of the Roman World*, p. 250.
11 Pliny, *Letters*, book 10, letters 96–7, trans. W Melmoth, rev. WML Hutchinson, vol. 2, William Heinemann, London, and GP Putnam's Sons, New York, 1927, pp. 401–7, www.archive.org/stream/letterswithengli02plinuoft#page/401/mode/2up, accessed 25/01/2014.
12 D Ayerst & AST Fisher, *Records of Christianity*, vol. 1, *In the Roman Empire*, Basil Blackwell, Oxford, 1971, p. 14, being a translation of letter (epistle) 96 of Pliny's *Book 10*.

same infatuation, but being citizens of Rome, I directed them to be carried thither.

These accusations spread (as is usually the case) from the mere fact of the matter being investigated and several forms of mischief came to light. A placard was put up, without any signature, accusing a large number of persons by name. Those who denied they were, or had ever been, Christians, who repeated after me an invocation to the Gods, and offered adoration, with wine and frankincense, to your image, which I had ordered be brought for that purpose, together with those of the Gods, and who finally cursed Christ — none of which acts, it is said, those who are really Christians can be forced into performing — these I thought it proper to discharge. Others who were named by that informer at first confessed themselves Christians, and then denied it; true, they had been of that persuasion but they had quitted it, some three years, others many years, and a few as much as twenty-five years ago. They all worshipped your statue and the images of the Gods, and cursed Christ.

They affirmed, however, the whole of their guilt, or their error, was, that they were in the habit of meeting on a certain fixed day before it was light, when they sang in alternate verses a hymn to Christ, as to a god, and bound themselves by a solemn oath, not to any wicked deeds, but never to commit any fraud, theft or adultery, never to falsify their word, nor deny a trust [i.e. a debt][13] *when they should be called upon to deliver it up; after which it was their custom to separate, and then reassemble to partake of food — but food of an ordinary and innocent kind. Even this practice, however, they had abandoned after the publication of my edict, by which, according to your orders, I had forbidden political associations. I judged it so much the more necessary to extract the real truth, with the assistance of torture, from two female slaves, who were styled* **deaconesses**: *but I could discover nothing more than depraved and excessive superstition.*

I therefore adjourned the proceedings and betook myself at once to your counsel. For the matter seemed to me well worth referring to you, — especially considering the numbers endangered.

---

13 D Ayerst & AST Fisher, p. 15.

> *Persons of all ranks and ages, and of both sexes are, and will be, involved in the prosecution. For this contagious superstition is not confined to the cities only, but has spread through the villages and rural districts; it seems possible, however, to check and cure it. 'Tis certain at least that the temples, which had been almost deserted, begin now to be frequented; and the sacred festivals, after a long intermission, are again revived; while there is a general demand for sacrificial animals, which for some time past have met with but few purchasers. From hence it is easy to imagine what multitudes may be reclaimed from this error, if a door be left open to repentance.*

This was the emperor's reply:

> *The method you have pursued, my dear Pliny, in sifting the cases of those denounced to you as Christians is extremely proper. It is not possible to lay down any general rule which can be applied as the fixed standard in all cases of this nature. No search should be made for these people; when they are denounced and found guilty they must be punished; with the restriction, however, that when the party denies himself to be a Christian, and shall give proof that he is not (that is, by adoring our Gods) he shall be pardoned on the ground of repentance, even though he may have formerly incurred suspicion. Information without the accuser's name subscribed must not be admitted in evidence against anyone, as it is introducing a very dangerous precedent, and by no means agreeable to the spirit of the age.*

Insights into Pliny's character

Knowing a person's motivation for writing brings to light many nuances about what they have written. Pliny's motivation for publishing copious letters seems to be a fairly benign expression of his self-importance and ambition. He wrote to his friend Titius Capito:

> *You are not singular in the advice you give me to undertake the writing of history; it is a work which many have frequently pressed upon me; and I strongly incline to it. Not that I have any confidence of success (which you would think presumptuous in a tiro [novice]), but because I hold it a noble task to rescue from oblivion those who*

> *deserve to be eternally remembered, and extend the fame of others, at the same time as our own. Nothing, I confess, so strongly affects me as the desire of a lasting name: a passion highly worthy of the human breast, especially of one, who, not being conscious to himself of any ill, is not afraid of being remembered by posterity. It is the continual subject therefore of my thoughts ...*[14]

Pliny wrote to over 100 different individuals,[15] and so the publication of these letters may have been his way of broadcasting that he had a large number of acquaintants, perhaps similar to the way some politicians use social media and the Internet.

When I first read Pliny's correspondence about Christianity, I found it startling that he considered obstinacy and stubbornness, in any situation, deserving of the death sentence. This certainly made me wonder why some called Pliny 'a humane man'.[16] However, upon closer scrutiny it turns out this compliment may have some validity, partly because it is always important to judge someone according to their times and customs, rather than ours. For instance, his three-fold interrogations of confessing Christians appears to many people today as being cruel. Yet early Roman proconsuls were known to offer periods of grace during which the accused could change their statement.[17] Furthermore, the change of a plea from guilty to not guilty created a loophole for the defendant, according to Roman law. This opportunity was due to the fact that a not guilty plea allowed for the introduction of evidence for and against the defendant. The governor was then free to 'attach whatever value to all this evidence that he saw fit'.[18]

Another sentiment expressed by Pliny that seems particularly pitiless is his lack of consideration of the age of the accused. In the context of Roman law, this was a reasonable question as their legislation 'did provide for a lessening of penalties in certain cases on account of the youth or female

---

14 Pliny, *Letters*, vol. 1, book 5, letter 8, p. 399, www.archive.org/stream/letterswithengli01plinuoft#page/398/mode/2up, accessed 03/01/2013.
15 F Gamberini, *Stylistic Theory and Practice in the Younger Pliny*, Olms-Weidmann, Hildesheim, Germany, 1983, pp. 134–5.
16 D Ayerst & AST Fisher, p. 13.
17 RF Clavelle, p. 35.
18 RF Clavelle, pp. 35–6.

sex of the accused'.[19] It is also a question that Pliny had asked Trajan before in relation to men of a variety of ages who had escaped their full punishment in the mines and other places.[20] These men were found out whilst working in the public service. Trajan's reply was that those who had grown old and infirm should be given a lighter workload.[21]

The final insight into Pliny's character that carries overtones of remorseless savagery is his torture of two girls. His motivations for these actions are discussed below. It will suffice to note here that during Roman times, the testimony of slaves 'was commonly, if not regularly, taken under torture'.[22]

A curious aspect of Pliny's letter about the Christians is his issuing of an 'edict' banning 'political associations (Latin: *hetaeriae*)'. *Hetaeriae* have also been translated as 'society meetings'.[23] Was this obedience to Trajan's command something that Pliny had in fact desired because he wanted to oppress his constituents? This edict was much more extensive than what many Westerners today would regard as reasonable, or even possible, to enforce in an ancient society. It transpires that Trajan was in fact against any type of society. At an earlier stage, Pliny was hoping that a fire brigade society could be formed in a certain city. However, Trajan opposed the idea of such *hetaeriae* on the grounds that:

> *Whatever title we give them [such societies], and whatever our object in giving it, men who are banded together for a common end will all the same become a political association before long.*[24]

---

19 RF Clavelle, p. 31 citing T Mommsen, *Römisches Strafrecht*, Verlag von Duncker & Humblot, Leipzig, 1899, pp. 928–9, 1042.
20 Pliny, *Letters*, vol. 2, book 10, letter 31, p. 315, www.archive.org/stream/letterswithengli02plinuoft#page/314/mode/2up, accessed 15/02/2013.
21 Pliny, *Letters*, vol. 2, book 10, letter 32, www.archive.org/stream/letterswithengli02plinuoft#page/316/mode/2up, accessed 15/02/2013.
22 RF Clavelle, pp. 46–7.
23 D Ayerst & AST Fisher, p. 15.
24 Pliny, *Letters*, vol . 2, book 10, letters 33 & 34, http://www.archive.org/stream/letterswithengli02plinuoft#page/318/mode/2up, 15/02/2013.

In short we can say that Pliny was a man driven by ambition, yet committed to following the letter of the law and obedience to his emperor. He was fully dedicated to the established religion of Roman gods, including the worship of the serving emperor. Although a prodigious writer, his legal training instilled a penchant to ensure he had his details correct.

Pliny's interest in the Christians

In Pliny's era, it seems that Christians were abhorred by large numbers of citizens and various governmental administrations. This hatred seems to have been based, at least in part, on the Christians' outspoken beliefs that there is only one God, and that the gods of all other religions were either non-existent man-made fabrications or demonic representations. This, of course, riled the majority of their fellow citizens, who believed and worshipped a multitude of gods simultaneously. To make matters worse, the majority believed that their gods would exact vengeance on all of the people for allowing such vile beliefs to go unpunished.[25]

In addition to these anti-Christian sentiments, popular opinion also alleged that Christians, in obedience to their religion, had been involved in certain 'sins and crimes'. It is apparent from the beginning of Pliny's letter that he wanted to know if this was the case. If their religion did not necessitate any criminal activity, he further wondered if they should be punished simply because they stated they were Christians. This second concern may seem strange to many present-day Western Christians, although Christians living in countries ruled by Islamic regimes, or communist hegemonies, unfortunately have an abundance of experience with such a state of affairs.[26]

Many Christians reading Pliny's letter for the first time approach it as if it represents a state-orchestrated, widespread persecution aimed at annihilating followers of Christ. Although such pogroms did take place, Pliny's letter does not support such a view. Instead, his letter

---

25 Further details regarding Christian and Jewish religious freedom within the Roman Empire are given in the appendix 'A brief background of first-century Judea' at the back of this book. See also the following for debates put forward by notable scholars as to why the early Christians were persecuted: MI Finey (ed.), *Studies in Ancient Society*, Routledge & Kegan Paul, London, 1974.
26 Refer to chapter 18 'Epilogue'.

indicates that his investigative methodology developed over time in response to changing circumstances.

The first method was in response to unidentified accusers who brought to him people alleged to be Christians. No other crime was given. What was the motive for presenting these people to Governor Pliny? One possibility is loss of business. It is apparent that the large number of people becoming Christians had resulted in a marked decline in worship at various pagan temples. As this worship involved sacred rites, perhaps requiring idols and accompanying animal sacrifices, various tradesmen and shopkeepers would have lost much business. It's therefore quite possible that the accusations made against this group of Christians were made by these same tradesmen and shopkeepers, goaded on no doubt by the temple priests. This consideration of motives is supported by Pliny's comments that the number of worshippers at temples and the sale of associated paraphernalia increased greatly after he had investigated and tortured Christians. Presumably there were those in the general public who suddenly felt it prudent to distance themselves from Christianity or even the mere possibility of being thought of as Christians by becoming visible patrons of the pagan gods.

As stated earlier, Pliny's use of threats was probably to persuade the defendants to change their plea from guilty to not guilty. If the defendants did change their plea to not guilty, then the law allowed Pliny to undervalue the evidence against the Christians, and so in effect to give them leniency. Roman law at that point of time did not allow a relaxation of punishment simply because a Christian denied their faith.[27] Those that didn't change their plea were promptly executed because of their sheer obstinacy.

Pliny's second method of investigation arose when larger numbers of people accused of Christianity were brought to Pliny. At least some of these had been named in an anonymous notebook. The defendants are grouped as follows:

- *Those who denied they had ever been Christians.* Pliny gave them the simple test of worshipping the pagan gods to prove that they were

---

27 RF Clavelle, pp. 34–6.

at least not Christians at the present time. If they passed, they were released. The simple test may have served a two-fold purpose. Firstly, it gave Pliny some measure of certainty regarding the defendant's plea. Secondly, it would have helped ensure that Emperor Trajan would consider the leniency given as appropriate and not excessive.

- *Those who declared that they were not followers of Christ, although they had been Christians in the past.* These too were given a simple test to show that they were not currently Christian believers. However, this group of self-declared apostates caused Pliny a great deal of consternation, probably because of popular rumours that the Christian faith necessitated various 'sins and crimes'. If the apostates had therefore participated in illegal activities in the past, then despite the apostates' recantations, these individuals should still face the judicial system. However, if they had not committed any crimes, should they still be punished because they had in fact been Christians? This problem explains why Pliny became so interested in the apostates' testimony, and why he would bother passing such favourable pro-Christian information onto Trajan. Pliny's level of uncertainty is clearly shown in the way he couched his original question, as can be more readily seen from a recent translation:

Should the penitent be pardoned, or should no mercy be shown a man who has recanted if he really has been a Christian? Should the mere name be reason enough for punishment however free from crime a man may be, or should only the sins and crimes that attend the name be punished?[28]

This questioning also explains why Pliny, after listening to the apostates' testimony, then considered it 'all the more necessary to find out the truth under torture'. After all, in Pliny's mind, the apostates may have hidden the criminal aspects of Christian practices for fear that they would then be trialled for these past actions.

It is also easy to imagine that the apostates themselves wanted to portray their sojourn in the Christian faith as one of innocence. It would have been very counter-productive for them to lie and frame

---

28 D Ayerst & AST Fisher, p. 14.

their former Christian colleagues, who they suddenly wanted to put at a distance, as criminals.

Does Pliny's letter reflect content found in the New Testament?

The overall picture of Christian belief painted by Pliny mirrors several themes found in the New Testament. The following points start with a statement drawn from Pliny's letter, followed by New Testament parallels:

1. **Christians sang to Christ.**
   'Sing and make music from your heart to the Lord, always giving thanks to God the Father for everything, in the name of our Lord Jesus Christ' (Ephesians 5:19–20).

2. **Christians regarded Christ as God.**
   This belief is mentioned and implied numerous times in the New Testament. The Gospel of John records that: 'Thomas [the disciple] said to him [Jesus], "My Lord and my God!"' (John 20:28).

3. **Christians praised Christ as they would a god.**
   It is interesting to note that the actual words stated here as coming from those who were once Christians are *carmenque Christo quasi deo dicere secum invicem*, which:

   > Pliny himself would doubtless have understood ... in the sense 'to Christ as if to a god'. If Pliny had regarded Jesus as a god comparable to Asclepius or Osiris, he would have written *Christo deo*, 'to the god Christ'.[29]

   The implication of this is that Pliny regarded this Christ as being a different god to the other known gods, possibly because Jesus was a real person who had lived on Earth recently.

   Of course, what the former Christians precisely said, as opposed to what Pliny surmises them as saying, no one can be sure. They may have said *Christo deo* 'to the god Christ'. Pliny may then

---

29 MJ Harris, 'References to Jesus in early classical authors', in D Wenham (ed.), *Gospel Perspectives, Vol. 5: The Jesus Tradition Outside the Gospels*, JSOT Press, Sheffield, UK, 1984, p. 346.

have re-worded this phrase when writing to Trajan so as to be more politically correct or unassuming. Alternatively, as the former Christians no longer worshipped Jesus, they may have revised their understanding from being *Christo deo* to *Christo quasi deo*, as not many would reject someone who they still regard as God.[30]

4. **Christians would not deny Christ.**
   'Therefore I want you to know that no one who is speaking by the Spirit of God says, "Jesus be cursed," and no one can say, "Jesus is Lord," except by the Holy Spirit' (1 Corinthians 12:3).

5. **Christians would meet regularly over a common meal.**
   'Every day they continued to meet together in the temple courts. They broke bread in their homes and ate together with glad and sincere hearts, praising God ...' (Acts 2:46–7).

6. **Christian moral standards stipulated paying debts, avoiding fraud, robbery, adultery, and bearing false witness.**
   Those who followed Jesus were acutely aware that they had to have new hearts cleaned — that is be 'born again' (John 3:3) — because Jesus taught that:

   > it is from within, out of a person's heart, that evil thoughts come — sexual immorality, theft, murder, adultery, greed, malice, deceit, lewdness, envy, slander, arrogance and folly. All these evils come from inside and defile a person. (Mark 7:21–3)

   Local Christian community leaders were to encourage their fellow Christians to:

   > be obedient, to be ready to do whatever is good, to slander no one, to be peaceable and considerate, and always be gentle toward everyone. (Titus 3: 1–2)

7. **Christians could be found in Bithynia-Pontus.**
   Peter, an apostle of Jesus Christ, To God's elect, exiles scattered throughout the provinces of Pontus, Galatia, Cappadocia, Asia and Bithynia ... (1 Peter 1:1)

---

30 MJ Harris, pp. 346–7, 362.

Lucian of Samosata also spoke of Pontus being filled with Christians, as mentioned in chapter 14.

8. **Christian popularity had negative impacts on idol worship.**
   The New Testament describes how the growing numbers of Christians in a particular city — Ephesus — was perceived as potentially having a large and negative impact on the sale of idols and visits to pagan temples:

   > About that time there arose a great disturbance about the [Christian] Way. A silversmith named Demetrius, who made silver shrines of Artemis, brought in a lot of business for the craftsmen there. He called them together, along with the workers in related trades, and said: 'You know, my friends, that we receive a good income from this business. And you see and hear how this fellow, Paul has convinced and led astray large numbers of people here in Ephesus and in practically the whole province of Asia. He says that gods made by human hands are no gods at all. There is danger not only that our trade will lose its good name, but also that the temple of the great goddess Artemis will be discredited; and the goddess herself, who is worshiped throughout the province of Asia and the world, will be robbed of her divine majesty.' (Acts 19:23–7)

9. **The Christian community included female deacons.**
   Paul praised a female deacon in his letter to Christians in Rome, writing: 'I commend to you our sister Phoebe, a deacon of the church in Cenchreae' (Romans 16:1).

10. **Christians were persecuted.**
    'Sometimes you were publicly exposed to insult and persecution; at other times you stood side by side with those who were so treated' (Hebrews 10:33).

11. **Christian Roman citizens were sent to Rome to face trial.**
    The New Testament tells of how Paul was brought by the Jewish authorities of Caesarea to stand trial in front of the Roman governor, Festus. The governor, attempting to impress his Jewish citizens, asked if Paul was willing to face judgment in Jerusalem. However, upon hearing Paul's request to appeal to Caesar, he granted his request and sent him to Rome (Acts 25:1 to 28:14).

The above eleven points show a striking similarity between Pliny's comments and the New Testament. However, before drawing conclusions from this, there is one issue that potentially undermines the worth of this comparison, namely the question of fraud. Did Pliny and Trajan originally pen these letters?

Authenticity of the letters

The genuineness of the letters of Pliny has been an area of great interest for many years.

It took only a brief search of the Internet to find people claiming that the letters were forgeries. However, the question of genuineness in the academic world is rarely focused on whether in fact Pliny was the author. Instead the question is aimed at determining whether Pliny wrote the letters as real correspondence, or whether he wrote them primarily as part of an exercise in artistic composition. Some, as far back as 1901, were so convinced of the idea that Pliny was using the letters primarily as a form of literary exercise that they considered that the addressee was sometimes totally irrelevant.[31]

Dr Federico Gamberini has extensively studied the literary characteristics of Pliny's letters. His PhD thesis was primarily on this topic. He wrote that: 'it may not be beyond imagination to suppose that some of them [Pliny's letters] may never have been sent to a correspondent'.[32] Instead they were intended all along to be included in a collection intended for publication. He highlighted the fact that the use of the word 'fictitious' to describe such letters is valid if it merely reflects this belief. So his label of fictitiousness wasn't intended to mean that the letters were not actually written by Pliny himself. He went on to make the comment: 'If on the other hand one supposes that the letters may have been [sent to their intended recipients, and] revised for publication, it is then no longer correct to speak of fictitiousness ... it is possible to unite the functions of artistic letter with those of real correspondence'.[33] This revision may have involved

---

31 H Peter, *Der Brief in der Römischen Literatur*, BG Teubner, Leipzig, 1901, p. 101. Cited by F Gamberini, p. 125.
32 F Gamberini, p. 130.
33 F Gamberini, pp. 130–1.

the addition of information that may have been superfluous for the recipient, but necessary for the reader of the published collection. Alternatively, it may have involved the omitting of details concerning financial matters.[34]

At the beginning of this section on authenticity, I mentioned that the 'academic world' has rarely focused on whether Pliny and Trajan were the original composers. I now want to investigate the nature of these concerns, the first of which question the entire collection of Book 10.

Dr R.F. Clavelle wrote his PhD thesis on issues relating to Book 10 of Pliny's letters, focusing on the letter of Pliny that referred to Christians. Dr Clavelle provided many refutations concerning allegations that others composed the letters of Book 10 in the fifteenth century, as opposed to Pliny and Trajan writing them in the second century. Some of the reasons for these allegations of fraud, and the essence of his responses are as follows:[35]

There was not enough time for such a multitude of letters to pass between the two correspondents.

It was not such a vast number, as 21 of Pliny's 60 letters[36] consisted of only 'short notes of commendation and congratulation, personal requests and short reports'.[37] The rest concerned problems and requests for approvals, necessitating larger formats. Looking at the numbers more closely, a pattern emerges which vouches even further for the authenticity of the letters. As Pliny gained experience as a governor, his need for advice tapered off, and this is reflected in the diminishing number of letters written. During the first five months of his first season in office, Pliny sent 15 serious reports or questions to Trajan, whereas in the first five months of his second season he sent only four letters.[38]

The style of Book 10 does not reflect Pliny's typical style.

---

34 F Gamberini, pp. 133.
35 All of the allegations covered in this book were made by Julius Held in 1835 (RF Clavelle, p. 11). The last was also made by Johan L. Ussing in 1860 (RF Clavelle, pp. 14–15).
36 This subset of 60 represents that portion of 68 that were written when Pliny was governor. See RF Clavelle, p.12.
37 RF Clavelle, p.12.
38 RF Clavelle, pp. 12–13.

This claim is unfounded as there is great consistency in 'the stylistic characteristics' of all 10 books. This is particularly noteworthy as the letters of Book 10 reflect 'official' correspondence whereas the others are of a 'literary' character.[39]

Trajan's replies were a forgery due to considerations of style and content.

Several meticulous studies carried out in the 1900s, did not:

> *conclude that the authorship of Trajan is to be denied even though here and there can be found some indications of a chancery style [that is, some portions may have come from Trajan's secretary or other governmental staff].*[40]

Since the 1800s and 1900s 'many of the details of provincial administration have been unfolding themselves.'[41] These findings illustrate the close parallels between such discoveries and the administrative procedures described in the correspondence between Pliny and Trajan.

Dr Clavelle continues on to say that 'although the genuiness of Book 10 is no longer contested',[42] there are those who contend that Epistle 96 (from Pliny) and 97 (from Trajan) concerning the Christians are forgeries. The following examples only touch on some of the arguments and counter-arguments referred to by Clavelle:

It has been claimed that the Latin words rendered into English as 'Sir', or 'Your Majesty',[43] are based on the term 'domine',[44] and this is a sign of forgery. This is because Trajan was known to dislike new honorific titles.[45]

---

39 RF Clavelle, p. 14. His footnote 25 at the end of this quote includes a reference to AN Sherwin-White, pp. 3–13.
40 RF Clavelle, p.15.
41 RF Clavelle, p.16.
42 RF Clavelle, p. 16.
43 D Ayerst & AST Fisher, p. 14.
44 W Harris, Pliny and the Christians, http://community.middlebury.edu/~harris/Classics/plinytrajan.html, accessed 15/01/2013. Harris translates 'domine' as Head of State. Dr William Harris was Professor Emeritus, Middlebury College, Vermont, US.
45 RF Clavelle, pp. 24–5.

Clavelle responded by noting that this same title had been used for an earlier emperor Domitian (r. 81–96 AD), so it was not a new title.[46] Further, over 60 of Pliny's letters to the emperor used this term of address, yet no one today suggests all these letters are forgeries.

From about the 1880s it has been suggested that either before, or around the time of, Tertullian (c. 145–220 AD) a Christian concocted the letters.[47]

Clavelle pointed out that this is highly implausible, because if the letter is a forgery designed to champion the cause of Christianity, it would not describe Christianity as a 'depraved and groundless superstition'. Nor would it promote the idea that Christians would become apostates, especially when some that did leave the faith did so decades earlier for no clearly stated reasons. Also it would seem impossible that a Christian forger could 'imitate so precisely the language and style of Pliny'.[48]

Pliny should have addressed his concerns on how to conduct trials on the Christians to provincial judges, rather than to the emperor.[49]

This is not a matter of concern, as Emperor Trajan had given Pliny permission to consult him whenever in doubt,[50] and there was a special nature to Pliny's mission to Bithynia-Pontus given Trajan had sent him with a specific mandate to stop wasteful spending.

Pliny's letter speaks of his banning of 'political associations [hetaeriae]' yet his previous letters do not mention this legislation.[51]

---

46 RF Clavelle, p. 24, citing Suetonius, *The Twelve Caesars: Book VIII Vespasian, Titus, Domitian*, ch. 13, 'His arrogance and presumption'. Refer to the English and Latin version at: www.poetryintranslation.com/PITBR/Latin/Suetonius8.htm#_Toc276122327, accessed 02/03/2013, and www.thelatinlibrary.com/suetonius/suet.dom.html#13, accessed 02/03/2013.
47 RF Clavelle, pp. 21-3, 205-7.
48 RF Clavelle, p. 21.
49 RF Clavelle, pp. 23-4.
50 Pliny, *Letters*, vol. 2, book 10, letters 3A & 31, http://www.archive.org/stream/letterswithengli02plinuoft#page/276/mode/2up, and http://www.archive.org/stream/letterswithengli02plinuoft#page/314/mode/2up, accessed 10/03/2013.
51 RF Clavelle, p. 45.

As mentioned on page 293, there is an instance in which the prohibition of *hetaeriae* had been discussed in an exchange of letters between Pliny and Trajan. Another instance is found in Letters 92 and 93 of Book 10.[52]

Conclusion

The above inquiry has revealed significant aspects about early Christian belief and behaviour. Pliny's letter mirrors 11 characteristics of Christianity found within the pages of the New Testament. Pliny's account shows that the Christians sang to Christ, whom they regarded as God, and consequently would not deny him. Their customs included meeting regularly over a common meal and keeping moral standards that stipulated paying debts, avoiding fraud, robbery, adultery, and bearing false witness. The community of Christians in Bithynia-Pontus was of such a large number that it caused a negative impact on idol worship. The community included female deacons. As a movement, the Christians were sometimes persecuted, and those that were Roman citizens could be sent to Rome to face trial. (For convenience, all these matching statements are presented in the appendix 'Points of agreement between biblical and non-biblical sources' at the back of this book.)

After careful investigation, I found that all the information from Pliny — a hostile, independent witness — is in accord with that found in the New Testament. Therefore, the evidence supports the claim that the bias of the New Testament authors has not interfered with their ability to write a reliable record of Christian beliefs and practices.

---

52 Pliny, *Letters,* vol. 2, book 10, letters 92 & 93, www.archive.org/stream/letterswithengli02plinuoft#page/396/mode/2up, accessed 15/02/2013.

16

Was Josephus a capable historian?

Another non-Christian historian who wrote about aspects of Christian belief was Josephus. His two short references to Jesus are particularly important because they were penned within about 60 years of Jesus' crucifixion. Apart from these direct references to Christianity, his books carry a vast amount of detail about Jewish and Roman society during the decades before and after Jesus lived. This material is useful when assessing and understanding the general political and cultural milieu found within the pages of the New Testament. His societal depictions are also valuable as they provide a means of making comparisons with those found in the New Testament.

Before I examined Josephus' writings and compared them to those in the New Testament, I wanted to learn more of his background and assess his capability as an historian. This is especially relevant as some have greatly disparaged his competencies, calling him a 'dull copyist who failed to impart any independent judgement or outlook on his material'.[1]

Who was Josephus?

Josephus had an amazing life, experiencing the benefits of aristocracy and the hardships of battle and imprisonment. He was born into a Jewish priestly family of royal descent in 37 AD. His father's family could be

---

1 S Mason, *Flavius Josephus on the Pharisees: A Compositional-Critical Study*, EJ Brill, New York, 1991, pp. 25 & 45.

traced back to a Jewish princess.[2] Although eventually considered a traitor by his fellow Jews, he had originally been placed in Galilee to organise the struggle against the Romans in the war of 66 AD when he was 29 years old. When defeat was inevitable, he and 39 others decided that voluntary death was better than capture. People drew lots to decide the order of killings, but when Josephus and one other were the only ones remaining, they surrendered.[3] He later obtained freedom and Roman citizenship, and even acted as interpreter for the Roman commander Titus (who later became emperor) when Titus' troops destroyed Jerusalem in 70 AD.

Josephus' main claim to fame today is as a historian. He most likely completed *The Wars of the Jews* (also known as *The Jewish War*) when Titus was emperor (79–81 AD), and finished three more works — *The Antiquities of the Jews* (a mammoth 20-book series), *Life* (an autobiography) and *Against Apion* — during the reign of Domitian (81–96 AD),[4] most likely during the last three years of this reign.[5] His *Antiquities* took at least 12 years to write, comprising more than 44,000 lines of Greek text.[6]

Josephus became somewhat of a legend in his own time. Two other Roman historians, Suetonius (b. 69 AD) and Cassius Dio (b. 163 AD) also mentioned Josephus by name.[7] Josephus states in his

---

2   T Rajak, *Josephus: The Historian and His Society*, Gerald Duckworth & Co., London, 1983, pp. 14–17. Chapter 1 of Rajak's book provides good explanations of alleged impossibilities regarding Josephus' description of his family background.
3   W Forster, *Palestinian Judaism in New Testament Times*, trans. GE Harris, Oliver and Boyd, London, 1964, p. 112.
4   AM Berlin & JA Overman, 'Introduction', in AM Berlin & JA Overman (eds), *The First Jewish Revolt: Archaeology, History, and Ideology*, Routledge, London, 2002, p. 1.
5   S Mason, 'Should any wish to enquire further (Ant. 1.25): The aim and audience of Josephus's Judean antiquities/life', in ed. S Mason, *Understanding Josephus: Seven Perspectives*, Sheffield Academic Press, Sheffield, UK, 1998, p. 100.
6   LH Feldman, 'Hellenizations in Josephus' *Jewish Antiquities*: the portrait of Abraham', in LH Feldman & G Hata (eds), *Josephus, Judaism, and Christianity*, Wayne State University Press, Detroit, US, 1987, p. 136.
7   Suetonius, *The Twelve Caesars, Book 8: Vespasian, Titus, Domitian*, ch. 5; Cassius Dio, *Roman History: Epitome of Book LXV (also called LXVI.1)*, trans. E Cary, vol. VIII, Harvard University Press, Cambridge, Massachusetts, US, 1968, pp. 259–60.

autobiography that the Emperor Titus himself signed Josephus' historical writings and ordered them to be published.[8] His material 'served as an important historical source not long after the publication of his work'.[9]

Why and for whom did Josephus write?

These are very important questions as the answers often help us discern why certain information was either included or excluded. Responses to these questions vary, depending on which book(s) of his are being studied.

Josephus' declared in the preface to his book *The Wars of the Jews* that he felt the need to write as earlier accounts of the Jewish war against the Romans were not factual. These false accounts had been motivated by either a desire to praise the Romans or to despise the Jews, and were being circulated amongst the Greeks and Romans.[10] To counter this situation, he decided to publish an account that 'will prosecute the actions of both parties [Jews and Romans] with accuracy'.[11] Josephus concluded this work by boasting that 'I shall not scruple to say, and that boldly, that truth hath been what I have alone aimed at through its [*The Wars of the Jews*] entire composition'.[12] These and similar claims served two purposes: firstly they provided credence to his work and its propositions, and secondly they helped him secure a place of fame alongside notable historians. This is because such expressions of impartiality were characteristic of ancient Greco–Roman historians.[13]

---

8   Josephus, *The Life of Flavius Josephus*, para. 65§363, in trans. W Whiston, *The Works of Josephus: Complete and Unabridged: New Updated Edition*, Hendrickson Publishers, Peabody, Massachusetts, US, 1987, p. 22.
9   JA Overman, 'The first revolt and Flavian politics', in AM Berlin & JA Overman (eds), *The First Jewish Revolt: Archaeology, History, and Ideology*, Routledge, London, 2002, p. 216.
10 Josephus, *The Wars of the Jews*, 'Preface', paras 1–6§1–18, in trans. W Whiston, *The Works of Josephus: Complete and Unabridged: New Updated Edition*, Hendrickson Publishers, Peabody, Massachusetts, US, 1987, pp. 543–4.
11 Josephus, *The Wars of the Jews*, 'Preface', para. 4§9, p. 544.
12 Josephus, *The Wars of the Jews*, book 7, ch. 11, para. 4§455, p. 772.
13 D Marguerat, *The First Christian Historian: Writing the 'Acts of the Apostles'*, trans. K McKinney, GJ Laughery & R Bauckham, Cambridge University Press, New York, 2002, p. 14.

However, whether Josephus achieved these aims will be investigated later in this chapter.

One scholar considered that in *The Wars of the Jews* Josephus aimed to demonstrate that the war arose:

> ... because a handful of would-be tyrants took advantage of the (admitted) egregious misrule of some Roman governors to incite sedition ... [Josephus' book was] ... aimed at defending the surviving Jews against widespread post-war animosity, perhaps even reprisals.[14]

Having completed *The Jewish War*, Josephus' self-proclaimed aim in writing *The Antiquities of the Jews* was in the hope that:

> ... it will appear to all the Greeks worthy of their study; for it will contain all our [Jewish] antiquities, and the constitution of our government ... [and] explain who the Jews originally were, — what fortunes they had been subjected to, — and by what legislator they had been instructed in piety, and the exercise of other virtues, — what wars also they had made in remote ages, till they were unwillingly engaged in this last with the Romans ...[15]

Josephus hoped that as a result of reading *The Antiquities of the Jews*, his readers would not only 'apply their minds to God; and to examine the mind of our legislator [Moses] ...'[16], but would also realise how previous Roman governors had allowed them to obey all of their laws and religious practices.[17] Josephus expected that both Jews and non-Jews would read this mammoth history. Whereas *The Jewish War* was primarily a defensive work, *The Antiquities of the Jews* was not.[18]

---

14 S Mason, 'Should any wish to enquire further (Ant. 1.25): The aim and audience of Josephus's Judean antiquities/life', p. 73.
15 Josephus, *The Antiquities of the Jews*, 'Preface', para. 2§5–6, in trans. W Whiston, *The Works of Josephus: Complete and Unabridged: New Updated Edition*, Hendrickson Publishers, Peabody, Massachusetts, US, 1987, p. 27.
16 Josephus, *The Antiquities of the Jews*, 'Preface', para. 3§15, p. 28.
17 Josephus, *The Antiquities of the Jews*, book 16, ch. 6, para. 8§174, p. 437.
18 S Mason, 'Should any wish to enquire further (Ant. 1.25): The aim and audience of Josephus's Judean antiquities/life', p. 101.

Josephus has at times been criticised for a lack of consistency in his various books, especially between *Life* and *The Wars of the Jews*. However one scholar has presented a very strong case that:

> *what discrepancies there are, beyond the trivial and the accidental, can be explained in terms of the literary form, and purpose of the narratives, and that it is inappropriate to speak of persistent, wilful distortion. In fact, in many cases we are dealing not even with real discrepancies, but with shifts in emphasis.*[19]

Similarly, another expert on Josephus wrote:

> *If we read the* War *[of the Jews] more completely and critically, however, its conflict with the Life is more apparent than real ... There are ... inconsistencies in Josephus but we may better understand them if we accept that* War *and* Life *were written at different times and with different points of view.*[20]

Another scholar, Dr Levine, has pointed out that discrepancies found between *The Wars of the Jews* and *The Antiquities of the Jews* reflect real changes that occurred during the time interval of the writing of these two works. As an example he stated that:

> *the radically different descriptions in* Antiquities *and* War *regarding the place of women in the Temple clearly indicate an increasing division between the sexes ... resulting in a severe limitation in women's access to the inner Temple ...*[21]

Dr Levine concluded that:

> *if our argument be granted, this Temple-related [archaeological and historical] material affirms the basic integrity of Josephus as an historian of first-century Jerusalem. His descriptions are*

---

19 T Rajak, p. 154.
20 RA Horsley, 'Power vacuum and power struggle in 66–7 C.E.', in AM Berlin & JA Overman (eds), *The First Jewish Revolt: Archaeology, History, and Ideology*, Routledge, London, 2002, pp. 89 & 114.
21 LI Levine, 'Josephus' description of the Jerusalem Temple: war, antiquities, and other sources', in F Parente & J Sievers (eds), *Josephus and the History of the Greco-Roman Period: Essays in Memory of Morton Smith*, EJ Brill, Leiden, The Netherlands, 1994, p. 245.

far from capricious, and apparent contradictions might often be explained by clarifying their historical circumstances and institutional contexts ...[22]

Josephus' accuracy in using other written sources

Josephus was well equipped as a historian in so far as he had access to the writings of many other historians. He made reference to at least 55 authors in his books, including Plato and Homer,[23] and Strabo, the Greek geographer and historian.[24] His works indicate that he was familiar with the writings of a wide range of historians, including Greek,[25] Syrian and Babylonian.[26] It was certainly reasonable for him to write that he had gone to great lengths to study the Greek literature.[27]

What is exciting about knowing which particular books Josephus used to compile his history is that we have copies of some of these same books. Cross-checking what he wrote with these sources of information produces an indication of Josephus' competency. The result of this comparison is that many scholars who specialise in Josephus have concluded that 'he remains loyal towards his sources as far as their substance, main contents, and their most essential data are concerned'.[28] As Josephus would have had to refer to written and/

---

22 LI Levine, p. 246.
23 LH Feldman, 'Hellenizations in Josephus' *Jewish Antiquities*: the portrait of Abraham', pp. 135–6.
24 Josephus quotes from him at times (*The Antiquities of the Jews*, book 14, ch. 3, para. 1§35, p. 367), calling him Strabo the Cappadocian.
25 Polybius (b. 203 BC), Alexander Polyhistor (b. 70 BC) and Dionysius of Halicarnassus (b. 60 BC).
26 Berossus (c. 290 BC), Nicolaus of Damascus (b. 64 BC).
27 Josephus, *The Antiquities of the Jews*, book 20, ch. 11, para. 2§263, p. 541.
28 P Bilde, *Flavius Josephus Between Jerusalem and Rome: His Life, His Works, and Their Importance*, Sheffield Academic Press, Sheffield, UK, 1998, p. 196; as cited by PR Eddy & GA Boyd, *The Jesus Legend: A Case for the Historical Reliability of the Synoptic Jesus Tradition*, Baker Academic, Grand Rapids, US, 2007, p. 185, n. 61.

or oral accounts when mentioning Jesus, then the issue of how fairly he used his various sources is very important.

In order to go deeper into this aspect, I looked at how he wrote about a particularly important event in Roman history. This event was how a general called Vespasian became Emperor of Rome in 69 AD; an occasion that Josephus predicted and witnessed. Not only do we have a description of this written by Josephus some time before 96 AD, but also descriptions written by the famous historians Tacitus and Suetonius in about 106 and 120 AD respectively. After comparing these various accounts, one scholar wrote that:

> *The narration by Josephus was written prior to the other two and published during the lifetime of Vespasian. (Would he have dared to do so had it been incorrect?) It is extremely realistic and abounds in detail ... Not only is Josephus' account superior in literary terms to the two others, it is also more convincing.*[29]

The above comment certainly gives great credit to Josephus, but I wanted to know if this favourable comparison wasn't just an isolated case. I found Josephus was of the family clan called Hasmoneans, who played a very important role in Jewish history. A consequence of their fame is that there is an extensive body of Jewish literature written about them, especially in the book called 1 Maccabees. Josephus would have extensively used 1 Maccabees as a source of information,[30] and we can still read it today. He would, of course, have heard family traditions about the Hasmoneans as well. Nearly everyone likes to boast about their ancestors, and Josephus was no exception, composing 2015 lines on them.[31] His re-working of this material provides a means of checking how fairly he did this. This cross-examination would be especially

---

29 M Hadas-Lebel, p. 105.
30 LH Feldman, 'Josephus' portrayal of the Hasmoneans compared with 1 Maccabees', in F Parente & J Sievers (eds), *Josephus and the History of the Greco-Roman Period: Essays in Memory of Morton Smith*, EJ Brill, Leiden, The Netherlands, 1994, pp. 42–3. Feldman states that the other books Josephus may have used include those by Nicolaus of Damascus, Polybius, Diodorus, Posidonius, Aristeas and Timagenes.
31 LH Feldman, 'Josephus' portrayal of the Hasmoneans compared with 1 Maccabees', p. 43.

valuable, for if anyone is likely to play loose with the truth, it most likely will be with the accomplishments of their own kith and kin.

The comparison indicates that Josephus did change the original material in several respects, which reveals certain trends. Looking at the way he portrayed the actions of God through this and other periods of Jewish history, Josephus greatly de-emphasised the role of God. So when 1 Maccabees has the Hasmoneans crying out to heaven, Josephus simply has them wailing. When the original has the hero reminding his troops how God's angel helped the Jews in past battles, Josephus has the hero encouraging the men without any mention of such an event.[32] Josephus also re-phrased his material so that it is not possible for others to consider the Jews as hating many other races. For example instead of referring to the Hasmonean opponents as 'enemies', he calls them 'nations'. Similarly he later changes the wording from 'heathen' to 'anyone'. He also omits details of how the Hasmonean victors destroyed the altars and idols of an enemy's town and instead writes how they destroyed the city. This is presumably because the destruction of idols would indicate disrespect for foreign religions, whereas destruction of an enemies' town would be expected in the course of war.[33] Josephus also paints some of the Hasmonean heroes in brighter colours than the original text. Whereas the original may simply say that the hero rekindled 'the spirit of his people', Josephus amends this 'by adding that from having been crushed in spirit through timidity they were now raised to a better spirit and good hope'.[34] Similarly 1 Maccabees has the hero and his men defeat the enemy, whereas Josephus has the hero being solely responsible for burning their war machines and slaughtering many enemy soldiers.[35]

From this analysis it appears that although Josephus appears to have changed the wording and, to some extent the meaning, he

---

32 LH Feldman, 'Josephus' portrayal of the Hasmoneans compared with 1 Maccabees', pp. 63–5.
33 LH Feldman, 'Josephus' portrayal of the Hasmoneans compared with 1 Maccabees', pp. 65–6.
34 LH Feldman, 'Josephus' portrayal of the Hasmoneans compared with 1 Maccabees', p. 63.
35 LH Feldman, 'Josephus' portrayal of the Hasmoneans compared with 1 Maccabees', p. 62.

didn't significantly alter the original accounts as to make his version unrecognizable. The basic facts are still there, albeit veiled. It is also possible to see a pattern in the way he re-worked his material to de-emphasise religious aspects, which allows us to take this into consideration when reading the rest of his historical books.

Josephus' accuracy as an eyewitness

Another way to test Josephus' reliability as a historian is to examine his ability to describe places and events he witnessed or in which he was a participant.

I decided to examine the accuracy of his descriptions as they relate to architectural details and military history. I chose these topics as they allow very specific comparisons to be made with what has been unearthed by archaeologists. Josephus did have a daunting task trying to document the history of the first Jewish revolt, as it was:

> far more complex than a simple anti-Roman revolt. It was instead a variety of interrelated and overlapping conflicts including urban-rural hostilities, class conflict within the cities, hostility toward and acquiescence in Roman and/or Herodian rule, and response to and rejection of Jerusalem authority — including plenty of mutual manipulation and negotiation and shifting alliances.[36]

Accuracy in portraying architectural details

Josephus provided a considerable amount of detail in his description of the harbour facilities at the ancient city of Caesarea Maritima. The picture illustrates the astounding engineering capabilities of that time:

> [Herod] adorned it [the city of Caesarea] with a haven, that was always free from the waves of the sea. Its largeness was not less than the [port built at] Pyraeum [at Athens]; and had towards the city a double station for the ships. It was of excellent workmanship ... This city [of Caesarea] is situate in Phoenicia

---

36 RA Horsley, p. 92.

> ... between Joppa and Dora, which are lesser maritime cities ... [Herod] effected [the building of the harbour] by letting down vast stones of above fifty feet [15.2 metres] in length, not less than eighteen [5.5 metres] in breadth, and nine [2.7 metres] in depth, into twenty fathoms [36.6 metres] deep; and as some were lesser, so were others bigger, than those dimensions. This mole which he built by the seaside was two hundred feet [61 metres] wide, the half of which was opposed to the current of the waves ... but the other half had upon it a wall, with several towers ... And the basis of the whole circuit on the left hand, as you enter the port, supported a round turret, which was made very strong, in order to resist the greatest waves; while on the right hand, as you enter, stood two vast stones, and those each of them larger than the turret, which was over against them: these stood upright, and were joined together.[37]

> At the harbour-mouth stood colossal statues, three on either side, resting on columns; the columns on the left of vessels entering port were supported by a massive tower, those on the right by two upright blocks of stone clamped together, whose height exceeded that of the tower on the opposite side.[38]

It had been stated by many sceptics that Josephus' description was either a sheer fabrication, or a gross exaggeration. However, 25 years of maritime archaeological research have largely confirmed Josephus' descriptions: According to Josephus, the dimensions of the foundational blocks were 15.2 metres by 5.5 metres by 2.7 metres; which is very similar to one of the stones revealed in 1983 to be 15 metres by 11.5 metres by more than 2 metres.[39] There is the very real possibility that if more stones are uncovered, some will have measurements identical to Josephus' description. Because of these discoveries, one archaeologist wrote that:

---

37 Josephus, *The Antiquities of the Jews*, book 15, ch. 9, para. 6§332–38, pp. 419–20.

38 Josephus, *The Jewish War*, book 1, ch. 21, para. 7, trans. H Thackery, vol. 2, William Heinemann, London, and Harvard University Press, Cambridge, Massachusetts, US, 1927, p. 195.

39 RL Vann, 'Caesarea Maritima', in ed. JP Delgado, *Encyclopedia of Underwater and Maritime Archaeology*, Yale University Press, London, 1997, p. 80.

> *The harbour plan... corresponds in its basic outline with the description of Josephus ... The extensive archaeological record at Caesarea reinforces this [Josephus'] literary description.*[40]

Although there are some differences, it can be seen that archaeology has confirmed that Josephus was able to convey quite accurate architectural details regarding dimensions and layouts.

Ability as a military historian

Josephus' descriptions of the battles fought by the Jews in the first war of the Jews have often been regarded as gross exaggeration at best, and deliberate fabrication at worst. It has been suggested that his motivations for such distortions were to paint a better picture of his ability to harness troops and to create a more flattering description of the Roman fighting machine.

Jotapata

The first major battle he recounted was at Jotapata (also called Yodefat), which also became the second bloodiest during the war and had the third-longest siege. One archaeologist, Dr Mordechai Aviam of the Israel Antiquities Authority, has examined the archaeological evidence to see how it compares with the details provided by Josephus. Aviam summarised the results as:

> *documenting [that is, affirming] many of the aspects of Josephus' narrative: (1) there was indeed a heavy battle around the hill of Yodefat in the mid-first century C.E.; (2) the town was surrounded with a wall hurriedly built in the early Roman period; (3) an earthwork [assault ramp] was made on the northern slope of the town; (4) weaponry, including bow and catapult arrows and ballista stones were shot into the town from all around; (5) many people died during the siege, battle, and fall.*[41]

---

40 RL Vann, p. 80.
41 M Aviam, 'Yodefat/Jotapata: The archaeology of the first battle', in AM Berlin & JA Overman (eds), *The First Jewish Revolt: Archaeology, History, and Ideology*, Routledge, London, 2002, p.132–3.

Despite Josephus providing an accurate overall picture of the town and battle tactics, he appears to have a propensity to exaggerate loss of life. Thus when Jotapata fell to the Romans in July of 67 AD, Josephus wrote of 40,000 being killed and 1200 being taken captive.[42] This contrasts markedly with modern estimations. Based on the size of the town, Aviam considered that there were probably only 7000 people in Jotapata at the beginning of the siege, though the number of captives may well have been 1200.[43]

Another occasion of exaggeration occurred when Josephus wrote about the death of a fellow Jew that was standing close to him near the wall of Jotapata during the siege. Josephus writes that suddenly the man's head was so powerfully knocked off by a stone hurled from a Roman war machine that it travelled a distance of three stadia (c. 470 metres).[44] However, ballistae (the Roman machines used to throw rounded missiles, or ballista) had an effective range of only between 350 to 450 metres.[45]

The above two examples of exaggeration, when considered alongside his overall accuracy, certainly don't greatly detract from his ability as an historian.

Gamala

Archaeology has also verified the truthfulness of another of Josephus' exploits. At the beginning of the Jewish revolt against the Romans, Josephus states that he built the city wall of Gamala (also called Gamla).[46] One archaeologist, Dr Danny Syon of the Israel Antiquities Authority, has summed up the findings regarding this wall:

---

42 Josephus, *The Wars of the Jews*, book 3, ch.7, para. 36§336–39, p. 654.
43 M Aviam, p. 131.
44 Josephus, *The Wars of the Jews*, book 3, ch. 7, para. 23§245, p. 650.
45 A Holley, 'The ballista balls from Masada', in D Barag et al., *Masada IV: The Yigael Yadin Excavations 1963–1965 Final Reports*, Israel Exploration Society, Jerusalem, 1994, pp. 349–65, cited by D Syon, 'Gamla: City of refuge', in AM Berlin & JA Overman (eds), *The First Jewish Revolt: Archaeology, History, and Ideology*, Routledge, London, 2002, p. 142.
46 Josephus, *The Wars of the Jews*, book 4, ch. 1, para. 2§9, p. 664; Josephus, *The Life of Flavius Josephus*, para. 37§186, p. 12.

> *The excavations proved without a doubt that the site [of Gamala] was indeed abandoned in ... 64 C.E. The excavations corroborated Josephus' account on many more points ... [The] wall was one of the surprises of the excavation. Josephus' claim that he* built *the city wall ... has been understood to mean that he* strengthened *and* reinforced *an existing wall ... The wall visible today is, in fact, a patchwork of pre-existing buildings ... with evidence of hasty construction closing the gaps between them ... the wall is anything but a straight line: it bulges, zigzags ... the fortification by Josephus included closing gaps between existing buildings ... and the thickening of existing building wall ... by the construction of a second wall behind them ... It also included the filling-in with stones of rooms along the course of the wall ...*[47]

Josephus' description of the actual battle at Gamala has also been remarkably verified by archaeology. Josephus states that 'the city had been filled with those that had fled to it for safety ... [The Romans brought] those machines [that] threw darts and stones ... and [brought] battering rams ...'[48] Archaeologists have found that:

> *[t]he excavations clearly show only one [breach] ... a huge number of arrow heads (some 300) and ballista balls (some 180) were found inside and outside of it ... The [breached] wall ... was thickened to 2.05 meters ... it was one of the weakest points in the wall ... [In total, approximately] 2000 ballista balls ... [and about] 1,600 iron arrow heads have been found to date [at Gamla] ... this number [of arrow heads] probably represents only a fraction of the arrows spent. Two areas in the city provided evidence of public places used by refugees...*[49]

Later Josephus made a seemingly fanciful remark when describing an event near the end of the battle, which occurred in September–October:

> *However, there arose such a Divine storm against them [the Jews] as was instrumental to their destruction; this carried the Roman*

---

47 D Syon, 'Gamla: City of refuge', in AM Berlin & JA Overman (eds), *The First Jewish Revolt: Archaeology, History, and Ideology*, Routledge, London, 2002, p. 135-6. Emphases in the original.
48 Josephus, *The Wars of the Jews*, book 4, ch. 1, paras 2–4, pp. 664–5.
49 D Syon, pp. 140–6.

> darts upon them, and made those which they threw return back, and drove them obliquely away from them.⁵⁰

This has received an intriguing corroboration by one archaeologist who noted that the area at this time of the year often experiences eastern gale force winds. When he and his team were at Gamala during those months, they felt sporadic blasts [which] could stop them from breathing, and make most objects airborne if they weren't made of stone or tied down. He concluded that 'the description of Josephus, even if embellished, is no doubt based on fact'.⁵¹

Despite this very favourable assessment of Josephus as a military historian, there is evidence that Josephus erred when he spoke of 5000 people in Gamala choosing mass suicide as the inevitable defeat drew near.⁵² Analysis of the site reveals that topographically it is unlikely that so many could have killed themselves by jumping off a summit. It is possible that Josephus genuinely misinterpreted the scene of people fleeing down a steep slope and trampling their fellows underfoot as a case of mass suicide, or he may have made a deliberate distortion or gross exaggeration.⁵³

This section on military history has confirmed that Josephus, although prone to exaggerate the loss of life and other numerical details, was able to present a very accurate overall picture of military events.

Did Josephus use other eyewitnesses?

I was also interested in whether there was any evidence that Josephus obtained information from eyewitnesses when he wasn't able to be part of the action himself. When writing about recent events in Roman history, was he diligent enough to seek out eyewitnesses?

It has been claimed that Josephus certainly did avail himself of the opportunity to listen to those who had direct access to the movers and shakers of Roman society. One scholar wrote:

---

50 Josephus, *The Wars of the Jews*, book 4, ch. 1, para.10§76, p. 667.
51 D Syon, p. 149.
52 Josephus, *The Wars of the Jews*, book 4, ch. 1, para. 10§80, pp. 667–8.
53 D Syon, pp. 149–51.

Josephus knew many witnesses to recent events of Roman history: not only King Agrippa II who had obtained accounts from his father [King Agrippa I], but also ... Epaphroditus, Nero's freedman ... [Epaphroditus] could have informed Josephus about political life in Rome under Nero ... There is ample reason to give credit to oral testimonies recorded by Josephus.[54]

Conclusion

Based on all the evidence considered so far, Josephus appears to have been a very reliable historian when dealing with military and political affairs, including those that he witnessed. This ability to be a reliable eyewitness is particularly relevant when examining the passages he wrote containing supplied information about Christians. This is because it is quite conceivable that he learnt about Christianity during his six-year stay in Jerusalem. This period of time, between 56 to 62 AD,[55] is about six years after a prominent meeting in Jerusalem of Jewish Christian leaders, including 'apostles and elders' and 'believers who belonged to the party of the Pharisees' (Acts 15:4–6). As Josephus became a Pharisee in Jerusalem when he was nineteen years old,[56] it is very plausible that he gained his knowledge about Christians from fellow Pharisees in Jerusalem.

With this knowledge of his competency as a historian, and his likely sources of information, it is now time to delve into his comments that

---

54 M Hadas-Lebel, 'Flavius Josephus, Historian of Rome', in F Parente & J Sievers (eds), *Josephus and the History of the Greco-Roman Period: Essays in Memory of Morton Smith*, EJ Brill, Leiden, The Netherlands, 1994, p. 102.

55 J Dickson, *Investigating Jesus: An Historian's Quest*, A Lion Book, Oxford, UK, 2010, p. 76.

56 Josephus, *The Life of Flavius Josephus*, para. 2§12, in trans. W Whiston, *The Works of Josephus: Complete and Unabridged: New Updated Edition*, Hendrickson Publishers, Peabody, Massachusetts, US, 1987, 2, p. 1. An idea, first promulgated in the 1800s, and again now by S Mason, is that Josephus was not actually a Pharisee. Refer to H Schreckenberg, 'Josephus in early Christian literature and medieval Christian art', in H Schreckenberg & K Schubert (eds), *Jewish Historiography and Iconography in Early and Medieval Christianity*, Fortress Press, Minneapolis, 1992, p. 27, n. 26. See also S Mason, *Flavius Josephus on the Pharisees: A Compositional-Critical Study*, EJ Brill, New York, 1991.

touch on the same subject matters as found in the New Testament. I wanted to know if his descriptions of the culture and people of Judea echo those in the New Testament. If so, then the authors of the New Testament can be considered as providing accurate portrayals that have not become spurious because of the authors' biases.

17

Josephus and the New Testament

The previous chapter established Josephus as a reliable historian. As Josephus wrote on many subjects that are also discussed in the New Testament, I will start with his two most famous comments, both of which pertain directly to Jesus, and then examine what his writings had to say about other New Testament people and events.

The first reference to Jesus: crucified by Pilate

The following passage, called the *testimonium flavianum*, is from Josephus' book *The Antiquities of the Jews*. Because this massive publication was finished before 96 AD, it may provide some of the earliest reflections penned by a non-Christian:

> *Now, there was about this time Jesus, a wise man, if it be lawful to call him a man, for he was a doer of wonderful works — a teacher of such men as receive the truth with pleasure. He drew over to him both many of the Jews, and many of the Gentiles. He was (the) Christ; and when Pilate, at the suggestion of the principal men amongst us, had condemned him to the cross, those who loved him at the first did not forsake him, for he appeared to them alive again the third day, as the divine prophets had foretold these and ten*

thousand other wonderful things concerning him; and the tribe of Christians, so named from him, are not extinct at this day.[1]

If all of this passage originally came from the hand of Josephus, it would provide independent support for many New Testament statements.

Authenticity of the first reference

What is particularly interesting is that some scholars dispute the authenticity of the *testimonium flavianum*; that is, they consider that Josephus did not originally write the passage. Other scholars accept that he authored the words either entirely, or with only small modifications.[2] Because of these differences of opinion, the *testimonium flavianum* has been the subject of an enormous and lengthy debate; apparently 87 studies were published on it just between 1937 and 1980.[3] One recent and well-referenced article is that by CE Price.[4] After considering many of the issues surrounding this question of authenticity, and due to considerations of space, I have chosen to write about just two of the questions that arise concerning the *testimonium flavianum*.

Is it out of context within Josephus' book?

One of the reasons frequently given for considering that the entire section about Jesus is spurious is that it interrupts the natural flow of events recounted by Josephus at this point in his book. This issue of

---

1 Josephus, *The Antiquities of the Jews* book 18, ch. 3, para. 3§63–4, in trans. W Whiston, *The Works of Josephus: Complete and Unabridged: New Updated Edition*, Hendrickson Publishers, Peabody, Massachusetts, US, 1987, p. 480. In order to study the Greek and English versions of any of Josephus' works, refer to Project on Ancient Cultural Engagement (PACE), http://pace.mcmaster.ca/york/york/texts.htm, accessed 10/02/2013.
2 FF Bruce, *The New Testament Documents: Are They Reliable?*, Wm B Eerdmans, Cambridge, UK, 1981, pp. 102–12.
3 S Mason, *Josephus and the New Testament,* Hendrickson Publishers, Massachusetts, US, 1992, p. 165.
4 CE Price, 'Firmly established by Josephus: What an ancient Jewish historian knew about Jesus', in JP Holding (ed.), *Shattering the Christ Myth: Did Jesus not Exist?*, Xulon Press, Maitland, Florida, 2008, pp. 21–46. See also C Price, *Did Josephus Refer to Jesus? A Thorough Review of the Testimonium Flavianum*, Bede's Library, http://bede.org.uk/Josephus.htm, accessed 10/02/2013.

context is reinforced in the minds of some people by the claim that Josephus would not have written the following words immediately after the paragraph about Jesus: 'About the same time another sad calamity put the Jews into disorder ...' At first sight, this logic seems reasonable because Josephus, being a non-Christian Jew, would be unlikely to consider the death of Jesus, a false Christ in the eyes of Jews, to be an unfortunate 'sad calamity'. In response to these concerns, I undertook an examination of the series of events surrounding the *testimonium flavianum*, which falls near the middle of chapter 3, from book 18 of Josephus' *The Antiquities of the Jews*.

This chapter 3 comprises five paragraphs:

- Paragraph 1 relates how the Roman governor, Pontius Pilate (r. 26–36 AD), brought idols into the city of Jerusalem at night. When the Jewish citizenry woke to find the idols, they pestered Pilate for six days. Pilate then confronted the protestors with his army but, instead of backing down, the protestors indicated they would willingly die without a fight in order to have Pilate remove the idols. Pilate then relented, without any blood being shed.

- The second paragraph speaks of how tens of thousands of Jews in Jerusalem started rioting over Pilate's plans to build a water supply to serve the city. They seemed to have become so incensed because the aqueduct was being built with money set aside for religious purposes. A terrible bloodbath resulted and Josephus concluded the narration of this event by saying that the carnage brought about the end of the 'sedition'.

- The third paragraph is the *testimonium flavianum*, as written out in full above.

- The fourth paragraph begins with the words: 'About the same time another sad calamity put the Jews into disorder; and certain shameful practices happened about the temple of Isis that was at Rome. I will now first take notice of the wicked attempt about the temple of Isis, and will then give an account of the Jewish affairs.' Josephus then immediately launches into the sad story of Paulina, a very wealthy and scrupulous married woman who was extremely devoted to the god Anubis. An extremely wealthy Roman knight, Mundus, had offered Paulina an enormous sum of money so that he could have sex with her for one night. Because Paulina refused, Mundus then bribed the local priests to convince Paulina that the god Anubis wanted to have her for himself for one night. Mundus later boasted to Paulina that he had pretended to be Anubis, and that it cost him much less to have her for the night than the money he originally offered her. The distraught Paulina then explained to her husband that they had been deceived, and he in turn complained to the Emperor Tiberius. The culpable priests were then crucified, the temple destroyed and Mundus banished. None of these events involved the Jews, Jerusalem or Pilate. Paragraph four in many ways is a large digression in that it takes up 55% of all the words in the chapter,[5] and yet the narrated events do not involve Jews, Pilate or even Judea.

- The fifth paragraph describes how four wicked Jewish men duped a wealthy woman living in Rome who had become a convert to Judaism. After the men succeeded in acquiring some of her gold, her husband relayed the news to Emperor Tiberius, who then banished all the Jews living in Rome. The only connections between paragraphs four and five is that dignified women were conned and the husbands of both (who happened to have the same name) were able to appeal successfully to the emperor for justice. This very loose linking of the two paragraphs further substantiates that paragraph four is a digression. This then implies that the opening words of paragraph four — 'About the same time another sad calamity put the Jews into disorder ...' — actually look forward to paragraph five.

Having finished this brief survey of Josephus' chapter 3, it is time to return to the question of whether the *testimonium flavianum* is within the context of narrated events. Reflecting on how Josephus' words 'Another sad calamity put the Jews into disorder ...' could apply to all the accounts (paragraphs) given in chapter 3, it seems that there is an explanation that binds four of the five together, namely that any action that resulted in the Jews being disordered was in fact a 'sad calamity'. This explanation is based on the following observations:

---

5   A total of 1069 words of the 1951 words found in the English translation provided by Whiston.

Josephus and the New Testament

- In the case of paragraph 1, the bloodless victory to get the idols removed involved Jews throwing themselves on the open ground in front of Pilate. This can be seen as a sad calamity in two ways: the Jews had to be disorderly to win their case against Pilate, and the idols had been brought into the city.

- In paragraph 2, 'many ten thousands' of Jews had 'made a clamour' against Pilate, clearly a case of disorder. Tellingly, Josephus referred to the protesting Jews as seditious, indicating that he did not approve of their action. This reinforces the concept that Josephus regarded any event, whether he sanctioned it or not, as a 'sad calamity' if it caused disorder among the Jews.

- Paragraph 3 tells of how some Jews gave their allegiance to a man that Pilate crucified 'at the suggestion of the principal men amongst us'. These Jewish followers of Jesus were disorderly as they continued in their loyalty to this criminal called Christ, even after his punishment had been brought about by Pilate and Josephus' colleagues. These disciples created a new and dishonourable sect, and this represented even more disorder. In Josephus' eyes, the sad calamity is the fact that some Jews followed Christ, not that Christ was crucified.

- Paragraph four is a large digression that has no bearing on Jews at all.

- Finally paragraph 5 describes the momentous disorder that occurred due to all the Jews in Rome being exiled.

Given the above analysis, the *testimonium flavianum* certainly appears to fit in with the overall context of the entire chapter. Interestingly, those scholars who believe that the *testimonium flavianum* is out of context, though still genuine, appeal to the tendency for Josephus to make digressions. Although my analysis makes it apparent that paragraph four is the only paragraph that is a digression, it is worth noting the words of one expert:

> *One feature of Josephus' writing which may be disconcerting to the modern reader and appear inartistic is the way in which at times the narrative is proceeding at a spanking pace when it is*

> *unceremoniously cut short by a paragraph or a longer passage of material unrelated or only marginally related to the subject in hand, and then resumed equally abruptly.*[6]

Appendix 1 at the end of this chapter looks at the issues of context and digressions more broadly in book 18 of *The Antiquities of the Jews*.

If Josephus knew about Jesus and the growing Christian community, then why didn't he write much more extensively about them?

This second question about the authenticity of the *testimonium flavianum* arouses even more curiosity when it is appreciated that Josephus had written a little earlier that:

> *The Jews had for a great while three sects of philosophy peculiar to themselves; the sect of the Essenes, and the sect of the Sadducees, and ... those called Pharisees ...*[7]

Some consider that this quotation indicates that Josephus knew nothing about Jesus or Christianity in general, because if he did he would have added them as yet another sect of philosophy. However, I discovered there are several reasons that would account for Josephus not mentioning the Christian sect when he wrote about the three other sects. These reasons also shed light on why Josephus would have been more reluctant to mention Christians other than his compulsion as a historian.

Firstly, the quote above makes it clear that Josephus set out to comment on only those sects that had been in existence 'for a great while'. From Josephus' perspective, Jesus and his followers were a very recent phenomenon as Jesus began teaching and healing only in about 30 AD. By contrast, Josephus mentions the Pharisees, Sadducees and Essenes[8]

---

6   Josephus, *The Jewish Wars*, trans. GA Williamson, rev. EM Smallwood, Penguin Books, Harmondsworth, Middlesex, UK, 1988, p. 20.
7   Josephus, *The Antiquities of the Jews*, book 18, ch. 1, para. 2§11, p. 477.
8   Josephus, *The Antiquities of the Jews*, book 13, ch. 5, para. 9§171, p. 346.

as already being in existence during the reign of the high priest Jonathan Maccabeus (c. 153–43 BC).[9]

Secondly, Josephus' reason for discussing these three sects stems from his desire to show that just as the Greeks had major philosophical schools, so too did the Jews. This is why he 'explicitly compares the Pharisees with the Stoics and the Essenes with the Pythagoreans, and implicitly compares the Sadducees with the Epicureans'.[10] It would not have been in his interest to mention the Christians in this context as that would have given them a degree of prominence and respectability.

Thirdly, Josephus' quote further narrowed his choice of interesting sects to those that were 'peculiar to themselves'; that is, religious groups that included only Jews. Long before Josephus had completed *The Antiquities of the Jews*, the Christian community included large numbers of non-Jews,[11] many of whom were in Rome. As Josephus had spent about 20 years in Rome leading up to the publication of his book,[12] he would have known of the large number of non-Jewish Christians residing there.

Fourthly, Josephus' motif throughout his books was to demonstrate that the Jews were, for the most part, a law-abiding nation. Josephus laboured to demonstrate in both *The Antiquities of the Jews* and *The War of the Jews* that the Jewish laws were 'especially admirable and that the Jews as a people adhere scrupulously to them even in the face of death'.[13] The gargantuan war against the Romans would never have eventuated if the activities of 'a handful of Jewish power-mongers …'[14] had been curtailed. Josephus documented that it was only two

---

9 Refer to *Jewish Encyclopedia* [online], 'Jonathan Maccabeus', 1901–06, www.jewishencyclopedia.com/articles/8773-jonathan-maccabeus#anchor2, accessed 25/03/2013.

10 SJD Cohen, *From the Maccabees to the Mishnah*, The Westminster Press, Philadelphia, 1987, p. 144.

11 See, for example, chapter 15 'Pliny the Younger'.

12 T Rajak, *Josephus: The Historian and His Society*, Gerald Duckworth & Co., London, 1983, p. 47.

13 S Mason, *Flavius Josephus on the Pharisees: A Compositional-Critical Study*, EJ Brill, New York, 1991, pp.105–6.

14 S Mason, *Flavius Josephus on the Pharisees: A Compositional-Critical Study*, p. 67. See also Josephus, *The Wars of the Jews*, Preface, para. 4, in trans. W Whiston, *The Works of Josephus: Complete and Unabridged: New Updated Edition*, Hendrickson Publishers, Peabody, Massachusetts, US, 1987, p. 544.

men who had started the movement that persuaded a great many of his countrymen to revolt over several decades. Both earlier and later in his chapter on the three sects, Josephus mentions this fourth Jewish philosophic sect under the leadership of Judas the Galilean. This strictly Jewish group is mentioned only in the context of having fomented many civil disturbances and wars, eventually being responsible for the monumental war against the Romans.

In the context of demonstrating that it was only a few who promulgated the great war, it would have been counter-productive to his cause for Josephus to list, in the same chapter as the quote mentioned above, another sect whose instigator was not only a Jew, but a convicted law-breaker who was crucified to death by the Romans. If he had done so, then two out of five, rather than one out of four, sects would have been considered as rebellious in nature.

Fifthly, throughout all his many books, Josephus was silent on other major Jewish religious movements:

> *Josephus, strangely enough, reports nothing worth mentioning about the institution of the synagogue and its importance for the survival of Judaism after [the war of the Jews against the Romans in] 70 [AD], although it was the synagogues ... where the liturgy and the traditions of Jewish religious communities developed, traditions which contributed to the unbroken continuity with which Judaism overcame the loss of the Temple [which was permanently destroyed by the war].*[15]

Moreover, a significant number of the citizens of Rome would have known of the existence of Christians and considered them disparagingly, partly because Emperor Nero had made great public spectacles of their torture in Rome in the 60s AD.[16] Josephus may have wanted to keep his description of the Christians brief and separate to the portrayals of the three main sects to downplay that Christianity originated in his

---

15 H Schreckenberg, 'Josephus in early Christian literature and medieval Christian art', in H Schreckenberg & K Schubert (eds), *Jewish Historiography and Iconongraphy in Early and Medieval Christianity*, Fortress Press, Minneapolis, US, 1992, p. 29.

16 See, for example, chapter 12 'Christian beliefs as revealed by Christian and non-Christian writers prior to 200 AD'.

homeland. Even in his short description of the Christians, Josephus makes it clear that not only Jews, but others also, had been lured into following Jesus.[17] One scholar elaborated on Josephus' desire to distance Judaism from Christianity by writing that:

> *In short: an extensive and objective description of the beliefs and goals of early Christianity could easily have disturbed his [Josephus'] apolitically well-rounded, grand picture of the Jewish religion and thereby have made it less attractive to Greeks and Romans. What remains therefore is only the briefest possible ... reference, doing no injury to Judaism's claim to truth and making no concessions to the new, still developing [Christian] movement.*[18]

Conclusion to the first reference about Jesus

Two of the common questions about authenticity that arise from Josephus' *testimonium flavianum* can be readily answered. These findings, as well as a thorough examination of the remaining questions, make it clear that Josephus did write about Jesus in the *testimonium flavianum*.

However, like many others, both Christian and non-Christian,[19] it seems to me that several additions and deletions were made by one or more Christian scribes as they copied Josephus' texts over the years.[20] Many scholars believe these scribes made only minimal changes, such as:[21]

> *The phrase 'if it be lawful to call him a man' was added;*
>
> *The phrase 'He was called the Christ' (ho legomenos Christos) had one word deleted so it became 'He was the Christ' (ho Christos);*

---

17 Josephus, *The Antiquities of the Jews*, book 18, ch. 3, para. 3§63, p. 480.
18 H Schreckenberg, 'Josephus in early Christian literature and medieval Christian art', pp. 37–8.
19 CE Price, 'Firmly established by Josephus: What an ancient Jewish historian knew about Jesus', p. 26.
20 Appendix 2 at the end of this chapter briefly discusses the matter of tampering by Christians in a more general manner.
21 CE Price, 'Firmly established by Josephus: What an ancient Jewish historian knew about Jesus', pp. 25–33.

> *The last phrase that begins with the words 'for he appeared to them alive...' originally had modifying words such as 'For it seemed to his followers that he appeared...'*

One scholar, who doesn't consider that the New Testament is perfectly accurate regarding historical matters, made the following summary that grants authenticity to a few minimal comments about Jesus:

> *The vast majority of commentators hold a middle position between authenticity and inauthenticity, claiming that Josephus wrote something about Jesus that was subsequently edited by Christian copyists. It would be unwise, therefore, to lean heavily on Josephus' statement about Jesus' healing and teaching activity, or the circumstances of his trial. Nevertheless, since most of those who know the evidence agree that he said* something *about Jesus, one is probably entitled to cite him as independent evidence that Jesus actually lived, if such evidence were needed.*[22]

After weighing all the evidence, and accepting all reasonable claims of doubt about authenticity, Josephus' original *testimonium flavianum* can be regarded as at least revealing that Christians were named after Jesus Christ, who was crucified by the Roman governor of Judea, Pontius Pilate. Josephus' words, therefore, perfectly echo these same well-known facts described in the New Testament (see Acts 11:26, 1 Peter 4:16, Luke 23 and Matthew 27:2).

The second reference to Jesus: James the brother of Jesus

Despite the brevity of this second reference, it substantiates six different facts found in the New Testament. It deals with the death of James, who was one of Jesus' brothers.[23] This happened in the three months between the death of the Roman procurator Festus (62 AD)[24]

---

22 S Mason, *Josephus and the New Testament*, pp. 173–4.
23 The other brothers were Joses, Judas and Simon. His sisters weren't named. See Mark 6:3.
24 M Avi-Yonah & E Stern (eds), 'Chronological tables', in *Encyclopedia of Archaeological Excavations in the Holy Land*, vol. 3, Oxford University Press, London, 1977, pp. 931–3.

and the arrival of the new one, Albinus. This interval allowed the new high priest called Ananus (whose father was also called Ananus) to do as he wished. He accomplished his plans by enlisting the help of the supreme council of Jewish judges called the Sanhedrin. Josephus wrote:

> *this younger Ananus ... was a bold man in his temper and very insolent; he was also of the sect of the Sadducees, who are very rigid in judging offenders, above all the rest of the Jews ... Festus was now dead, and Albinus was out upon the open road; so he [Ananus] assembled the sanhedrin of the judges and brought before them the brother of Jesus, who was called [legōmenos, λεγομενος] Christ, whose name was James, and some others;*[25] *and when he had formed an accusation against them as breakers of the law, he delivered them to be stoned ...*[26]

This passage is important as it records the existence of Jesus 'who was called Christ'.

It is perfectly natural that Josephus needed to indicate which Jesus he was referring to as more than one individual went by this name. Josephus mentions at least six different individuals by this name in his *Antiquities* alone, two of which appear within a few paragraphs after the one quoted above. Even the New Testament mentions a 'Jesus, who is called Justus' (Colossians 4:11). It is also to be expected that Josephus referred to the Jesus of the Christians as someone 'called [legōmenos] the Christ' as this was one of the most common ways for Christians to refer to Jesus. Jesus is called the Christ numerous times in the New Testament alone. It has also been said that the phrase 'brother of Jesus who was called Christ' was used for several reasons, one being to convey to the reader that '... this man [James] was the brother of the one I mentioned before'.[27]

The quotation about James dovetails with other facts from the New Testament: 'Is not this the carpenter, the son of Mary, and the brother of

---

25 The translator of this passage inserts at this point '[or, some of his companions]'.
26 Josephus, *The Antiquities of the Jews*, book 20, ch. 9, para. 1§199–200, pp. 537–8.
27 S Mason, *Josephus and the New Testament*, p. 178.

James and Joses and Judas and Simon? Are not His sisters here with us?' (Mark 6:3, NASB). James is also referred to as 'the Lord's brother' in Galatians 1:19. Although some denominations teach that after Jesus was born his mother didn't have any more children, other denominations accept that the New Testament provides strong support that he did.[28]

The fact that it was Jesus' brother James that was chosen by Ananus reinforces the truthfulness of the New Testament statement that James had become a prominent figure in the Christian community. Ananus would have been especially keen to destroy Christian leaders rather than ordinary ones. James acted as a spokesperson for the apostles and elders meeting in Jerusalem (Acts 15:1–21).

Josephus' account of James supports the New Testament's strong association of James with Jerusalem, mentioned in Acts 1:13–14 and 15:1–21. James would have attracted further interest from the high priest because of this association, given that the high priest was intimately linked to Jerusalem. The high priest 'had one house attached to the Temple ... and another in the city of Jerusalem ... [and it was] required that he should spend most of his time in the Sanctuary ...'.[29]

The description of the Sadducees as judgemental and Ananus being their leader and the mastermind behind the death of James reinforces the portrayal of them found in the New Testament book of Acts. The Sadducees in Jerusalem had not only arrested the disciples Peter and John on two separate occasions (Acts 4:1–3; Acts 5:17–18), they wanted to kill them as well (Acts 5:33).

The stoning of James indirectly endorses the veracity of the stoning of one of the early Christian leaders called Stephen (Acts 6:12 – 7:60). As the Jews stoned James, it is reasonable to conclude that they may have stoned others. This corroboration is important, as some have argued

---

28 Some argue that the Greek word used for 'brother' in relation to Jesus includes the meaning of cousin. The normal meaning, though, is brother. Also 12 of the references to Jesus' brothers are coupled to a reference to his mother, and sometimes Joseph as well, indicating a very close relationship. Also there is a Greek word for cousin, and it is not used in these passages.

29 *Jewish Encyclopedia* [online], 'High priest', 1901–06, www.jewishencyclopedia.com/articles/7689-high-priest, accessed 11/08/2008. Sanctuary refers to the temple in Jerusalem.

that Jews were not allowed to execute anyone under Roman rule. This contention appears to be nullified by the fact that a variety of Jewish religious literature, including the Mishnah and Tosepta, speaks of the religious execution of offenders.[30] This literature, together with:

> ... Acts, and Josephus suggests that in the first century C.E. the Jewish court could decree capital punishment in religious matters but not in political ones or when the public order was threatened.[31]

It is even possible that Josephus was an eyewitness to the stoning of James as he would have been 25 years old, and still acting as a priest in Jerusalem. According to his autobiography, Josephus left Jerusalem for Rome when he was 26.

Authenticity of the second reference

There have been voices claiming that all of the above passage, or at least critical parts of it, have been inserted by Christians who copied Josephus' original works. I discovered at least six good reasons for accepting this passage as being written by Josephus himself. Collectively these reasons make a convincing case that all of it is from the hand of Josephus:

- The phrase doesn't express any admiration about Jesus or James. If a Christian had inserted these comments then they almost certainly would have taken the opportunity to add a compliment of some sort.

- The weight of scholarly opinion, including those who would be accepted as having no perceived bias towards Jesus, is in favour of its authenticity. One very famous Jewish scholar, Dr Joseph Klausner (1874–1958), stated that there is no foundation for doubting that Josephus wrote the words of this second reference to Jesus, and he

---

30 Tosefta t Sanhedrin 10:11, Mishnah m. Sanhedrin 7:2, according to JJ Rousseau & R Arav, *Jesus and His World: An Archaeological and Cultural Dictionary*, Fortress Press, Minneapolis, US, 1995, p. 265. For English translations of this Jewish literature refer to www.toseftaonline.org/seforim/tractate_sanhedrin_mishna_and_tosefta_1919.pdf and www.emishnah.com/PDFs/Sanhedrin%207.pdf, respectively, accessed 20/04/2013.
31 JJ Rousseau & R Arav, p. 265.

refers to several other scholars who agree.³² Dr Klausner was the chief editor for *The Hebrew Encyclopedia*, a committed Zionist (i.e. a proponent for the establishment of modern Israel as a political homeland for Jews), and a professor of Hebrew Literature, and later Jewish History, at Hebrew University of Jerusalem.³³ Clearly he was not going to unfairly try to establish the existence of Jesus and James from the works of Josephus.³⁴ It has been said that the 'overwhelming majority of scholars' consider the portion that reads 'the brother of Jesus called Christ' is authentic.³⁵

- At least as early as the second century, Christians had a very different version of how James died compared to Josephus. Although both Christians and Josephus recall that he was stoned, at least some Christians believed that it was at the hands of Pharisees and scribes, and that James was finally killed when a stick hit his head during the stoning. This account of James' martyrdom is based on the writings of the Christian historian called Hegesippus, who wrote between 165–175 AD.³⁶ So if Christians had added words to Josephus' account, they probably would have mentioned the clubbing and the Pharisees.

- The entire passage is in keeping with the natural flow of the history that Josephus was writing: Ananus calling the judges together

---

32 J Klausner, *Jesus of Nazareth*, trans. H Danby, George Allen & Unwin, London, 1927, pp. 42f & 58f.

33 E Kaplan & DJ Penslar (eds), *The Origins of Israel, 1882–1948: A Documentary History*, University of Wisconsin Press, Madison, Wisconsin, US, 2001, p. 185.

34 DF Sandmel, 'Into the fray: Joseph Klausner's approach to Judaism and Christianity in the Greco-Roman world', 1 January 2002. Dissertation available from ProQuest, paper AAI3043948, http://repository.upenn.edu/dissertations/AAI3043948, accessed 20/04/2013.

35 R Van Voorst, *Jesus Outside the New Testament*, William B Eerdmans, Grand Rapids, US, 2000, p. 83. Similarly, it has been said that 'most scholars' consider the words 'Jesus called the Messiah', found in the testimonium flavianum, to be authentics. Z Baras, 'The Testimonium Flavianum and the martyrdom of James', in LH Feldman & G Hata (eds), *Josephus, Judaism, and Christianity*, Wayne State University Press, Detroit, US, 1987, p. 341.

36 Hegesippus, 'Fragments from his five books of commentaries on the Acts of the Church', *Early Christian Writings*, http://earlychristianwritings.com/text/hegesippus.html, accessed 20/04/2013.

resulted in various Jews complaining to the procurator Albinus. Albinus responded by writing to Ananus, reminding him that such a gathering first needed his [Albinus'] consent. King Agrippa then removed Ananus from his position of high priest after he had been in place for only three months. Thus Josephus needed to mention James in order to provide adequate explanation for Ananus' short stint. Josephus continues in later paragraphs to describe the rise and fall of other high priests, and even how they threw stones at one another![37]

- The phrase 'the brother of Jesus' also indicates that Josephus himself wrote these words rather than a Christian scribe copying *The Antiquities of the Jews*. This is because it appears that Christians never described James in this way. In the New Testament, James is never referred to as 'brother of Jesus'. Rather he is designated as 'brother of the Lord' (Galatians 1:19), or simply as James (Acts 12:17, 15:13, 21:18). When the New Testament authors want to highlight his importance they refer to him and two other disciples as 'pillars' (Galatians 2:9). James refers to himself as 'a servant of God and of the Lord Jesus Christ' (James 1:1). Other Christian literature calls him 'brother of the Lord' or 'cousin of the Lord'.[38]

- It is expected that Josephus would use the Greek word *legōmenos* (λεγομενος) in reference to Jesus when he wrote 'Jesus, who was called Christ'. This is not only because it alludes to his earlier mention of Jesus, but also because it distances Josephus from the idea that this Christ may be the actual Christ the Jews were waiting for in the future. After all, Josephus never became a follower of Jesus. As far as Josephus was concerned, Jesus had a grandiose appellation, but that does not necessarily mean that Josephus thought he deserved such a name. The definition of *legōmenos* includes 'the so-called'.[39] This is not to say that *legōmenos* always has a negative connotation.

---

37 Josephus, *The Antiquities of the Jews*, book 20, ch. 9, para. 4§213, pp. 538–9.
38 CE Price, 'Firmly established by Josephus: What an ancient Jewish historian knew about Jesus', p. 47.
39 The term *legōmenos* was searched using the Liddell-Scott-Jones (LSJ) Greek–English lexicon (at www.persus.tufts.edu, accessed 20/04/2013) and the third semantic field for the lexical form *legō* gave *legōmenos* as an example that means 'the so-called'.

As with most words, its meaning depends on the context. The word is used a number of times in the New Testament, and many of these occasions it has a neutral tone (Matthew 10:2, Matthew 26:14, Luke 22:47, John 4:25, John 9:11), but other times it clearly means 'alleged', as in 1 Corinthians 8:5.

Some have argued against the authenticity of this second reference by pointing out that if this were the first time Josephus used the word 'Christ', then he would have given an explanation for the term. This idea assumes that Josephus did not pen the earlier reference to Christ. However, Josephus is merely using the term 'Christ' to designate to which Jesus he is referring. In a similar fashion he referred to a leader of one of his nation's enemies as '… Antiochus, who was called Epiphanes …'[40] This Antiochus had chosen the title/epithet (Theos) Epiphanes (in about 174 BC, after he took the Seleucid throne in 175 BC[41]), as a way of publicising that he was the manifestation of a Greek god called Phanes, and to distinguish himself from several previous rulers called Antiochus. Josephus' lack of explanation for the derivation of 'Christ' is no more surprising than his silence over the origins of 'Epiphanes'. Josephus' choice of the term 'Christ' reflects the fact that Jesus of Nazareth was well known amongst Christians and non-Christians[42] as Jesus Christ, or even just Christ.

Conclusion to the second reference about Jesus

There appears to be no reasonable basis for disputing the authenticity of this second reference to Jesus. Josephus' writings run in parallel with various teachings found in the New Testament, namely that Jesus Christ had a brother called James (Mark 6:3, Galatians 1:19). Individual Christians were punished, partly because of the attitudes of members of the Jewish sect called the Sadducees (Acts 4:1–3 and

---

40 Josephus, *The Wars of the Jews*, book 1, ch. 1, para. 1§31, in trans. W Whiston, *The Works of Josephus: Complete and Unabridged: New Updated Edition*, Hendrickson Publishers, Peabody, Massachusetts, US, 1987, p. 546.

41 *Wikipedia*, 'Antiochus IV Epiphanes', http://en.wikipedia.org/wiki/Antiochus_IV_Epiphanes, accessed 10/04/2013. See also Polybius, *The Histories*, book 26, p. 353, http://archive.org/stream/historiespolybi00hultgoog#page/n369/mode/2up, accessed 20/04/2013.

42 Refer to chapters 12 to 15.

5:17–18). Sometimes the Jewish authorities authorised the stoning of Christians (Acts 6:12 – 7:60).

Josephus' comments about other New Testament people

Having investigated Josephus' comments about Jesus, I wanted to now focus on some of his other references to people or events that are mentioned in the New Testament. Once more I was interested to see if Josephus' writings revealed any harmony with the New Testament accounts.

Josephus and John the Baptist

Josephus writes of how there was a Herod Antipas, who was ruler of the provinces of Galilee and Perea.[43] Later he states that Herod killed 'John, that was called the Baptist'[44] by sending him to prison, and describes John as one 'who was a good man, and commanded the Jews to exercise virtue, both as to righteousness towards one another, and piety towards God, and so to come to baptism ...'[45] This is very similar to the New Testament, which relates that:

> *In the fifteenth year of the reign of Tiberius Caesar — when ... Herod [was] tetrarch of Galilee ... [John] went into all the country around the Jordan, preaching a baptism of repentance for the forgiveness of sins. (Luke 3:1-3)*

John the Baptist's teaching included instructing people to share their clothes and food with the poor, and to treat everyone justly (Luke 3:10–14). Elsewhere the New Testament describes his fate:

> *Now Herod had arrested John and bound him and put him in prison ... and had John beheaded in the prison. (Matthew 14:3–10)*

What I found notable about Josephus' passages on Jesus and John the Baptist is the absence of any connection between these two prominent Christian figures. This link between the two characters is very

---

43 Josephus, *The Antiquities of the Jews*, book 17, ch. 11, para. 4§318, p. 473.
44 Josephus, *The Antiquities of the Jews*, book 18, ch. 5, para. 2§116, p. 484.
45 Josephus, *The Antiquities of the Jews*, book 18, ch. 5, para. 2§117, p. 484.

prominent in the New Testament, which relates how John the Baptist taught that:

> '*After me comes the one more powerful than I, the straps of whose sandals I am not worthy to stoop down and untie. I baptize you with water, but he will baptize you with the Holy Spirit.*' (Mark 1:7–8)

One explanation for Josephus' silence on this point is simply that he did not know how the two related to each other.[46] This is particularly likely, as even the four New Testament Gospels do not describe Jesus and John the Baptist as being frequently together. On the other hand, Josephus may have not described their interactions simply because it was not his intent to provide a significant history of the beginning of Christianity.[47] Whatever the reason, this lack of connection points in favour of the authenticity of Josephus' words on these two personalities. This is because if a Christian copyist had been significantly adding words, then there is a high likelihood that the copyist would have inserted the common history of Jesus and John.[48] As with 'the brief reference to James' the brother of Jesus, this 'more elaborate account' of John the Baptist is regarded by 'most scholars' as genuine.[49]

Josephus and the beliefs of the Sadducees

Josephus' teachings on what the Sadducees believed echoes those found in the New Testament. Josephus states that the Sadducees believed that the soul dies with the body, and there are no punishments or rewards after death.[50] The New Testament notes that they didn't believe in the resurrection of the dead (Matthew 22:23–34, Luke 20:27).

---

46 This has been suggested by others, such as: H Schreckenberg, 'Josephus in early Christian literature and medieval Christian art', pp. 38–9.
47 Refer to chapter 16, 'Was Josephus a capable historian?'.
48 CE Price, 'Firmly established by Josephus: What an ancient Jewish historian knew about Jesus', p. 34.
49 H Schreckenberg, 'Josephus in early Christian literature and medieval Christian art', p. 39.
50 Josephus, *The Antiquities of the Jews*, book 18, ch. 1, para. 4§116, p. 477; *The Wars of the Jews*, book 2, ch. 8, para. 14§165, p. 608.

Josephus and the New Testament's descriptions of legal proceedings

Josephus' writings also support aspects of the trial of Jesus that led to his crucifixion. This is because Josephus' description of the trial of another person tends to corroborate the broad sequence of events leading to Jesus' crucifixion. Josephus related the peculiar life and death of a Jew called Jesus, the son of Ananus. This Jesus had begun to infuriate the populace of Jerusalem in about 63 AD, as he incessantly called out a warning cry '... a voice against Jerusalem and the holy house ... and a voice against this whole people'.[51] Some of the most eminent in the community then 'gave him a great number of severe stripes', but as he still persisted they then turned him over to the 'Roman procurator, where he was whipped till his bones were laid bare ...'[52] The procurator then asked him who he was, decided he was a madman, and dismissed him.[53]

There are five different elements in this sequence of events that mirror what happened to Jesus of Nazareth:

- Jesus Christ was first arrested by the 'most eminent in the community', namely Jewish chief priests, officers of the temple guard and the elders (Luke 22:47–52).

- They then beat him (Luke 22:63–5, John 18:22).

- Then they took him to the Roman procurator, Pilate (Luke 23:1).

- Pilate asked him about his identity: 'Are you the King of the Jews?' (Luke 23:1–3, John 18:33). Pilate then sent Jesus to Herod, who then returned Jesus to Pilate. Pilate the procurator then wanted to merely punish Jesus and release him (Luke 23:15–17).

- Pilate then had Jesus flogged (whipped) and questioned him about his identity once more (John 19:1–12). Finally Pilate handed Jesus over to be crucified (John 19:16, Luke 23:23–4).

---

51   Josephus, *The Wars of the Jews*, book 6, ch. 5, para. 3§300–1, p. 742.
52   Josephus, *The Wars of the Jews*, book 6, ch. 5, para. 3§302–4, p. 742.
53   Josephus, *The Wars of the Jews*, book 6, ch. 5, para. 3§305, p. 743.

Whilst discovering these great similarities about criminal trials, I did come across concerns over whether the Jews would have demanded the crucifixion of Jesus, as recorded in Luke 23:20–3. This is because capital punishment in Jewish law normally involved stoning, burning, decapitation and strangulation.[54] However, what is set down in law doesn't always dictate what actually transpires. Josephus narrated how a Jewish leader had ordered mass crucifixion in Jerusalem many years before Jesus' crucifixion. Josephus wrote that the Jewish high priest and ruler, Alexander Janneus (r. 103–76 BC), while:

> *feasting with his concubines ... ordered about eight hundred of them [Jews who had opposed him] to be crucified; and while they were living, he ordered the throats of their children and wives to be cut before their eyes.*[55]

Also, the Jewish sect called Essenes appeared to have instituted crucifixion as punishment for treason.[56] Before the time of Jesus, a crucified person was also referred to by Jews metaphorically as 'one hanged alive on the tree'.[57] This metaphor is used several times in the New Testament to refer to the crucifixion of Jesus (Acts 10:39 and 13:29, 1 Peter 2:24, Galatians 3:13, ASV and ESV for all verses).

Did Luke copy information from Josephus' books?

The great extent to which Josephus' works are mirrored in the New Testament does raise the question as to whether the similarity is because Josephus made use of some of the writings from the New Testament, or vice versa. The only New Testament author considered

---

54 Mishnah m. Sanhedrin 7:2, www.emishnah.com/PDFs/Sanhedrin%207.pdf, accessed 20/04/2013.
55 Josephus, *The Antiquities* of the Jews, book 13, ch.14, para. 2§380, p. 361.
56 JA Fitzmyer, 'Crucifixion in ancient Palestine, Qumran literature, and the New Testament', *The Catholic Biblical Quarterly*, vol. 40, 1978, pp. 493–513. Fitzmyer refers in particular to the Qumran text 11QTemple.
57 JA Fitzmyer, pp. 493–513. The phrase originally referred to the practice of hanging from a tree the corpse of an executed criminal (Deuteronomy 21:22–3).

by some to have made use of Josephus' works is Luke, although this idea runs counter to the strong evidence that Luke completed his books decades before Josephus started his first publication. Nevertheless, as I wanted to be certain that the similarity was not simply because one author borrowed from other, I carried out an investigation allowing for the possibility that Luke wrote his books after Josephus published *The Antiquities of the Jews*. Given that this question of borrowing has in itself resulted in many large books, I will look at only one historical account that was described by both authors:

Then Herod [Agrippa I] went from Judea to Caesarea and stayed there. He had been quarrelling with the people of Tyre and Sidon; they now joined together and sought an audience with him. After securing the support of Blastus, a trusted personal servant of the king, they asked for peace, because they depended on the king's country for their food supply. On the appointed day Herod, wearing his royal robes, sat on his throne and delivered a public address to the people. They shouted, 'This is the voice of a god, not of a man.' Immediately, because Herod did not give praise to God, an angel of the Lord struck him down, and he was eaten by worms and died (Acts 12:19–23).

Now when Agippa had reigned three years over all Judea, he came to the city of Caesarea, which was formerly called Strato's Tower; and there he exhibited shows in honor of Caesar, upon his being informed that there was a certain festival celebrated to make vows for his safety. At which festival, a great multitude was gotten together of the principal persons, and such as were of dignity through his province. On the second day of which shows he put on a garment made wholly of silver, and of a contexture truly wonderful, and came into the theatre early in the morning; at which time the silver of his garment being illuminated by the fresh reflection of the sun's rays upon it, shone out after a surprising manner ... and presently his flatterers cried out ... that he was a god ... Upon this the king did neither rebuke them, nor reject their impious flattery. But as he presently afterward looked up, he saw an owl sitting on a certain rope over his head, and immediately understood that this bird was the messenger of ill tidings ... and fell into the deepest sorrow. A severe pain also arose in his belly,

> *and began in a most violent manner. He therefore looked upon his friends, and said, "I whom you call a god ... and ... immortal, am immediately to be hurried away by death." ... Accordingly he was carried into the palace, and the rumor went abroad every where, that he would certainly die in a little while. But the multitude presently sat in sackcloth, with their wives and children ... and besought God for the king's recovery ... And when he had been quite worn out by the pain in his belly for five days, he departed this life ...*[58]

It is difficult to accept that Luke borrowed from Josephus for several reasons, for if he had:

Why did Luke include the conflict with Tyre and Sidon, as Josephus never associates these cities with Agrippa I.[59] There is no theological reason for Luke inventing this conflict, in fact Tyre and Sidon had previously only been mentioned by Luke when describing how Jesus regarded their citizens as more sensitive to God's message than Jews.[60]

Why would Luke incorporate the character Blastus, who is not mentioned in any of Josephus' writings?

Why include these cities and Blastus when he could have strengthened his lesson about God's rebuking of pride by writing how Agrippa was still punished by God despite admitting his humanness?

Why play down the divine-like quality of Agrippa's clothing? Especially when he had recounted earlier that God sometimes reveals himself in the midst of blinding light (Luke 9:29).

These unanswerable questions point even more strongly to the conclusion that Luke did not borrow from Josephus when it is appreciated that Luke's account is much shorter than Josephus'. Based on an extensive comparison of these two accounts, one scholar wrote:

---

58 Josephus, *The Antiquities of the Jews*, book 19, ch. 8, para. 2§343–50, pp. 523–4.
59 Josephus had not mentioned Tyre since describing its beginnings during the time of Hyrcanus (d. 175 BC) in *The Antiquities of the Jews*, book 12, ch. 4, para. 11§233, p. 322. Sidon had not been mentioned since book 1 of *The Antiquities of the Jews*.
60 Luke 10:13–15; Acts 12:6–8.

> *When we consider both the differences and the agreement in many details of the information in the two accounts, it is surely better to suppose the existence of a common source on which Luke and Josephus independently drew [rather than to conclude that Luke had read Josephus' books].*[61]

Similarly, another scholar concluded that:

> *After examining the texts myself, I must conclude with the majority of scholars that it is impossible to establish the dependence of Luke-Acts on* Antiquitates *[i.e.* The Antiquities of the Jews*]. What is clear is that Luke-Acts and Josephos shared some common traditions about the recent history of Palestine.*[62]

Finally, one very famous scholar on the works of Josephus was not only convinced that the two authors wrote independently of each other, but that their respective writings do not commonly contradict each other:

> *It seems probable that Luke and Josephus wrote independently of one another; for each could certainly have had access to sources and information, which he then employed according to his own perspectives. A characteristic conglomerate of details [found within their writings], which in part agree, in part reflect great similarity, but also in part, appear dissimilar and to stem from different provenances, accords with this analysis. Presumably the two authors use neither the same sources nor each other. It is probable, 'that in historical matters, Luke and Josephus are equally reliable witnesses, who cannot be played off against each other. In fact, the historical reports of Josephus and the Lucan writings supplement and illuminate each other much more than they contradict each other.'*[63]

---

61 H-J Klauck, *Magic and Paganism in Early Christianity: The World of the Acts of the Apostles*, trans. B McNeil, T&T Clark, Edinburgh, 2000, p. 43.
62 GE Sterling, *Historiography and Self-definition: Josephos, Luke-Acts, and Apologetic Historiography*, EJ Brill, Leiden, The Netherlands, 1992, pp. 365–6.
63 H Schreckenberg, 'Josephus in early Christian texts', in H Schreckenberg & K Schubert (eds), *Jewish Historiography and Iconography in Early and Medieval Christianity*, Fortress Press, Minneapolis, US, 1992, pp. 51–2. His quotation refers to: 'Flavius Josephus und die lukanischen Schritten', pp. 206 ff, in W Haubeck & M Bachmann (eds), *Wort in der Zeit*, FS K.H. Rengstorf, Leiden, 1980.

Although the above is only a very brief investigation, it does illustrate that Josephus and the New Testament authors are considered to have written independently.[64]

Conclusion

Josephus' portrayal of Christianity included several facts that are echoed in the New Testament. For example, that Christians were named after Jesus Christ, who was crucified by the Roman governor of Judea called Pontius Pilate. This Jesus had a brother called James. Christians were punished, sometimes, at least in part, because of the attitudes of members of the Jewish sect called Sadducees, who did not believe in a life after death. The Jewish authorities authorised the stoning of individual Christians. Finally, Josephus tells of how King Herod imprisoned, and then killed, a good man called John the Baptist, who had encouraged virtuous behaviour and baptism.

Josephus' writings also provide strong support for the sequence of events that led up to Jesus' crucifixion, namely: the arrest being made by leaders of the Jewish community, who then beat him before presenting him to the Roman procurator, who after questioning the identity of the accused desired to merely pronounce harsh punishment before releasing the victim. From these parallel accounts, it is apparent that there are no factual reasons for believing that the bias of the New Testament authors caused them to corrupt the truth.

As with other chapters in part IV of this book, I have placed these similarities between Josephus and the New Testament in the appendix 'Points of agreement between biblical and non-biblical sources' at the end of this book.

Having explored several major issues concerning the recording and preservation of Jesus' life and teachings, I now wanted to delve into the implications of the New Testament being a reliable source of information about Jesus. This is the topic of the next chapter.

---

64 H Schreckenberg, 'The Works of Josephus and the Early Christian Church', trans. H Regensteiner, in LH Feldman & G Hata (eds), *Josephus, Judaism, and Christianity*, Wayne State University Press, Detroit, US, 1987, p. 317. For an elaboration of the debate, refer to JP Holding, 'Did Luke borrow from Josephus?', Tekton Education and Apologetics Ministry, [no date], www.tektonics.org/lp/lukeandjoe.html.

Appendix 1
Digressions in book 18 of The Antiquities of the Jews

Although Josephus originally wrote his *The Antiquities of the Jews* in 20 books,[65] he probably did not divide it further into chapters. This implies that entire books, rather than chapters, may be more relevant when studying aspects of context and digressions. However, there is not always any relationship between where Josephus placed his book divisions and the contents of a particular book. Evidently he 'imposed his book divisions on his narrative rather than fitting his narrative into the book divisions'.[66] Because of these facts, it seems that a better understanding of whether the *testimonium flavium* is in or out of context would be achieved by examining a larger portion of book 18. To do this, I have chosen the events that fall between the first and last references to Pontius Pilate.

The second paragraph in chapter 2 of book 18 mentions the activities, or sometimes just the names, of several successive procurators of Judea, namely Coponius, Annius Rufus, and Valerius Gratus. It also introduces Pontius Pilate with no more than the simple fact that he was Gratus' successor.

Paragraphs 3, 4 and 5 are very disconnected from each other. Paragraph 3 immediately digresses to describe the building activities of Herod the tetrarch — the Roman client king of Galilee and Perea — including how he won the favour of the people of Galilee, a province to the north of Judea. No reference is made to Pilate.

Paragraph 4 covers, in a very lengthy fashion,[67] events within the empire of Parthia, which was roughly centred over present-day Iran. These events had no direct bearing on the lives of the Jews, Pontius Pilate, the provinces of Judea and Galilee, or even Herod the tetrarch.

Similarly, paragraph 5 deals, albeit very briefly, with events that had no direct relationship to the Jews, their procurator or Herod. It basically notes that the Roman general Germanicus had taken over the small

---

65 Josephus, *The Antiquities of the Jews*, book 20, ch. 11, para. 11§267, p. 542.
66 G Sterling, p. 248.
67 Based on the English translation by Whiston, paragraph 4 is 869 words.

kingdom of Commagene, which abutted Syria's northern border. A Roman governor then poisoned Germanicus.

The contents of chapter 3 have already been discussed.

The first two paragraphs of chapter 4 discuss Pilate's brutal actions in thwarting an armed gathering of Samaritans, a group distantly related to the Jews. They also provide Pilate's last mention, namely his inglorious eviction from Judea occasioned by the Samaritans' successful complaint to the Roman governor of Syria.

The above brief outline illustrates how frequently Josephus will digress when writing about a particular province, governor or king.

Appendix 2
Deliberate changes by Christian copyists?

One of the issues that concerned me when dealing with the debate about authenticity was the allegation that Christians of the first few centuries had deliberately changed the original text, even if it was to only a minor extent. I wanted to know whether this was of significant concern to historians. The following statement, penned by a scholar who does believe that Christian scribes altered the *testimonium flavianum*, helped put the situation into perspective:

> ... *in general, Christian copyists were quite conservative in transmitting texts. Nowhere else in all of Josephus' voluminous writings is there strong suspicion of scribal tampering. Christian copyists also transmitted the works of Philo, who said many things that might be elaborated in a Christian direction, but there is no evidence that in hundreds of years of transmission, the scribes inserted their own remarks into Philo's text ... [In] the cases of Philo and Josephus, whose writings are preserved in their original language and form, one is hard pressed to find a single example of serious scribal alteration. To have created the* testimonium *out of whole cloth [i.e. out of nothing] would be an act of unparalleled scribal audacity.*[68]

---

68 S Mason, *Josephus and the New Testament*, pp. 170–1.

It is likely that the only evidence of pro-Christian tampering of Josephus' text that can be verified happened nearly 1000 years after Josephus wrote his books. This relates to the translation of much of Josephus' texts into the Old Russian language, which became a book called *Slavonic Josephus*. This Slavonic book should probably not even be considered a translated version of Josephus as such. This is because not only did it add many phrases to the *testimonium flavianum*, but it also inserted and omitted many other parts of Josephus' works, so that it is more a re-written history book. This Slavonic book did not become the basis for other handwritten copies translated into Greek or Latin.

18

Implications

The research in this book has provided very solid reasons for concluding that the New Testament contains a true and accurate record of Jesus' life and teachings. But what does it mean for us?

The answer to this question will very much depend on what other beliefs are already held. Because there are a myriad of beliefs about the nature of God, or even if there is a God, then the number of possible responses is enormous. When this fact is coupled with the knowledge that people make decisions based on their emotions and circumstances, and not just what they intellectually agree with, then it is impossible to answer this question in an all-encompassing manner. Instead I have decided on a three-fold approach. The first is how this certainty has affected me. The second is to map out a hypothetical set of responses that I hope would occur in someone who is not a Christian and is not even certain that there is a God. The third is to investigate the implications for followers of the Islamic faith who accept that the New Testament can be trusted.

What about me?

I have believed in Jesus as God the Son, the creator of the universe, for many years. I have experienced countless times his power and life-transforming spirit liberating me from my evil heart. Yet the findings contained in this book have still had a powerful impact on me. Now when I read Jesus' words it feels more like I am hearing Jesus' words. Picking up the New Testament now is like collecting an instant ticket to a time-and-space shuttle, able to transport me to his land of dusty roads and bringing me within earshot of his spoken words.

I also have an even stronger desire to articulate to others why it is reasonable to believe in Jesus as revealed in the New Testament. Like a man who has in his wife the greatest living treasure, I feel prouder than ever that I have the opportunity of introducing him to those around me. I also feel more ashamed than ever on those occasions when I back away from attempting to enter into a mutually enjoyable conversation about Jesus with people I meet.

A hypothetical map for those who are interested in investigating Jesus

Step 1: The first step may simply be to read the New Testament Gospels and consider that Jesus' claims should be seriously examined. However, in order for this to happen, some may have to cast aside what they want to be true — which is a type of bias — in order to accept what is true. The existence of such a bias is evident in the following candid admission made by Thomas Nagel while he was Professor of Philosophy at New York University:

> *I want atheism to be true and am made uneasy by the fact that some of the most intelligent and well-informed people I know are religious believers. It isn't just that I don't believe in God and naturally, hope there is no God! I don't want there to be a God; I don't want the universe to be like that.*[1]

Step 2: Having read the Gospels, the next step would be to contemplate that Jesus' main message was not that we should follow his set of moral values and so be good citizens, but that our hearts need to be changed:

> *[Jesus] went on: 'What comes out of a man is what makes him "unclean". For from within, out of men's hearts, come evil thoughts, sexual immorality, theft, murder, adultery, greed, malice, deceit, lewdness, envy, slander, arrogance, and folly. All these evils come from inside and make a man "unclean".' (Mark 7:20–3)*

It is because all people start with an intrinsically flawed nature that Jesus declared:

---

1 T Nagel, *The Last Word*, Oxford University Press, New York, 1997, p. 130.

> *'I tell you the truth, no-one can see the kingdom of God unless he is born again ... For God so loved the world that he gave his only Son, that whoever believes in him should not perish but have eternal life.' (John 3:3, 16)*

Jesus' promise of eternal life was not meant to convey that we would have to wait until we physically die before we can start living with him, because he also gave a strong invitation for people to know him as the living God before they die:

> *Jesus replied, 'If anyone loves me, he will obey my teaching. My Father will love him, and we will come to him and make our home with him.' (John 14:23)*

This last claim of Jesus' warrants more space than is possible in this book. Suffice to say that it is not only Christians who can see the benefit of having a living relationship with God, as shown by the following quote from Matthew Parris. This prolific author of books on travel and politics won the Orwell Prize for Journalism in 2005. In 2008 he wrote:

> *But travelling in Malawi refreshed another belief, too: one I've been trying to banish all my life, but an observation I've been unable to avoid since my African childhood. It confounds my ideological beliefs, stubbornly refuses to fit my world view, and has embarrassed my growing belief that there is no God ...*
>
> *Now a confirmed atheist, I've become convinced of the enormous contribution that Christian evangelism makes in Africa: sharply distinct from the work of secular NGOs, government projects and international aid efforts. These alone will not do. Education and training alone will not do. In Africa Christianity changes people's hearts. It brings a spiritual transformation. The rebirth is real. The change is good.*
>
> *I used to avoid this truth by applauding — as you can — the practical work of mission churches in Africa. It's a pity, I would say, that salvation is part of the package, but Christians black and white, working in Africa, do heal the sick, do teach people to read and write; and only the severest kind of secularist could see a mission hospital or school and say the world would be better without it. I*

would allow that if faith was needed to motivate missionaries to help, then, fine: but what counted was the help, not the faith.

But this doesn't fit the facts. Faith does more than support the missionary; it is also transferred to his flock. This is the effect that matters so immensely, and which I cannot help observing ...

The Christians were always different. Far from having cowed or confined its converts, their faith appeared to have liberated and relaxed them ...

Christianity, post-Reformation and post-Luther, with its teaching of a direct, personal, two-way link between the individual and God, unmediated by the collective, and unsubordinate to any other human being, smashes straight through the philosophical/spiritual framework I've just described. It offers something to hold on to for those anxious to cast off a crushing tribal groupthink. That is why and how it liberates.[2]

Step 3: Understanding this fundamental life-changing message leads to the final step in accepting Jesus' words as found in the Gospels. One famous theologian used an analogy to describe this final step:

We can grasp Jesus as the Christ, the Son of God, the only saviour, only if our hearts are opened for him and by him. The meaning of his death on the cross can be seen and understood only if we ourselves are identified with that death, and this is exactly what faith in the cross means ... I will use an analogy ... A reporter goes to Korea to provide the people at home in America with a true picture of what is happening in the Korean war ... But if he ... [merely goes to the headquarters] he will not be a good reporter. The good war reporter goes into the front lines. He exposes himself to the shells of the enemy. He shares the life of the soldier. Then he can give a true picture of what happens in the Korean war. Now this is what happens with the cross of Jesus Christ and you. You can't understand the cross of Christ without going there into the

---

2   M Parris, 'As an atheist, I truly believe Africa needs God', *The Times* Online, 27 December 2008, www.timesonline.co.uk/tol/comment/columnists/matthew_parris/article5400568.ece.

> *front line where God meets you ... [The New Testament writers] say that in order to understand Jesus Christ crucified you have to be crucified yourself. You have to die with Christ on the cross.*[3]

Although these words may seem dramatic, they do echo Jesus' own words:

> *'If anyone would come after me, he must deny himself and take up his cross daily and follow me. For whoever wants to save his life will lose it, but whoever loses his life for me will save it. What good is it for a man to gain the whole world, and yet lose or forfeit his very self?' (Luke 9:23–5)*

Implications for followers of Islam

There are a several reasons why I wanted to investigate what the implications might be for a Muslim who accepts that the New Testament can be trusted as accurately conveying the words and actions of Jesus. Firstly, the book regarded as sacred by Muslims, namely the Quran,[4] mentions Jesus. Secondly, I have friends who were once Muslims but their search for truth has led them to ask Jesus to become their master and rescuer.

Muslims are those who follow Islam as described in the Quran, which Muhammad wrote during the intervening years between 610 AD and his final year of life in 632 AD.[5] Muhammad claimed that an angel with 600 wings revealed the words of the Quran to him.[6] Because of this a Muslim believes that the words of the Quran are the words of the God who made the world, who they call Allah. Although Christians and Muslims both believe that their God created the universe, they have extremely different beliefs about other aspects of the nature of

---

3   E Brunner, *Faith, Hope, and Love*, Lutterworth Press, London, 1957, pp. 26–7.
4   Quran is also spelt as Qur'an and Koran.
5   D Scot, *Windows in the Qur'an: Volume 1: Medinan Suras in Chronological Order in the Light of Muhammad's Life, Qur'anic Text, and Ahadith*, Ibrahim Ministries International, 2011, pp. 10–11.
6   Sahih Bukhari, book 4, vol. 54, no. 455, trans. from www.quranexplorer.com/Hadith/English/Index.html, accessed 30/06/2013.

this creator.[7] Other authoritative Islamic books include those found in a very large collection called the hadith.[8]

Surprisingly, deciding to trust in the New Testament would not change some of the beliefs in Jesus that a follower of Islam should already acknowledge, as the Quran contains some teachings that are in agreement with the New Testament. For example:

- Jesus was born from a virgin called Mary.[9]
- Jesus healed people that were born blind and others that had leprosy.[10]
- Jesus brought the dead back to life.[11]
- Jesus is called 'His [Allah's] Word'.[12]
- Jesus is a sign from Allah for all people.[13]

What I found even more surprising than these similarities is the claim that the Quran itself teaches that the Gospels are a revelation from the God who created the universe. In order to verify this startling conclusion, I embarked on the following study of the relevant verses found in the Quran. Because the Quran was originally written in Arabic, and as various English translations differ to each other, I have made use of at least two English translations of each Quranic verse and have used only those that have been listed in a pro-Islamic website as being generally accepted translations. These verses sometimes contain words enclosed in curved brackets (parentheses) that represent the translator's additions.

I started with a Quranic verse stating that there are other books revealed from God, not just the Quran, and that these books should be respected in the same way as the Quran:

---

7 D Scot & M Abdulhaq, *Share the Gospel with Muslims*, Ibrahim Ministries International, 2009, pp. 129–40.
8 The plural of hadith is sometimes given as ahadith.
9 Sura 19:19–21, 21:91, 66:12. For online translations of these verses from the Quran, refer to www.islamawakened.com/ and click 'The Qur'an' link for an index to suras in the Quran. Sura is a word used to denote a chapter in the Quran.
10 Suras 3:49, 5:110.
11 Suras 3:49, 5:110.
12 Sura 4:171. However, Allah is not identical to the God of the Bible.
13 Sura 21:91. However, Allah is not identical to the God of the Bible.

> *We believe in Allah, and in what has been revealed to us and what was revealed to Abraham, Ismail, Isaac, Jacob, and the Tribes, and in (the Books) given to Moses, Jesus, and the prophets, from their Lord: We make no distinction between one and another among them ... (Sura 3:84, Yusuf Ali, 1985)*

> *Say: 'We believe in Allah, and in what has been sent down to us and what was sent down to Ibrahim (Abraham), Ismail (Ishmael), Ishaq (Isaac), Yaqoub (Jacob), and the tribes, and in (the Books) given to Musa (Moses), Isa (Jesus), and the prophets, from their Lord: We make no distinction between one and another of them, and to Allah do we surrender our will (in Islam).' (Sura 3:84, Syed Vickar Ahamed)*

Although at first sight it would seem that the Quran is here referring to a book given to Jesus rather than the Gospels written about Jesus, there are strong reasons for believing otherwise. For example, Christians living at the time of Muhammad, and in the same geographical regions as Muhammad, did not acknowledge the existence of a book that was supposedly written by Jesus. Those Christians acknowledged only one set of authoritative books, namely the Bible containing the Old and New Testaments. The Old Testament contains the books of the Jewish Torah and the New Testament contains the books of the Gospel. The Quran considers these books as containing the truth because it declares that those Jews and Christians who were alive at the same time as Muhammad could find descriptions of the illiterate ('unlettered') Muhammad in their books:

> *'Those who follow the messenger, the unlettered Prophet, whom they find mentioned in their own (scriptures), — in the law and the Gospel; — for he commands them what is just and forbids them what is evil ...' (Sura 7:157, Yusuf Ali, 1985)*

> *Those who follow the messenger (Mohammed), the Prophet who can neither read nor write, whom they will find described in the Torah and the Gospel (which are) with them. He will enjoin on them that which is right and forbid them that which is wrong.[14] (Sura 7:157, M Pickthall)*

---

14 Sura 7:157.

Despite attempts by several Muslim authors, it is quite apparent that neither Muhammad's name, nor a person having his likeness, are mentioned in the prophecies found in the Old and New Testaments.[15]

Elsewhere in the Quran there is a verse that goes even further in its endorsement of the scriptures that the Jews and Christians had in their possession at that time. This verse notes that it came to confirm (i.e. uphold) the scriptures of the Jews and Christians.

> *And when there comes to them a Book from Allah, confirming what is with them, — although from of old they had prayed for victory against those without Faith, — when there comes to them that which they (should) have recognised, they refuse to believe in it but the curse of Allah is on those without Faith. (Sura 2.89, Yusuf Ali, 1985)*

> *Now when there has come to them a Book from Allah confirming the Holy Books of Torah and Gospel which they already have — even though before this they used to pray for victory against the unbelievers — when there came to them that which they very well recognize, they knowingly rejected it; Allah's curse is on such disbelievers. (Sura 2.89, Farook Malik)*

Similarly, the following verse from the Quran simultaneously confirms the scriptures belonging to the Jews and Christians that were alive during Muhammad's lifetime, and warns them that they should follow the Quran:

> *O people of the Book (Jews and Christians)! Believe in what We have now revealed (The Qur'an), confirming your own scriptures, before We obliterate your faces and turn them backward, or lay Our curse on you as We laid Our curse on the Sabbath-breakers: and remember that Allah's command is always executed. (Sura 4:47, Farook Malik)*

> *O you who were given the Book (before)! Believe (sincerely) in (the whole of) what We have been sending down (on Muhammad), confirming what (of the truth) you already possess, before We obliterate faces so as to deprive them of seeing, hearing, speaking*

---

[15] J Gilchrist, *Is Muhammad Foretold in the Bible?*, Answering Islam, www.answering-islam.org/Gilchrist/muhammad.html, accessed 30/07/2013.

and smelling, or exclude them from Our mercy as We excluded the Sabbath-breakers. (Bear in mind that) God's command is always executed. (Sura 4:47, Ali Ünal)

These verses are making a profound comment about the Gospels and the Torah that were being used by Christians and Jews respectively at the same time as when Muhammad was alive, namely, that they were truthful revelations. This flows out of the fact that Allah's book could hardly be said to uphold them if they were blatantly incorrect. Moreover, the truth found in the Gospels and the Torah is of such a profound nature that the Quran instructs that Christians and Jews should obey the Gospels and the Torah that they had in their possession:

Say: 'O followers of the Bible! You have no valid ground for your beliefs —unless you [truly] observe the Torah and the Gospel, and all that has been bestowed from on high upon you by your Sustainer!' Yet all that has been bestowed from on high upon thee [O Prophet] by thy Sustainer is bound to make many of them yet more stubborn in their overweening arrogance and in their denial of the truth. But sorrow not over people who deny the truth. (Sura 5:68, Muhammad Asad)

Say, 'Oh people of the book! You are not at all rightly guided unless you put into practice the Torah, the Gospel, and other revelations sent to you by your Lord.' (Oh Muhammad, SAW) the fact is, what your Lord has revealed to you has rather increased the (attitude of) rebellion and disbelief in most of them. Do not grieve or feel sorry for the unbelieving nation. (Sura 5:68, Munir Munshey)

Because this book has demonstrated that the New Testament Gospels have not changed over the hundreds of years before the time of Muhammad, and have not changed since the time of Muhammad, then it can be concluded that the Quran considers that the Gospels are synonymous with the 'books given to Jesus' mentioned earlier. This conclusion can be seen in the following words of Ibn Ishaq, who wrote the earliest biography of Muhammad:

Among the things which have reached me about what Jesus the Son of Mary stated in the Gospel which he received from God for the followers of the Gospel, in applying a term to describe the apostle of God, is the following. It is extracted from what John the

Apostle set down for them when he wrote the Gospel for them from the Testament of Jesus Son of Mary.[16]

Summing up, the historical reliability of the New Testament, as revealed in the research found in this book, should further encourage Muslims to respect the New Testament Gospels and not discourage Christians from obeying the Gospels. However, the historical reliability of the Gospels may create a dilemma for some Muslims, as the Quran appears to teach some things about Jesus that are opposite to those found in the Gospels. For example, the Quran appears to teach that Jesus was not crucified:

And because they said (in boast): "We killed the Messiah, Isa (Christ, Jesus) the son of Maryam (Mary), the messenger of Allah;" — But they did not kill him, nor crucified him, but so it was made to appear to them, and those who differ in this (matter) are full of doubts, with no (certain) knowledge; They follow nothing but idle talk, for sure they did not kill him:— But! Allah raised him up to Himself, and Allah is Exalted in Power, All Wise— (Sura 4:157–8, Syed Vickar Ahamed)

(We punished them because of) their (blatant and boastful) statement, 'We killed Jesus, the son of Mary, the Massiah, the messenger of Allah!' But they did not kill him, and they did not crucify him! It just appeared to them to be so! Those who differ are certainly in doubt about that matter. They do not have a definite knowledge. (They have nothing) except their assumptions and conjectures. They definitely did not kill him! The fact is, Allah raised him (towards Himself) and Allah is the most Powerful, the Wisest. (Sura 4:157–8, Munir Munshey)

However, it has been suggested that it was not the crucifixion that only 'appeared' to have occurred, but rather what 'appeared' to be so was that the enemies of Jesus had crucified him by their own will, whereas it was Allah who orchestrated the killing.[17] This interpretation is partly

---

16 Ibn Ishaq, *Sirat Rasoul Allah*, translated as *The Life of Muhammad* by A. Guillaume, Oxford University Press, Karachi, 1998, pp. 103–4, www.justislam.co.uk/images/Ibn Ishaq - Sirat Rasul Allah.pdf, accessed 29/06/2013.

17 *The 'Shame of the Cross' and its Glory*, Answering Islam, www.answering-islam.org/Cross/shame3.html, and also M Anderson, *Jesus the Light and the Fragrance of God*, Answering Islam, www.answering-islam.org/Mna/frag4_1.html, both accessed 22/07/2013.

based on those verses that indicate that it was Allah who killed Jesus — who some translators call Isa or Iesa:

(And remember) when Allah said: O Jesus! Lo! I am gathering thee and causing thee to ascend unto Me, and am cleansing thee of those who disbelieve and am setting those who follow thee above those who disbelieve until the Day of Resurrection. Then unto Me ye will (all) return, and I shall judge between you as to that wherein ye used to differ. (Sura 3:55, M Pickthall)

Behold! Allah said: 'O Iesa! Certainly I am the Giver of death to you and the Raiser of you towards Me and the Protector to you against those who rejected (you), and the Maintainer of those who have followed you above and higher to those who have rejected (you) — till the Day of Resurrection. Afterwards, towards Me is your returning place, then I will pronounce judgement between you people in whatever you used to create differences of opinion. (Sura 3:55, Kamal Omar)

Recall what time Allah said: O 'Isa! verily I shall make thee die, and am lifting thee to myself and am purifying thee from those who disbelieve, and shall place those who follow thee above those who disbelieve until the Day of Resurrection; thereafter unto Me shall be the return of you all, then I shall judge between you of that wherein ye were wont to differ. (Sura 3:55, Abdul Majid Daryabadi)

This alternative interpretation has not gained much ground, as most Muslims are taught to believe that Jesus was not crucified. Instead, many Muslims believe it was a substitute person, not Jesus, that was crucified.[18] This belief in a substitute then mandates that the Gospels are not historically reliable. However, if they are not reliable, there does not seem to be any adequate explanation for why the Quran instructs Christians to 'practice' them[19] and Muslims to 'believe' in them and to 'make no distinction' between the Quran and the books of Jesus.[20] This is particularly poignant when, as this book has shown, the Gospels that Christians were using at the time of Muhammad are the same as those that existed for over 300 hundred years before his time,

---

18 M Anderson, www.answering-islam.org/Mna/frag4_1.html, accessed 22/07/2013.
19 Sura 5:68, Munir Munshey, as discussed earlier.
20 Sura 3:84.

and are still in existence today. Perhaps it is this dilemma that is part of the reason that many people have ceased following Muhammad and given their lives to Jesus. Certainly there are many different reasons why those who were Muslim have become Christians.[21] If Islamic law (also called Sharia or Shari'a), based on the Quran and the hadith, did not insist on killing those who wish to convert away from Islam,[22] perhaps the number of such converts would be immense.

Conclusion

If you are someone who is not sure about what to believe about God, or a member of another religious group, I hope that this book will play a large part in affirming the accuracy and trustworthiness of the New Testament. I further hope that you will read it in such a way that you will see your need for Jesus to forgive you and give you life in abundance. If you already have given your life to Jesus, I hope that the words of the New Testament will be more alive to you than ever before. As Jesus of Nazareth said:

> 'Everyone who drinks this water [from a well] will be thirsty again, but whoever drinks the water I give them will never thirst. Indeed, the water I give them will become in them a spring of water welling up to eternal life.' (John 4:13–14)

> I am the gate; whoever enters through me will be saved. They will come in and go out, and find pasture. The thief comes only to steal and kill and destroy; I have come that they may have life, and have it to the full. (John 10:9–10)

---

21 Refer to the list on the Answering Islam website (www.answering-islam.org/Testimonies/index.html, accessed 22/07/2013) for some of these reasons.

22 For further discussion on how Sharia law teaches that converts (or apostates) must be condemned to die, see: JM Arlandson, *Undistinguished Nonsense from a Distinguished Professor: Bassiouni and the Non-reform of Non-Islamic Non-apostasy Laws*, Answering Islam, www.answering-islam.org/Authors/Arlandson/bassiouni_apostasy.htm, accessed 30/06/2013; P Sookhdeo, *Freedom to Believe: Challenging Islam's Apostasy Law*, Isaac Publishing, McLean, Virginia, US, 2009.

END-OF-BOOK APPENDICES

Appendix 1

A brief background of first-century Judea

This sketch describes the political and religious setting in and around first century AD Judea. A very large number of publications have been produced on this topic, so the following is only the briefest of introductions. This content is arranged topically, rather than chronologically.

The geographical extent of the early Christian movement was generally under the control of the Roman Empire. This empire included a vast area of the world, and many of the monuments of its conquered nations, such as the Great Pyramid of Giza in Egypt and the Acropolis in Athens, still create a sense of awe today. Even those architectural wonders no longer visible were equally impressive. For example, the Lighthouse of Alexandria was about 30 metres taller than the Statue of Liberty,[1] which is an impressive feat given it was built between 280 and 247 BC. The empire also constructed its own enduring monuments, from the Colosseum in Rome to the Great Theatre of Ephesus, which could hold 25,000 spectators. These structures attest to a level of technological skill, organisation and achievement that mitigate against any tendency to assume that first century AD Greco–Romans citizens had inferior intelligence.

---

1   The lighthouse was 120–140 metres high. In comparison, the Statue of Liberty is 93 metres tall from the ground to the tip of its torch.

Political control

In about 333 BC the Greek army of Alexander the Great conquered Persia and the region of Judea and surrounding countries.[2] (Judea refers to the land of the Jews, or Israel.) Although Greek rule lasted for only 200 years, some would argue that the Greek influence on culture lasted for nearly 900 years. Towards the end of this Greek rule, the Macedonian king of Syria, Antiochus IV, tried to abolish the Jewish religion. Worship at the Temple in Jerusalem by Jews was halted for three years, with the populace forced to worship the pagan god of Zeus in the year 167 BC. The Jews finally overthrew their oppressors and there followed a period of 80 years of national independence. Unfortunately, the Jewish leaders of this time became almost as tyrannical as the previous rulers.[3]

The Roman armies followed next, eventually taking control of Judea and entering Jerusalem in 63 BC. The Parthians, with an empire based in what is now Iran and Turkey, invaded Judea in 40 BC and temporarily interrupted the Roman conquest. This caused Herod, a governor in the northern area of Judea called Galilee, to flee and seek help from the Romans. The Roman senate appointed Herod king of the Jews, even though Herod himself was not a Jew by birth, but belonged to a related nation. With the help of the Roman armies in 37 BC, this puppet king was able to conquer Jerusalem, capital of the region of Judea. King Herod subsequently greatly expanded his kingdom to encompass surrounding regions and embarked on a major building campaign.

When Herod the Great died in 4 BC, Emperor Augustus divided Herod's region into two, appointing Herod Antipas I to rule over Galilee and southern Transjordan[4] until 39 AD. Antipas was therefore king over the area where Jesus spent his youth and of much of the land in which Jesus had travelled. Antipas tried to remove Jesus from

---

2 SJD Cohen, *From the Maccabees to the Mishnah*, The Westminster Press, Philadelphia, 1987, pp. 14–5.
3 FF Bruce, *The Spreading Flame*, Paternoster Press, Devon, UK, 1964, p. 28.
4 Transjordan included areas east of the Jordan River, east of the Dead Sea and east of the Arabah. American-Israeli Cooperative Enterprise, *Transjordan*, Jewish Virtual Library, www.jewishvirtuallibrary.org/jsource/judaica/ejud_0002_0020_0_19996.html, accessed 20/06/2013.

his territory (Luke 13:31–2), and later questioned Jesus in court in the old Maccabean palace (Luke 23:6–12). Herod Antipas had previously imprisoned John the Baptist when John had outspokenly criticised him and then had him beheaded (Matthew 14:1–11).

About 18 years after the beginning of the reign of King Herod Antipas, Tiberius Caesar Augustus became the Roman emperor, ruling from 14 AD until his death in 37 AD. Therefore, for most of Jesus' life Tiberius was the emperor, as Jesus was born in 5 to 7 BC and was most likely crucified on 7 April 30 AD.[5] As with many Roman provinces, the emperor exerted his rule over them by appointing governors. Governors were variously called procurators or prefects and had primarily a military function. The governor Pontius Pilate presided over the trial and crucifixion of Jesus Christ. His administration was noted for its: 'Venality, violence, robbery, persecutions, wanton malicious insults, judicial murders without even the formality of a legal process, and cruelty …'[6] Pilate's cruelty against rebels was probably not that unusual; the governor of Syria, Quintilius Varus, in 4 BC crushed a revolt in Judea and crucified 2000 people.[7]

A major war against the ruling Romans by the local population in Judea broke out in May 66 AD. It can be considered as starting when the Roman procurator, Florus, sent troops to ransack a part of Jerusalem.[8] Initially the Romans were defeated, but by 68 AD nearly all of the country except Jerusalem was re-conquered by the Roman armies

---

5 R Riesner, *Paul's Early Period: Chronology, Mission Strategy, Theology*, trans. D Stott, WB Eerdmans Publishing Company, Grand Rapids, Michigan, US, 1998, pp. 52–8.
6 A Edersheim, *The Life and Times of Jesus the Messiah*, vol. 1, book 2, MacDonald Publishing Company, McLean, Virginia, US, (1886) 1988, p. 262.
7 Josephus, *The Antiquities of the Jews,* book 17, ch. 10, para. 10§295, p. 471, in trans. W Whiston, *The Works of Josephus: Complete and Unabridged*, Hendrickson Publishers, Massachusetts, US, 1989. See also FF Bruce, *The Spreading Flame*, Paternoster Press, Devon, UK, 1964, p. 36.
8 AM Berlin & JA Overman, 'Introduction', in AM Berlin & JA Overman (eds), *The First Jewish Revolt: Archaeology, History, and Ideology*, Routledge, London, 2002, p. 7. Other scholars consider that the flash point for the start of the war may have been a violent outburst between Jews and Gentiles in Caesarea Maritima in 66 AD. See Josephus, *The Wars of the Jews*, book 2, ch. 13, para. 7§266–270, pp. 614–5 and Josephus, *The Antiquities of the Jews*, book 20, ch. 8, paras 7–9§173–81, p. 536.

under the immediate command of Titus. The battle for Jerusalem was one of the bloodiest in history, made incredibly worse by the warring of various factions within the walls whilst trying to fight the Romans outside the walls.[9] Josephus related that the famine within Jerusalem resulted in one mother committing cannibalism upon her own child,[10] and the streets were filled with the dead bodies of the aged.[11] Many tried to escape the siege only to be frequently caught by the Romans, who at one stage crucified about 500 every day in sight of the city walls.[12] The final death toll when Jerusalem fell in 70 AD was 1,100,000.[13] Survivors were sold as slaves, some being sent to Egypt when it fell. Josephus states that a total of 97,000 Jews were taken captive during the entire war.[14] Jerusalem's Jewish temple was thoroughly demolished and the city nearly totally destroyed. Much property was confiscated. Its status as a capital city was reduced because Caesarea Maritima became the capital of the region of Judea.[15]

Despite the crushing defeat of Jerusalem, the final stance of the Jews against the might of the Romans happened a few years later in 73 AD at Masada, which was about 60 kilometres (37 miles) south of Jerusalem. Masada was basically a fortress, and when the rebels could see that their defeat was imminent, a contemporary historian described how they slaughtered 960 of their own men, women and children. Such a quick death was considered preferable when compared to becoming

---

9 There were four different groups from various districts warring with each other. RA Horsely, 'Power vacuum and power struggle in 66–7 C.E.', in AM Berlin & JA Overman (eds), *The First Jewish Revolt: Archaeology, History, and Ideology*, Routledge, London, 2002, p. 106.
10 Josephus, *The Wars of the Jews*, book 6, ch. 3, para. 4§201–9, p. 737.
11 Josephus, *The Wars of the Jews*, book 5, ch. 12, para. 3§512–3, p. 723.
12 Josephus, *The Wars of the Jews*, book 5, ch. 11, para. 1§450, p. 720.
13 Josephus, *The Wars of the Jews*, book 6, ch. 9, para. 3§420, p. 749. This is the number killed in Jerusalem since the city had removed the Roman forces from its walls in 66 AD. Some consider that Josephus exaggerated the number killed in the first battle of the revolt, but not the number of slaves taken. M Aviam, 'Yodefat/Jotapata: the archaeology of the first battle', in AM Berlin & JA Overman (eds), *The First Jewish Revolt: Archaeology, History, and Ideology*, Routledge, London, 2002, p. 131.
14 Josephus, *The Wars of the Jews*, book 6, ch. 9, para. 3§420, p. 749.
15 JJ Rousseau & A Arav, *Jesus and His World: An Archaeological and Cultural Dictionary*, Fortress Press, Minneapolis, US, 1995, p. 30.

slaves or being unable to help each other when tortured as captives. Each man was responsible for the killing of his own wife and children.[16] However, some scholars are questioning whether archaeological evidence supports the final defeat ending in a mass suicide.[17]

Surprisingly, it wasn't too long before the Jews in Judea mounted another major war against the Romans, this time in 132 AD. When the Romans under Emperor Hadrian regained control about three years later, thousands of people had been killed or enslaved once again. The Romans were keen to ensure that such an uprising wouldn't happen again so they rebuilt Jerusalem as a pagan city, renamed it Colonia Aelia Capitolina, and Caesarea Maritima became the capital of the entire country, which was renamed as Palestine.[18] The site of the ruined Jewish temple was used to build a new pagan temple, complete with statues of the Emperor Hadrian and the god Jupiter. This last Jewish revolt against the Romans brought about the end of Jews being part of the Christian movement in Jerusalem because all Jews were banned from entering Jerusalem.

Emperor worship

Rome had already fully embarked on the road to worshipping its leaders well before Jesus' lifetime. As early as 44 BC, the Roman dictator Julius Caesar permitted a statue of himself to have the inscription *Deo Invicto* (unconquered god).[19] In 29 BC the city of Pergamum built the first temple to the godhead of the Emperor Augustus.[20]

---

16 Josephus, *The Wars of the Jews*, book 7, ch. 9, para. 1§389–90, p. 769.
17 K Stubbs, *Is the Truth About Masada Less Romantic?*, George Mason University's History News Network, http://hnn.us/articles/25292.html, accessed 02/08/2013.
18 JJ Rousseau & A Arav, p. 30. This wasn't the first time that Palestine was used as the name for the region. Refer to J Sarfati, *Origins of the Word 'Palestine'*, Creation Ministries International, http://creation.com/atheist-deconversion-and-palestine-word-origins, accessed 31/07/2013.
19 Tacitus, *The Annals*, book 4, ch. 37, in AJ Church & WJ Brodribb (eds), *Complete Works of Tacitus*, Random House, New York, 1942, from the Perseus Digital Library, www.perseus.tufts.edu/hopper/text?doc=Perseus%3Atext%3A1999.02.0078%3Abook%3D4%3Achapter%3D37, accessed 20/06/2013. See also P Barnett, *Revelation in its Roman Setting*, http://paulbarnett.info/2011/04/revelation-in-its-roman-setting/, accessed 20/06/2013.
20 BL Shelley, *Church History in Plain Language*, 2nd edn, Word Publishing, Dallas, 1995, p. 43.

Worship of the Roman emperors as gods did not mean that the general populace considered them as gods who would intervene to help them as individuals. As one writer put it: '... the emperors for all their trappings of divinity were not generally felt as gods who answered prayers or gave oracles and cures'.[21]

Despite being honoured with divine titles, the actual process of becoming a god — called deification or apotheosis — was regarded as commencing only after the death of an emperor. Julius Caesar was not officially deemed to have become a god by the Roman Senate until 42 BC, nearly 2 years after his death.[22] Because apotheosis happened only after death, when Emperor Vespasian (r. 69–79 AD) was mortally ill, he jokingly said: 'I suppose I shall soon be a god'.[23] However, other emperors were impatient to enjoy the benefits of being a god. Emperor Caligula (r. 37–41 AD) constructed several temples dedicated to himself. Emperor Nero (r. 54–68 AD) claimed he had a miraculous and divine birth, perhaps being the first emperor to insist on godhood before his death.

Despite emperor worship being government policy, the empire was generally very accommodating to the religious practices of its citizens and of those who had been conquered. This was under the provisos that they willingly included the emperor as a god to be worshipped and that their beliefs did not detract from giving the emperor their highest allegiance.

Roman religion's use of books

Roman religion does not appear to have been based on sacred books. One scholar concluded that:

---

21 CP Jones, *Culture and Society in Lucian*, Harvard University Press, London, 1986, p. 38.
22 L Kreitzer, Apotheosis of the Roman Emperor, *Biblical Archaeologist*, 53(4), 1990, pp. 211–17.
23 Suetonius, 'Life of Vespasian (Divus Vespasianus)', ch. 23, in trans. A Thomson, *The Lives of the Twelve Caesars; An English Translation, Augmented with the Biographies of Contemporary Statesmen, Orators, Poets, and Other Associates*, Gebbie & Co., Philadelphia, 1889, www.perseus.tufts.edu/hopper/text?doc=Perseus%3Atext%3A1999.02.0132%3Alife=ves.%3Achapter=23, accessed 20/06/2013.

Appendix 1

> *As there is no evidence at all about [the existence of] these books, one has to accept the fact that Roman religious tradition was mainly oral. Further, all scholars agree that this tradition concerned only rituals ... There was no religious teaching other than practice and assistance to the divine services. By the day of his majority [i.e. the day he legally became an adult], every young male had to be capable of sacrificing or performing a consultation of the gods. He learned these procedures, like all the other features of social life, during the preceding years at the side of his father or a friend of his family.*[24]

Although their religion had no books purporting to have been revealed from a god, one part of Roman religion that was put into writing was their prayers. These booklets, called *libelli*, appear to have often been dictated to the celebrant by a priest. Related to this lack of holy scripture is the concept of the origin of ethics. Christians and Jews regard their holy scriptures as dictating ethical behaviour, whereas:

> *... [i]n the Graeco-Roman world ethics were discussed by philosophers but were not, as a rule, thought to have divine sanction, while the Jews thought that the rules governing treatment of 'the neighbour' and 'the stranger' were given by God to Moses.*[25]

The only religious texts, apart from these booklets, were the annual proceedings (commentaries) of the priests, which covered such matters as problems arising with applications of ritual. Priests had to consult with a magistrate because they did not have any independent powers. Decisions made in the course of discussions with the magistrate were written into the format of an edict from a magistrate. These covered '... isolated decisions adapting ... ritual rules to new situations. As a result, the written public tradition about [the Roman] cult was not exhaustive ... [the relevant] archives were [largely] restricted to the priests ...'[26]

---

24 J Scheid, 'Oral tradition and written tradition in the formation of sacred law in Rome', in C Ando & J Rupke (eds), *Religion and Law in Classical and Christian Rome*, Franz Steiner Verlag, Stuttgart, Germany, 2006, pp. 17–18.

25 EP Sanders, *Judaism: Practice and Belief: 63 BCE – 66 CE*, SCM Press, London, 1992, p. 50. The Old Testament commands Jews to love their neighbour and strangers as they love themselves (Leviticus 19:18, 33–4), and specifies that traders are to use honest measuring standards (Leviticus 19:35).

26 J Scheid, p. 19.

Jewish religious freedom

In about 64 BC, Jewish religious freedom was made universal in the Roman Empire under Julius Caesar. This allowed the Jews to assemble for worship and to build synagogues. They were also exempt from participation in the imperial cult (emperor worship), which was said to follow automatically from their religion being a protected cult.[27] However, the Jews were expected to make a daily sacrifice, in their own temple, of two lambs and a bull for the emperor's wellbeing. This substituted for the sacrifices that would normally be made directly to the emperor.[28] Christians, however, were not given this exemption. Even after the Jewish war of 66–70 AD, '... Rome made no attempt to punish the Jews by stamping out, or even imposing restrictions on, their cult'.[29] However, because the Temple was destroyed in the war, the Temple tax collected from the people was consequently diverted to Rome, supposedly for the benefit of the temple of the Roman god Jupiter Capitolinus. This could be understood as Jews throughout the Roman Empire having to pay their way out of worshipping the emperor by paying a '... subscription to Jupiter'.[30]

The Temple in Jerusalem wasn't rebuilt, perhaps because of a lack of funds, a lack of suitable leadership for such a project or, perhaps, because the Temple site was polluted with Roman religious symbols and shrines. The destruction of the Temple resulted in the cessation of sacrificial animal worship and all other aspects of Temple ritual.[31] This was of major consequence to the Jews because the Temple was at the heart of their culture, including their social and political life,[32] and the

---

27 EM Smallwood, *The Jews Under Roman Rule: From Pompey to Diocletian: A Study in Political Relations*, EJ Brill, Leiden, The Netherlands, 1981, pp. 134–7. Smallwood was Professor of Romano-Jewish History at Queen's University of Belfast.
28 EM Smallwood, p. 148. Herod the Great may have introduced the substitution.
29 EM Smallwood, p. 344.
30 EM Smallwood, pp. 344–5.
31 EM Smallwood, pp. 346–7.
32 LI Levine, 'Josephus' description of the Jerusalem Temple: war, antiquities, and other sources', in F Parente & J Sievers (eds), *Josephus and the History of the Greco-Roman Period: Essays in Memory of Morton Smith,* EJ Brill, Leiden, The Netherlands, 1994, p. 233.

place that possibly hundreds of thousands of Jews from many parts of the world went for festivals.[33]

Christian freedom and persecution

From a spiritual point of view, Christianity grew out of Judaism as a plant grows out of a seed — the incarnation of Jesus Christ being that point of transition. From a cultural point of view, Christian communities became separated from mainstream Judaism due to political forces. The first split occurred at the time of the battle of Jerusalem (66–70 AD). This developed as the leaders of the Jerusalem church acted on a vision that they should flee the city at the start of the revolt. Obviously many Jews would have considered them as deserters. This alone resulted in a major schism between Jews and Jews who had become Christians. The second split occurred some years later when Jewish synagogues banned Christian Jews. The two groups became isolated.

During the first 300 years after Jesus' birth, Christians experienced wide variations in Roman policy. At one extreme there was tolerance; at the other a desire to have them eliminated systematically. Persecutions against Christians typically involved torture and death, although at other times it was more in the form of discrimination. For example, Christians were banned from the army and the court system in 299 AD.[34]

---

33 S Safrai, *Pilgrimage at the Time of the Second Temple*, Am Hasefer (Hebrew), Tel-Aviv, 1965, pp. 42–122. Cited by LI Levine, p. 245.
34 ED Digeser, 'Religion, law and the Roman polity: the era of the Great Persecution', in C Ando & J Rupke (eds), *Religion and Law in Classical and Christian Rome*, Franz Steiner Verlag, Stuttgart, Germany, 2006, p. 73.

Appendix 2
Points of agreement between Biblical and non-biblical sources

Area of Interest	Biblical Source	Non–Biblical Source
The person of Jesus		
Jesus was an impressive teacher.	Mark 1:22	Lucian
	Matthew 5:27–8	Lucian
	James 1:25	Lucian
Jesus was a lawgiver.	Galatians 6:2	Lucian
	Colossians 1:1	Josephus
Jesus was called the Christ.	Philippians 1:1	Josephus
Jesus began the Christian religion and his followers were called Christians.	Acts 11:26, 26:28	Lucian, Josephus
	1 Peter 4:16	Pliny, Tacitus
Jesus was crucified.	Mark 15:33–7	Lucian
Jesus was crucified in Judea (i.e. Palestine).	Matthew 27:2	Lucian
Jesus was executed when Tiberius was emperor and Pontius Pilate was governor of Judea.	Luke 3:1–3	Tacitus

Jesus was crucified by Pontius Pilate, a Roman governor.	Matthew 27:2–26	Josephus
Jesus was crucified because of his relationship to the new cult.	Luke 22:66–70	Lucian
	Matthew 21:4–6	Lucian
	Matthew 27:37	Lucian
Jesus' crucifixion was accompanied by an unusual darkness.	Matthew 27:45	Thallus
	Luke 23:44	Thallus
Jesus had a brother called James.	Mark 6:3	Josephus
Other New Testament individuals		
There was a man called John the Baptist.	Matthew 3:1	Josephus
John the Baptist was a good man.	Matthew 11:7–11	Josephus
	Luke 3:10–14	Josephus
John the Baptist encouraged virtuous behaviour.	Luke 3:10–14	Josephus
John the Baptist encouraged baptism.	Mark 1:7–8	Josephus
John the Baptist was imprisoned and killed.	Matthew 14:3–9	Josephus
King Herod was responsible for killing John.	Luke 9:7–9	Josephus
At some stage after the crucifixion, the brother of Jesus called James could already be said to have become a Christian.	Acts 1:14, 15:13	Josephus
	Galatians 1:19	Josephus
Christian beliefs and culture		
Christians worshipped Jesus in the same way people worship God(s).	Luke 24:51–2	Lucian
Christians worshipped Jesus by singing.	Ephesians 5:19–20	Pliny

Appendix 2

Christians regarded Christ as God.	John 20:28	Pliny
Christians read from 'sacred books', which were interpreted and explained.	2 Timothy 3:16	Lucian
Christians believed they would be immortal and live forever.	John 3:16, 5:24	Lucian
	Romans 6:4–5	Lucian
Christians denied the Greek gods.	1 Corinthians 6:9–11	Lucian
Christian leaders were in Judea (Palestine).	Acts 15:1–30	Lucian
Christians revered their leaders greatly.	1 Thessalonians 5:12	Lucian
	1 Timothy 3:8	Lucian
Christian leaders were lawgivers.	1 Timothy 4:11, 5:17	Lucian
Christians become brothers only after worshipping Jesus.	Romans 8:9–17	Lucian
Christian moral standards stipulated avoiding fraud, robbery, adultery, bearing false witness and not paying debts.	Mark 7:21–3, Titus 3:1–2	Pliny
Christians shared their belongings and were not materialistic.	Acts 4:32–5, 9:36, 11:29	Lucian
Christians had regulations about food.	1 Corinthians 8:4–13	Lucian
Christians included simple folk.	1 Corinthians 1:26	Lucian
	1 Timothy 5:3, 9–10	Lucian
Some Christians were widows.	James 1:26–7	Lucian
The Christian community included female deacons.	Romans 16:1	Pliny

Christians met regularly over a common meal.	Acts 2:46–7	Pliny
Christian persecution and history		
Christians were imprisoned for their faith.	Acts 12:1–4, 16:16–40	Lucian
Individual Christians were punished because of the attitudes of the Sadducees.	Acts 4:1–3, 5:17	Josephus
Christians were sometimes stoned because of their beliefs.	Acts 6:12–7:60	Lucian, Josephus
Christian Roman citizens were sent to Rome to face trial.	Acts 25:1–28:14	Pliny
Christianity as a movement		
Christianity spread from Judea to Rome.	Acts 1:4	Tacitus
	Acts 28:14–31	Tacitus
Christians were in Bithynia–Pontus and Rome.	1 Peter 1:1–2	Lucian, Pliny
	Romans 1:7	Lucian, Pliny
Christian popularity had negative impacts on idol worship.	Acts 19:23–7	Pliny
Other historical facts recorded in the New Testament		
The Jewish sect of the Sadducees did not believe in the resurrection of the dead.	Luke 20:27	Josephus
The trial of Jesus mimicked Jewish legal proceedings		
The arrest was made by the most eminent in the community.	Luke 22:47–52	Josephus
A severe beating was given to the accused.	Luke 22:63–5	Josephus
The accused was handed over to a Roman governor.	Luke 23:1	Josephus

The Roman governor questioned the identity of the accused.	John 18:33	Josephus
The Roman governor ordered the accused to be whipped.	John 19:1–12	Josephus

Appendix 3

Did Jesus really grow up in the town of Nazareth?

Although the previous chapters have described a wealth of information to support the reliability of the New Testament, I was surprised to discover that there were assertions made by some atheists that one particularly important town did not exist during Jesus' life. This town is Nazareth, where, according to the New Testament, Jesus' parents were living prior to his birth. It is also the place to which his family returned after living as refugees in Egypt while Jesus was an infant. Nazareth is the town where Jesus grew from boyhood to manhood.

The existence or otherwise of Nazareth is an important issue to resolve because if basic biblical information about Jesus is incorrect, many of the conclusions arrived at through the course of this book would be weakened.

It appeared that the case for the non-existence of Nazareth during Jesus' lifetime in atheist literature and websites often prominently relied on the absence of literary evidence for the town during this period of time. One of the publications speaks of this in the first page of its introduction and repeats it five times later in the book.[1] This line of reasoning was a logical place to start my investigations.

---

1   R Salm, *The Myth of Nazareth: The Invented Town of Jesus: Scholars Edition*, American Atheist Press, Cranford, New Jersey, US, 2008, pp. xi, xiii, 64, 212, 286, 291. Salm is described on the back cover of his book as a pianist and mental health professional, though no qualifications are given.

Nazareth and the argument from silence

The argument from silence has been presented this way:

> ... some liberal scholars wondered why the town was not mentioned in the Jewish scriptures [Old Testament], nor in the Talmud, nor even once in the prolix [lengthy] writings of the first-century Galilean general, Josephus ... Why, they asked, did the first Christian generations either completely ignore the place, or appear to not know where it was.[2]

Similarly, the self-proclaimed atheist Zindler asserts that:

> Nazareth is not mentioned even once in the entire Old Testament, nor do any ancient historians or geographers mention it before the beginning of the fourth century. The Talmud, although it names 63 Galilean towns, knows nothing of Nazareth. Josephus, who wrote extensively about Galilee (a region roughly the size of Rhode Island) and conducted military operations back and forth across the tiny territory in the last half of the first century, mentions Nazareth not even once — although he does mention by name 45 other cities and villages of Galilee. This is even more telling when one discovers that Josephus does mention Japha, a village which is just over a mile from present-day Nazareth! Josephus tells us that he was occupied there for some time.[3]

Various atheistic internet sites add other Jewish writers, such as Philo, to the above list of writers who did not mention Nazareth. However, using a lack of evidence to say that a certain town does not exist can be a weak argument. Such an approach is called an argument from silence and should be used only in certain settings.

One of the problems with using an argument from silence concerning the existence of a physical place is that writers of history often have a narrow focus. For example, the famous giant Sphinx in lower (northern) Egypt is 73 metres long and 20 metres high, and was built by

---

2   R Salm, p. xi.
3   FR Zindler, 'Where Jesus never walked', *American Atheist*, 2009 www.atheists.org/Where_Jesus_Never_Walked, accessed 28/03/2009.

the pharaoh Khafre sometime around 1800 BC.[4] Khafre had previously built a 136-metre-high pyramid, which is only 420 metres (460 yards) from the Sphinx. These two colossal structures are located only a short distance from the Great Pyramid built about 100 years earlier by the pharaoh Khufu (called Cheops by the Greeks). The renowned Greek historian Herodotus visited Egypt in about 450 BC and wrote about the Great Pyramid (which stood 146 metres high). Herodotus wrote much about Cheops and the building of his pyramid, a total of nearly 360 words when translated into English. He also mentioned a number of other pyramids that were built before and after Cheops' reign, as well as a manmade causeway and lake. Yet Herodotus didn't mention the Sphinx located only 300 metres (330 yards) from the Great Pyramid.[5] It would be a great mistake to conclude that the Sphinx didn't exist during or before Herodotus' lifetime simply because he failed to refer to it.[6]

The Old Testament: silent about what?

Let's now look at the specific weaknesses in the argument from silence when applied to the existence of Nazareth. The Old Testament does not have a section devoted to providing a complete list of all the towns that existed in the region of Galilee. So stating that it doesn't mention Nazareth as if this is important is misleading. Even if it did have such a list, it would be fairly irrelevant as the Old Testament's

---

4 Structural and chronological details used in this paragraph are from J Ashton & D Down, *Unwrapping the Pharaohs: How Egyptian Archaeology Confirms the Biblical Timeline*, Master Books, Green Forest, Arkansas, US, 2006, pp. 36–53.
5 Herodotus' only mention of a sphinx is to say that King Amasis '… dedicated great colossal statues and man-headed sphinxes very large, and for restoration he caused to be brought from the stone-quarries which are opposite Memphis, others of very great size from the city of Elephantine …', from Herodotus, *An Account of Egypt*, trans. GC Macaulay, www.gutenberg.org/files/2131/2131-h/2131-h.htm, 5th last para., accessed 16/06/2013.
6 The basics of this illustration (as well as several others) about using the argument from silence came to my attention from reading this excellent book: EA Parsons, *The Alexandrian Library: Glory of the Hellenic World: Its Rise, Antiquities, and Destruction*, Cleaver-Hume Press, London, 1952, pp. 375–7. To see four possible reasons why Herodotus did not mention the sphinx, see JT Katz's review (at http://bmcr.brynmawr.edu/2003/2003-05-11.html, accessed 16/06/2013) of C Zivie-Coche, *Sphinx: History of a Monument*, trans. D Lorton, Cornell University Press, Ithaca, US, 2002.

history finishes about 400 years before the time of Jesus. So it is possible for the town of Nazareth to have grown during that 400-year period.

Some websites provide a specific reason as to why the Old Testament should have mentioned Nazareth. This relates to lists of priests provided in the Old Testament. One of the lists referred to by such websites is 1 Chronicles 24:7–18. This provides the names of 24 family leaders found amongst the descendants of Aaron, one of the main leaders in early Old Testament history. These priests took turns to serve in the temple in Jerusalem, each leader and his family assistants being referred to as a division. When each division was called up, they would leave their homes in Judea or Galilee and serve in Jerusalem for one week out of every 24, plus the pilgrimage festivals.[7] One of the names on this list eventually became associated with Nazareth, so there could be an expectation that this town would be mentioned on this list. However, this list does not provide any names of towns at all, so expecting it to name Nazareth is unwarranted. What is exciting though is how this list corresponds with archaeology, for this biblical list refers to how 'the eighteenth [lot fell] to Happizzez'. Happizzez is a name found inscribed in stone in Caesarea Maritima, and this stone is discussed later in this appendix.

The other list of priestly leaders is found in the Old Testament book of Nehemiah. This list has also been referred to as supporting evidence for why the Old Testament should have mentioned Nazareth. Since the time of the list in Chronicles (discussed above), the empire of Babylon had invaded Israel and all the surviving Jews had been taken captive and deported to Babylon. The temple and palaces in Jerusalem were burnt in 586 BC, and the wall around Jerusalem broken. Forty-eight years later in 538 BC, Cyrus, the king of Persia, captured Babylon and the account of Nehemiah records how Cyrus gave the Jews permission to return from exile to their homeland, where they rebuilt their temple in Jerusalem and the walls around the city. Nehemiah then provides a catalogue of priestly names: the heads of 22 priestly families are

---

7   EP Sanders, *Judaism: Practice and Belief 63 BCE – 66 CE*, SCM Press, London, 1992, p. 170; S Safrai, *A Priest of the Division of Abijah*, Jerusalem Perspective website, 1 February 1989, citing Mishna, Ta'anit 4:2, www.jerusalemperspective.com/2304/, accessed 24/06/2013.

given in Nehemiah 12:1–7 from the days of Jeshua, and 20 names of priestly leaders in 12:12–21 from a different period of time, in the days of Joiakim.[8] Once again no towns are mentioned at all. As no towns are mentioned in either list, it seems deceitful to proclaim that the Old Testament would have mentioned Nazareth if it had existed at that time.

One other section of the Old Testament that some websites claim should mention Nazareth is that found in Joshua 19:10–16. This section mentions towns and villages that were in the vicinity of modern Nazareth. However, the book of Joshua records events that occurred over 1200 years before Jesus' birth, which allows plenty of time for Nazareth to appear in the intervening years. Also while the text in Joshua names only the towns, it does refer to unnamed villages. Nazareth may well have been one of those villages. The above research convinced me that there is no relevance in using the Old Testament as part of the argument from silence to discredit the existence of Nazareth in the New Testament.

Josephus' silence concerning Nazareth

The next piece of evidence I will examine concerns Josephus, the military leader and historian of the first century AD. His writings are used as part of the argument from silence because while Josephus mentions 45 cities and towns in Galilee,[9] he does not mention Nazareth. However, when I read Josephus' works, it is apparent that he did not intend to name all the towns in the region. Many of the Galilean towns and cities that he does name are found in his account of the war between the Jews and the Romans. (It was during this war that Josephus became a very prominent commander.) Josephus does make it obvious that the 45 named Galilean towns were not the only towns in Galilee, for he states in his biography that there were over 240

---

8   The latter list repeats all the names of the former list except the name of Hattush. No explanation is given in these texts. These two lists refer to different periods of time.
9   I found many authors referred to the number of villages as 45, but have yet to find the original source for this reckoning.

cities and villages in Galilee![10] This figure of 240 has been indirectly substantiated in recent times.[11]

Another indicator that Josephus didn't intend to name all the settlements in Galilee can be found in the quote from Zindler's book provided at the beginning of this chapter. Zindler states that the Talmud, a collection of Jewish teachings, speaks of 63 towns and yet Josephus names only 45. It would seem self-evident that Josephus didn't name all of the habitations.

Even a casual read of Josephus' book on the war makes it plain to his readers that he is not mentioning all the villages and smaller cities that were destroyed by General Vespasian as he brought Israel back under Roman control. For example, Josephus states that after the citadel of Joppa was taken, Vespasian erected a military camp there so that:

> *the horsemen might spoil the country that lay around it, and might destroy the neighboring villages and smaller cities. So these troops overran the country, as they were ordered to do, and every day cut to pieces and laid desolate the whole region.*[12]

Another geographically broad statement was made earlier in Josephus' *War of the Jews* specifically in regards to Galilee. In this case, Josephus had enraged the Romans by trying to take the Galilean city of Sepphoris, whose residents had earlier sided with the Romans. Their allegiance to Rome was openly declared only after Josephus had given them consent to build a wall to keep out the Romans in the first

---

10 Josephus, *The Life of Flavius Josephus*, para. 45§235, in trans. W Whiston, *The Works of Josephus: Complete and Unabridged: New Updated Edition*, Hendrickson Publishers, Peabody, Massachusetts, US, 1987, p. 15. He states elsewhere that: 'the cities lie here [in Upper and Lower Galilees] very thick; and the very many villages there are here, are everywhere so full of people ... that the very least of them contain above fifteen thousand inhabitants' (in *The Wars of the Jews,* book 3, ch. 3, para. 2§43, in trans. W Whiston, *The Works of Josephus: Complete and Unabridged: New Updated Edition*, Hendrickson Publishers, Peabody, Massachusetts, US, 1987, p. 641. Some commentators have 204 instead of 240 cities and villages.

11 BJ Capper, 'Essene community houses and Jesus' early community', in JH Charlesworth (ed.), *Jesus and Archaeology*, William B Eerdmans Publishing Company, Grand Rapids, Michigan, US, 2006, pp. 472–502, esp. pp. 474–6.

12 Josephus, *The Wars of the Jews*, book 3, ch. 9, para. 2§430–1, p. 658.

place! Josephus failed in his quest to conquer this city, which is only 5 kilometres north of Nazareth.[13] He described how:

> *the Romans, out of the anger they bore at this attempt, [did not] leave off either by night or by day, burning the places in the plain, or stealing away the cattle that were in the country, and killing whatsoever appeared capable of fighting perpetually, and leading the weaker people as slaves into captivity: so that Galilee was all over filled with fire and blood; nor was it exempted from any kind of misery or calamity; for the only refuge they had was this, that when they were pursued, they could retire to the cities which had wall[sic] built ... by Josephus.*[14]

I was still curious as to why Josephus named certain towns in Galilee, and not others. After reading widely I found that certain tendencies appeared. Many towns were named simply because they helped describe the borders of Galilee,[15] and obviously not every town along the border needs to be named. This is especially so as the village of Nazareth wasn't even on a major Roman road.[16] Eleven towns are named because they have a military relevance and simultaneously highlight Josephus' importance. This is because Josephus fortified these towns with walls, and gave permission to two other towns to build walls.[17] Such naming of towns indicates that he did not name towns simply because they existed in Galilee.

Another apparent reason why Josephus named only some towns is that he concentrated on only the significant battles with the Romans. These battles were generally between the Jews living within their

---

13   JL Reed, *Archaeology and the Galilean Jesus: A Re-examination of the Evidence*, Trinity Press International, Harrisburg, US, 2002, p. 115. Although Nazareth is not on the plains (being 500 metres above sea level), it is lower than Sepphoris, and the Jezreel Plain is 'only a short [steeper] jaunt to the south' which is itself 150 metres above sea level. (p. 115).
14   Josephus, *The Wars of the Jews*, book 3, ch. 4, para. 1§62–3, p. 642.
15   Josephus, *The Wars of the Jews*, book 3, ch. 3, para. 1§35–40, p. 641.
16   JL Reed, p. 117. Reed has carried out archaeological excavations at Sepphoris.
17   Josephus, *The Wars of the Jews*, book 2, ch. 20, para. 6§572–5, p. 634.

walled cities or when there were large numbers of people involved.[18] Walls gave the Jews such a great advantage that it sometimes resulted in the Romans' withdrawal. This occurred once quite early in the Roman attempt to recapture the region. Josephus describes how the commander Placidus:

> *who had overrun Galilee, and had besides slain a number of those whom he had caught ... saw that the [Jewish] warriors ran always to those cities whose walls had been built by Josephus, he marched furiously against Jotapata, which was of them all the strongest ... [The Jews] fought the Romans briskly when they least expected it ... so Placidus, finding himself unable to assault the city, ran away.*[19]

Later Jotapata came under attack again, this time by General Vespasian with his 60,000-strong army over an eight-week period.[20] During this battle, Vespasian sent his commander Trajan against a double-walled city called Japha, which lay about 16 kilometres to the south of Jotapata,[21] with 1000 horseman and 2000 footmen re-assigned to this task. Now Nazareth lies a little to the east of a direct line connecting Japha and Jotapata. When the city of Jotapata looked like it was ready to fall, Trajan received help from Titus (Vespasian's son), who came with 500 horseman and 1000 footmen. As a result of this battle, no males remained alive except for infants, a total of 15,000 Galileans were killed and 2130 were taken away as captives.[22] It is easy to see that Josephus wouldn't at this point in his narrative bother to mention a smaller skirmish between these two larger battles, even though it may well have happened as either Trajan or Titus moved between the two towns of Japha and Jotapata. Nazareth at the time of Jesus may have had a population as small as 480.[23] Others estimate it to have been larger with a significant Roman population. Either way

---

18 A battle that did not involve a walled city, but is nevertheless described, is the one on Mount Gerizzim, where 11,600 Samaritans were killed in one day after refusing to surrender (Josephus, *The Wars of the Jews*, book 3, ch. 7, para. 32§307–315, p. 653.
19 Josephus, *The Wars of the Jews*, book 3, ch. 6, para. 1§110–114, pp. 644–5.
20 Josephus, *The Wars of the Jews*, book 3, ch. 4, para. 2§64–9, p. 642; book 3, ch. 7, para. 4§145–9, p. 646.
21 CL Rogers, *The Topical Josephus: Historical Accounts That Shed Light on the Bible,* Zondervan, Grand Rapids, Michigan, US, 1999, p. 140.
22 Josephus, *The Wars of the Jews*, book 3, ch. 7, para. 31§305, p. 653.
23 J Strange, 'Nazareth', in *Anchor Bible Dictionary*, Doubleday, New York, 1992.

it wasn't going to offer up much resistance. Of course, Nazareth may have been largely wiped out earlier than this, perhaps during the battle at Sepphoris or by Placidus at the first battle of Jotapata.

Given this lack of detailed discussion, it is only to be expected that Josephus would not particularly bother naming a place like Nazareth that he hadn't fortified and that didn't qualify as a major city.

The silence of the Talmud concerning Nazareth

The Talmud is a collection of authoritative Jewish teaching in two main sections, the Mishnah and the Gemara. These were committed to written form in about 200 and 500 AD respectively. The Talmud covers civil and ritual laws, folklore and the interpretation of biblical texts. It concentrates on legislation (*halakhah*) and theology (*aggadah*) — in fact, 'historical facts are mentioned incidentally only'.[24] The Talmud has many sayings that seem peculiar to modern Western readers:

> *Rabbi Yehuda said ... Most donkey-drivers are wicked, most camel-drivers are righteous, and most sailors are pious. The best of doctors are destined for hell ...*[25]

Like the Old Testament and the books of Josephus, the Talmud never aims to make a register of all the towns in Galilee or anywhere else. So although the Talmud names 63 towns in Galilee,[26] its 'silence' concerning Nazareth doesn't carry any great significance.

One of the reasons why the Talmud (and the Tosepta — which is a collection of Jewish sayings from 70 to 200 AD[27]) mentions a

---

24 B Isaac, *The Near East Under Roman Rule: Selected Papers*, Brill, Leiden, The Netherlands, 1998, p. 225.
25 HH Friedman, *Ideal Occupations: The Talmudic Perspective*, Jewish Law Articles: Examining Halacha, Jewish Issues and Secular Law, www.jlaw.com/Articles/idealoccupa.html, accessed 24/06/2013.
26 I found many authors referred to the number of villages as 45, but have yet to find the original source for this reckoning.
27 J McDowell & B Wilson, *Evidence for the Historical Jesus: A Compelling Case for His Life and His Claims*, Harvest House Publishers, Eugene, Oregon, US, 1993, pp. 54–6.

number of towns in Galilee is because these towns were some of the places where the priests in Galilee lived. But as one famous Jewish archaeologist has noted: 'these passages are sporadic and do not form a complete list'.[28]

That the Talmud is no geographical treatise is shown by the following description of the borders of Galilee:

> *From the village of Hananiah and upwards, every part in which the sycamore tree does not grow is Upper Galilee. And from the village of Hananiah and lower down, where any sycamore tree grows, is Lower Galilee. And the neighbourhood of Tiberias is the Vale.*[29]

Compare the above description to that of Josephus, who named five towns when he described the borders of Lower Galilee.[30]

Another indication that the authors of the Talmud did not intend to provide thorough geographic and historical information is that the Talmud does not mention the palace-fortress complex of Masada. Yet archaeologists in the 1960s discovered coloured frescoes from the palace built by King Herod the Great (r. 39 – 4 BC).[31] The discovery shows that Masada was occupied almost 200 years before the Talmud was compiled. The ignoring of Masada by the Talmud is very relevant to this discussion because Masada, unlike Nazareth, was historically significant to the Jews. This is because it is where the Jews fought their last great battle against the Romans in the first Jewish revolt. The battle in 73 AD resulted in the slaughter of 960 Jewish men, women and children by their own hands.[32]

Philo's silence concerning Nazareth

As for Philo of Alexandria (c. 20 BC – 45 AD), he was a Jewish philosopher who certainly didn't set out to write a comprehensive treatise on the geography of Galilee. That geography plays a very small part in

---

28 M Avi-Yonah, 'The Caesarea inscription of the twenty-four priestly courses', eds EJ Vardaman & JL Garrett Jr, *The Teachers Yoke: Studies in Memory of Henry Trantham,* Baylor University Press, Waco, Texas, US, 1964, p. 51.
29 J Barclay (trans.), *The Talmud,* ch. 9, para. 2, 1878, www.sacred-texts.com/jud/bar/bar029.htm, accessed 24/06/2013. Sections from the Talmud, the Mishna, Treatise II 'On the Sabbatical Year'.
30 Josephus, *The Wars of the Jews,* book 3, ch. 3, para. 1§38–40, p. 641.
31 E Ashkenazi, 'Restoring the glory of Herod the Great', *Haaretz,* 20 July, 2013.
32 Josephus, *The Wars of the Jews,* book 7, ch. 9, para. 1§400, p. 769.

his writings is evident by simply examining them. Amongst the 45 works of his that have been translated into English, Jerusalem is mentioned in only two of them, with a total of only four mentions altogether. Galilee is cited only once amongst the 45 books, and its capital Tiberias, which was built in about 20 AD,[33] is totally neglected.[34] Similarly, while the Idumaeans (people who lived in the region of Idumaea) are mentioned 138 times by Josephus, Philo doesn't refer to them at all,[35] yet King Herod the Great who ruled over Judea was an Idumaean.

Some antagonists mention other literature from about the time of Jesus that is similar in its silence with respect to Nazareth, but what has been said about the arguments from silence above applies equally to these other sources. This is because none of the sources attempt to write a comprehensive list of all the places in Galilee. It should be evident by now that care is needed when basing a case on an argument from silence.

Other scholars who specifically mention the absence of Nazareth in the writings of the Old Testament, Josephus and the Talmud do not come to the conclusion that Nazareth didn't exit during Jesus' lifetime. Rather they draw the quite reasonable conclusion that Nazareth was 'absolutely insignificant'.[36]

Variable Greek spellings of Nazareth

Apart from the argument from silence, I came across another fact that has been used to discredit the notion of Nazareth being present during

---

33 The study of coins found in Tiberias reveals it was founded between 17 and 22 AD. JH Charlesworth, 'Jesus research and archaeology: a new perspective', in ed. JH Charlesworth, *Jesus and Archaeology*, William B Eerdmans Publishing Company, Cambridge, 2006, p. 21. Charlesworth here refers to publications by M Avi-Yonah and Y Meshorer.
34 These figures were obtained by performing an online search using words that contain the strings 'salem', 'gal' and 'tiber' of *The Works of Philo Judaeus: The Contemporary of Josephus*, trans. CD Yonge, HG Bohn, London, 1854–90, digital copy available at www.earlychristianwritings.com/yonge/, accessed 24/06/2013. Jerusalem was found in the books *On Dreams, That They are God-Sent* and *On the Embassy to Gaius*. Galilee was found in the latter of these two books.
35 B Isaac, p. 267.
36 JD Crossan & JL Reed, *Excavating Jesus: Beneath the Stones, Behind the Texts*, HarperSanFrancisco, San Francisco, 2001, p. 52.

the time of Jesus: namely that the New Testament writers were not consistent in their Greek spelling of Jesus' hometown. Some atheist publications then use this evidence to conjecture that three different writers over three different time periods were responsible for writing these various names in the New Testament book of Matthew.[37] The variable spelling is purported to bolster the contention that there was no town of Nazareth during Jesus' lifetime, as otherwise they feel it would've been spelt more consistently.

Certainly it is true that Jesus' hometown was sometimes spelt as Nazareth (Ναζαρεθ) (Matthew 21:11; Luke 1:26; Luke 2:4, 39 and 51; and Acts 10:38),[38] other times as Nazaret (Ναζαρετ) (Matthew 2:23, Mark 1:9, John 1:45–6), and twice as Nazara (Ναζαρα) (Matthew 4:13, Luke 4:16).[39] One reasonable explanation for this variability is that these are all valid alternate Greek transliterations. This is based on the fact that other places also have alternate names.[40] In Joshua 19:12 the writers of the Greek translation of the Hebrew Old Testament, called the Septuagint, transliterate the Hebrew town called Daberath as Dabiroth (Δαβιρωθ), but a few chapters later in 21:28 as Debba (Δεββα). Similarly in 2 Chronicles 18:19 they transliterate the Hebrew place Ramoth Gilead as Ramoth Galaad (Ραμωθ Γαλααδ), but a few chapters later in 22:5 as Rama Galaad (Ραμα Γαλααδ).

Sometimes a town was spelt in two different ways by authors who wrote within about the same time. Josephus spelt the town Mabartha, whilst Pliny the Elder spelt it Mamortha.[41]

Similarly, Jerusalem is spelt in Greek in a variety of ways. Sometimes it is transliterated from the Hebrew with a rough breathing mark (Hierousalhm, Ἱερουσαλήμ), sometimes with a smooth one (Ierousalhm, Ἰερουσαλήμ). These transliterated forms are the technically correct spellings, and the breathing marks affect only the pronunciation. In other places, the city is sometimes given more normal forms of spelling (for

---

37 R Salm, pp. 301–2.
38 Matthew 21:11, Luke 1:26, Luke 2:4,39 & 51 and Acts 10:38.
39 One manuscript (P70 from the third century) has 'Nazara' instead of 'Nazaret' at Matthew 2:23.
40 BC Smith, *Rejection at Nazareth*, in Text Excavation, www.textexcavation.com/synrejnaz.html, accessed 24/06/2013. This article provides several other examples as well.
41 B Isaac, pp. 165–6.

Greek speakers), such as Ierosoluma (Ἱεροσόλυμα) and Hierosalhma (Ἱεροσάλημα).[42] Jerusalem is even spelt in the plural form more than 60 times in the New Testament but no one suggests that this means there was more than one city called Jerusalem. Certainly the various spellings of Jerusalem don't indicate that that there were several different places with slightly different names. Also the variations are never used to contend that the city never existed at that time.[43]

Where did the Z in Nazareth come from? From Hebrew to Greek.

Another argument based on the spelling of Nazareth has been used to discredit the teaching that Jesus was from Nazareth. It partly relates to the discovery of the ancient Hebrew spelling of Nazareth inscribed in marble, amongst the ruins of a synagogue in the town of Caesarea Maritima.

Before delving into this argument further, it is important to note that Hebrew reads from right to left, and so in the following paragraphs whenever Hebrew fonts are used, I have adopted this format. So that readers do not need to learn Hebrew letters, I have sometimes supplied only the names of the letters in the following paragraphs, and in these cases I have kept to the English system of placing them in order reading from left to right. Although written Hebrew consisted of twenty-three consonants, it didn't originally have a set of symbols for vowels. Vowels were, of course, spoken and the reader of a Hebrew script simply added the appropriate vowels from memory. Vowel-signs were eventually standardised and added to the written Hebrew language in about 900 AD. They were then represented by a system of dots and dashes above or below the line of consonants. This incorporation did not become compulsory, as evident by the printing of modern Hebrew newspapers without these vowel-signs.[44]

Returning to the marble inscription, which is dated to about 355 AD, this confirmed that the Hebrew spelling of Nazareth definitely

---

42 RJ Decker, *Jerusalem: Some Notes on the Greek Spelling*, New Testament Resources, http://ntresources.com/blog/?s=Jerusalem+some+notes+on+greek+spelling, accessed 24/06/2013.
43 RJ Decker, http://ntresources.com/blog/?s=Jerusalem+some+notes+on+greek+spelling, accessed 24/06/2013.
44 FF Bruce, *The Books and the Parchments: Some Chapters on the Transmission of the Bible*, Pickering & Inglis, London, 1978, pp. 41–2.

contained a *tsade*, being spelt 'nṣrt' (*nun-tsade-resh-taw*, תרשנ). This Hebrew spelling of Nazareth has caused some to accuse the Greek New Testament writers of having spelt Nazareth wrong. They argue that the normal way of transliterating the Hebrew letter *tsade* into Greek was to use the Greek letter *sigma* (σ). Because the New Testament writers used the Greek letter *zeta* (ζ) to transliterate *tsade* when spelling Nazareth (Ναζαρεθ), instead of using *sigma*, the sceptics consider this a spelling mistake. These sceptics further contend that the use of *zeta* by the New Testament authors harks back to those authors changing an original unknown story of Jesus being a Nazirite (a Jew who had taken special religious vows) into the story of Jesus being from Nazareth. The Hebrew consonant spelling for Nazirite is 'nzr' (*nun-zayin-resh*, רזנ).[45] So based on the notion that the Hebrew letter *zayin,* used in spelling Nazirite, is normally transliterated into Greek as *zeta*, the sceptics contend that this is evidence that the *zeta* used by the New Testament authors originally came from Jesus being a Nazirite rather than a Nazarene.

The pivotal point in the argument is that Hebrew *tsade* should always be transliterated into Greek as *sigma*. So what I found particularly revealing was that using *sigma* to transliterate *tsade* is not the only permissible transliteration, and sometimes Greek *zeta* is used.

The following examples[46] taken from the Septuagint illustrate this: Genesis 13:10 writes the name of a town in Hebrew as *tsade-ayin-resh*, which was transliterated into Greek as Ζογορα (Zogora) and into English as Zoar. Similarly Genesis 22:21 writes the name of a man in Hebrew as *ayin-waw-tsade*, which was transliterated into Greek as Ωξ (Ox), and into English as Uz. In Genesis 36:42 the Hebrew chief Mibṣar can be found transliterated into Greek in the Codex Alexandrinus (a fifth-century AD manuscript) as Mazar.[47]

---

45 J Strong, 'A concise dictionary of the words in the Hebrew Bible; with their renderings in the Authorized English Version', in S Zodhiates (ed.), *The Hebrew-Greek Key Study Bible*, Word Bible Publishers, Iowa, US, 1988, p. 77. As Hebrew reads from right to left, writers would write the word in the reverse direction. However, Young has 'nzyr' (*nun-zayin-yod-resh*).
46 BC Smith, www.textexcavation.com/synrejnaz.html, accessed 24/06/2013. This article provides several other examples as well.
47 MO Wise, 'Nazarene', in JB Green & IH Marshall (eds), *Dictionary of Jesus and the Gospels* , Intervarsity Press, Downers Grove, US, p. 572.

Some of this variability in transliterating Hebrew into Greek was due to the various Greek writers having different preferences to others. For instance, in Judges 8:5 the writers of the Septuagint transliterated the Hebrew name of a king called *tsade-lamed-mem-nun-ayin* into Greek as Σελμανα (Selmana), turning a *tsade* into a *sigma*, whereas Josephus transliterated it as Ζαρμουη (Zarmoune),[48] turning a *tsade* into a *zeta*. Our English texts write the name as Zalmunna. It is pertinent to note that *tsade* is regarded by authorities as having an 'ancient pronunciation [that] is difficult to determine accurately'.[49] As the Greek of the New Testament does not have a letter exactly corresponding to the Hebrew letter *tsade*, it is quite reasonable for the Greek New Testament writers to use the letter *zeta* in the case of Nazareth.[50]

Nazareth, not Nazirite

There are other strong reasons for being certain that Jesus was from Nazareth, rather than originally being described as a Nazirite. Each of the four writers of the New Testament Gospel accounts make the point that Jesus was from a place called Nazareth very clear, as is obvious from the following quotes:

> *... he went and lived in a town called Nazareth. (Matthew 2:23)*

> *At that time Jesus came from Nazareth in Galilee and was baptized by John in the Jordan. (Mark 1:9)*

> *In the sixth month of Elizabeth's pregnancy, God sent the angel Gabriel to Nazareth, a town in Galilee. (Luke 1:26)*

> *He went to Nazareth, where he had been brought up... (Luke 4:16)*

---

48 Josephus, *The Antiquities of the Jews,* book 5, ch. 6, para. 5§228, p. 142.
49 RL Harris, GL Archer & BK Waltke, *Theological Wordbook of the Old Testament*, Moody Press, Chicago, US, 1980, p. ix. It has been suggested that since it is written in a different form when placed at the end of a word, it had at least two different pronunciations.
50 RB Allen, 'Does anything good come from Nazareth?, *DTS Magazine*, 7 July 2006, www.dts.edu/read/does-anything-good-come-from-nazareth-ronald-b-allen/, accessed 20/07/2013; and in Mounce Reverse-Interlinear New Testament version (e.g. Matthew 2:23, Mark 14:67, Luke 24:19).

> *'Nazareth! Can anything good come from there?' Nathanael asked. (John 1:46)*

The case for Jesus coming from a place called Nazareth as opposed to being a Nazirite is so strong that two scholars, one of whom was a professor of foreign languages, wrote that:

> *there is no reason to believe that the Greek* nazoraios *of the three later canonical Gospels [Matthew, Luke and John], as opposed to the* nazarenos *of [the Gospel of] Mark, implied that Jesus was a member of a Jewish sect of 'observants' and not an inhabitant of Nazareth. The authors of the Gospels in whatever form they used it, understood the term as synonymous with the phrase 'the one from Nazareth' (*o apo nazareth*; Matt. 12:11; Mark 1:9; John 1:45; also Acts 10:38) ... Was Nazareth the birthplace of Jesus as his very name, Jesus of Nazareth, would indicate? [The Gospel of] Mark specifies that Jesus went to preach to his own* patrida, *a Greek word that means 'family from the father's side, clan, native place' (Mark 6:1).*[51]

Another reason why it seems implausible that Jesus was a Nazirite is that he did not act like a Nazirite throughout his entire ministry as he drank wine,[52] in contrast to his cousin John the Baptist (Luke 7:32–4).

Nazareth: a village or a city

I found one other line of literary evidence used to contend that Nazareth wasn't there before Jesus was crucified. The argument raised is that as Nazareth is referred to in the New Testament as a city, and as cities are so much bigger than villages, it should have been noted in the non-Christian literature stated above. This is simply another argument from silence and has been dealt with above. However, my curiosity was sparked about whether the New Testament describes Nazareth as a city or a village, and what the difference was between these forms of settlement.

---

51 JJ Rousseau & R Arav, *Jesus and His World: An Archaeological and Cultural Dictionary*, Fortress Press, Minneapolis, 1995, p. 215. For further details about the authors, refer to footnote 64.

52 Just before he was crucified, he did reject wine after tasting it (Matthew 27:34).

Appendix 3

The New Testament describes Nazareth as a city (*polis*) in several places (Matthew 2:23, Luke 2:4 and 39). However, large and small places are called *polis*, such as the large city of Jerusalem and the much smaller place of Bethlehem (Matthew 21:10, Luke 19:41 and 2:4).

Other places in the New Testament are referred to as a village (*kome*), such as two unnamed villages in Matthew 21:2 (village with a donkey) and Luke 8:1 (Jesus travelled from one town and village to another). Similarly small places are found in Luke 9:52 (Samaritan village), Luke 10:38 (home of Martha and Mary) and Luke 24:13 (Emmaus).

However, the terms city and village are not used with absolute precision in the Bible or in Hellenistic [Greek] periods and languages.[53] An example of this can be found in the works of Josephus, where he sometimes refers to the same place using both terms, *polis* and *kome*.[54] It has been stated that 'the term *polis* in Josephus designates towns of widely varying sizes'.[55] Another scholar has also emphasised that not too much should be read into the terms *polis* and *kome* when reading ancient literature.

> *The character of poleis [plural form] in antiquity has been difficult to establish. As is clear from ancient sources, no clear-cut definition for* polis *or* kome *existed. Pausanius, for example derides [the place of] Panopeus for claiming status as a polis when the city had no government buildings, gymnasium, theatre, marketplace or water descending to a fountain.*[56]

---

53 CC McCown, 'City', *Interpreter's Dictionary of the Bible A-D*, Abingdon, New York and Nashville, 1962, p. 632, cited by JF Strange, DE Groh & TRW Longstaff, 'The location and identification of Shikhin, part 1, *Israel Exploration Journal*, vol. 44, nos 3–4, 1994, p. 222, ref. 23.

54 Josephus used both terms to refer to the one town called Garisme (*The Life of Flavius Josephus*, para. 71§395) or Garis (*The Wars of the Jews*, book 3, ch. 6, para. 3§129, p. 645). Data obtained from Strange et al., 1995, p. 224.

55 JF Strange, DE Groh & TRW Longstaff, p. 225.

56 D Edwards, 'The socio-economic and cultural ethos in the first century', in LI Levine (ed.), *The Galilee in Late Antiquity*, Jewish Theological Seminary of America, New York, 1992, p. 322.

After the Jewish wars, the Christian historian Eusebius (c. 263–339 AD) described Nazareth as 'a small Jewish village'.[57] It seems that only in the seventh century that 'Nazareth and its area received the official status of *polis* (Helenopolis)'.[58]

Archaeology of Nazareth

Having looked at the evidence used to claim that Nazareth didn't exist during the time of Jesus, it's appropriate to look into the evidence used to assert that it did exist at that time. This positive evidence is important to examine as it has been claimed that archaeological evidence conclusively shows that the village of Nazareth did not exist before 100 AD.[59] The archaeological discoveries are only touched on here due to lack of space.

Early Nazareth has been difficult to study as, unlike Capernaum (another important place in Jesus' life), 'later and modern buildings largely obscure the site'.[60] Also Nazareth was the site of several battles over the centuries, and after its destruction was ordered by the Sultan Baybars in 1263, it remained in ruins until the seventeenth century.[61] Despite the negative impact of these factors, first-century Nazareth has been discovered to have had a 'winepress ... beautifully constructed stone walled-terraces ... and three circular stone towers ...'[62] The Israeli Antiquities Authority issued a press release describing the excavation of a residential building that:

> consisted of two rooms and a courtyard ... The artifacts recovered from inside the building were few and mostly included fragments of pottery vessels from the Early Roman period (the first and second

---

57 JJ Rousseau & R Arav, p. 214, referring to Eusebius', *Onomasticon*, 138:24.
58 JJ Rousseau & R Arav, p. 214.
59 R Salm, pp. 206-7.
60 JDG Dunn, 'Did Jesus attend the synagogue?', in JH Charlesworth (ed.), *Jesus and Archaeology*, William B Eerdmans Publishing Company, Cambridge, 2006, p. 221, n. 77.
61 B Bagatti, 'Nazareth', in M Avi-Yonah & E Stern (eds), *Encyclopedia of Archaeological Excavations in the Holy Land*, vol. 3, Oxford University Press, town not specified, 1977, pp. 919–22.
62 JH Charlesworth, 'Jesus research and archaeology: a new perspective', in JH Charlesworth (ed.), *Jesus and Archaeology*, William B Eerdmans Publishing Company, Cambridge, 2006, p. 38.

Appendix 3

centuries CE). In addition, several fragments of chalk vessels were found, which were only used by Jews in this period because such vessels were not susceptible to becoming ritually unclean.

Another hewn pit, whose entrance was apparently camouflaged, was excavated and a few pottery sherds from the Early Roman period were found inside it. The [excavation director], Yardenna Alexandre, said, 'Based on other excavations that I conducted in other villages in the region, this pit was probably hewn as part of the preparations by the Jews to protect themselves during the Great Revolt against the Romans in 67 CE.' [63]

Professor John McRay has given the following broad statement regarding the archaeology of Nazareth in the first century:

The excavations conducted by Bagatti, revealed that Nazareth of Jesus' day was an agricultural settlement with numerous winepresses, olive presses, caves for storing grain, and cisterns for water and wine ... Pottery found in the village ... [includes] Roman pieces from the time of Christ. [64]

Professor McRay is not only an expert scholar in the field of archaeology, he also has a strong belief in Jesus. He wrote the following words regarding his book on the archaeology of the New Testament: 'If it stimulates its readers to further research, reflection, and respect for the New Testament as the historical revelation of the Word of God, it will have fulfilled its author's hopes'.[65]

---

63 Israel Antiquities Authority, 'For the very first time: a residential building from the time of Jesus was exposed in the heart of Nazareth', press release, 21 December 2009, www.antiquities.org.il/article_Item_eng.asp?sec_id=25&subj_id=240&id=1638&module_id=#as, accessed 20/07/2013.

64 J McRay, *Archaeology and the New Testament*, Baker Academic, Grand Rapids, US, 1991, pp. 157-8. John McRay, Professor Emeritus of New Testament and Archaeology at Wheaton College, studied at 'Hebrew University ... in Jerusalem, Vanderbilt University Divinity School, and the University of Chicago [where he obtained his Ph.D]... McRay is also a former research associate and trustee of the WF Albright Institute of Archaeological Research in Jerusalem; a current trustee of the Near East Archaeological Society.' L Strobel, *The Case for Christ*, Zondervan, Grand Rapids, Michigan, US, pp.125–6.

65 J McRay, p.14.

Some may claim that such an admission of bias should automatically make his claims about Christian archaeological sites invalid. However, if an author's favourable bias about a contentious topic is regarded as sufficient reason in itself to discount the evidence presented by that author, and if this was to be accepted as a universal axiom, then meaningful evidence-based debate would cease. Of course, the words of any scholar discussing their own field of expertise should not be dismissed lightly simply because they admit to having a bias; rather the reader should objectively weigh up the validity of the author's statements based on the evidence provided. Bias does not necessarily result in an author playing loose with the truth. In many cases, any bias an author may have is a direct result of convictions borne by the very evidence they write about, in which case the bias has followed in the footsteps of the evidence. One way to assess the validity of McRay's statements is to compare them with those from other archaeologists. The following comment relating to the existence of Nazareth is from two archaeologists,[66] one of whom has a bias quite the opposite to that of McRay's as he does not believe that miracles, including the resurrection of Jesus, have ever happened:[67]

> *There is no doubt about the existence and location of Nazareth in the time of Jesus ...*[68]

The other archaeological piece of evidence that I'd like to mention is the marble inscription mentioned earlier in this chapter, which is dated to about 355 AD. This was found in 1962 amongst the ruins of a synagogue in the town of Caesarea Maritima. A very masterful

---

[66] The two archaeologists are Rami Arav and John J Rousseau. In 2004, Rami Arav was professor of religion and foreign languages at the University of Nebraska at Omaha. (Refer to *Bethsaida: A City by the North Shore of the Sea of Galilee*, vol. 3, Truman State University Press, Kirksville, US , 2004, p. 295.) Arav was a research associate at the Zinman Institute of Archaeology, University of Haifa, and he participated in the archaeological survey of Israel. He now directs the Bethsaida excavation. Rousseau was a research associate at the University of California, Berkeley, a Fellow of the Jesus Seminar and Co-director of the Bethsaida excavations.

[67] This and other details about the Jesus Seminar can be found in PR Eddy & GA Boyd, *The Jesus Legend: A Case for the Historical Reliability of the Synoptic Jesus Tradition*, Baker Academic, Grand Rapids, Michigan, US, 2007, p. 28.

[68] JJ Rousseau & R Arav, p. 215.

analysis has revealed that it formed a list relating various priestly groups (called courses or divisions) to different towns, one of them being Nazareth.[69] This list served as a reminder to the Jews of the situation that existed sometime around 135 AD, or perhaps even as early as just after the destruction of the temple in 70 AD. Each priestly course would serve for a week, and do so twice a year. In this way the list also functioned as a type of calendar. The inscription indicates that Nazareth was functioning in this manner at least as early as 135 AD.

A cliffhanger ending

Nazareth is not only famous as the town in which Jesus grew up. It is also infamous for being the place of the first attempt on Jesus' life. The account of this attempted assassination is found in Luke 4:28–30 (NASB):

> *And all the people in the synagogue were filled with rage as they heard these things [that Jesus taught]; and they got up and drove Him out of the city, and led Him to the brow of the hill on which their city had been built, in order to throw Him down the cliff. But passing through their midst, He went His way.*

Knowing of this event, I was startled when I came across the assertion that no such cliff exists. The two modern-day authors quoted in the above section state: 'There is no site corresponding to the description in Luke 4:29 of a brow of a hill from which Jesus could have been thrown headlong'.[70]

However, others have found a cliff site that matches the description. It is pertinent to recall that the assassination attempt happened at a cliff that was located outside of the city, but on the same hill on which the city was built. As one apologist wrote: 'Nazareth was and still is partially situated in a hollow against the slopes of a mountain, so that

---

69 Avi-Yonah, M, 'The Caesarea inscription of the twenty-four priestly courses', in EJ Vardaman & JL Garrett, Jr (eds), *The Teacher's Yoke: Studies in Memory of Henry Trantham*, Baylor University Press, Waco, Texas, US, 1964, pp. 46–57.

70 JJ Rousseau & R Arav, p. 214.

it is enclosed on three sides by portions of the mountain'.[71] A further description of the cliff site is as follows:

> *[Nazareth] lies on the north-western side of a wad'y [a creek bed that is dry unless there is rainfall], and extends from the bed of the wad'y about half-way up the slope. The top of the ridge is about 300 feet [91 metres] perpendicular above it ... Near the other extremity of the town [namely the south-western end], however, and at about the same level on the hillside [as the upper edge of the town] is a natural precipice about 40 feet [12 metres] high, and evidently of ancient origin. A few houses now stand above it, and on the level platform of rock at its base stands a Maronite chapel. Here in the imperishable rock, unchanged by human hands, is the spot where this tragic event occurred ... True, the spot is now within the limits of the city, but it is obvious at a glance that all the houses near the precipice are of modern construction ... many new houses were in course of erection when the author was there in 1879.*[72]

This south-west cliff certainly seemed to be a suitable candidate to match up with the one mentioned in the murder attempt.

But the almost-cliffhanger ending of Jesus at Nazareth raises another question. What was Jesus teaching that so angered his hometown crowd that they wanted to kill him? The inability to accept that these townsmen would turn on one of their own has so vexed some that it is one of the reasons given for disbelieving that Nazareth was even there at that time.[73] However, it is not impossible or unprecedented for a home crowd to turn on one of its own. Jesus' speech to the people in Nazareth was more than enough to make them homicidal. Professor

---

71 JP Holding, *Shattering the Christ Myth: Did Jesus Not Exist?*, Xulon Press, 2008, p. 365.

72 JW McGarvey, *Lands of the Bible: A Geographical and Topographical Description of Palestine, with Letters of Travel in Egypt, Syria, Asia Minor and Greece*, The Standard Publishing Company, Cincinnati, 1880, ch. 7, pp. 313–39, digital copy available at www.dabar.org/McGarvey/Lands/P2_C07.htm, accessed 16/07/20013. The title page reads 'Sometime Professor of Sacred History in the College of the Bible, Lexington, Ky'.

73 TK Cheyne, 'Nazareth', in TK Cheyne & J Sutherland (eds), *Encyclopaedia Biblica: A Critical Dictionary*, Adam and Charles Black, London, 1889, columns 3358 to 3362.

of Middle Eastern New Testament studies, Kenneth Bailey, re-phrased Jesus' inflammatory remarks to the people as:

If you [people of Nazareth] want to receive the benefits of the new golden age of the Messiah ... I am not asking you merely to tolerate or accept them [certain Gentiles]. You must see them as your spiritual superiors and acknowledge that they can instruct you in the nature of authentic faith.[74]

Prof. Bailey later on adds:

Jesus knew that the town's agenda was to reclaim land from Gentiles who had moved into ... [their region]. He must have known that these stories would upset the congregation before him. But he told them anyway and the room exploded in anger! Settler types often see religion and politics as a single passage. When Jesus disagreed with their political economic goals they decided to kill him.[75]

Conclusion

The research findings involved in this chapter indicate that much of the evidence used to dismiss the existence of Nazareth during the lifetime of Jesus has very little foundation. One of the most touted pieces of evidence, namely the argument from silence, has been shown to be irrelevant because it is based on ancient writings that never purported to comprehensively list towns and villages. Other lines of evidence, such as the variability in the spelling of Nazareth and the related contention that Jesus was a Nazirite, have been found to provide no firm foundation for doubting the existence of Nazareth as a place during Jesus' lifetime. Despite claims to the contrary, there is archaeological evidence showing that Nazareth was functioning as a village when Jesus' parents left there for Bethlehem, and also when the villagers tried to kill Jesus approximately three decades later. Although many websites and books confidently proclaim that Nazareth did not exist during Jesus' lifetime, a deeper look at their evidence, as well as other markers, points strongly in the opposite direction.

---

74 KE Bailey, *Jesus through Middle Eastern Eyes: Cultural Studies in the Gospels*, IVP Academic, Downers Grove, 2008, p. 165.
75 KE Bailey, p. 167.

www.ingramcontent.com/pod-product-compliance
Lightning Source LLC
Chambersburg PA
CBHW052128010526
44113CB00034B/1025